MW00559012

COMMUNITY VOICES

COMMUNITY VOICES

Health Matters

Henrie M. Treadwell, Marguerite J. Ro, and
Leda M. Pérez, Editors

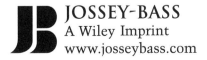

JOSSEY-BASS
A Wiley Imprint
www.josseybass.com

Published by Jossey-Bass
A Wiley Imprint
989 Market Street, San Francisco, CA 94103-1741—www.josseybass.com

Jossey-Bass books and products are available through most bookstores. To contact Jossey-Bass directly call our Customer Care Department within the U.S. at 800-956-7739, outside the U.S. at 317-572-3986, or fax 317-572-4002.

Jossey-Bass also publishes its books in a variety of electronic formats. Some content that appears in print may not be available in electronic books.

Library of Congress Cataloging-in-Publication Data
Community voices : health matters / Henrie M. Treadwell, Marguerite J. Ro, and Leda M. Pérez, editors.—1st ed.
  p. ; cm.
 Includes bibliographical references and index.
 ISBN 978-0-470-93498-2 (cloth)
 1. Community health services—United States. 2. Medical policy—United States. 3. Health services accessibility—United States I. Treadwell, Henrie M. II. Ro, Marguerite J. III. Pérez, Leda M.
 [DNLM: 1. Community Health Services—methods—United States. 2. Health Policy—United States. 3. Health Services Accessibility—United States. 4. Healthcare Disparities—United States. 5. Men's Health—United States. WA 546 AA1]
 RA445.C648 2010
 362.12—dc22
                                                    2010040036

Printed in the United States of America
FIRST EDITION

HB Printing 10 9 8 7 6 5 4 3 2 1

CONTENTS

To all of those who have touched our lives
and kept us on the path

FOREWORD

There has never been a more opportune time for the publication of the book *Community Voices: Health Matters*. The past year has been one of contentious debate over health insurance reform in the United States. On March 23, 2010, President Obama signed the Patient Protection and Affordable Care Act into law, enshrining "the core principle that everybody should have some basic security when it comes to their health care."[1] As historic as this occasion may be, it is only the beginning of a process aimed at improving health care and controlling attendant costs in this country. That is why this book holds such promise.

The opening quote by former Supreme Court Justice Louis D. Brandeis in which he envisioned the states as "laboratories of democracy" is consonant with the "learning laboratories" notion embraced by Community Voices, except that a mix of geographically and politically varied sites are the pioneering change agents in the latter. Part One of the book *Community Voices: Health Matters* provides reflections from each of the eight constituent learning laboratories—(1) Baltimore, Maryland; (2) Denver, Colorado; (3) Ingham County, Michigan; (4) Miami, Florida; (5) New Mexico; (6) Pinehurst, North Carolina; (7) northern Manhattan, New York; and (8) Oakland, California—regarding their ongoing efforts to bring about health insurance and health system reform. Critical analysis of what works, what doesn't, and why will be essential in the ongoing mission to promote health and provide holistic care to everyone in U.S. society, regardless of the ability to pay for services.

Other parallels between the enduring legacy of Brandeis as the people's attorney and the ongoing mission of Henrie M. Treadwell, Ph.D., and her Community Voices collaborators as champions of health care for the underserved merit comment here. According to biographer Melvin I. Urofsky, Brandeis lived and worked in the real world.[2] Likewise, the members of the Community Voices coalition believe that "practical examples that reach real people where they live, work, and seek health care services are better guides for policy-makers than untested solutions" (see http://www.communityvoices.org/about.aspx).

Brandeis famously held true to his ideals, even as he was usually in the minority on the Supreme Court. In *Gilbert* v. *Minnesota* (1920), he dissented while standing up for freedom of speech even in wartime "because of its educational value and the importance to democracy."[3] Similarly, for more than a decade, Community Voices has steadfastly advocated for oral health and mental health as part of overall health and well-being, and for increased attention on prison health and reentry issues, even though these positions are rarely endorsed and included in proposed legislation. Nonetheless, the dissenting opinions of Brandeis have since become the law of the land. How long will it take the U.S. federal government to expand rights and extend protections to the most vulnerable populations as part of U.S. health reform? As Brandeis demonstrated throughout his life, it is never the wrong time to be on the right side of social justice.

Significantly, Brandeis was a pragmatist who created tools that enabled lawyers to turn theory into practice. The Brandeis brief, which has become commonplace today, not only presents the court with an analysis of legal precedents but also marshals current factual material—statistics, scientific experiments, governmental records—to demonstrate a reasonable basis for its position.[4] And so it is with the Community Voices leadership, which contends, "It is not enough to implement programs without establishing a framework for how they operate, an evaluation process, and methods to document those findings so that adjustments can be made" (see http://www.communityvoices.org/about.aspx). Accordingly, Part Two of the book chronicles authoritative peer-reviewed publications and groundbreaking policy briefs that emanated from the Community Voices initiative and are part of the scientific and online record.

Dr. Treadwell and her fellow contributors are well qualified to write this book. They have been engaged in health reform in underserved communities for the long term to foster primary care, emphasize prevention, preserve and strengthen the health care safety net, implement stronger health care delivery systems, and develop best practices that adapt to unique contexts (see http://www.communityvoices.org/about.aspx). *Community Voices: Health Matters* makes a distinctive contribution to the field because the assembled contributors are not strictly academic authorities or policy analysts, even as David Satcher, M.D., Ph.D., former U.S. Surgeon General and former director of the Centers for Disease Control and Prevention, wrote the Preface for this volume. Rather, the authors of this book have been supporting one another in an ongoing way, as each has sought solutions on the ground in their own communities around priorities such as men's health, community health workers, oral health, case management, and mental health. Indeed, through the advocacy of Community Voices, certain of these topics are now more fully integrated into the public health discourse.

At this moment in time, our nation is confronting the unconscionable gaps in coverage that have resulted in an estimated forty-five thousand premature deaths each year and have forced more than a million people into bankruptcy.[5] Regardless of the final bill that emerges from the U.S. Congress and is signed into law by President Obama, it won't create a just, efficient, and workable system of health care. Moreover, it won't address the social determinants of health such as education throughout the lifecourse, safe and affordable housing, locally grown nutritious food supplies, places to engage in daily physical activity, and living wages for all workers that will prevent needless pain and suffering for the majority of Americans who lack these basic necessities for living healthy lives. No piece of legislation, however sweeping, can be expected to rectify so complicated an issue as genuine health reform, but there is historical precedence on how to move forward.

According to Arthur M. Schlesinger Jr., Franklin Roosevelt once said of the New Deal, "Practically all of the things we've done in the federal government are like things Al Smith did as governor of New York."[6] David Osborne argues that other states deserve credit as well, and that many of Roosevelt's initiatives, such as unemployment compensation, massive public works programs, deposit insurance, and social security, were modeled after successful state programs.[7] Further, "[t]he groundwork for much of the New Deal social agenda was laid in the states during the Progressive Era."[8] How can successful historical examples of states as laboratories of democracy be applied to health reform?

A hopeful vision was offered recently offered by Atul Gawande, who likened the pilot programs offered in the current health reform bill to those that transformed the U.S. agricultural system in the past century. In his words, "The task [to improve care and control costs] will require dedicated and talented people in government agencies and in communities who recognize that the country's future depends on their sidestepping the ideological battles, encouraging local change, and following the results."[9] The answers to many of the questions being sought to transform the nation's health care and public health systems are to be found in the pages of *Community Voices: Health Matters*. Readers seeking to bring about change in their own communities, institutions, states, and nations will want to listen to the voices of those who have been involved in the struggle for more than a decade, and who understand that health reform is worth our very best efforts, even if some of our experiments fail. No less a reformer than

Brandeis wrote, "There must be power in the States and the Nation to remold, through experimentation, our economic practices and institutions to meet changing social and economic needs. . . ."[10]

Even a problem of the immensity of health reform may be solved over time with the ingenuity and commitment of all of us. We need the evidence contained in this volume to steer us through the travails ahead, and to continue to add to the experiments being carried out at the local, state, and regional levels to inform national public policy. The time to act on the results of pilot programs is now, even if we don't have all of the answers, because health matters.

Mary E. Northridge, Ph.D., M.P.H.
Professor of Clinical Sociomedical Sciences (in Dental Medicine)
Columbia University Mailman School of Public Health
Editor-in-Chief, *American Journal of Public Health*
January 2, 2011

Notes

1. S. G. Stolberg and R. Pear, "Obama Signs Health Care Overhaul Bill, with a Flourish," New York Times, March 23, 2010. Available at: http://www.nytimes.com/2010/03/24/health/policy/24health.html. Accessed August 2, 2010.
2. M. I. Uroksy, *Louis D. Brandeis: A Life* (New York: Pantheon Books, 2009).
3. B. A. Murphy and M. A. Fekete, "Brandeis, Louis Dembitz (1856–1941," in John R. Vile (ed.) *Great American Judges: An Encyclopedia*, Volume 2 (Santa Barbara, Calif.: ABC-Clio, Inc., 2003, p. 129.
4. A. M. Dershowitz, "The Practice," *The New York Times*, Sunday Book Review, September 25, 2009. Available at http://www.nytimes.com/2009/09/27/books/review/Dershowitz-t.html.
5. A. Gawande, "Testing, Testing," *The New Yorker*, December 14, 2009, pp. 34–41.
6. A. M. Schlesinger Jr., *The Age of Roosevelt. Volume III: The Politics of Upheaval* (Boston: Houghton Mifflin, 1960), p. 520.
7. D. Osborne, *Laboratories of Democracy: A New Breed of Governor Creates Models for National Growth* (Boston: Harvard Business School Press, 1990).
8. Osborne, *Laboratories of Democracy*, p. 1.
9. Gawande, "Testing, Testing," p. 41.
10. L. Brandeis, *New State Ice Co.* v. *Liebmann*, Dissenting Opinion, 1932.

PREFACE

When Community Voices: Healthcare for the Underserved was launched in 1998, I had just been appointed by President Bill Clinton as the 16th Surgeon General of the United States. However, I became directly engaged with Community Voices when we released the first-ever *Surgeon General's Report on Oral Health* in 2000. The report addressed the state of oral health in America and the significant disparities in the oral health of our citizens. It was then that someone at the W.K. Kellogg Foundation contacted me to talk about an exemplary program in oral health— the Community Voices New Mexico initiative, which began in 1999. Indeed the W.K. Kellogg Foundation had established programs in thirteen cities and counties across the nation. The product of a few audacious leaders at the Foundation, this ambitious initiative was born in the context of a country that had just recently engaged in government-led attempts at health care reform which, despite great efforts, did not achieve a system that would provide quality health care to all of its residents.

Notwithstanding the political environment around health reform and very much because of it, Community Voices established roots in very diverse cities, with the conviction that change could come through other means. Change would not be top-down; rather change would come from the communities that were themselves living the realities of little-to-no access to quality health care and the leaders who interfaced with them daily. Community Voices would be heard clearly on the needed reforms to eliminate health disparities in both practice and policy.

Throughout my forty-plus years of service and my efforts to raise awareness about the overwhelming health disparities experienced in the United States, I have found the convictions set forth by Community Voices to be essential to ensuring access to quality health care for all—that is, that the best understanding of what must be done to improve health care and well-being comes directly from those most affected and that sustainable solutions are possible only when people are met where they are. It was in that spirit in 2002, during my tenure as director of the National Center for Primary Care (NCPC) at the Morehouse School of Medicine (MSM), that I wholeheartedly agreed when Kellogg Foundation leadership asked me to consider collaborating in building a permanent home for Community Voices at the NCPC. This was a natural marriage of, on one hand, a steadfast movement focused on eliminating health disparities and opening the doors of access to all, and on the other, an institution whose mission includes among other things improving the health and well-being of individuals and communities through programs in education, research, and service. The subsequent and current organizational placement of Community Voices under the Satcher Health Leadership Institute, established in 2006 at the MSM, has also been a natural fit.

Over the course of a ten-year history, Community Voices has produced myriad lessons regarding promising programs and policies and specific recommendations for improving health and quality health care access for all. Community Voices has contributed to the body of information on how best to address the crisis of health disparity, including men's health—the "silent crisis," mental health, and oral health. While the overarching goal of the initiative was always to ensure access to quality health care, especially for the most vulnerable, it was clear that there were a number of different pathways for addressing the issues. Given this, significant work was developed around providing credibility for the value and contribution of community health workers, employing solid care management methodologies; developing insurance products; and deploying facilitated enrollment strategies for those eligible for public programs.

Each Community Voices site was unique, and after the first five years, Kellogg re-funded eight of the original thirteen sites. The logic of funding so many different places was particularly attached to the notion of the "learning laboratory," such that lessons and best practices would derive from each of the communities involved, offering numerous alternatives in practice and in policy. While certainly there are common elements among all, each site also has had different experiences in the manner in which programmatic and policy changes have been implemented.

The leadership and tenacity of Kellogg and MSM leaders have championed the causes established in the first-ever *Surgeon General Report on Oral Health* and *Surgeon General's Report on Mental Health,* both released during my tenure, by ensuring that traditionally neglected areas such as oral health, mental health, and men's health were put on the map of primary care. Today, as you will read here, there is traction and success in all of these areas of work. The importance of good oral health has been embraced by both communities and foundations alike and by local and state governments, with the understanding that primary care can play a significant role. Men's health is finally being understood as directly related to community health—to the health of families, women, and children. Men's health now sits squarely on the table of health policy discussions and is no longer an issue that can be ignored. More emphasis has been placed on mental health and the need to reduce the stigma associated with mental disorders and mental illness and on the inappropriate treatment of people who are incarcerated or recently released from jails and prisons.

This book summarizes the extensive work of the Community Voices initiative. While Community Voices' leaders have published in a number of the country's top journals, its history has not been collected in one place. In addition to the Introduction and Afterword, the book is divided into two major parts. Part One introduces and highlights the work of the eight Community Voices sites. Part Two provides a brief description of the major issues addressed as well as policy briefs and reprints of some publications. We hope that this book will not only raise awareness of the significant work of Community Voices but also serve to motivate those of us who believe in health equity to explore the roles we each can play in eliminating health disparities throughout the world. Let this be the starting point.

David Satcher, M.D., Ph.D.
Director, The Satcher Health Leadership Institute and
The Center of Excellence on Health Disparities
Poussaint-Satcher-Cosby Professor of Mental Health
Morehouse School of Medicine
Atlanta, Georgia
16th Surgeon General of the United States
January 2011

ACKNOWLEDGMENTS

This book is the product of many minds and many hands. It is the sum of years of work; the body of evidence of an odyssey toward improving health care access for so many. No one person alone could have accomplished such a task; rather, many thanks must be given to a number of institutions and individuals.

We thank the W.K. Kellogg Foundation for its vision and commitment to this work over the years. In particular, we are ever grateful to Ms. Barbara Sabol, former Program Officer, who was one of the key leaders who crafted and implemented this work throughout the country, never taking "No, it's not possible" for an answer. Likewise, we thank Dr. Gloria Smith, former Vice President, for her overall support and confidence in the power of communities to make change. We are grateful, also, to our colleagues at the National Center for Primary Care (NCPC) and the Morehouse School of Medicine for supporting Dr. David Satcher's initial "Yes!" to this work and believing enough in its mission to carry it through and provide a permanent home for the initiative. We personally thank Dr. Georges C. Benjamin, Executive Director, American Public Health Association, for his valued counsel and support over the years. Finally, we acknowledge the other work that has served to advance the Community Voices story from the perspective of different places across the country, among them Northern Manhattan Community Voices' publication of *Mobilizing the Community for Better Health: What the Rest of America Can Learn from Northern Manhattan*, Columbia University Press, forthcoming, and *Taking Care of the Uninsured*, Voices of Detroit Initiative, 2009.

None of the actual accomplishments, of course, would have ever happened had it not been for the thoughtful and incisive leadership of the project directors who engaged in this adventure to find that change was truly possible. Our heartfelt thanks and solidarity go to Dr. Laura Herrera, Mr. Dennis Cherot, Ms. Sherry Adeyemi, Dr. Nicole Jarrett, Ms. Michelle Spencer, and Mr. Vincent DeMarco of Baltimore Community Voices; Dr. Elizabeth Whitley and Dr. Patricia Gabow of Denver Health Community Voices; Ms. Melany Mack, Mr. Doak Bloss, and Mr. Bruce Bragg of Ingham County Community Voices; Ms. Elise Linder, Dr. Pedro Jose "Joe" Greer Jr., and Mr. Rod Petrey of Community Voices Miami; Mr. Wayne Powell, Dr. Dan Derkson, and Dr. Arthur Kaufman of Community Voices of New Mexico; Mr. Charles Frock, Ms. Lisa Hartsock, Ms. Barbara Bennett, Ms. Roxanne Leopper, and Ms. Angela Conner of FirstHealth Community Voices; Ms. Jacqueline Martinez, Dr. Allan Formicola, and Mr. Moises Perez of the Northern Manhattan Community Voices Collaborative; and Ms. Luella Penserga, Ms. Sherry Hirota, Ms. Jane Garcia, and Mr. Ralph Silber of Oakland Community Voices. Without these leaders, individually and collectively, the work you will read about here would simply not have been possible. Their patient and devoted contributions to making this book factual and useful to public health students and policymakers alike is much appreciated. To all of these leaders and so many others whom we may not have mentioned directly by name here, those who helped conceive of the ideas that have brought us to where we are today—we pay tribute to you and give thanks knowing that without you and the visible leadership of project directors throughout the country, this work would have remained only as a worthy goal in the minds of a few courageous leaders.

Last, we give thanks to the many invisible hands at both NCPC and Jossey-Bass that brought this work to life. We thank you all for your tenacity in this endeavor, as we are sure many future students of community public health will too.

THE AUTHORS

The Editors

Henrie M. Treadwell

Dr. Henrie M. Treadwell, Ph.D., is Director and Senior Social Scientist for Community Voices, a special informing policy initiative that is funded by the W.K. Kellogg Foundation. She is also a full-time research professor in the Department of Community Health and Preventive Medicine at Morehouse School of Medicine. Her work includes formulation of health and social policy options, oversight of programs designed to address health disparities and the social determinants of health, and special programs to facilitate reentry into community of those engaged with the criminal justice system. She is the founder of the Freedom's Voice Symposium and the Soledad O'Brien Freedom's Voice Award, an award to recognize mid-career individuals doing significant work to improve global society. Dr. Treadwell also oversees dissemination of policy briefs, fact sheets, and other media products to inform the policymakers and the public and communities of policy and program options to improve health access. She has been featured on many major media outlets, such as CNN's *Lou Dobbs Tonight* and the Campbell Brown show. She frequently appears on various syndicated radio and television networks aired throughout the world. Dr. Treadwell most recently co-authored *Health Issues in the Black Community*.

Marguerite J. Ro

Marguerite Ro, Dr.PH., is Deputy Director of the Asian & Pacific Islander American Health Forum (APIAHF), a national health policy organization dedicated to strengthening policies, programs, and research to improve the health and well-being of Asian Americans, Native Hawaiians, and Pacific Islanders. Formerly an assistant professor at Columbia University, she held appointments in the College of Dental Medicine, the Mailman School of Public Health, and the Center for Community Health Partnerships. Dr. Ro has worked on national and state initiatives aimed at improving access to health care and reducing disparities for underserved and vulnerable populations. She was the senior policy analyst for the Community Voices: Healthcare for the Underserved Initiative. Recently, Dr. Ro has been appointed to serve on the Advisory Committee on Minority Health for the U.S. Department of Health and Human Services. Dr. Ro received her master's degree and doctorate from the Johns Hopkins School of Hygiene and Public Health.

Leda M. Pérez

Leda M. Pérez, Ph.D., is Vice President for Health Initiatives at the Collins Center for Public Policy in Miami, Florida, where she leads efforts to promote promising practices and policies to improve access to quality health care for the people of Florida and the nation. In 1999–2003 she was the project director for Community Voices Miami, based at Camillus House, a not-for-profit organization in the service of homeless people. In 2003, Dr. Pérez joined the Collins Center for Public Policy, where she continued to lead Community Voices Miami until 2008. Prior to Community Voices, Dr. Pérez worked on issues related to Latin American development and human rights. She has published on a number of community health issues, including men's health, prison health, and the power of community health workers as part of the integrated system of care. Dr. Pérez has consulted for the United Kingdom's Department for International Development (DFID)-funded Medicines Transparency Alliance (MeTA) in Peru. She earned a Ph.D. in international studies with specializations in Interamerican studies and development from the University of Miami in 1996. She holds a Master of Arts degree in international affairs and a Bachelor of Science degree in communication.

The Contributors

Georges C. Benjamin

Georges C. Benjamin, M.D., FACP, has been Executive Director of the American Public Health Association (APHA), the nation's oldest and largest organization of public health professionals, since December 2002. He came to that post from his position as Secretary of the Maryland Department of Health and Mental Hygiene. Dr. Benjamin became Secretary of Health in Maryland in April 1999, following four years as Maryland's Deputy Secretary for Public Health Services. As Secretary, Dr. Benjamin oversaw the expansion of and improvement in the state's Medicaid program.

Dr. Benjamin is a graduate of the Illinois Institute of Technology and the University of Illinois College of Medicine. He is board-certified in internal medicine and a Fellow of the American College of Physicians; a Fellow of the National Academy of Public Administration, Fellow Emeritus of the American College of Emergency Physicians, and an Honorary Fellow of the Royal Society of Public Health.

At APHA, Dr. Benjamin also serves as the publisher of the nonprofit's monthly publication, *The Nation's Health*, the association's official newspaper, and *The American Journal of Public Health*, the profession's premier scientific publication. He is the author of over one hundred scientific articles and book chapters. Dr. Benjamin also serves on the boards of Research!America, Partnership for Prevention, and the Reagan-Udall Foundation, and is a member of the Institute of Medicine of the National Academies. In 2008 he was named one of the top twenty-five minority executives in health care by *Modern Healthcare* magazine in addition to being voted amongst the one hundred most powerful people in health care in 2007 through 2009 and one of the nation's Most Powerful Physician Executives in 2009.

Barbara Bennett

Barbara Bennett, R.N., B.S.N., M.S.N., L.N.C., is Administrative Director for Regional and Community Health Services and has been in this position with FirstHealth of the Carolinas since April of 2006. She serves as the overall leader and manager of community benefit activities for FirstHealth of the Carolinas (FHC). She also serves as the administrator for Home Health, Hospice, Health and Fitness Centers and leads several initiatives, including FirstFit, the FirstHealth employee wellness program.

Before accepting the position with Community Health Services, Ms. Bennett was the corporate risk manager and administrative director for all risk activities for seven years starting in April 1999. Prior to this position she served as the director for Behavioral Services for FHC for twelve years, during which time she developed the full continuum of Behavioral Services.

Ms. Bennett received a Bachelor of Science degree in nursing from UNC-Greensboro in 1976 and was the recipient of the Faculty Award for Nursing in her class; she received a master's degree in community mental health from the University of Kentucky in 1982. She has ten years of experience in teaching nursing, including curriculum development and an assistant professorship at Western Carolina University in Cullowhee, North Carolina.

Traci N. Bethea

Traci N. Bethea, M.P.A., is currently a doctoral candidate in the Department of Environmental Health at Boston University School of Public Health. Her dissertation focuses on the role of place in health by investigating differences in self-rated health by urban and rural status and the effect of neighborhood factors on the incidence of head and neck cancer. Her research interests include the influence of the built environment on health, exposure, and chronic outcomes among correctional populations, and the social factors that have an impact on health disparities. Since 2008, she has been a teaching assistant in environmental health and epidemiology courses and, since the following year, has been a guest lecturer at both Boston University and Northeastern University. Prior to doctoral study, she completed a Bachelor of Arts degree at Duke University and a Master of Public Administration degree at Columbia University's School of International and Public Affairs.

Doak Bloss

Doak Bloss, B.A., is a writer and facilitator. Since 1998 he has worked for the Ingham County Health Department (ICHD), where he served as the project coordinator for Ingham Community Voices until 2002. As Health Equity and Social Justice Coordinator for ICHD, he leads a team of twenty facilitators conducting four-day workshops on health equity and social justice for the department's employees and interested community members. His coordination of the Social Justice Project for Ingham County Health Department is detailed in a chapter of the 2007 publication *Tackling Health Inequities: A Handbook for Action,* published by the National Association of City and County Health Officials, and updated and reissued in 2010 by Oxford University Press.

Bruce Bragg

Bruce Bragg, M.P.H., was director of the Ingham County Health Department (ICHD) for over thirty years until his retirement in 2007. ICHD serves a population of about three hundred thousand with a staff of three hundred and a budget of over $30 million. ICHD provides a broad range of services, including operation of a network of Federally Qualified Health Centers, which provide primary care services to twenty-five thousand low-income, uninsured Medicaid and Medicare individuals. ICHD also provides categorical public health services, communicable disease prevention and control, and environmental hazard prevention and control services. ICHD has actively engaged the community through community health assessment and improvement and environmental health assessment and improvement initiatives, and through its coordinating role in the implementation of a Robert Wood Johnson

Foundation grant to ensure access to health care for the uninsured and a W.K. Kellogg Foundation "Community Voices" grant. Presently Mr. Bragg is an outreach specialist/assistant professor in the College of Human Medicine at Michigan State University. He also consults with the Michigan Department of Community Health in the development of infrastructure capacity of local health departments.

Ronald L. Braithwaite

Ronald L. Braithwaite, Ph.D., is currently a professor in the Departments of Community Health and Preventative Medicine, Psychiatry, and Family Medicine (and director of research in Family Medicine) at Morehouse School of Medicine. He received his B.A. and M.S. degrees from Southern Illinois University in sociology and rehabilitation counseling and a Ph.D. in educational psychology from Michigan State University. He has done postdoctoral studies at Howard University, Yale University, and the University of Michigan School of Public Health and Institute for Social Research. He has held faculty appointments at Virginia Commonwealth University, Hampton University, Howard University, Rollins School of Public Health of Emory University, and the School of Public Health at the University of Cape Town, South Africa.

His research involves HIV intervention studies with juveniles and adults in correctional systems, social determinants of health, health disparities, and community capacity building.. He also served as a senior justice fellow for the Center for the Study of Crime, Culture, and Communities. Dr. Braithwaite also serves on the National Institute of Drug Abuse-African American Scholars and Research group. His research spans the globe to Africa, where he has conducted HIV prevention projects in Ghana, Kenya, Swaziland, Zimbabwe, Senegal, Gambia, Ethiopia, Malawi, Tanzania, and South Africa.

Dennis G. Cherot

Dennis G. Cherot has an extensive background in health care management, with expertise in primary care managed care, hospital administration, and public health administration. He currently serves as president and CEO of Total Health Care, a Federally Qualified Health Center, serving thirty thousand patients at nine Primary Care sites throughout Baltimore City. He has previously served as vice president and senior vice president, respectively, at Liberty Medical Center in Baltimore and Interfaith Medical Center in Brooklyn, New York.

Previous positions include serving as a member of the Mayor's Cabinet in Newark, New Jersey, as director of the Department of Health & Welfare, the largest health care municipal department in the state of New Jersey.

Gail C. Christopher

Gail C. Christopher, D.N., is vice president for programs at the W.K. Kellogg Foundation in Battle Creek, Michigan. In this role, she serves on the executive team that provides overall direction and leadership for the Kellogg Foundation and provides leadership for Food, Health & Well-Being, and Racial Equity programming. She is a nationally recognized leader in health policy, with particular expertise and experience in the issues related to social determinants of health, health disparities, and public policy issues of concern to African Americans and other minority populations. A prolific writer and presenter, she is the author or co-author of three books; a monthly column in the *Federal Times;* and more than 250 articles, presentations, and publications. Prior to joining the Kellogg Foundation, Dr. Christopher was vice president of the Joint Center for Political and Economic Studies' Office of Health, Women and Families in Washington, D.C. She holds a doctor of naprapathy degree from the Chicago National College of Naprapathy in Illinois and completed advanced study in the interdisciplinary Ph.D. program in holistic health and clinical nutrition at the Union for Experimenting Colleges and Universities at Union Graduate School of Cincinnati, Ohio.

Daniel Derksen

Daniel Derksen, M.D., is a professor in the Department of Family & Community Medicine and Senior Fellow for the Robert Wood Johnson Foundation Center for Health Policy at the University of New Mexico (UNM). He sees patients and teaches medical students and resident trainees at UNM and at the First Choice South Valley Health Commons in Albuquerque, New Mexico. Dr. Derksen was president of the NM Medical Society in 2009 and worked on medical homes legislation, culminating in the enactment of HB 710. He was appointed to a four-year term on the American Academy of Family Physicians Commission on Governmental Advocacy in 2010. Dr. Derksen completed an RWJ Health Policy Fellowship in 2008. His Capitol Hill assignment was with Senator Jeff Bingaman (D-NM). Dr. Derksen worked on S.790, "The Health Access and Health Professions Supply Act of 2009," parts of which appear in the Senate health reform bill HR 3590. The legislation calls for the creation of a National Health Workforce Commission, grants, and programs to increase the supply of health professionals to rural and underserved areas, and funding for Teaching Health Centers.

Allan J. Formicola

Allan J. Formicola, D.D.S., is a professor of dentistry and former dean of the Columbia University College of Dental Medicine (1978–2001). He is the founder of the Center for Community Health Partnerships, which merged into the Center for Family and

Community Medicine at Columbia University. Dr. Formicola brought together the collaboration between Columbia University Medical Center, the Alianza Dominicana, and the Harlem Hospital Medical Center to establish Northern Manhattan Community Voices Collaborative. Under his leadership as dean of the College of Dental Medicine, the Community DentCare network was developed and the Thelma Adair Medical/Dental Center was established. He currently directs or co-directs a number of national foundation projects dealing with oral health disparities and a lack of access to dental care.

Jane Garcia

Jane Garcia, M.P.H., is the chief executive officer of La Clínica de La Raza, a federally qualified health center with twenty-five locations, headquartered in Oakland, California. La Clínica de La Raza has an annual operating budget of over $65 million and serves over fifty-five thousand individuals, the majority of whom are low income, working, and uninsured. *Hispanic Business* recognized La Clínica de La Raza as the seventh largest nonprofit in the U.S. in service to Latinos. Ms. Garcia is a recipient of the National Medical Fellowship's Distinguished Public Service Award and the San Francisco Foundation's Community Leadership Award. In 2003, Congresswoman Barbara Lee paid tribute to Ms. Garcia "for her twenty-five years of service to the community," which resulted in an entry into the Congressional Record. Ms. Garcia received her B.A. degree from Yale University and her master's degree from the University of California at Berkeley School of Public Health. Ms. Garcia is originally from El Paso, Texas.

Mary Guevara

Lisa G. Hartsock

Lisa G. Hartsock, M.P.H., is the National Executive Director for Assistance League, a national nonprofit organization that puts caring and commitment into action through community-based philanthropic programs. Assistance League has 122 chapters with nearly twenty-six thousand volunteers in seventeen states. Prior to this national position, Ms. Hartsock has worked with health and human service organizations in leadership roles to oversee grants management, program development, and philanthropy. She was the project director for FirstHealth of the Carolinas Community Voices from 1998 through 2004. Ms. Hartsock earned her Bachelor of Science degree from the University of Iowa and her Master of Public Health degree from the University of North Carolina at Chapel Hill with the focus of health policy and administration.

Sherry Hirota

Sherry Hirota is the chief executive officer of Asian Health Services, a nationally recognized multicultural and multilingual federally qualified health center located in Oakland Chinatown, California. Under the executive leadership of Ms. Hirota since 1983, Asian Health Services has grown to serve more than twenty thousand patients, with a staff of 220 and an annual budget of $18 million. Ms. Hirota's board and advisory affiliations include The California Endowment; Advisory Committee on Research on Minority Health; Advisory Board of the Bureau of Primary Health Care's National Center for Cultural Competence; the Dellums' Commission: Expanded Pathways of Young Men of Color; Workforce Committee of the California Primary Care Association; Alameda Alliance for Health; Community Health Center Network; and the Alameda Health Consortium. Ms. Hirota is a recipient of The California Wellness Foundation's 2005 Champions of Health Professions Diversity Award; Outstanding Woman of the Year in Health—Alameda County Women's Hall of Fame; Robert Wood Johnson Community Health Leadership Award; and Woman of the Year, 16th Assembly District of California.

Kisha Braithwaite Holden

Kisha Braithwaite Holden, Ph.D., is Associate Director for Community Voices: Healthcare for the Underserved and an assistant professor of clinical psychiatry at Morehouse School of Medicine. She earned her doctorate degree from Howard University in counseling psychology and completed an NIMH funded postdoctoral research fellowship at The Johns Hopkins University in the school of medicine and school of public health. Dr. Holden brings several years of experience as a clinician, evaluator, and researcher conducting community-based studies focused on mental health disparities and depression among African American women. She is committed to promoting the health and well-being of culturally diverse families and the development of strategies for informing mental health policy.

Arthur Kaufman

Arthur Kaufman, M.D., is Distinguished Professor for the Department of Family and Community Medicine at the University of New Mexico and Vice President for Community Health. Before joining the faculty at the University of New Mexico in 1974, he served in the Indian Health Service in South Dakota and New Mexico. He has devoted his career to innovations in medical education and clinical service directed at health needs of underserved, rural, and marginalized populations. Models of service he has championed include the "Health Commons," which offers one-stop shopping where primary care, behavioral health, case management and public health are integrated. He has also helped develop the concept of "Health Extension Rural Offices" in New Mexico, whereby field health agents link community health priorities with university resources. He was chair of the Department of Family and Community Medicine for fifteen years before assuming his new role as Vice President for Community Health.

Roxanne Leopper

Roxanne Leopper, M.S., is the policy director for Community Health Services of FirstHealth of the Carolinas in Pinehurst, which serves as a Community Voices learning laboratory. Ms. Leopper works in conjunction with community partners to develop and implement plans for policy work at the local, state, and federal levels in the areas of access to care, men's health, mental health, tobacco, community health workers, and oral health. She also serves as a liaison to state and federal executive and congressional offices along with state government agencies. She has oversight responsibility for data tracking and identifying areas of opportunity with regard to community health initiatives, implementation of outreach programs, coordination of marketing campaigns, and evaluation of programs. Ms. Leopper serves in leadership positions for various community collaboratives to include Moore Health and the North Carolina Alliance for Health. She received her Bachelor of Science degree from West Virginia University and her Master of Science degree from The American University.

Elise M. Linder

Elise M. Linder, M.S.W., began her career at Camillus Health Concern serving Miami's homeless population in 1995 after moving to Miami, Florida. She became the supervisor of case management services until 1998, when she joined Community Voices Miami at Camillus House, focusing her attention on infrastructure development, building and facilitating community collaboratives, policy development, and research and data collection. Ms. Linder has authored publications regarding access to health care through school-based settings and state policy for providing oral health services to children with Medicaid in Florida. She facilitated local stakeholder collaboratives in school-based health and oral health, which led to the development of strategic planning to improve policies and programs for services provided to people without health insurance or without appropriate coverage. Ms. Linder is currently developing a private practice and pursuing a career in health psychology. She received her bachelor's degree from Emory University and her master's degree in social work from the University of Georgia.

Melany Mack

Melany Mack, M.S.W., serves as Director of Public Health Services at the Ingham County Health Department in Lansing, Michigan. She oversees Community Health Assessment, Health Promotion, and Public Health Services, which includes Public Health Nursing and Family Outreach Services. She is actively engaged in the department's Building Healthy Communities Initiatives. Beginning in 2002, Ms. Mack was project coordinator for the Ingham County Community Voices Initiative, serving as liaison to community groups and providing administrative oversight for outreach contracts. She is responsible for overseeing enforcement of Ingham County's tobacco licensing regulation. Ms. Mack completed an M.S.W. degree at Michigan State University and is intensely interested in issues of community, health, and social justice.

Stephen Marshall

Stephen Marshall is Senior Associate Dean for Extramural Programs at the Columbia University College of Dental Medicine (CDM). Since 1988, Dr. Marshall has held various positions at the CDM, including Acting Director for the Division of Community Health, Director of Clinical Business Affairs and Managed Care, Chairman of the Quality Assurance Committee, and Assistant Dean for Patient Care Programs. He is currently responsible for the Community DentCare Program, the ElderSmile Program, hospital relationships, dental plans, and continuing education programs.

Jacqueline Martinez

Jacqueline Martinez, M.P.H., is the senior program director at the New York State Health Foundation. She serves as a key adviser to the president and CEO and leads two of the Foundation's program areas. Prior to joining the Foundation, Ms. Martinez served as the executive director for the Northern Manhattan Community Voices Collaborative at Columbia University's Center for Community Health Partnerships, where she implemented and evaluated health programs in obesity prevention, mental health, case management, and childhood asthma. Under the leadership of the National Community Voices initiative, she worked to mobilize national, state, and local resources to promote policy changes to address the health care concerns addressed by the program. Ms. Martinez has also served as program manager for Alianza Dominicana, Inc., and has been a National Institutes of Health (NIH) fellow in Yucatan, Mexico, and an assistant coordinator for Beginning with Children, a Brooklyn-based charter school. Ms. Martinez holds a Master of Public Health degree from Columbia University and a Bachelor of Science degree from Cornell University. She has served as adjunct professor of sociology at the Borough of Manhattan Community College, board director of the Institute for Civic Leadership, and board member of the National Alliance on Mental Illness-New York City Metro.

Michael Murnik

Mary E. Northridge

Mary E. Northridge, Ph.D., M.P.H., is a professor of clinical sociomedical sciences (in dental medicine) at Columbia University. Professor Northridge holds joint appointments in the Mailman School of Public Health (MSPH) and the College of Dental Medicine. In addition, she is a faculty member in the Department of Sociomedical Sciences at the MSPH and the Urban Planning Program at the Graduate School of Architecture, Planning and Preservation, and teaches a course titled Interdisciplinary Planning for Health. In 2008, Professor Northridge was reappointed as editor-in-chief of the *American Journal of Public Health* (AJPH) for her fourth three-year term. She first collaborated with Henrie M. Treadwell and Community Voices in bringing to fruition the May 2003 issue of the AJPH, devoted to men's health. Professor Northridge has enduring interests in social and environmental determinants of health, and an emerging focus on the utility of systems science to integrate and sustain holistic health and health care.

Joyce H. Nottingham

Joyce N. Nottingham, M.S., Ph.D., graduated from Spelman College with a B.A. degree in biology. Dr. Nottingham earned an M.S. degree in counselor education from Southern Connecticut State University and a Ph.D. in educational psychology from Georgia State University. She attended leadership programs at both Harvard University and Bryn Mawr College in Pennsylvania.

Dr. Nottingham has taught at the elementary, secondary, and college levels. Most of her professional career has been in higher education administration, including at Morehouse College as testing director, Associate Director of the Office of Health Professions, Director of Institutional Research, and Associate Vice President for Institutional Research and Planning. Dr. Nottingham also served as Vice President of Institutional Research, Planning, and Effectiveness, at Life Chiropractic College.

For the past six years, Dr. Nottingham has worked at the Morehouse School of Medicine as a consultant with the Community Voices Program and with the sixteenth Surgeon General, Dr. David Satcher. She has also worked as an educational and management consultant in the private sector. More recently, Dr. Nottingham has served as Associate Director of the Satcher Health Leadership Institute at the More-house School of Medicine and as the Institute's Communications and Fundraising Specialist.

Luella J. Penserga

Luella J. Penserga, M.P.H., has worked for almost twenty years in the field of public health and health services. She is the project director of Community Voices—Oakland, a collaborative project of Asian Health Services and La Clínica de La Raza, two community health centers, and the Alameda Health Consortium, an association of eight community health centers in Alameda County, California. Previously Ms. Penserga worked at the Asian & Pacific Islander American Health Forum and at the University of California—Los Angeles (UCLA) Center for Health Policy Research. She has directed projects on numerous issues, including access to care, the uninsured, emergency department use, women's health, domestic violence, tobacco control, and cancer survivorship. She is a former board president of the Asian Women's Shelter in San Francisco, and worked and volunteered for numerous organizations, including The San Francisco Women's Foundation and the Alameda Alliance for Health. She received her M.P.H. degree from UCLA and her B.A. degree from Oberlin College in Ohio.

Wayne Powell

Wayne Powell, B.A., M.A., serves as the associate director for the Office of the Vice President for Community Health (OVPCH), University of New Mexico, Health Sciences Center; the associate director for the Institute for Public Health, OVPCH; and the project director for Community Voices New Mexico. He started his professional career as a community service coordinator and caseworker in rural New Mexico. He was appointed first Cabinet Secretary of the New Mexico Children Youth and Families Department; served as Deputy Secretary of the NM Human Services Department, and held numerous other positions in state and local governments, as well as serving on boards and committees. He provides consultation to county and local communities on local policy development, intergovernmental relations, and technical assistance. He has co-authored articles for the *American Journal of Public Health, Journal of Health Care for the Poor and Underserved,* and publications of the W.K. Kellogg Foundation.

Fornessa Randal

Fornessa Randal is Executive Director of the Coordinated Systems of Care Community Access Program of New Mexico and Director of Innovative Community

Engagements for the University of New Mexico's Office for Community Health. She has spent the past eight years spearheading three major statewide initiatives providing access to health care for uninsured and underinsured populations in New Mexico. She was lead inventor of the Primary Care Dispatch (sm), the Field Case Management program, and NurseAdvice (sm) New Mexico.

Melva Robertson

Melva Robertson, M.A.P.W., is Communications Manager for Community Voices of Morehouse School of Medicine. She is an experienced public relations officer with comprehensive skills developing effective communications to include media kits, speeches, publications, and website content. Prior to her time at Morehouse School of Medicine, Melva was Media Specialist II for the Department of Public Affairs at Grady Health System, in Atlanta, Georgia. There she served as liaison between the health system and international, national, and local media outlets. Through her media relations efforts, she maintained a positive image for the health system by coordinating internal and external hospital publicity, media coverage, commercials, and television shows. A graduate of Morris Brown College with a Bachelor of Arts degree in mass media arts, Melva is also experienced in news writing, reporting, and editing through freelance projects. She received her Master of Arts degree in professional writing from Kennesaw State University.

Barbara J. Sabol

Barbara J. Sabol, R.N., recently retired from her position as a program director for the Food, Health and Well-being and Policy teams at the W.K. Kellogg Foundation in Battle Creek, Michigan, where in her many years of leadership there she worked to develop and review programming priorities and recommended proposals for funding. Prior to Barbara's retirement, she worked closely with the vice president in implementing goals and strategies that support the Foundation's vision and mission.

Before joining the Foundation, Barbara was president and CEO of NorthStar Group in Washington, D.C. She also was commissioner for New York City's Human Resources Administration, serving more than one million New Yorkers and managing a budget of more than $15 billion and over fifteen thousand employees. In that position, she was responsible for the programs and policies in welfare, Medicaid, child welfare, and services for homeless adults and families.

Barbara is a registered nurse with management skills in operation, budget, program, and policy development. She has held appointments in government as a policymaker, manager, and cabinet officer. She has served on the board of directors for the New York City Health and Hospital Corporation, the largest public hospital system in the nation. Barbara gained national recognition for going underground as a welfare recipient to experience the system she administered from the client's point of view.

She holds a master's degree in counseling and guidance and a bachelor's degree in psychology, both from the University of Missouri at Kansas City. She received her registered nurse certification from Kansas City General Hospital and Medical Center.

David Satcher

David Satcher, M.D., Ph.D., is Director of The Satcher Health Leadership Institute, which was established in 2006 at the Morehouse School of Medicine in Atlanta, Georgia. The mission of the Institute is to develop a diverse group of public health leaders, foster and support leadership strategies, and influence policies toward the reduction and ultimate elimination of disparities in health. Dr. Satcher was sworn in as the 16th Surgeon General of the United States in 1998. He also served as Assistant Secretary for Health in the Department of Health and Human Services from February 1998 to January 2001, making him the second person in history to have held both positions simultaneously. Dr. Satcher graduated from Morehouse College in Atlanta, Georgia, in 1963. He holds M.D. and Ph.D. degrees from Case Western Reserve University in Ohio. A proponent of healthy lifestyles through physical activity and good nutrition, Dr. Satcher is an avid runner, rower, and gardener.

Ralph Silber

Ralph Silber has a masters degree from UC Berkeley in Public Health, with a concentration in health policy and planning. He has more than twenty-five years experience in community health, primary care, and health policy. For almost twenty years, he has served as the executive director of the Alameda Health Consortium, the association of eight nonprofit community health centers in Alameda County, California. He is also the chief executive officer of the Community Health Center Network, a managed care and practice management organization with more than forty-five thousand managed care members.

Mr. Silber is a founding member of the board of directors of the California Primary Care Association and a member of the Legislative Committee of the National Association of Community Health Centers. He has served on numerous government advisory committees at the federal, state, and county levels and has delivered presentations at numerous national conferences. He has held research and teaching positions at both UC Berkeley and Stanford University. He has authored articles in the *American Journal of Public Health* and *Medical Care*.

Betty Skipper

Betty Skipper, Ph.D., is a professor of biostatistics and epidemiology in the Department of Family and Community Medicine at the University of New Mexico. She teaches Evidence-Based Medicine—Medical Curriculum Phase IB and is a mentor for medical student research projects.

Michelle L. Spencer

Michelle L. Spencer, M.S., has been Chief of Staff of the Baltimore City Health Department since 2005. She has previously worked for the Maryland Department of Health and Mental Hygiene, Memorial Sloan-Kettering Cancer Center, and the Addiction Research and Treatment Corporation. Past contributions include presentations to the Baltimore City Mayor's Office of Minority and Women-Owned Business Development and the Maryland Council on Cancer Control.

Elizabeth Whitley

Elizabeth Whitley, Ph.D., R.N., is Director of Denver Health Community Voices (DHCV), the public health care safety net for Denver, Colorado. She leads a learning laboratory dedicated to discovering new ways to increase access to health care, decrease health disparities among the underserved, and influence health policy through experimentation, transformation, linkages, and leveraging resources. She has extensive experience in establishing collaborative community-based programs and research, particularly in the areas of community outreach and patient navigation. She has created and tested models that have become best practices and are replicated nationally. Dr. Whitley is currently a co-principal investigator for the NCI-funded patient navigation research program to determine the efficacy of patient navigators on decreasing time to diagnosis and treatment for breast, colorectal, and prostate cancer patients. She is also conducting research on the return on investment of community outreach workers and patient navigators.

INTRODUCTION

THE POWER OF COMMUNITIES

Breaking a Legacy of Inequity and Disparity

Henrie M. Treadwell and Marguerite J. Ro

The founding of our nation was based upon the premise of "life, liberty, and justice for ALL," a nation where men, women, and their families would be free to
pursue the American Dream. The Dream is based on the idea that every person has
an equal opportunity to achieve the impossible, or at least to fulfill his or her potential. At a minimum, each man and woman should be able to take care of his or her
family and participate and contribute to his or her community and our American
society. A grand vision, but one not yet based in reality. And why not? Answers to
this lie in our nation's history of slavery, indentured servitude, and the continuing
structural discrimination that compounds issues of race and ethnicity, social class, and
gender, resulting in health disparities and inequities for too many.

While advances in science and technology have allowed people to travel to the
moon, to clone animals, and to extend life through technology and organ transplants,
millions of Americans continue to die early, experience preventable illnesses, and are
barred from seeing a doctor for basic health needs. This contradiction was—and
is—unacceptable to leaders at the W.K. Kellogg Foundation, who view health care
as a basic human right and who firmly believe in racial and social equity. Guided by
the unequivocal conviction that our country had to do better and that it was not only
possible—but imperative!—to improve health and health care, the Kellogg Foundation created the Community Voices: Healthcare for the Underserved initiative.

In the 1990s, Kellogg's tagline was "helping others help themselves." This reflected the strong belief that communities have untapped knowledge, assets, and

power that can be directed toward solving some of our nation's most basic problems. Communities can and should be the architects for change in promoting healthy communities with health care systems that reflect their needs. In the 1990s, as today, many communities (indigenous, low-income, rural, and, particularly communities of color) experienced the burden and pain of health disparities and inequities disproportionately. Given the tremendous diversity of our nation, there is no one solution or strategy that can resolve these issues. The solutions and strategies that move us toward health equity must then reflect the political, social, and economic context of communities, lifting up the experiences of those most unserved and underserved. For, if all people are to have access to quality care, if all are to improve their likelihood of being free from disease, if equity among our communities and populations are to be achieved, then we need to learn carefully what is working and what is not, especially for those most underserved.

Community Voices: Healthcare for the Underserved was launched in 1998 following a failed attempt at national health care reform that was focused primarily on the issue of health insurance coverage. Access, in the health care reform debate, was defined as having or not having health insurance. This was and remains contrary to the experiences of underserved communities for whom access is hindered due to a needlessly complex health care system, cultural and linguistic barriers, and lack of comprehensive health care services that include the mouth and mind as part of the body. It was clear, then, that Community Voices would have to address the myriad challenges that presented barriers to care.

This book is about the remarkable accomplishments of eight Community Voices communities, or "learning laboratories," that took on the challenge of improving and ensuring health care for the underserved. What you will read here is the compilation of a decade of thought, work, and action about the kinds of interventions and policies that it will take to ensure health and well-being for millions in the nation. The sum of many voices and issues, this work was successful in bringing to the fore contextually relevant solutions for health care access.

Leadership was stimulated on myriad levels. Leaders emerged in the unlikely and unusual partnerships between community-based organizations and academia; between political leadership and providers and consumers of health care; between the neighbor "next door" and the legislator at the capitol. This leadership, in turn, uncovered issues that had not previously been clearly seen or understood—issues including not only the race and ethnic disparities in health care but also the gender disparities between women and men, the latter having limited access to most services. This leadership was—is—unrelenting. Throughout the course of the initiative, the tenacity of those doing the work would serve to provide a deep understanding of who was and was not receiving care and some critical answers for why not. This book, then, represents a collection of the best that is known about how to address inequities and disparities in health and health care from across the Community Voices diaspora, including a selection of the most important published work, on issues ranging from the promising practices for ensuring health care access to some of the calls to action in policy. This is an extraordinary history of what is possible when communities are free to lead the way. This is the story of Community Voices: Healthcare for the Underserved.

1998: Health Care Access on the Verge of an Earthquake

By the late 1990s, as the W.K. Kellogg Foundation launched Community Voices: Healthcare for the Underserved, the number of uninsured in the country had risen to an astounding forty-three million individuals! Any notion of health reform had fallen off the national policy agenda, and the public safety net was on the brink of a crisis, with our nation's poorest families and communities bearing the brunt. In the near-decade between 1989 and 1998, uninsurance among non-elderly adults and children grew substantially. Between 1989 and 1993, the rate of the non-elderly uninsured grew by 2 percent, and between 1994 and 1998, it grew again from 17.3 percent to 18.2 percent. In both cases, declines in Medicaid coverage fueled this trend, and in the period between 1994 and 1998 the uninsured rate might have been yet higher had it not been for the increase in employer-sponsored coverage for some.[1] What this meant for low-income populations, however, is that they were still the most likely to be uninsured, as they were the least likely to benefit from employer-sponsored coverage, in some cases because of the inability to be employed or in many cases because employers did not offer health insurance, particularly for those who worked for small businesses or who worked part-time jobs. The disparity in the rise in uninsurance by ethnic or race breakdown during the period 1994–1998 was shocking: for white non-Hispanics, 3.4 percent; for black non-Hispanics, 17.4 percent; and for Hispanics, 21.5 percent.[2]

This period, following the defeat of the Clinton plan in the early 1990s, also witnessed the rise of health maintenance organizations and managed care in which insurance companies—not the medical and public health community—became gatekeepers for who received care and who did not. In this "managed care" environment, even those fortunate enough to have health insurance experienced limitations as to what their insurance would cover. In this model, primary health care ultimately included very little. Oral and mental health treatment, for example, were not—and are still not in many parts of the country—considered essential health care and were therefore not covered.

In oral health, despite the knowledge that billions of dollars were being spent on treatment of preventable dental caries and oral cancers and that low-income African Americans and Mexican Americans were more likely to have untreated decaying teeth than other non-Hispanic, white populations, oral health was still not integrated into primary health care or insurance coverage. In total, 90 percent of adults in the country were affected by tooth decay, a fact only bolstered by the release of the Surgeon General's Oral Health Report in 2000.[3] Among low-income children the situation was particularly acute, with one-third of these suffering from untreated caries in primary teeth.[4]

In the beginning of the new century, 20 percent of the country lived with a mental health issue, a substance issue, or both, but less than a third of those affected would actually receive treatment. Not unexpectedly, barriers included the lack of coverage available as well as the high price of medicines.[5] With managed care capitation rates, it was difficult to determine the quality of care for those who actually were able to get treatment. For the poorest, however, mental health coverage and care was limited, and instead, the jails and prisons received more people with mental illness or substance issues than did community-based centers for treatment, a trend that has continued to this writing.[6] This was due in great measure to the closure of psychiatric hospitals, resulting in a loss of state psychiatric beds and the inability of under-funded community services to provide adequate support and services for those with mental illness or those with substance dependency.[7]

Into the new millennium, the numbers of uninsured began to rise even more, as did health care spending. By fiscal year 2001, there was double-digit growth in Medicaid spending (10.9 percent in fiscal year 2001).[8] By fiscal year 2003, forty states had experienced Medicaid shortfalls, and nearly all states were seeking to contain their Medicaid spending.[9] By fiscal year 2004, the total medical expenditures for the now forty-four million uninsured individuals was estimated at nearly $125 billion, more than $41 billion of which was attributed to uncompensated care.[10]

An Initial Response to the Earthquake

It was during this political, economic, and social "earthquake" that Community Voices emerged in the late summer of 1998. The inability of so many to access basic health services and the disparities experienced by the same had reached a critical juncture. If national statistics regarding the soaring number of uninsured people in the country were not enough, when we dissected that data by race and ethnicity, looked at income levels, and looked specifically at the gaps in care (such as in oral health and mental health) even for those with health insurance, and when we considered the almost nonexistent care for low-income men, it was clear that the challenges were complex and deep and that a "one-size fits all" solution would not be sufficient.

It would be necessary, moreover, to provide the time, commitment, and resources to ensure that communities could devise solutions that addressed the myriad challenges and problems with the health care system and develop strategies and innovations that would promote the health of communities. We knew that whatever the answers or solutions would be, they would have to address the social, economic, and political determinants of the public's health. And we knew that only through sustained effort in communities over time would it be possible to get to the heart of the problems and to test innovations in practice and in policy to create the evidence base for change.

The Kellogg Foundation initially supported the work of thirteen community-based "learning laboratories" whose goal was to develop, implement, and refine strategies for catalyzing sustainable improvements that would make quality health care accessible to those who needed it most. To glean the best possible picture of the issues facing the country, the learning laboratories were based in areas home to some of the nation's most underserved populations, such as those living in poor urban and rural areas, Native Americans, immigrants, the formerly incarcerated, and the homeless. Each community where a learning laboratory was based faced its own unique issues and considerations, as well as shared cross-cutting challenges such as the lack of affordable insurance and lack of culturally appropriate care.

The initial thirteen learning laboratories were based in Alameda County/ Oakland, California; Albuquerque, New Mexico; Baltimore, Maryland; California, with a focus on Native Americans; Denver, Colorado; Detroit, Michigan; El Paso, Texas; Lansing/Ingham County, Michigan; Miami, Florida; North Carolina (select rural counties); northern Manhattan, New York; Washington, D.C., and West Virginia. These learning laboratories were led by various entities including health centers, public health departments, academic institutions, health care systems and networks, a policy advocacy organization, and an Indian health board. Together with support from a national resource team that provided policy technical assistance, communication support, and evaluation services, Community Voices set forth on an ambitious change agenda to tackle access and quality issues in the health care system at local, state, and national levels. The four broad outcomes for Community Voices were to

- Create a sustained increase in access to health services for the underserved and uninsured with a focus on primary care and prevention
- Ensure a preserved and strengthened health care safety net in the community within the context of an improved community
- Promote a changed delivery system in which care is delivered in a more cost-effective way and quality remains high
- Promote established models of best practices that provide examples of different approaches and strategies other communities can select from and adapt to their own unique circumstances.

In 2003, in an effort to institutionalize the efforts of the previous five years and build sustainability for the work, the National Center for Primary Care (NCPC) at the

Morehouse School of Medicine in Atlanta accepted leadership of the Community
Voices' program office (see the Conclusion for further discussion). With renewed
funding and a completion of the agenda of some of the original thirteen Community
Voices learning laboratories, the number of participating Community Voices sites was
reduced to eight: Alameda County/Oakland, California; Albuquerque, New Mexico;
Baltimore, Maryland; Denver, Colorado; Lansing/Ingham County, Michigan;
Miami, Florida; North Carolina (select rural counties); and northern Manhattan. During this final phase, with NCPC leading and coordinating efforts, areas of major
emphasis were mental health and substance abuse treatment; promotion of community health workers (CHWs); promotion of care management methodologies; a continuation of oral health direct services promotion; and men's health, prison health,
and reentry.

Community Voices: Getting to the Heart of the Matter

The charge for Community Voices was to catalyze systems changes that would ensure
improved delivery of health services, secured with policy changes that would sustain
the improvements in care. Community Voices sought to transform the health care
system to one that is more equitable by linking programs with policies. Moreover, the
goal was to lift up these local strategies and solutions to inform and stimulate change
at the national level. As part of the process for change, a series of "core principles"
was conceived to help guide the work of the participating communities. These principles became the "roadmap" for improving health care access and highlighting often
ignored but critical areas of community well-being.

A plan and capacity for informing the public and marketplace policy. It was understood from
the outset that the work developed would have to be relevant for both public and
private systems. We knew that it would be essential to inform policy decisions at different levels and that solutions might have to include a combination of approaches.
Sites such as Denver and North Carolina (see Chapters Two and Six), which operated
in the context of hospital systems, experimented with health insurance plans for small
businesses on one hand while developing strong care-management protocols for
chronically ill patients on the other. Often it was these kinds of combined approaches
that surfaced across the country as communities experimented with a number of possible practical and policy-oriented solutions.

A plan and strategy for development or refinement of a cost- effective delivery system. Along
these lines, a number of promising practices were developed. A strong line of work
promoted across all of the eight learning laboratories was in the CHW model. With
the knowledge that part of the access problem is based on the inability of many to
successfully navigate across a number of fragmented systems, the evolution of this
model was effective in raising awareness about the value of CHWs themselves as

connectors to care in a highly complex maze. In Denver, Ingham County, and New York, for example (see Chapters Two, Three, and Seven), CHWs led the way in critical efforts to enroll people in public and private health insurance plans while helping them to negotiate a large and often unfriendly system. On the basis of their success, work was also published in order to continue to inform policymakers (see Chapters Two, Three, and Seven, and Part Two). Yet in other sites, efforts were devoted to creating an employment pathway for these "natural helpers," oftentimes themselves part of the population of the underserved (see Chapters Four and Five), or to offering special training in order to ensure that care would be provided in culturally competent ways (see Chapter Eight).

Linkages to public health. Two learning laboratories functioned either in partnership, or directly out of a public health department (see Baltimore, Chapter One, and Ingham County, Chapter Three). As this work was conceived, it would be critical to demonstrate the larger public health needs often not seen clearly through a model focused exclusively on ensuring coverage. Moreover, because of the highly important role that public health departments play in underserved communities, there would be an opportunity to help strengthen these models of care and highlight the necessary changes. In Baltimore, in its initial partnership with the Baltimore City Health Department, it became clear that there was a dearth of services for men. In this context and with this knowledge through Baltimore Community Voices, the nation's first full-time men's health center was established, something that would come to be replicated elsewhere in Baltimore as well as in other places across the country (see Chapter One). Ingham County's health department took to heart the philosophy that communities should lead, and indeed they did as the Ingham County Health Department and Ingham Community Voices proceeded to successfully insure more people while improving access to services for those not receiving care (see Chapter Three).

Community involvement that includes all the key members of the community. Certainly, community participation and leadership were the cornerstones of Community Voices. Community Voices Miami (See Chapter Four) functioned only because of the simultaneous participation of community members and political leadership alike. In Ingham County a constant community dialogue process that in essence became the norm for the way in which the county's public health department operated was the basis for a number of critical change efforts in mental health, social and economic justice, and health disparities (See Chapter Three).

Clear plans and capability to hold the provider and community network together through infrastructure that includes management information systems, legal agreements, and established and expanded relationships. One of the best examples of this principle was demonstrated through the Northern Manhattan Community Voices Collaborative (see Chapter Seven) as well as in New Mexico Community Voices (see Chapter Five). In Northern Manhattan a formal partnership was established between a university, a hospital, and a community-based organization, the latter known for its strong history of activism in the community. Through this unlikely partnership it was possible to advance in a number of key policy areas, including mental health, improved information technology, and chronic diseases (such as diabetes and obesity). In New Mexico, through the "Health Commons" approach established in partnership with the University of New Mexico and the University of New Mexico Medical Center, a strong, community-based method of creating viable pathways for care for vulnerable populations was made possible (see Chapter Five).

Explicit responsiveness to the community's culture and environment for creating health and wellness. Indeed, in all of the Community Voices sites, there was a concern to ensure that the culture of the community be carefully considered as practical, and policy interventions were designed and implemented. For example, Oakland Community Voices, based in Alameda County and the home to one of the country's most diverse communities, led a number of efforts regarding cultural competency on the ground and ensured that the complex issues of the populations it served were brought to the policy forefront. The "California Uninsured Survey" was a one-of-a-kind effort to look deep into the community and provide solid data about its members and their needs (see Chapter Eight).

Effective use of resources to attain systems change. A clear insight was that resources would always be limited and thus change efforts would need to consider the most efficient and effective courses of action in order to be successful. New Mexico Community Voices (Chapter Five) was, in many ways, a model to other Community Voices laboratories and communities across the country. The New Mexico story is really one of constant leveraging of resources through solid partnerships and powerful engagement at the legislative level. Similarly, Northern Manhattan and North Carolina brought about unexpected changes in policies through systematic efforts devoted to creating the evidence base and the policy arguments (see Chapter Seven on Northern Manhattan's successful efforts with Medicaid and Chapter Six on North Carolina's efforts in changing tobacco legislation).

Demonstrated readiness of the organization(s) that will spearhead the project. The stakes were too high in this work, and it was essential that those who participated be committed to the process and the projected outcomes. Beyond this, "readiness" was mostly about the willingness of each site to step forward and engage in the work. It was about working with different contexts and understanding that the solutions emerging would not be the same for every place, but that some solutions would be universal.

The capacity to function and serve as a laboratory for systems change in which new approaches can be tested and through which others can learn. A fundamental principle for Community Voices, the "bottom line" of the work beyond working to obtain access to care and services for so many, was the learning. Kellogg's notion of each of the sites as "learning laboratories" was a conscious effort to experiment constantly and extract from these experiences the very best there was to give. Community Voices, as in the scientific method, produced a number of experiments, some which were more successful than others. But at the end of this ten-year journey there is now a body of work from which others may learn and continue the work.

The Community Voices Way of Working: A Word on Campaigns

Another critical aspect of the Community Voices learning laboratories work was the development and implementation of campaigns for specific policy targets (such as men's health, CHWs, mental health, and oral health). Together with the national resource team, three stages of each campaign were considered: formulation, awareness, and action.

Formulation

During the formulation stage, learning laboratories created the public engagement and messaging or evidence base for change campaigns. Sites worked to realign and collect more information where needed, spread the word about the issue, and forge lasting alliances. This entailed conducting research and analysis at local, state, and national levels on the problem or need, and answering the questions, Why is this issue a threat to the fiscal viability of the overall health care system? What is the current state of the issue with regard to programs, services, and policies? What systems changes are needed? What are the needed changes in the health care and social services systems? and, What strategic partners are needed to resolve the problem? It was important to answer these questions at both the local and national levels to link common priorities and to demonstrate that strategically (and tactically) these issues were integral to resolving the problem of lack of services for low-income communities and communities of color, especially. Ultimately, the idea was to support the voices of many from across the nation—from local, state, and national levels—in the development of a national campaign or movement. We knew it would be difficult to achieve broad-based change without this kind of momentum!

Also important was having these questions answered by key agencies, organizations, and individuals who reaffirmed, and in some cases strengthened, the credibility of the analyses from their disciplinary or practice perspective. For example, partnerships with academic researchers, policy think tanks, and peer-reviewed journals (see Part Two) were critical to developing issue materials and disseminating the same across a wide array of community and policy-oriented publics alike. Also, at the local level, learning laboratories produced materials that resulted in legislative studies (see North Carolina, Chapter Six, and New Mexico, Chapter Five). Another significant way of working was in the production of factsheets, briefs, reports, and presentations, which helped to provide clear and concise answers to key questions about mental health, men's health, CHWs and other areas of interest (see Chapters Two, One, and Seven, respectively). Hardcopy and electronic materials were made available to diverse groups of stakeholders, including community members, providers, health systems, insurers, policy advocates, think tanks, government agencies, policymakers, and other decision makers and opinion leaders.

These materials were part of the formulation to gain the "buy-in" and support for these issues from key stakeholders, including community leaders, policymakers, providers, leaders from faith-based organizations, researchers, and other opinion leaders. With this support, the learning laboratories were able to tackle these otherwise invisible issues.

Awareness

To catalyze change on issues such as men's health or oral health, raising awareness and visibility was critical. It was precisely the attention given to, and the awareness created around, the issues, emphasizing the disparities in care and the impact on families and communities, that would sustain and support the programmatic strategies and policy improvements.

Various communication and social marketing strategies and tools were adopted to gain earned media (that is, coverage in national news outlets). Key to achieving visibility was identifying public figures and celebrities who voiced support and participated in media activities for the various issue campaigns (for example, Surgeon General David Satcher and Senator Jeff Bingaman [New Mexico], Alonzo Mourning [professional basketball player], Danny Glover [actor]) and taking advantage of opportunistic events (such as the release of the Surgeon General's reports on oral health and mental health). These public awareness activities helped to catapult Community Voices as a recognizable entity in addressing issues such as the lack of available services for men or the inadequacy of mental health and oral health treatment, and encouraged other stakeholders to build relationships with Community Voices. Of key importance, messages were developed that would gain traction with policymakers, those working on the specific target issue, and the lay community.

At both the local and national levels, a sustained effort to bring visibility to the issues was critical. At the local level, holding meetings and conferences was critical to engaging communities in dialogue to help shape and support policy goals. Briefings at which communities invited local legislators to see and engage in ongoing efforts were important, as were briefings on Capitol Hill for legislators and their staffers. And maintaining an up-to-date web presence from both the national program office and the learning laboratories became a highly effective method for disseminating information, particularly as the Internet became a primary source of data.

Another key strategy was to build the evidence base in peer-reviewed literature. This was a major learning curve for all of the learning laboratories that were not based at academic institutions. Making writing a priority and then learning how to write for the journals was challenging, but ultimately very rewarding. Special issues of the *American Journal of Public Health*, the *Journal of Healthcare for the Poor and Underserved*, and articles in journals such as *Health Affairs*, the *Journal of Men's Health and Gender*, and the *International Journal of Men's Health* documented the work and impact of the learning laboratories, again lending value and credence to the work of communities.

Action

Success was benchmarked in various ways. Some of the most notable benchmarks included policy formulation and the adoption of legislation at federal and state levels; leveraging of new resources and financing; new opportunities to support future work; significant contributions in specific fields or areas of work; and, not of least significance, the number of vulnerable individuals who accessed care. Highlights of four of the campaigns (oral health, community outreach, mental health, and men's health), including the kinds of achievement that dedicated community efforts can accomplish, are the core of this text. There were so many successes in this work and, though they are not all captured here, some highlights should be underscored nevertheless. Detailed examples of the activities of the learning laboratories serve as the basis for chapters in Part One.

Onward: Beyond Community Voices

The agenda begun by Community Voices in the late 1990s is still not finished. As noted earlier, and as you will read in the forthcoming chapters, while there were a great many accomplishments, part of the "success" is that each learning laboratory was able to bring light to issues that had previously not been seriously considered. Thus, priority must now be given to current efforts devoted to addressing those issues. With this in mind, this book has been written with the hope that those who read it will come away inspired by what can be accomplished and with a stronger knowledge of what remains to be done.

Within the chapters of this book are critical lessons about leadership, building partnerships, and fomenting change. Leadership, as it is reflected in the work of the Community Voices sites, was diverse in terms of where individuals were housed and what roles individuals played in making change happen. Leadership was much more than title or status and was more about being mavens and connectors. These leaders sought to build new partnerships in providing services and in developing an advocacy base to support policy and systems changes. Working with local industry, well-established and successful national social service programs such as Head Start, youth groups, local businesses, and many others, Community Voices sites went beyond the traditional routes of working within health to expanding the group of stakeholders who made health a priority and a lens for community change. By taking the risk of forging innovative ways of working with new partners; by shining the light on critical health care issues that had been mostly ignored, including the limited access to primary care for men and the inadequate oral health and mental health treatment available, Community Voices was able to experiment, strategize, and make change happen. These are crucial lessons for every community, but also for us as a nation.

Organization of This Book

Part One contains eight chapters, each dedicated to one Community Voices site that participated in the initiative in the period 2003–2008. A description of each site's development, challenges, and successes is provided, as well as an abstract with learning objectives at the beginning of each chapter and a final section on lessons learned meant to help the reader extract the key points.

Each chapter highlights the specific social issues experienced in each site and how these were addressed as well as how the momentum was maintained for the larger national Community Voices initiative priority areas. Finally, Part One shares the calls to action expressed over the years by the sites as well as the current concerns and recommendations related to specific policy target areas as well as for the larger goals of the initiative.

Part Two compiles some of Community Voices' most cutting-edge publications. As noted before, part of the Community Voices "approach" was to seek out different spaces through which to tell the story of the issues being uncovered and the possible solutions for the same.

The book ends with a Conclusion and Afterword, the latter written by Dr. Gail C. Christopher, current vice president for programs at the Kellogg Foundation, a veritable call to action for the agenda that remains.

Notes

1. "Why Does the Number of Uninsured Americans Continue to Grow? Results," *Medscape Today*. Retrieved February 2, 2010, from http://www.medscape.com/viewarticie/409823_3.
2. Ibid.
3. H. Treadwell, C. Casares, and K. Norris, "Oral Health: Who Cares? Who Should Care?" *Community Voices*, 2006.
4. "Promoting Oral Health: Interventions for Preventing Dental Caries, Oral and Pharyngeal Cancers, and Sports-Related Craniofacial Injuries," Centers for Disease Control,

November 30, 2001. Retrieved February 2, 2010, from http://www.cdc.gov/mmwr/preview/mmwrhtmllrr5021a1.htm.

5. M. Ro and L. Shum, "Forgotten Policy: An Examination of Mental Health in the U.S.," W.K. Kellogg Foundation, May 2001, p. 1.

6. R. Daly, "Prison Mental Health Crisis Continues to Grow," *Psychiatric News*, 2006, 41(20), 1.

7. See Bazelon Law Center, http://www.bazelon.org/.

8. D. J. Boyd, "The Bursting State Fiscal Bubble and State Medicaid Budgets," *Health Affairs*, 2003, 22(1), 55.

9. V. Smith, K. Gifford, R. Ramesh, and V. Wachino, "Medicaid Spending Growth: A 50-State Update for Fiscal Year 2003," Kaiser Commission on Medicaid and the Uninsured, January 2003.

10. J. Hadley and J. Holahan, "The Cost of Care for the Uninsured: What Do We Spend, Who Pays, and What Would Full Coverage Add to Medical Spending?" Kaiser Commission on Medicaid and the Uninsured, May 2004.

COMMUNITY VOICES

PART ONE

CHAPTER ONE

BALTIMORE COMMUNITY VOICES

Serving the Uninsured and Underserved Through Coalition-Building and Special Attention to Men's Health[1]

Dennis G. Cherot and Michelle L. Spencer

This chapter provides a review of Maryland's coalition-building efforts for health care access as well as the development of men's health programming and policy in Baltimore City. In both instances, coalition leaders and men's health service providers alike engaged myriad communities to educate and mobilize them around issues of concern. This chapter showcases the success of Maryland's Health Care for All! Coalition and shares the process and the tools used to establish and develop the first full-time men's health center in the country. After reading this chapter, the reader will

- Learn about the work of the Maryland's Health Care for All! Coalition and its political success in improving health care access for Marylanders
- Understand the context and issues facing men in Baltimore, an underserved subpopulation
- Learn about the kinds of services required to improve access to health care for underserved men around the country
- Learn about the kinds of tools used to attract men to a specialized health center as well as to inform policymakers about gaps in the system

- Learn about likely and unlikely partnerships toward improving access to care for vulnerable populations
- Identify barriers to care and learn how to develop strategies and models to overcome them

Introduction

It was impossible to know in 1998 when Community Voices first funded the Baltimore City Health Department (BCHD) that its work would become synonymous with men's health and the largest coalition in the state to reform health care. Perhaps it was Baltimore Community Voices' (BCV's) deep understanding of the issues faced by some of the poorest people in the area and an uncompromising sense of what needed to be done. But after nearly a decade of work, BCV established itself as a leader in this city as well as around the country in terms of its visionary efforts for improving access to health care for underserved populations, especially men. Its overriding strength was derived from an unequivocal commitment to grassroots efforts devoted to engaging communities and allowing the same to inform about those most affected by the inadequacies of the health care system.

Together with a diverse group of partners and collaborators, BCV identified barriers to access to care and developed strategies and models to overcome them. As part of Community Voices (CV), BCV opened the nation's first full-time men's health center; mobilized support to change the face of health care delivery in the state of Maryland; held conferences to address the urgent needs of newly released prisoners; formed partnerships for the delivery of comprehensive oral health services; demonstrated a promising model for reducing infant mortality rates; and improved access to on-demand substance abuse treatment. The sum of these parts is that BCV played a critical role in developing a model for coalition-building to have an impact on health care reform, while leading the nation in spotlighting and addressing the issues facing vulnerable men. Today, the Baltimore Men's Health Center is a part of a functioning and thriving federally qualified community health center (FQHC) serving the comprehensive needs of some of Baltimore's most vulnerable populations. This model has inspired the opening of other men's health centers in the city and in the country.

Need and Vision: Origins and Factors That Called for Change

At the time of the initial CV funding and to date, Maryland has been considered affluent. In 2002, it was deemed the state with the highest median income and lowest poverty rate.[2] In sharp contrast, however, the city of Baltimore had tremendous disparities in wealth, with approximately 22 percent of its children living in poverty.[3]

...in other parts of the nation, concentrated poverty in the city was an over-looked issue. But researchers would not be deterred from seeking out the most vulnerable populations in the city to identify and address the gaps in health care services. One of these gaps was in men's health, particularly that of low-income men. As a result, one of its key pillars of work, BCV chose to target a population of 10,500 people in the Sandtown-Winchester area, representing one of the city's most impoverished neighborhoods, including a predominantly African American community experiencing significant levels of substance abuse, an unemployment rate of more than 17 percent, and high incidences of formerly incarcerated people living within this seventy-two-block area.

BCV's focus on Sandtown-Winchester, then, was not only logical, it was critical to showcasing a highly underserved community with deep health and social challenges, sandwiched in the middle of a bustling urban area that might have obscured this reality had it not been for the insistence and leadership of those at BCHD and BCV. It was in this context that BCV leaders' vision of the importance of advocating for men, a highly marginalized subpopulation became a central issue, as did the overarching concern about the high numbers of uninsured, the central focus of the CV national initiative.

Building the Work: Infrastructure and Policy Factors

With the BCHD as the main anchor of this work, two partnerships were forged, paving the way for key policy directions. One collaboration, the Maryland Citizens Health Initiative Fund, was the platform from which the Health Care for All! Coalition was born. The other association was with the Men's Health Center (MHC), a public-private partnership based at the BCHD. The decisions to partner and the subsequent activities resulted in significant impacts over the years, thereby amplifying the work of BCV and improving access to health services for Baltimore's residents.

Health Care for All!

The Health Care for All! Coalition in Maryland was established through the initial foundation of a not-for-profit organization, the Maryland Citizens Health Initiative Fund (MCHI) that was created in 1999 to educate Marylanders about access to quality health care.[4] Beginning in 2000, BCV gave substantial support to the MCHI Health Care For All! Coalition's effort to achieve quality, affordable health care for all Marylanders. With this support MCHI was able to build a coalition of more than two thousand faith, community, labor, business, and health care organizations from across the state committed to this goal. Since then, this Coalition has achieved much success in Maryland, bringing the state from forty-fourth in the country to twenty-first in health care coverage for adults.

Over the years in which it was associated with BCV, the Coalition won major victories for health care consumers in Maryland (see Exhibit 1.1). Through the Coalition's efforts, Maryland has allowed young people up to age twenty-five to stay on their parents' health care plans; reduced prescription drug prices for seniors; increased reimbursement rates for Medicaid providers; significantly expanded dental care for children on the State Children's Health Insurance Program (SCHIP), and, by increasing by a dollar the state cigarette tax (which substantially reduced smoking in the state), increased the state's Medicaid eligibility level from 40 percent of the poverty level to 116 percent, providing health care coverage for more than forty-seven thousand uninsured adults as of July 1, 2008.

EXHIBIT 1.1. HEALTH CARE FOR ALL! SUCCESS CASES.

Required Large Companies to Do Their Fair Share on Health Care
A law passed in 2005 prevented Maryland's largest and most profitable companies from dumping their employee health care costs on the taxpayers. This was the first law in the nation requiring large companies to contribute a minimum amount toward their employee's health care.

Won Lower-Cost Prescription Drugs for the Uninsured
HB 1143, passed in 2005, was expected to provide the largest prescription drug discount for the uninsured in the nation. Uninsured or underinsured people living below 200 percent of the federal poverty line in Maryland [$19,600 (individual), $40,000 (family of four)] would soon have access to discounts of 40 percent or higher off the cost of name-brand drugs.

Built a Stronger and More Sturdy Safety Net
HB 627, passed in 2005, increased funding for health care centers that serve the uninsured; required Maryland hospitals to create a uniform financial assistance application; helped federally qualified health centers obtain capital grants to grow; expanded uninsured people's access to more affordable prescription drugs; and created a legislative task force to study how to achieve health care for all Marylanders.

Won More Fair Reimbursement for Physicians
With the passage and override of the governor's veto on HB 2, passed in 2004, more than six hundred thousand Marylanders received assistance through the State's Health Choice Program (Medicaid), including better access to physicians. A "fair wage" was negotiated for physicians treating patients in this program.

Prevented Massive Health Care Cuts
Prior to the 2005 legislative session, the Department of Health and Mental Hygiene announced that it was considering $483 million in cuts to health care services in Maryland. With education and strong grassroots pressure, MCHI convinced the governor not to make these wholesale cuts.

As a result of the Coalition's extensive outreach and educational campaigns, the Maryland General Assembly passed several key components of the Health Care for All! plan into law, increasing access to health care and providing more affordable prescription drugs for tens of thousands of uninsured Marylanders. Most notable are two state laws hailed as firsts in the nation—one that required large employers to spend 8 percent of payroll on health care for their employees and another that established the nation's best prescription drug discount program for the uninsured. While the first law was ultimately struck down in the courts in January 2007, the legislation did succeed in drawing attention to the number of employed yet uninsured Marylanders in need of expanded access to health care.

Health Care for All! also made important gains through its education of Maryland residents. It was only through massive citizen and legislative outreach that it was able to pass such significant legislation as the Healthy Maryland Initiative, which succeeded in reducing the number of teen smokers while providing approximately fifty thousand Marylanders with access to quality, affordable health care.

Men's Health Initiative

BCV leaders were convinced that disparities in morbidity and mortality in men of color and other marginalized populations were woefully misunderstood. They knew—and wanted to demonstrate—that poor health status of men of color is socially derived, stemming from deeply embedded and complex issues of poverty, unemployment, labor mismatch, psychological distress, incarceration, discrimination, poor education, and under-resourced communities.

As part of its efforts to address the underlying issues affecting men's health, BCV worked to establish a service delivery model centered on the whole man. Concerned that poor men of color are undervalued, discounted, and viewed as dispensable, BCV, through its development of a Men's Health Center (MHC), adopted the motto, "Building Healthy Families . . . One Man at a Time." BCV made a commitment to the men and families of Baltimore City to implement a series of strategies including developing, implementing, and evaluating a service delivery model through the MHC that improves access to care for men; building community capacity through education, outreach, and establishing and maintaining collaborations; and, finally, informing practice and policy on how to improve access to care for men on local, state, and national levels.

Ethnic, Racial, and Gender Health Disparities

Ethnic minorities and men are at particular risk for being uninsured. While African Americans and Hispanics constitute about two-thirds of Baltimore's population, they account for more than half of the uninsured. Adults without dependent children—most often men—account for 61 percent of the uninsured. Approximately 10 percent of women and 14 percent of men are uninsured in the state. Deep disparities exist, especially for men of color who have the lowest life expectancies. While the age-adjusted death rates (for all causes of death) for male Marylanders is lower than for their female counterparts, black males face a death rate 1.4 times higher than white males as a result of higher rates for cancer, stroke, accidents, diabetes, HIV, homicide, and heart disease. In 2004, the life expectancy of a black male at birth in Baltimore was 11.5 years shorter than that of a white female. For the state of Maryland, the life expectancy of black males at birth was 70.6 years as opposed to 76.7 years reported for white men in 2007.[5]

BCV and MHC leaders worked diligently to highlight this situation, creating a better understanding locally and nationally about the fact that being uninsured and male increases barriers to medical care. Sandtown-Winchester, the place where the MHC was physically located, was characterized by high levels of poverty and crime and an area to where many men newly released from prison return (60 percent of the MHC's clients had been in prison). Approximately half of the men receiving care at the Center had a history of substance abuse. Because these men typically were less prepared for reintegration due to limited availability of jobs, housing, and social services in the community, service to them was not only an obvious need but an emergency. The top three issue areas that surfaced for men in this neighborhood were access to primary care, help with medication, and oral health care (Table 1.1). Another key challenge was access to substance abuse and mental health services.

TABLE 1.1. TOPICS ADDRESSED DURING MHC OUTREACH (2006).

	%
Getting primary care	76
Help with medication	54
Dental health	50
Retention in health plan	37
Health promotion	36
Smoking cessation	31
Food resources	25
STI/HIV	24
Substance abuse	20
Mental health	16

The Needs

The typical client of the MHC is an unmarried African American man in his 40s with education less than a high school diploma (Figure 1.1). In 2005, seven of ten clients were single, and only 10 percent were married. African Americans made up nearly 100 percent of those who sought care at the Center.

A significant proportion of MHC clients represented the working poor. Approximately 40 percent of all clients reported being employed at the time of their initial visit to the Center. Three-quarters of the men reported a monthly income of below $500 a month. Only 3 percent reported a monthly income above $1,500.

As time progressed in Baltimore and in other sites across the country, it became evident not only that these statistics were compelling realities in Baltimore but that there appeared to be a similar "profile" to the kinds of men presenting for services in different cities. In many cases, as Baltimore demonstrated, these men were not uninsured because they were not employed. They simply were not in the kinds of jobs that offered health insurance. Working with this population afforded BCV an opportunity to learn about the issues having an impact on these particular men. It also allowed Baltimore to refine its interventions and strategies for bringing men to care and providing services to them once they were at the Center.

Working also with formerly incarcerated men, MHC established partnerships with the Baltimore City Ex-Offender Initiative and the Maryland Re-Entry Partnership to make primary health care an integral component of community reentry for newly released men. In many ways, Baltimore, through its MHC, was an important forerunner in this work that has brought light to the issues facing incarcerated and formerly incarcerated people, their needs, and the needs of their communities. The MHC has worked to build strong links between prison and community health services. The prescient goal in this work was to ensure that a prisoner would have a physical health exam prior to being released, helping to create a pathway for continuity of care.

FIGURE 1.1. BALTIMORE MEN'S HEALTH CENTER CLIENTS BY AGE.

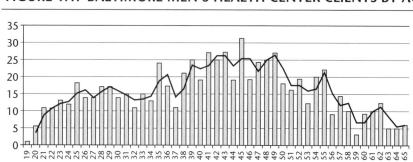

Building a Service Delivery Model That Works

The nation's first men's health center was established in Baltimore in 2000 and has served thousands upon thousands of men since it opened its doors. Since its opening a decade ago, the Center made a transition from the Division of Adult, School and Community Health to the Division of Clinical Services in an effort to implement improved quality assurance. It later developed a key partnership with Total Health Care, a Federally Qualified Health Center. Since the transition to Total Health Care in 2007, the MHC has provided a full range of preventative, primary, and subspecialty services. Indeed, this move institutionalized the MHC into the Baltimore delivery of care system and made it possible to increase the breadth and depth of services provided.

Upon establishing itself, the MHC sought to demonstrate effective ways to improve access to health care to uninsured men between the ages of nineteen and sixty-four in Baltimore City. It was resolved that men who receive care at the Center must be seen as an integral part of families and communities, recognizing that their physical, mental, and social needs are entwined. In addition to the primary health care services provided, the Center expanded the services provided over the years. It learned quickly that co-locating services (such as substance abuse detoxification and mental health services) is an important strategy for improving access to care.

Focus on Primary Care

From the beginning, the MHC Service Delivery Model was based on primary care with a focus on prevention. This had a significant impact on the health of MHC clients. When MHC first opened its doors, the top diagnosis was hypertension, but in 2004, four years later, the MHC reported that the main reasons for visits were for health maintenance. Further analyses have shown that the Center's approach resulted in increased and improved access to primary care. Between 2000 and 2003 the percentage of all non-emergency hospital emergency room (ER) admissions in Baltimore increased by 3 percent. As was expected, neighborhoods with a disproportionate number of low-income families experienced the greatest increases. However, in the neighborhoods in which MHC had its highest penetration of services, the increase was only 1 percent, 2 percent lower than the increase found citywide. More than seven thousand men in Baltimore had found a medical home at the Center in 2005, making it possible for them to avoid sporadic and costly ER care.

MHC leaders also realized the importance of providing a congenial, supportive, nonthreatening environment for their clients and of understanding their need to feel a "sense of belonging." Contrary to many beliefs, BCV and MHC leaders saw first-hand that the men presenting for services at the Center were concerned about their own health and were not looking for a "free ride." To establish a connection to their clients and provide a "sense of belonging" for them, the Center developed a medical card that was provided to them, identifying the Center as their medical home (Figure 1.2).

On-Site Substance Abuse Treatment

Approximately half of the men who received care at the Center have a history of substance abuse. Loss of referrals and long waiting lists for treatment slots spurred an inquiry into developing a model of effective treatment at the MHC. In September 2004, BCHD received federal funding (Center for Substance Abuse Treatment Grant Program) for thirty outpatient treatment slots at the MHC for assessment, referral, counseling, case management, and detoxification. A licensed physician monitored the administration of Buprenorphine, a drug for treatment of opioid dependence (the most common type of dependence among adults treated in Baltimore).

Clients of the program participated in group education, received intensive case management by the on-site Certified Addictions Counselor, on-site medication monitoring, and a smooth transition to a support network of providers through the local hospital Bon Secours Next Passage for follow-up and additional treatment.

FIGURE 1.2. "CHECK UP OR CHECK OUT."

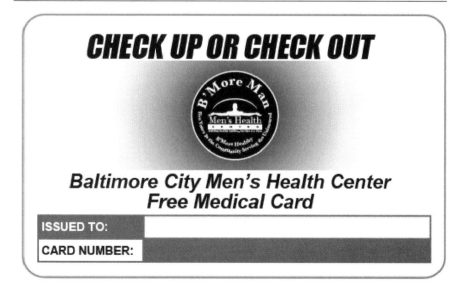

On-Site Mental Health Services

The MHC was clear about integrating mental health care as part of overall primary health care. As part of its services programming, the MHC partnered with The Mental Health Policy Institute for Leadership and Training in the development and implementation of the "Poverty and Depression Project." The goal of the Project was to improve services to people suffering from depression and living in traumatic conditions and to better integrate mental health services with primary health care together in the community in which people are living. The MHC is one of four sites in Baltimore where mental health and other services are provided. At each of these sites, as at the Center, outreach, screening for depression, treatment for depression, and education for paraprofessionals and consumers were offered. Also, training was offered to medical professionals in subjects related to mental health and depression. The Institute and its parent organization Baltimore Mental Health Systems, Inc. (BMHS) contracted with Bayview Medical Center to provide the clinical services.

The intervention was a multifaceted approach to provide outreach and identification, treatment, and education in innovative settings. This included a small team of mental health professionals who would outreach to the community to provide clinical services at two sites: the MHC and the Rose Street Community Center. In addition to clinical services, there was also an educational program for both the recipients of services and the staff at these sites to provide basic education about depression, substance abuse, violence prevention, and services in the community, thereby creating a heightened awareness of the issues and the solutions.

HIV Intervention

There were emergency health situations among the population of Baltimore that MHC staff simply could not ignore. The City of Baltimore has the third highest rates of HIV and AIDS among metropolitan areas within the United States. In Baltimore, many communities are affected, but racial minorities, particularly African Americans, are hardest hit, are at greatest risk, and have the most difficulty accessing resources for preventing and treating HIV/AIDS. While there has been success in addressing HIV/AIDS in Baltimore, inadequate coordination and innovation have hampered efforts to sufficiently address HIV/AIDS and its comorbidities, which include drug addiction, sexually transmitted diseases, homelessness, and poverty. Baltimore City's African American population accounts for 64 percent of the total city population. However, African Americans represent nearly 90 percent of all residents living with HIV/AIDS in Baltimore City, with more than three in one hundred African American males affected with HIV in Baltimore.

Between 2002 and 2004, the MHC tracked the HIV tests performed at the Center and determined that of tests performed, 4 percent were positive. The revelation was that there were many people in Baltimore City who were living with HIV but were unaware of their serostatus.

Formerly Incarcerated Men

In 2005 nearly nine thousand people, most of whom were men, were leaving the Maryland prison system to return to Baltimore City. Prisoners and formerly incarcerated people are at risk for higher rates of infectious diseases, chronic conditions, mental health problems, substance abuse, and dental problems. A history of incarceration presents a barrier to medical care by reducing employment opportunities, especially for those jobs that provide health benefits.

The Sandtown-Winchester community has a high concentration of newly released inmates. In 2003, more than 10 percent of released prisoners returning to Baltimore returned to Sandtown-Winchester, where the Center resides. In 2002, 221, or 13 percent, of the 1,669 men to whom the Center provided health care identified themselves as having been released from prison within the past year as documented on their patient encounter form.

The MHC sought to build strong links between jail and community health services. It was observed by MHC staff that men who were leaving jail and prison sought health care at the same rate as the general patient population. Thus, it was clear to the MHC in its own work and future policy advocacy that primary health care must be a part of the community reentry process for men. In addition to providing services for this population, the MHC helped to bridge the gap in access to care for these men through its participation on the Baltimore City Ex-Offender Task Force.

The goal of the Task Force was to promote change and enhance and improve the scope of services delivered to Baltimore City's formerly incarcerated people. In July 2005, the Baltimore City's Reentry Center (ReC) was opened. The ReC provides training opportunities, career development, office resources, employment linkages, child support, driver's license reunification, assistance with retrieval of needed identification, and referrals to housing. In addition, the MHC staff is on-site at the ReC to provide information regarding services offered at the MHC and to make medical referrals to the Center.

The role of BCV and the MHC in highlighting the connection between the health of poor men and prison cannot be understated. Their work was groundbreaking in terms of underscoring the need to address the issues facing vulnerable men as a deterrent to prison. For those coming out of corrections, the MHC was careful to make a case for having their needs met, in some ways acting as a protective factor against recidivism.

Building Community Capacity Through Education, Outreach, and Collaboration

Uninsured men typically are isolated from the health care system. MHC leaders found that with their population, even when financial barriers are removed, issues of distrust, disengagement, lack of knowledge still persisted, and special efforts needed to be made to bring men into the Center. The MHC addressed this in various ways, including employing Community Health Workers (CHWs) and establishing collaborations with likely and unlikely partners.

The MHC employed CHWs from the start. On the front line, canvassing neighborhoods, serving as ombudsmen to the Center, helping the men of Baltimore navigate the health care system, and providing linkages to social services, the MHC CHWs are indigenous to the communities they serve and have been successful in providing one-on-one guidance and encouragement to men that come to the Center (Exhibit 1.2). At one point, outreach by the CHWs accounted for a third of the Center's new registrants.

Collaborative Efforts in the Community

Located in a Health Professional Shortage Area (an area that has been declared to have a shortage of primary care medical physicians, dentists, and mental health professionals), the MHC was intent on improving access to primary care for a medically underserved population by providing primary care to uninsured men between the ages of nineteen and sixty-four years old. To address these challenging issues, BCV engaged in a series of partnerships. Beyond the aforementioned Health Care for All! Coalition and MHC, BCV counted on a number of powerful partners, including the University of Maryland Dental School; Johns Hopkins University; the Maryland Society of Sight; and, of great significance to the target population, the Baltimore Mental Health Systems (BMHS) and Baltimore Substance Abuse, Inc. (BSAS).

EXHIBIT 1.2. COMMUNITY HEALTH WORKERS IN ACTION!

- Act as patient navigator by assisting MHC clients with the registration process, filling out applications for emergency and transitional housing, and pharmacy assistance, and lending a listening ear for Center clients as necessary.
- Conduct and engage outside speakers for group sessions and classes for MHC clients (including smoking cessation, family planning and reproductive health, domestic violence training, diabetes and hypertension education, health screenings, and substance abuse counseling). Represent the Center at community health fairs.
- Provide employment, literacy training, and education linkages and referrals for MHC clients.
- Refer eligible clients to the City's Reentry Center for additional services.

A strength in the MHC has been its ability to link men to services on- and off-site. It is also a model of public-private cooperation, as the BCHD reorganized to include the MHC under the purview of its clinical division. The end result of this collaboration was a thriving new model in which a health department partnered with a community-based organization in operating the MHC. It is precisely this partnership, in addition to collaborative agreements with mental health projects (The Mental Health Policy Institute for Leadership and Training and the "Poverty and Depression Project") and substance abuse providers (Center for Substance Abuse Treatment Grant Program), that made it possible for uninsured men to receive screenings, primary health care, and health education.

The belief of the Center has been, and continues to be, that in order to provide access to care to men reluctant to seek health care, we have to meet them where they are, and be willing to listen to their needs. Having the MHC anniversary event outdoors was advantageous in that we were able to attract the curious onlookers that otherwise probably would not have come into the Center on their own.

After the event, I remained outdoors to provide assistance to the city workers who were disassembling the stage and thanked them for their assistance throughout the event. I began reflecting on the success of the day and the number of lives touched by the Center, when I was approached by a young man who appeared to be in his late twenties or early thirties. By his side was a little girl who looked to be approximately five years old. I would learn later that this little girl was his daughter. He apologized for having to "bother" me, but indicated that I looked like someone he could talk to. He was intimidated by the crowd earlier, so he watched the festivities from afar instead.

I spent more than twenty minutes on the street with this young man who described myriad problems, all of which probably seemed insurmountable to him. I asked him if he would be willing to come with me to the Center because I was certain that we would be able to help him with his medical needs as well as point him in the right direction for assistance with the other socioeconomic issues that plagued him. He agreed. I gave him a business card and told him to contact me if there was anything else I could do for him.

Weeks later he did call and thanked me for taking the time to listen. He reported that his medical needs were being taken care of at the Center and he was making progress in bringing resolution to some of the other problems in his life.

It is encounters such as these that really magnify the importance of safety net providers in the community. The health and well-being of a community is only as solid as its individual membership.

—Sherry Adeyemi, Baltimore Community Voices project director

In a national context in which poor, unemployed men are most likely to be uninsured, this model has made important inroads to broadening the discussion of what low-income men need to be well and live successful lives. Through outreach and the organization's commitment to serving the whole man, the Center has been successful in building upon a service delivery model that has bridged the gap to accessing health care and has served as a safety net provider in the community (Figures 1.3 and 1.4).

The MHC worked over the years to improve access to health care for underserved men, including increased enrollment of new clients; enhancement of Center processes; development of a stronger referral base; community engagement; and identification of MHC clients who would advocate for men's health issues and dissemination.

FIGURE 1.3. BALTIMORE COMMUNITY VOICES OUTREACH TOOLS AND PRODUCTS.

SCREENING AND IMMUNIZATIONS GUIDELINES FOR MEN

Ask your doctor or nurse practitioner if a specific test is right for you based on your personal and family history.

Test	When to Start	How Often	Result and Date
Blood Pressure	Age 18	Yearly	
Weight (BMI)		Discuss with your doctor or nurse	
Cholesterol • Total • HDL • LDL	Age 20	Discuss with your doctor or nurse	
Blood Sugar		Discuss with your doctor or nurse	
Testicular Exam	Age 15, self-exam	Discuss with your doctor or nurse	
STD tests, including HIV (if Sexually active)	Both partners, before each new relationship		
Colonoscopy (ask your doctor about other tests)	Age 50 or earlier with risk factors	Every 10 years	
Digital Rectal Exam or PSA		Discuss with your doctor or nurse	

Immunizations	Tetanus Booster	Hepatitis B (series)	Flu Vaccine	PPD (test for TB)	
	Every 10 years	If not Already immunized	Yearly	Yearly, if at risk	
Date Given					
Next Due					

6 Tips for Men's Health
1. Find a doctor and know your numbers.
   • For a referral call Baltimore HealthCare Access at (410) 649-0512.
2. Know your HIV status.
   • Free testing and treatment daily at: 1515 W. North Ave. (410) 396-0176; 620 N. Caroline St. (410) 396-9410
3. Exercise and eat healthy.
   • For activities near you call Recreation and Parks at (410) 396-7900.
4. Take steps to avoid violence.
   • Report illegal drug activity to (410) 666-DRUG (3784).
   • Resolve arguments peacefully through Community Mediation (410) 467-9165
   • Prevent domestic violence by calling (410) 889-7884
5. Avoid Tobacco.
   • 1-800-QUIT-NOW (1-800-784-8669)
6. Know how to access treatment for addiction.
   • For treatment call Baltimore Substance Abuse Systems, Inc. at (410) 637-1900.

First Annual
Men's Blue Suit
Health Awareness Weekend
September 14-16, 2007

Wear BLUE and be true to yourself by taking better care of your health

Keep a list of your current prescriptions and take it with you when you visit your doctor or nurse.

Name of Medicine	Dosage

Men's Health Card

Baltimore City Health Department
www.baltimorehealth.org
(410) 396-4398

Sheila Dixon
Mayor

Joshua M. Sharfstein, M.D.
Commissioner of Health

FIGURE 1.4. BUS ADVERTISEMENT.

With the transition of the MHC to a FQHC, additional services have been made possible, not only improving access to care but also providing more comprehensive care. The transition to the FQHC improved care for a wider range of patients, including the uninsured as well as clients in Maryland's new Primary Adult Care program for men living below poverty and patients with Medicaid. Expanded hours also allowed for those men who work to gain access to care without taking time away from work and possibly losing compensation. The addition of 24/7 telephone coverage provided clients expanded access to a clinician, resulting in cost containment due to the decrease in emergency room use. Finally, the availability of routine oral health services through referrals to nearby clinics affiliated with the FQHC or to a dental provider of the client's choice was made possible as was transportation through free bus tokens for those referred to other sites, often a formidable barrier to care.

Informing Men's Health Policy and Practice

Beyond the critically needed services provided by the MHC, one of the things that made BCV's work so powerful is its work in actively informing men's health policy. This is a notable achievement, considering that prior to the MHC there was very little discussion, if any, regarding the barriers to care facing low-income men. BCV's work in this area has created a broader national awareness that the need of Baltimore's men is not the isolated concern of one clinic.

As a result, beyond urban centers such as Washington, D.C., Detroit, and Miami, awareness of men's health is also beginning to take hold in some unexpected settings. Indian health clinics in rural California, for example, have examined the cultural notions of care that are attached to men in the community. North Carolina's state legislature now considers a men's health report card as it examines public health policy in the state. Closer to home, the MHC model was adopted by other community organizations, inspiring them to realize the importance of men's health. One example in Baltimore is the opening of the Men's Health Clinic by the Park Heights

Community Alliance, a nonprofit coalition of community associations, individual residents, health care providers, and human services agencies. Examples of this and other similar replications around the country are a testament to the legacy of Baltimore's MHC and how it is being duplicated as a model of systems change and caregiving.

Other systems and policy changes were made possible due to the visionary leadership and dedication of the MHC's staff. Due to the Center's advocacy and legislative efforts, the Maryland Commission on Men's Health was established. At the local level, Baltimore's City Council passed a resolution to reconvene the Commission on African American Males in the Baltimore Metropolitan Area (Exhibit 1.3).

In the community, leaders from the MHC attended countless health fairs and other community outreach events. Because of a comprehensive approach to health, efforts on behalf of the MHC were instrumental in crime reduction within Baltimore City, effectively lowering homicide and shooting rates in Baltimore neighborhoods. Bon Secours, the closest hospital to the MHC, saw a 1.4 percent increase in ER visits

EXHIBIT 1.3. INFORMING MEN'S HEALTH POLICY.

Maryland to Create a Commission Focused on Men's Issues

On April 7, 2005, legislation (HB 681/SB 824) was adopted to create the Maryland Commission for Men. The goal of the commission was to develop strategies and programs including community outreach and public-private partnerships designed to raise public awareness of men's issues, encourage the participation of men's healthy behaviors, review the health status of men in the state, and focus on health outcomes including oral cancer, depression and diabetes, and to recommend policy changes to further goals of the Commission.

Baltimore Commission on African American Males to Be Reconvened

On March 6, 2006, the Baltimore City Council adopted a resolution (Council Bill 05-0090R) to reconvene the Commission on African American Males in the Baltimore Metropolitan Area. The charge of the commission was to assess the current health, welfare, social, and spiritual condition of African American males in the Baltimore Metropolitan area. The Commission was originally established in 1995 and released the Report on the State of African American Males in Baltimore City and the Baltimore Metropolitan Area, 1996. The report concluded with recommendations focused in eight areas: leadership, noncustodial fathers, education status, employment and economic development, welfare reform, health and health care, criminal justice, and religious involvement. The reconvened Commission, consisting of representation from the health department, police department, Mayor's Office, and nine local colleges and universities, was to determine the progress made since the report and identify the issues to be addressed to improve the long-term well-being of African American males.

from the first quarter of 2006 to the first quarter of 2007, compared with a 2.5 percent average increase for all hospitals in the city. A belief among MHC leaders as well as in the CV national initiative is that such a change was only possible because of the access to health care offered at the MHC for non-urgent medical issues that historically have been evaluated in local ERs.

BCV's work on men's health was a true catalyst for change, not only in the state of Maryland but across the country, in its influence of opinion leaders and policymakers. Because of the success and lessons learned from Baltimore, future programming by the W.K. Kellogg Foundation, for example, insisted that other funded sites include a men's health component to their work. The current work of the National Center for Primary Care at the Morehouse School of Medicine, where the CV national initiative is currently headquartered, is also one of the country's leaders on this issue. As a result, it has generated much political and community interest and has since served as a model to other CV sites across the country, as well as a promising practice for many communities nationwide. Seen in this light, BCV's work with the MHC was seminal to current efforts.

Lessons Learned

BCV's lessons over the years were both macro and micro; about what to do and what not to do. Through a process of trial and error, much was learned in terms of both building collaboratives and transferring men's health services to Total Health Care. Following are some of those poignant lessons.

- *Place matters in providing service!* Making the transfer to Total Health Care made it possible for the Men's Health Center to obtain more referrals to other services through the federally qualified community health center (FQHC) network. It now has better referrals to oral health care, for example, as well as a pharmacy on-site. It also is now serving some women, as it wants them to be involved in men's health care.
- *Multiple providers are often required.* To meet the comprehensive primary health care needs of the population, including primary prevention, behavioral health, and oral health care, a number of different providers may be required.
- *The evidence base must be established in order to effect change.* Systemic changes are integral to improved access to quality health care. To achieve this, much of the work devoted to improving access must also be devoted to creating the evidence base for policy alternatives.
- *Model the change you want to see!* For Baltimore, this was done through the Men's Health Center, which provided comprehensive services to an underserved population, while consistently informing decision makers about the gaps in the system that needed to be addressed.

- *A focused mission is powerful!* The work of BCV concentrated on two simultaneous but intertwined missions: achieving health care for all and improving and sustaining services to men, an underserved subpopulation. BCV did not waver in its commitment to these goals, ensuring that its policy discussions and recommendations always included possible solutions in both practice and policy.

- *Highlight the findings and disseminate.* One of the discoveries in Baltimore was that a significant number of men being seen at the MHC also had had experiences with the criminal justice system. BCV's work shone a steady spotlight on this issue, helping to provide some particularly needed services, including mental health and substance abuse treatment, while also sharing with policymakers the needs of incarcerated people and those returning home.

- *Work with everyone!* BCV leaders worked with myriad communities, including the grassroots, criminal justice, policymakers, health and social service providers, and known celebrities. They were strategic in their knowledge that all are potential pathways to create awareness about the issues, while improving connections with other providers and policymakers. Such an approach ultimately yields better service for the client, as well as informs decision makers about what needs to be done.

- *Use outreach as a strategic tool.* BCV was careful to employ its CHWs as both connectors to care and disseminators of information in the community at large and in policymaking circles. The use of social marketing tools to bring people into care and to inform decision makers cannot be undervalued.

- *Be creative in financing partnerships.* While the Kellogg Foundation and others played important supportive roles, no one organization could have sustained BCV throughout all of its years of work. Rather, BCV leaders created strategic partnerships with other providers and other systems of care. Where funding was hard to find, BCV devoted efforts to informing decision makers about the gaps and needs in specific areas such as on-demand substance abuse treatment and the value of this model versus incarceration.

Conclusions

There were many factors that made it possible for the Health Care for All! Coalition to create changes in policy and for the MHC to provide health care to several thousand men over the past decade. In the previous pages, we have provided an overview of the context, resources, processes, and tools that enabled these changes. In working in tandem with Maryland's Healthcare for All! and the development of the MHC, BCV succeeded in bringing attention to the larger issue of the uninsured as well as in putting a specific spotlight on a highly underserved population, men. Because of its efforts, Maryland has passed several significant laws that improve access to care for uninsured populations, and today the MHC is part of a recognized FQHC that continues to provide much needed services and referrals to underserved men and their families. At the same time, BCV has served as an inspiration to other Community Voices sites and other communities across the country, particularly in its efforts devoted to putting men's health and well-being on the social and political map.

Notes

1. This chapter has been adapted from Baltimore Community Voices Phase III, Annual Reports: September 1, 2004–August 31, 2005; September 1, 2005–August 31, 2006; and September 1, 2006–August 31, 2007. We acknowledge here the work of Sherry Adeyemi, Nicole Jarrett, Vincent DeMarco, and Laura Herrera.
2. E. Massey, "Maryland: High Income, Low Poverty," *Baltimore Business Journal*, 2002. Retrieved July 23, 2010, from http://baltimore.bizjournals.com/baltimore/stories/2002/07/22/daily25.html.
3. Maryland Budget & Tax Policy Institute, *Frequently Asked Questions About Poverty*, 2002. Retrieved July 23, 2010, from http://www.marylandpolicy.org/html/research/POVERTYfaq2002.asp.
4. Vincent DeMarco (personal correspondence, September–October 2009).
5. Men's Health Network, *The State of Men's Health Maryland*, 2007. Retrieved July 23, 2010, from http://www.menshealthnetwork.org/states/MD.pdf.

CHAPTER TWO

DENVER HEALTH COMMUNITY VOICES

Working to Improve Health Through Experimentation, Linkages, Leveraging, and Transformation[1]

Elizabeth Whitley

This chapter provides a review of Denver Health Community Voices' work to improve access to health care for Denver's residents. After reading this chapter, the reader will

- Learn about the Denver Health Community Voices process of experimentation, linkages, leveraging, and transformation
- Learn about effective community outreach and outreach worker education strategies
- Learn about specific tools and best practices employed by a health care safety net in expanding coverage to publicly sponsored health insurance programs for underserved and vulnerable populations
- Learn about specific models and best practices employed to manage care and provide navigation for patients with chronic illnesses
- Learn about the role and applicability of evidence-based research in providing practice and policy alternatives
- Learn about effective evaluation strategies to build the evidence base for new practice and policy strategies that increase access for the underserved.

Introduction

The conception of Community Voices by the W.K. Kellogg Foundation gave Denver Health the freedom and "space" to be creative, take risks, and invite others to share in the process to increase access to health care and reduce health disparities among Denver residents. Denver Health Community Voices (DHCV) served as the learning laboratory to stimulate discoveries, model community engagement, and motivate change.

Over the past ten years, DHCV has grown into a program of innovative community-based initiatives that addresses gaps in the safety net through what Denver Health CEO and Medical Director Patricia Gabow termed *experimentation, linkages, leveraging, and transformation*. As examples, DHCV has experimented with subsidizing health insurance for small businesses and their employees and is conducting a randomized clinical trial on patient navigation. DHCV has formed linkages with community and faith-based organizations, as well as created academic partnerships. DHCV also leverages resources, particularly funding for community health workers (CHWs) across programs and partners. DHCV has transformed the Denver Health (DH) system and the Denver community in many ways.

Most, but not all, experiments have been successful. However, valuable lessons have been learned and continue to inform the work. Consistent with DHCV's commitment to test new approaches and provide evidence-based recommendations to policymakers, several research studies were conducted as a part of its efforts. These, together with DHCV's ongoing documentation and sharing of best practices, have made it possible for other communities and safety nets to replicate the models and implement the strategies, best practices, and lessons learned by DHCV.

Finally, DHCV committed to the principle *"relationships are primary and all else is derivative,"*[2] which has guided the organization in the establishment of new connections and collaborative partnerships, as well as in the strengthening of existing relationships among DHCV and community stakeholders that extend beyond the Initiative.

Origin and Factors That Called for Change

The City and County of Denver is one geopolitical unit that covers 154,636 square miles at 5,280 feet above sea level. Denver comprises 77 discrete neighborhoods, recognized by both the City and residents. The population of Denver comprises 554,636 individuals, of which 51.9 percent are Non-Hispanic whites, 31.7 percent are Hispanics, 10.8 percent are African Americans, and 5.6 percent fall under the category of "others." It is here where DHCV came to life in the context of an urban public hospital system. Embedded directly into DH, the city's primary safety net, DHCV took on numerous real-time challenges in improving access to health care for some of the most vulnerable populations.

DH is an independent governmental authority categorized as a political subdivision of the state. DH's highly integrated health care system includes the 911 emergency medical response system, a 477-bed acute care hospital with a Level 1 trauma center for adults and children, nine federally qualified community health centers, twelve school-based clinics, a 100-bed nonmedical detoxification center, the Denver Department of Public Health, three dental clinics, the Rocky Mountain Poison Center, a twenty-four-hour-a-day nurse advice line, and a health maintenance organization (HMO).

In 1997, DH served 120,000 individuals, or one in five Denver residents, of which 70 percent were racial and ethnic minorities. Of the patients, 20 percent had Medicaid and 53 percent were uninsured, of which 20 percent were eligible for the state sliding-fee discount program. At that time, Denver had 2.8 percent unemployment; 17 percent of the residents lived in poverty and 16.5 percent were uninsured.

DHCV was first funded in 1998 by the W.K. Kellogg Foundation and The Colorado Trust, a local private foundation. DHCV was designed to address gaps in the fabric of Denver's intricately woven safety net. Although DH was a vertically integrated, highly effective health care delivery system, prior to DHCV, community outreach was limited; care for chronically ill, uninsured adults was fragmented; and low enrollment of eligible patients into publicly sponsored insurance programs was of great concern. Given that, DHCV committed to two essential goals: (1) improve access to health care for Denver's medically underserved; and (2) inform and change public policy related to health program funding at local, state, and federal levels.

Infrastructure

DHCV is an "umbrella" for numerous community-based, mostly grant-funded initiatives. During the first five years, DH CEO and Medical Director Patricia Gabow, M.D., provided leadership and direction for DHCV. Oversight and direction were also provided by a policy board and a multicultural steering committee.

Currently, DHCV resides within Community Health Services at DH and is directed by Elizabeth Whitley, Ph.D., R.N. Dr. Whitley is responsible for development, program oversight, fundraising, donor relations, and dissemination. Together with two program managers, an operations manager, and a senior secretary, approximately forty employees are associated with DHCV at any given time.

Policy Factors

Throughout the life of this initiative, DHCV has participated in educating policymakers and stimulating and influencing necessary health policy changes at local, state, and federal levels. Often, the work was aimed at preserving the safety net by minimizing state and federal cuts in funding, especially Medicaid. Continued challenges to the sustainability of the safety net include concentration of vulnerable populations to a few providers; growing numbers and costs of the uninsured (especially pharmaceutical and technology costs); revenue streams not keeping pace; complexity of enrollment into publicly funded programs; and lack of funded care and services for undocumented immigrants. Access to capital, workforce supply costs, and regulatory burdens are also sustainability-related policy issues. Federal policy improvements that would help the safety net include coverage or funding for the uninsured, simplification of enrollment processes, special technology or pharmaceutical pricing, the creation of a capital fund for the safety net, loan repayment for safety net employees, one regulatory body, and simplification of regulations.

There were some local and state incremental health policy successes, such as DH capital expansion on the November 2002 ballot; securing Medicaid Administrative Activities for enrollment in 2004; eligibility modernization such as eliminating the Medicaid assets test; simplification of the enrollment process and on-site Medicaid eligibility determination; increasing for Child Health Plan Plus (CHP+) at 205 percent of poverty; and, the passage of Citizens for a Healthier Colorado (tobacco tax initiative) in 2005, resulting in approximately $170 million per year for health care for the poor.

However, one constitutional amendment continues to cripple Colorado's fiscal policy—the Taxpayer's Bill of Rights (TABOR). TABOR, passed by the voters in 1992, limits government growth and requires voter approval on all tax increases. One of the most difficult provisions of TABOR is that it creates a ratcheting effect, which means that every time services are cut, that level becomes the base from which all future increases are calculated. DHCV continues to work with policy partners within limitations imposed by TABOR while also working to change the same.

Community Partnerships, Outreach, and Care Management

Key to the success of community outreach has been DHCV's work with its community partners. Community partners include businesses, schools, leaders, churches, and other gathering places located in DH's primary zones of influence. Community health workers (CHWs) identify, invite, and negotiate the relationships with individuals and organizations that serve as community partners in their neighborhoods. Currently numbering more than two hundred, the community partners distribute health information and promote awareness of how and where to access services. DHCV also contributes to the work of other projects, organizations, and coalitions.

The Community Outreach program provides culturally sensitive outreach to underserved individuals and communities, increases enrollment of eligible individuals into health coverage, disseminates health information and education, conducts basic health screening, and provides systems navigation. Specifically, CHWs are deployed through a free pregnancy testing program, the family neighborhood health program, DHCV's school-based health centers, men's health, community health centers, outreach programs aimed at enrolling individuals in publicly funded health insurance, and the barbershop cardiovascular disease prevention program, among other programs.

Free Pregnancy Testing

One of DHCV's CHWs suggested that free pregnancy testing be offered. This idea became the basis for barrier-free pregnancy testing, which is offered by CHWs one day per week at all but two of the DH Community Health Centers. Figure 2.1 demonstrates the increasing volume since 2003, and Table 2.1 summarizes the demographics of participants for 2007.

DHCV completed 14,579 pregnancy tests between 2003 and 2007. Approximately 70 percent of the tests resulted in a positive outcome. The program continues to see repeat testers, but 93 percent of tests in the reporting period were for unique women.

The majority of women receiving free pregnancy tests during the reporting period were Hispanic and Spanish-speakers. Almost one-third of the women are married, and the mean age was almost twenty-five years.

FIGURE 2.1. FREE PREGNANCY TEST RESULTS AT DENVER HEALTH, 2003–2007 YTD.

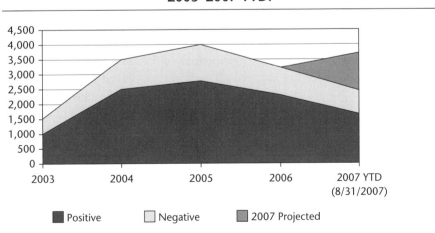

TABLE 2.1. DEMOGRAPHIC CHARACTERISTICS FOR WOMEN RECEIVING A FREE PREGNANCY TEST, 9/1/06–8/31/07.

Characteristic	Number	%
Test Result		
Positive	2,072	70
Negative	890	30
Borderline	4	less than 1
Language		
English	1,353	46
Spanish	1,518	51
Other/Unknown	95	3
Ethnicity		
African American	380	13
Asian	71	2
Hispanic	2,247	76
Native American	24	1
White	167	6
Other/Unknown	77	3
Marital Status		
Divorced	59	2
Married	891	30
Separated	157	5
Significant Other	543	18
Single	1,201	40
Other/Unknown	115	4
Age (Mean[SD])	24.79 (6.46)	

The program evaluation demonstrated that the free pregnancy testing program increased access to early prenatal care for underserved pregnant women, increased the number of DH deliveries, and increased revenue due to an increase in Medicaid-reimbursed deliveries of approximately $250,000 per year. Since then, the free pregnancy testing program has been incorporated into DH Community Health Services operations, which offer in addition family planning services for women with negative pregnancy tests.

Family Neighborhood Health Model

DHCV was one of the learning laboratories that participated in and benefited from international exchange trips organized by Community Voices. In Trujillo, Peru, for example, Dr. Whitley observed the Family/Neighborhood Health Model (UNI Trujillo project, Moche District) and recognized its applicability in Denver neighborhoods.

Trujillo's "family health care model," developed in conjunction with the health system and surrounding impoverished communities, was based on a CHW outreach program that dramatically decreased preventable mortality and improved overall health. Through employment of the concepts of family surveillance and protection, one of the goals of this work was to increment the number of "protected families" by ensuring that these received all health measures intended to inform, prevent, promote, and provide for well-being. CHWs conducted an assessment among families in their neighborhoods to identify the most common health issues and needs, working closely with individuals and families to achieve protection through this process.

In 2005, DHCV succeeded in adapting and replicating the family/neighborhood health model for use in underserved Denver neighborhoods with a two-year grant from the Office of Health Disparities, Colorado Department of Public Health and Environment, for five West Denver neighborhoods. Recognizing the link with neighborhood revitalization efforts, in 2007 the City of Denver funded the program for a sixth neighborhood, where more than 1,100 surveys were completed, representing approximately 10 percent of the adult population in that neighborhood.

The main conditions that CHWs assess and monitor include cardiovascular disease, diabetes, cancers, and associated risk factors. CHWs visit each household in their neighborhoods and conduct a brief risk and health assessment for each adult family member. This service is also provided at community gatherings, churches, and schools. Blood pressure, height, weight, and body mass index (BMI) are offered to each individual interested in participating. Appropriate health education and referrals to screening and primary care also take place.

The CHWs subsequently follow up with individuals to monitor the completion of screening, reassess for health issues or concerns, and provide other resources. As a last step, they meet with community groups to report aggregate survey results and encourage residents in their efforts to improve their health. Data resulting from this outreach revealed that one of the most common needs of participants is enrollment in publicly funded health coverage. In response to this need, DHCV provided community-based enrollment facilitation.

School-Based Health Centers

DH school-based health centers (SBHCs), located in twelve Denver elementary, middle, and high schools, provided health and mental health services to more than 7,700 students in the 2007–2008 school year, resulting in more than 30,340 patient visits. CHWs are assigned to the schools to facilitate enrollment in publicly funded health insurance (described in more detail further on) and to assist with a dental sealant program for second and third graders.

Adult Care Management

The Adult Case Management Program was designed to demonstrate that case management of chronically ill adults across funding streams and clinical disciplines improves health outcomes and lowers costs. DHCV's work in care management began in 1999 when staff analyzed medical records from adult patients with three or more annual admissions to the hospital and discovered that 460 patients in one year accounted for $24,527,388 in charges, most of which was not covered by any payer source. Furthermore, it was discovered that many of these patients with frequent admissions had no primary care home and suffered from multiple chronic diagnoses such as mental illness and diabetes.

Between 1999 and 2003, DHCV conducted a randomized controlled trial with uninsured adults who were hospitalized three or more times in one year at DH. Patients admitted to DH for the third time in one year received a visit from a registered nurse (RN) or a licensed clinical social worker (LCSW) case manager and were invited to participate in the study. Specific challenges for these patients included the prevalence of substance abuse and behavioral health issues, lack of transitional housing, insufficient resources, and the undocumented status of several of the clients.[3] Although there were significant limitations to the study, DHCV concluded that case managing a chronically ill, transient population with an RN/LCSW model *was not* cost-effective.

Innovation and experimentation characterized DHCV's work in this area, as it soon proceeded to discover more cost-effective models of care. The work developed in the first years of DHCV was continued via funding through the Health Resources and Services Administration (HRSA) Healthy Communities Access Program (HCAP) grant and continues with the Men's Health Initiative. Through DHCV's efforts, DH has effectively made the transition from a costly RN/LCSW model to the patient navigator model employed by the Men's Health Initiative, described in the following sections.

Men's Health Initiative

The goal for the Men's Health Initiative (MHI) is to increase access and affordability, reduce disparity, and improve seamlessness of health care to underserved men in Denver. At the beginning of DHCV's work on men's health, men's focus groups were conducted to uncover attitudes and beliefs about health care access among underserved men. The six groups were stratified by age, race and ethnicity, and language.

The focus groups revealed that financial barriers—particularly the lack of health insurance coverage—were the paramount concerns of underserved men of color. Many nonfinancial barriers to health care access were also identified, including racism, communication difficulties, fear, and beliefs about manhood. These findings in turn were useful to program planning efforts for improving health outcomes and reducing disparities, and to informing policymakers about men's health issues.[4]

This is a story of man I met at the Denver County Jail over a year ago. When I first talked to "Floyd" he was close to being released after serving several months for a DUI.

We talked for a pretty long time, and he told me he had spent over half his life in prisons and jails—how his family was done with him and how he had used them. We also talked about his many years of "drinking and drugging." He said he was ready to turn his life around. (I usually don't ask why or how long people are in jail, but will listen if they want to talk about it.)

A few days later, "Floyd" called me up and he came to my office, where we talked some more. I referred him to some programs and tried to help him stay positive. We also got him an appointment with Jack (one of our very good primary care providers). At the appointment he received medicines for high blood pressure, cold medicines, and Prozac. I saw him a couple of days later, and he was pretty down. "Floyd" was living in his car but did not have any gas money. Again, I encouraged him to enroll in a program. He took the information and left. Like a lot of the guys I work with, he took a piece of my heart. I know their lives are hard.

As time passed, I did not hear from him and things got real busy here at the Men's Health Initiative, but I often wondered how he was doing. To tell the truth, I just figured he was either back in jail or using again. What chance did he have? The odds were against him. Last week he showed up in my office, with a white shirt and a tie. His medical card had run out, and he wanted it renewed. As we talked, he told me that things were going well; he was working part time at a local newspaper, and wasn't using. He was still seeing Jack and taking his meds.

Now, I'm not saying everything was perfect, but he had not been to jail or used in over a year (both records for him)! He tried to give me credit for helping him, but I can't take it. As I told him, he did all the work. But I am glad I was there to encourage him and give some direction.

— Merrill Carter, Men's Health Initiative Patient Navigator

A marketing campaign was created to increase awareness about men's health and the MHI among African American and Hispanic men, as well as to encourage men to access preventive health care (Figure 2.2). The "It's not your time" (to die) campaign was created on the basis of the results of the men's focus groups and communicated two messages: men of color die younger from preventable diseases than other men, and the DH MHI offers affordable and accessible preventive health care for men in Denver. During the quarter following the launch of the campaign, 1,500 new men accessed the DH system. In addition, in 2007, DHCV published the first Denver Men's Health Report Card for use with policy- and grantmakers.

Two patient navigators (PNs) conduct outreach to men in the community and in the city and county jail. During 2008, 1,293 new participants were enrolled in the Men's Health Initiative. As of August 31, 2008, 8,140 total men had been enrolled in the program. Demographics for all participants and the new enrollees are summarized in Table 2.2. Participants' ethnicity remains fairly evenly split between African American, Hispanic, and white, although slightly more white men have enrolled in the program. The majority of participants are either homeless or in jail.

Incarceration continues to be a common experience for many of the participants. Among the new enrollees, 33 percent (n = 428) listed jail as the place where they last received health care. The majority of men described their health status as fair and stated that they do not have a regular doctor. The average age of participants is forty-one years.

FIGURE 2.2. IT'S NOT YOUR TIME.

TABLE 2.2. MHI DEMOGRAPHICS.

	All MHI Participants (n = 8,140)		New MHI Participants (n = 1,293)	
Ethnicity				
African American	2,347	29%	362	28%
Asian	52	1%	10	1%
Hispanic	2,514	31%	364	28%
Native American	175	2%	35	3%
White	2,944	36%	500	39%
Other/missing	108	1%	22	2%
Living arrangement				
Homeless	3,717	46%	839	65%
Jail	2,180	27%	187	14%
Independent	949	12%	177	14%
Other/missing	1,204	15%	90	7%
Health Status				
Good	2,184	27%	234	18%
Fair or poor	5,444	67%	1,013	78%
Missing	512	6%	46	4%
Regular Doctor				
Yes	1,461	18%	180	14%
No	6,326	78%	1,083	84%
Missing	353	4%	30	2%
Age at intake (mean years [SD])	41.2	(11.3)	43.0	(10.6)

During 2008, 2,228 men received services through the MHI. PNs tracked 4,507 total encounters with clients for an average 2.0 encounters per client and an average 2.4 services per client. The MHI provided 519 copays or fees (medical visit, prescription, or fee for a picture identification card), supplied over thirteen thousand bus tokens, and scheduled or coordinated seventy-nine medical or enrollment specialist visits. The PNs also took over 1,500 applications for the Colorado Indigent Care Program (CICP) and logged 762 hours through that process. General conversations or meetings with clients to check on basic needs and insurance status are the most frequent service and encompassed 762 hours of PN time during the reporting year.

A return on investment (ROI) analysis for the MHI was completed and is described in detail in a previously published article.[5] Briefly, the analysis revealed that the MHI has increased access to primary and specialty care for underserved men, while also helping men use safety net services more appropriately. The study's authors observed that inpatient, urgent care, and behavioral health visits decreased for men participating in the program, resulting in cost savings.

Community Reentry from Jail

The MHI PNs visit the jail several times a week and meet with men who are due to be released in the near future. They take applications for CICP. They also assess the individual's needs and try to help address issues before they reenter their communities. Upon release, they meet with their clients to help them access primary care, medications, support groups, and so on.

Through a grant from Morehouse School of Medicine (MSM), Center for Primary Care, Community Voices, DHCV was able to assist reentry clients with transportation and in accessing mental health services through DH's partner, the Mental Health Center of Denver (MHCD). The PNs refer clients who are likely to benefit from an evaluation and limited therapy to MHCD, which has proven to be an excellent partner and is collaborating with DHCV on the evaluation of this project. The MHI care management program has led to linkages with the Denver Crime Prevention and Control Commission, where DHCV is leveraging resources and improving the mental health care for men who are incarcerated, easing the transition back to community and collaboratively influencing public policy.

Community Cardiovascular Disease Prevention Program

Through a grant from the Colorado Department of Public Health and Environment to reduce the risk of cardiovascular disease among adult residents in Colorado communities, DHCV employs CHWs and PNs to promote awareness of modifiable risk factors and provide community-based screening and referrals to primary care and other resources. Over the first three years just less than eighteen thousand individuals in fourteen Colorado communities were screened, 81 percent of which did not know their risk prior to the screening.

The Barbershop Program

As a part of the Community Cardiovascular Disease Prevention Program, DHCV sponsors the Barbershop Program in Denver, targeting primarily African American males because of the prevalence of cardiovascular disease (CVD), risk, and health disparities in this population. Two African American men were hired as PNs and trained to work in the barbershops, where they conduct health screenings, provide basic counseling and education on CVD risk, and refer individuals at moderate or high risk to a primary care provider and community resources. The PNs also follow up with clients to maximize follow-through and continued engagement. A unique feature of this CVD screening program is that PNs use pen-tablet computers to enter all screening and other client data. The software system helps the PN manage their work by guiding them through the screening process, calculates a Framingham risk score, tracks both medical and community referral resources, and tracks actual referrals made at the individual level. It creates follow-up reminders as well as provides management reports so that PN activities can be monitored.

Over the course of the first three years, the two PNs screened a total of 2,836 people in twenty-two barbershops. As shown in Table 2.3, over half of the clients screened were male (57 percent), and three-quarters were African American (75 percent). Interestingly, the screened population was fairly young, with only 41 percent over the age of fifty. More than one-quarter (29 percent) of participants reported having no health insurance, and 28 percent did not have a medical home.

TABLE 2.3. DEMOGRAPHIC PROFILE OF 2,836 CLIENTS SCREENED IN BARBERSHOPS.

Age	
Under 35	26%
35–50	33%
Over 50	41%
Gender	
Male	57%
Female	43%
Race or Ethnicity	
African American	75%
White	8%
Hispanic/Latino	14%
Other	3%
Insurance Status	
Insured	71%
Uninsured	29%
Have Medical Home	
Yes	72%
No	28%

Table 2.4 illustrates the risk status of screened clients. The screening results indicate that clients visiting barbershops are indeed at risk for CVD and other health conditions. Almost 18 percent had a medium, and 15 percent a high Framingham risk score (that is, risk for CVD in the next ten years). In terms of modifiable risk factors, more than a quarter of screened clients were current smokers (26 percent) and more than one-quarter had blood pressure above the normal range (20 percent considered to have mildly high, 10 percent moderately high, and 1 percent severely high blood pressure). Further, only 23 percent were considered to be of a healthy weight (39 percent were overweight and 36 percent obese) according to BMI measures. Finally, 58 percent were found to have desirable, 32 percent borderline high, and 10 percent high cholesterol levels.

TABLE 2.4. CVD RISK STATUS OF CLIENTS SCREENED IN BARBERSHOPS.

General	
Family history of heart disease	21%
Family history of diabetes	27%
Currently smoke cigarettes	26%
Total Cholesterol	
Desirable	58%
Borderline	32%
High	10%
Blood Pressure/HTN	
None	69%
Mild	20%
Moderate	10%
Severe	1%
Framingham Risk Score	
Low	67%
Medium	18%
High	15%
BMI	
Underweight	2%
Healthy weight	23%
Overweight	39%
Obese	36%
Knowledge of risk	
Yes	53%
No	47%

Of particular interest, 53 percent of screened clients reported having no knowledge of their CVD risk before the screening—a finding that supports the value of using CHWs to screen clients and to educate them about risk and risk reduction in community screenings such as barbershops. Of import, DHCV's findings indicate that these screenings did more than just provide information and education: PNs referred 517 clients to health and health care resources in the Denver area (such as QuitLine) and had more than 1,900 follow-up visits with the same clients over time. Of note is that 64 new patients accessed services at DH following the screening.[6]

Promoting Community Health Workers and Patient Navigators

DHCV understood the CHW and PN roles as potential pathways out of poverty for individuals from underserved Denver communities. In addition to providing full employment and benefits, DHCV wanted to help to build capacity in employees while continuing to promote their effectiveness. Focus was provided in three areas: CHW education, career-building, and patient navigation training (see Exhibit 2.1).

CHW Education

In an effort to standardize and elevate the preparation of CHWs, DH and the Community College of Denver (CCD) collaborated on creating, implementing, and evaluating a standardized, academic education certificate program. Following a needs assessment conducted with forty organizations employing outreach workers in Denver, DHCV developed a seventeen-credit-hour certificate training program in partnership with CCD. The creation of the curriculum for this program was informed by the Annie E. Casey study (The National Community Health Advisor Study), the Community Health Works in San Francisco, and DHCV's own experience with CHWs.

The sixth CCD CHW certification course was offered in 2009. For the fourth time, the reach of the program extended beyond the Denver metropolitan area, and students from Steamboat Springs, Pueblo, Vail, and Colorado Springs completed the course. In fact, three of the six required courses can be taken at any community college in the state.

All students are employed and given work release time to attend school. In addition, the students receive full scholarships for tuition and books from grants. The seventeen credit hours that each student earns are applicable to an advanced degree from all colleges in the State.[7]

EXHIBIT 2.1. EVALUATING THE SUCCESS OF COMMUNITY HEALTH WORKERS AND PATIENT NAVIGATORS.

Denver Health's sophisticated information system made it possible for Denver Health Community Voices (DHCV) to develop and implement a robust local evaluation, particularly of the work of community health workers (CHWs) and patient navigators (PNs).

"Goldmine," a sales database, was adapted for use by the CHWs and PNs to track all activities and contacts made with program participants. Because all Denver Health patients have a unique medical record number, the hospital is able to link Goldmine data to individual patient encounter files to examine systemwide utilization patterns and charges. Clinical information is held in Denver Health's Lifetime Clinical Record (LCR). Payer source and reimbursement information is obtained from patient accounting and finance. Data on enrollment status in publicly funded health coverage are obtained from HealthTrack, the enrollment tracking system.

All data sources get leveraged for research, evaluation, and quality-improvement efforts. Data from DHCV clients' electronic medical records, including service utilization, number and type of visits, charges, payer source, and reimbursement of charges, were used to determine return on investment of CHW and PN programs.

Career Pathway

A career pathway for CHWs and PNs was developed, resulting in the official titles of CHW, PN I, and PN II. The career pathway allows CHWs to advance to the role of PN and beyond. At DH, PNs are CHWs who have advanced training in the psychosocial and medical experiences of a particular condition and who provide care coordination, guidance, and assistance to clients in overcoming financial, systemic, cultural, and linguistic barriers to care. At DH, PNs must have the CHW certification or possess an advanced degree or credentials. In addition, DHCV developed competency assessment tools for both the CHW and PN roles. These tools are used in training and education, and as performance evaluations for staff serving in these roles.[8]

Patient Navigation Training

Expanding on the work of DHCV and CCD, the Colorado Patient Navigator Training Collaborative was formed to create a PN training curriculum with DH partners at the University of Colorado Denver to better enable PNs to implement evidence-based strategies to overcome health disparities. Currently, the courses are offered online and via face-to-face workshops. This curriculum, which builds upon the CHW program, is also offered through CCD and may provide college credit in addition to a certificate (see www.patientnavigatortraining.org). In addition, PN training is

RV interviewed for a patient navigator job in 2006. RV is from Mexico and had a bachelor's degree in human resources from the Instituto Tecnológico de Chihuahua. She had immigrated to the United States five years previously and was bilingual in English and Spanish. She had worked as a secretary in a local church for the past four years. RV was in her mid-twenties and had two children, ages two years and two months. She had recently separated from her husband.

I hired her because she was obviously very bright and she desperately needed the job. As she said, "I don't just want a job, I want a career."

RV has been working as a patient navigator for more than three years. She is responsible, caring, and professional—an exemplary employee. When her salary is increased, RV must negotiate the number of hours she can work per week without losing child care assistance, without which she would be unable to work.

RV has completed the Community Health Worker Program at the Community College of Denver and the Patient Navigator Training Program. She is currently in school taking prerequisites for nursing school.

—Elizabeth Whitley, director, Denver Health Community Voices and Men's Health Initiative

occurring at a national level as part of a collaboration between the National Cancer Institute, the American Cancer Society, and the Centers for Medicare and Medicaid Services. Finally, as a means of informing practice and policy, DHCV leaders are spearheading research to provide the evidence base for employing PNs.

Patient Navigation Research Program (PNRP) Dr. Whitley and Dr. Peter Raich are conducting a two-group, randomized controlled trial of a multidimensional patient navigation intervention at DH, funded by the National Cancer Institute to test the efficacy of patient navigation assistance from the point of an abnormal screening or diagnosis through treatment for prostate, colorectal, and breast cancers. To date, more than 1,100 individuals have been enrolled in the five-year multisite study.

Reducing Health Disparities Through Patient Navigation A grant funded by the Office of Health Disparities, Colorado Department of Public Health and Environment and led by Dr. Whitley focuses on improving health outcomes for underserved individuals with chronic diseases and associated risk factors. Three PNs located at three community health centers contact DH patients on the diabetes or hypertension registries who are not up to date on their cancer screening and assist them in accessing screening, diagnostic, surveillance, and treatment services. This crosscutting, culturally appropriate PN project decreases health disparities by improving health outcomes for patients with chronic conditions and associated risk factors. To date, the results of this project demonstrate that PNs increase access to diagnostic, surveillance, and treatment services, particularly with completion of cervical and colorectal cancer screening. In addition, patients who are followed by PNs in clinics have improved diabetes control (as indicated by HGBA1C level) and LDL cholesterol levels.

Improving Access to Health Insurance Coverage

Through research and the employment of some common practices for increasing enrollment, DHCV succeeded in covering thousands of people, while also experimenting with less traditional ways of expanding health insurance coverage.

Facilitated Enrollment

The purpose of the facilitated enrollment program is to increase enrollment of eligible individuals into publicly sponsored insurance programs. In addition, DHCV aimed to make insurance more affordable to small business employers and employees. To do this, DHCV conducted research to study the effect of premium subsidies on enrollment and retention in small employer and child health plans.

DHCV investigated further the impact of being uninsured among users in the DH system. It compared the access to and quality of health care between Medicaid and uninsured adult patients (n = 791) who were utilizing DH between August and November 1999. DHCV evaluated access to care and quality by reviewing medical charts and determining the frequency with which an array of *Healthy People 2000* parameters occurred in the two populations. Significant differences existed between self-pay and Medicaid patients for six of the eight parameters. There was no significant difference in obtaining pap smears or lipid profiles in diabetic patients, for example, but significant differences between these two payer categories receiving mammograms, achieving hypertension control, and in four diabetic indicators such as the ordering of eye exams. Although the study did not provide information as to the cause of this disparity, it mirrors other studies that have shown a difference in access and quality between uninsured and Medicaid patients.

This difference between uninsured and Medicaid patients was particularly relevant, since nationally 43 percent of children are eligible for Medicaid and did not enroll and 50 percent of children were eligible for CHP+ and did not enroll.[9] This was particularly true in Denver, where almost 64 percent of children eligible for CHP+ were not enrolled.[10] Almost two thirds of new Medicaid recipients lost coverage within twelve months, and of these individuals, 54 percent had no insurance the following month.[11] Therefore, a significant need existed to enroll eligible individuals in Medicaid and CHP+ in Denver.

Welfare reform and the delinking of Temporary Assistance to Needy Families (TANF) and Medicaid eligibility in 1996 resulted in increasing rates of uninsurance, particularly for the working poor. Over a three-year period since welfare reform, Denver's TANF Medicaid eligibles had declined by 27 percent.[12] Moreover, in a study examining health insurance coverage of former welfare recipients, a year or more after leaving welfare, 49 percent of women and 30 percent of children were uninsured. Although the majority of women were working, only 33 percent obtained health coverage through their jobs. Rates of uninsurance increased with the number of months since leaving welfare and with declines in Medicaid coverage.[13] In 1999, DHCV also conducted a survey to identify and examine barriers to enrollment in publicly sponsored insurance programs. The survey of five hundred uninsured DH patients revealed that the primary barrier to enrollment was the lack of awareness about Medicaid and CHP+. These data on both lack of awareness regarding governmental programs and access and outcome differences between uninsured and Medicaid patients led to DHCV's assessment that failure to enroll in applicable government health coverage programs represented one of the major and most remediable gaps in health care in Denver.

This lack of coverage for health needs has a negative impact on individuals' personal health and the overall health of the community, as well as the financial health of DH. In looking for new ways to address this issue, DH embarked on a process of facilitating enrollment into the public health coverage programs that were available, such as Medicaid, CHP+, and the state-funded adult discount program Colorado Indigent Care Program.

Enrollment Redesign

With the help of state and county partners, the process of enrollment was redesigned in 1999 to include centralized application assistance and enrollment support. In addition, the development of a comprehensive web-based tracking database called AppTrack (now HealthTrack) was completed and shared with some of DHCV's partners.

One aspect of the redesign included the creation of enrollment specialists—staff that undergo extensive four-week training in available programs and who enroll individuals and families. There are now forty enrollment specialists, with at least one available at every DH site. Deployment of two bilingual outreach enrollment specialists further enabled DH to enroll individuals and families in community settings (described further on).

DHCV collaborated with its partners in revising and simplifying the Medicaid/ CHP+ application in 2000–2001. DH also became a Medical Assistance (MA) eligibility determination site, which accepts medical assistance applications and determines eligibility for applicants using the Colorado Benefits Management System (CBMS), the state's computerized benefit system, which was implemented in 2004.

Outreach Enrollment

Outreach enrollment is offered by CHWs and enrollment specialists in community-based settings such as schools, churches, and community-based organizations. Applications for Medicaid, CHP+, and CICP are taken and entered into the CBMS. Applicants are informed at the time of application of their eligibility and given a temporary card so that they can access services immediately. During 2008–2009, outreach enrollment was responsible for 1,127 applications and 3,336 beneficiaries.

Revenues from enrollment were significantly enhanced as a result of DHCV activities and support. Current funding for DH enrollment is through federal dollars drawn down via certification of public expenditures at 50 percent match on cost. Progress in the facilitated enrollment initiative is the result of collaborative relationships with state and county officials from Medicaid, Human Services, Health Care Policy and Financing, and the Department of Insurance as well as numerous community-based organizations and coalitions.

CHP+ Premium Subsidy Program

CHP+, the non-Medicaid, children's health insurance program (SCHIP), was launched in Colorado in April of 1998. Colorado children eighteen and under who were not eligible for Medicaid, whose family income fell between 100 and 185 percent of the Federal Poverty Level (FPL), were eligible for CHP+. The subsidy was available to families who enrolled their children in CHP+ and chose the Denver Health Medical Plan (DHMP).

Between 1998 and 2000, the DHCV premium subsidy program paid the monthly premiums. Beginning in January 2001, a nominal enrollment fee replaced the monthly premium. The DHCV subsidy program and study were discontinued in 2002. A comparison of DH health services utilization of CHP+ children and uninsured children revealed that CHP+ children used more preventive services and fewer emergency services than uninsured children.[14]

Small Business Premium Subsidy Program

DHCV aimed to make insurance more affordable to small business employers and employees by offering a small business plan. The small business premium subsidy was available to small businesses that chose to contract with DHMP for the Small Business health maintenance organization (HMO) and who met the following eligibility criteria:

- Employer enrolling in DHMP must have two to fifty employees.
- Business net income for the previous year must be less than $50,000.
- Employer must have been uncovered for at least ninety days.

The subsidy covered 20 to 50 percent of the monthly premium for both the employer and the employee and was determined by a sliding scale on the basis of the business net income of the previous year. As of December 2000, twenty-one small businesses from service and professional industries were enrolled in the study and receiving the subsidy. These twenty-one businesses included sixty-six subscribers and 108 members.

The small business premium was discontinued in 2002 because of continued losses. The medical loss ratio of 140 percent over premium cost, plus administration, sales, and marketing all contributed to the negative financial status. Affordable health insurance coverage for small business owners and employees continues to be a major policy issue.

Lessons Learned

DHCV has evolved into a program of innovative community-based initiatives that is sustained by diverse funding sources. Resources are maximized by linking and leveraging funds across programs and partners. In achieving these results, DHCV has learned myriad lessons over the years. Though all the lessons are too numerous to list here, following are some key observations:

- *Relationships are primary*! Ron David's keynote address at the first CV meeting provided an important frame for the CV work when he stated, "Relationships are primary; all else is derivative." DHCV used this philosophy to guide all efforts, resulting in numerous shared successes.
- *Committed, engaged leadership is required.* High-performing, action-oriented leadership was necessary and effective in articulating the vision, encouraging dialogue at all levels, tolerating ambiguity, and creating the environment for discovery and change.
- *Experimentation, linkages, leveraging, and transformation are effective ways of operating.* The CV initiative provided a space in which to experiment with some approaches that worked and others that did not. However, the idea that DHCV was a learning laboratory helped guide a willingness to take risks. In this process, linkages (or

partnerships), together with the leveraging of resources, positioned DHCV as a force of change and transformation. These methods are employed to the present day at DHCV.

- *Thoughtful community engagement has improved DH's and DHCV's partnerships with the communities they serve.* Building on the understanding that relationships are primary, this concept is especially powerful in community engagement. DHCV's commitment to establish meaningful partnerships with its communities has served to ensure that practical and policy solutions are grounded in the realities of people's real-life experiences, building credibility for DHCV and DH along the way.
- *Although additional financial and human resources are always welcome, change within a large bureaucracy is challenging.* Change in large organizations is often a slow and difficult process, even when it increases access to care for the underserved. Sometimes evolution is preferable to revolution!

Conclusions

Despite challenging economic and political times, the DHCV learning laboratory has been successful in increasing access to health care for underserved populations, educating policymakers as well as stimulating and participating in local, state, and national policy change. However, the recent economic recession, rising costs, and the state government's continuing fiscal crisis combine to threaten access to health care for Denver's residents. Denver's unemployment rate is 7.8 percent, more than 17 percent of Denverites are uninsured, and almost one-quarter of the children in Denver have no health insurance.

Denver Health serves one in four of the 554,636 Denver residents, of which 64 percent are Hispanic, 17 percent are white, 15 percent are African American, one percent are Asian/Pacific Islander, one percent are Native American, and two percent are Other. In 2008, 46 percent of DH's patients were uninsured, and the hospital provided $318 million in uncompensated care. The growing cost of caring for the un- or underinsured coupled with shrinking funding streams has threatened Denver's health care safety net.

In this current context of health care reform at both the national and state levels, DHCV will continue to experiment, create linkages, and leverage resources wherever possible in an effort to transform the safety system. To date, the learning laboratory experience through DHCV has contributed to increasing access to health care for the underserved, strengthening the safety net, establishing evidence-based best practices for replication, and changing health policy. It will require thoughtful policy decisions to ensure that those gains are not lost.

Notes

1. Denver Health Community Voices is grateful to the W.K. Kellogg Foundation, which provided a wealth of resources for a length of time that allowed the organization to fully develop as a learning laboratory and produce outstanding results. With appreciation to Henrie Treadwell, Ph.D., Barbara Sabol, R.N., Patricia A. Gabow, M.D., Denver community partners, and fellow Community Voices participants nationwide.

2. At the Initiative's opening conference in Stowe, Vermont, in August 1998, Professor Ron David of Harvard University provided the Keynote Address in which he shared this concept.

3. K. Black and E. Whitley (eds.), *Misery and Grace* (Denver: Denver Health Community Voices, 2006). (A book of stories told by case managers about their chronically ill patients that was produced for distribution to policy- and grantmakers.)

4. E. M. Whitley, B. A. Samuels, R. A. Wright, and R. M. Everhart, "Identification of Barriers to Healthcare Access for Underserved Men," *Journal of Men's Health and Gender*, 2005, 2(4), 421–428.

5. E. M. Whitley, R. M. Everhart, and R. A. Wright, "Measuring Return on Investment of Outreach by Community Health Workers," *Journal of Health Care for the Poor and Underserved*, 2006, 17, 6–15.

6. D. Main, E. Whitley, P. Arevalo Rincon, J. McGloin, M. Hocker, S. Thomas, and P. Iwasaki, "Cutting Cardiovascular Risk in Barbershops," *Journal of Men's Health*, 2009, 6(4), 325–330. doi:10.1016/j.jomh.2009.07.006.

7. E. M. Whitley, J. Drisko, R. M. Everhart, and B. A. Samuels, "Standardized Academic Education Prepares Competent Community Health Workers," *American Journal of Health Studies*, 2007, 22(2), 121–126.

8. Kaiser Commission on Medicaid and the Uninsured, *Medicaid and Children: Overcoming Barriers to Enrollment Findings from a National Survey* (Washington, DC: Kaiser Commission, 2000). Retrieved October 2009 from http://www.kff.org/medicaid/upload/Medicaid-and-Children-Overcoming-Barriers-to-Enrollment-Report.

9. Kaiser Commission, *Medicaid and Children*.

10. Colorado Child Health Advocates.

11. O. Carrasquillo, D. Himmelstein, S. Woolhandler, et al., "Can Medicaid Managed Care Provide Continuity of Care to New Medicaid Enrollees? An Analysis of Tenure of Medicaid," *American Journal of Public Health*, 1988, 464–466.

12. Colorado Department of Health Care Policy and Financing (1997–1999).

13. DataWatch, *Health Affairs*, 2000, 175–184.

14. S. Eisert, and P. Gabow, "Effect of Child Health Insurance Plan Enrollment on the Utilization of Health Care Services by Children Using a Public Safety Net System," *Pediatrics*, 2002, 110(5), 940–945.

CHAPTER THREE

INGHAM COMMUNITY VOICES

Health Coverage and Health Equity Through Public Health Leadership and Community Building

Doak Bloss, Melany Mack, and Bruce Bragg

This chapter discusses Ingham Community Voices, funded through the Ingham County Health Department. It describes the unique dynamic of a local health department promoting new coverage strategies for the uninsured, and the use of facilitated dialogue to build new relationships with the community in support of these strategies. Reading this chapter, the reader will

- Learn how a local health department operating within county government adopted a proactive role in creating social change at the systems level
- Identify shifts in the relationship between public entities and the communities they serve that can identify and mobilize new resources to improve community health
- Learn how community dialogue processes engaged diverse stake-holders in working for improved health and health coverage, and for the recognition and elimination of the root causes of health inequity
- Learn about outreach strategies used to reach vulnerable populations
- Learn about a health coverage model for low-income people that was replicated in counties throughout Michigan.

Introduction

Ingham Community Voices (ICV) was unique among the learning laboratories launched in the fall of 1998 in that it was the only one exclusively led by a local health department—a government entity charged with preserving and protecting the health of the people of Ingham County, Michigan. Among county health departments in Michigan, however, this department had always been unique. The Ingham County Health Department (ICHD), using its own general funds, had provided primary health care services to uninsured and indigent residents for several decades. In 1998, the department leveraged this local investment in health to forge an innovative partnership with the state Medical Services Office and two local hospital systems, creating the Ingham Health Plan, a unique coverage model that enrolled over sixteen thousand people within four years and has ensured access to health care for over sixty-six thousand different people since its inception.

Through Community Voices, ICHD pioneered the use of dialogue as a vehicle for engaging and mobilizing the community around health care reform at the local level. Over the course of a decade, ICV staged community gatherings both large and small, in neighborhood focus groups of ten or fewer participants and in town hall meetings attended by hundreds. Resulting action plans and community campaigns are credited with giving traction not only to the Ingham Health Plan but to neighborhood-based community health workers (CHWs); improved access to oral health, mental health, and substance abuse treatment, and the county's decision to tackle issues of racism, class exploitation, and gender discrimination as root causes of health inequity.

Moreover, each of these accomplishments has been achieved through shared responsibility among community stakeholders, and shared investment of both human and financial resources.

Public Health as a Catalyst for Social Change

Prior to its Community Voices initiative, ICHD had been proactive in advancing new programs to improve access to health care and promote health. With the advent of ICV, the department shifted its energies toward finding *systemic* solutions to long-standing health risk factors and health access barriers. For example, prior to 1998 the network of health centers run by ICHD provided care to six thousand uninsured people on a regular basis, but this care was delivered in haphazard fashion and ICHD was seen by many patients as the "provider of last resort" rather than as a bona fide medical home. Community support for the Ingham Health Plan was built around the concept that health care in the county should be a social right, and uninsured persons deserved to belong to an *organized system of care*. Similarly, the county had for many years released information on health risk behaviors and ways an individual could take responsibility for improving one's health status. Through Community Voices, ICHD began *asking* residents (especially people of color and people of low socioeconomic status) what constituted community health from their perspective, and to shape its health promotion strategies accordingly (Figure 3.1).

FIGURE 3.1. COMMUNITY HEALTH DEFINED AND PROMOTED IN COLLABORATION WITH THE COMMUNITY.

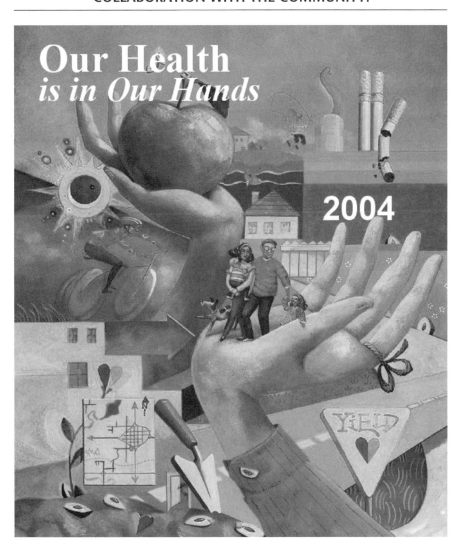

In this new role as a catalyst for more systemic and community-grounded change, ICHD was one of the few local health departments in Michigan that recognized an opportunity in the late 1990s to work with the state's Medical Services Administration to explore creative ways to finance care to the uninsured. Over the course of more than a year, the department's leadership negotiated with local hospital systems and state and local government to create a unique funding model for managing care to uninsured residents. The model used the county's local $2 million investment in health care for the indigent to draw down additional public funds for the creation of an independent nonprofit entity, the Ingham Health Plan Corporation (IHPC). While the funding mechanism for the plan has changed several times during the eleven years the plan has been in existence, it was the creation of this independent corporation that established a sustainable, collaborative, and systemic response to the medical needs of the uninsured.

The birth and growth of the Ingham Health Plan was a complicated endeavor, and one that could not have been easily understood by the community without ICV's strategic engagement of all sectors of the community. Early in the initiative, ICHD staff interviewed over fifty key informants from four stakeholder groups—health care consumers, providers, insurers, and purchasers—and compiled findings into a comprehensive "story" summarizing each group's perspective on the problem of lack of insurance. The resulting document became the cornerstone for the first ICV town hall meeting in February 2000, and cemented in the minds of participants the notion that even though stakeholders might disagree on who was obstructing health care reform on the national stage, all were equally committed to ensuring access to care at the local level. Five principles emerged from this gathering, the first of which laid the foundation for all that would follow: *Access to health care is a right for all citizens. Upholding this right in our community entails responsibilities that the entire community must bear.*[1]

A year's worth of learning sessions, focus groups, and grassroots community health summits followed, and led to the formulation of the *Action Plan for an Organized System of Care in the Capital Area* in February 2001 (Figure 3.2). Building upon the two-year-old Ingham Health Plan coverage model, this document laid out thirty-six key actions (each with its own designated "lead entity") organized under seven broad goals: coverage, zero disparity, ownership, oversight, outreach, oral health, and mental health/substance abuse services. Not only did this plan marshal the resources of the community behind a campaign for access to health care, it provided benchmarks for progress as various stakeholders gathered to share the status of the plan's objectives in ensuing community briefing events.

The Community Health Summits that were part of this process also produced individual Action Plans for Lansing neighborhoods and communities of color in Ingham County, which in turn led to exciting new grassroots-driven outreach and programming. (A fuller description of these summits can be found in the next section.) As a consequence, ICHD as a public health institution began to rethink its strategy for

FIGURE 3.2. COMPREHENSIVE ACTION
PLANNING FOR ACCESS TO CARE.

allocating and using resources. At the programmatic level, the department gained a new appreciation of the value of having neighborhood residents actively working to achieve the department's community health goals in such areas as smoking cessation, enrollment in coverage, and cancer prevention and detection. More fundamentally, department administrators began to ask two strategic questions of themselves, and to urge other institutions to do likewise (see Figure 3.3).

ICV's impact in transforming the practice and perspective of a local health department is clearly reflected in the overarching goals of the initiative as they were articulated in 2001 (Exhibit 3.1). These goals were formulated by community members, not delivered to the community by public health "experts." Moreover, they reflect a new understanding that the work of public health is not confined to regulatory functions or categorical programming. It is inextricably intertwined with the perceptions, the strengths, and the self-defined needs of the community itself.

Community Engagement Through Dialogue

Even more than the accomplishments of Ingham Community Voices in terms of access to care and community capacity building, it is important to understand how ICV used dialogue as a vehicle for illuminating and empowering the collective will of the community. Although access to health care and grassroots health promotion were the first issues ICHD tackled through facilitated dialogue, dialogue subsequently has become the methodology of choice for nearly all the department's collaborative planning work. There is also evidence that facilitated dialogue has become a standard

FIGURE 3.3. STRATEGIC QUESTIONS FOR PUBLIC HEALTH AS CHANGE AGENT.

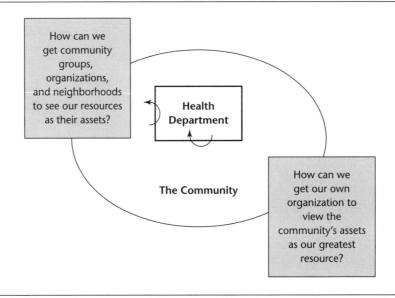

practice for a number of other institutions in Ingham County as a direct result of its successful application through ICV.

Dialogue as it was used to engage the community in Ingham County must be understood as much more than *conversation*, and in some ways as the opposite of a much more familiar form of public discourse: *debate*. Unlike conversation, dialogue involves a vigorous and directed exploration of a critical issue or question, and welcomes differences in perspective in doing so. Unlike debate, dialogue illuminates the collective will of diverse participants and seeks multiple, complementary solutions rather than one "right" or one "best" answer.

The dialogue method used in ICV was a modified version of the Technologies of Participation model taught by the Institute for Cultural Affairs[2]; however, the origins of this approach extend much further back, to the theories and practices of the Brazilian educator Paulo Freire (1921–1997). Freire insisted that education be a mutual transaction in which teacher and student are essentially equal partners in the search for what is true. In his *Pedagogy of the Oppressed*, he also argued that no educational process is values-free; unless it encourages an honest, critical examination of present reality, education will inevitably work to sustain the status quo, which is frequently oppressive to those who are "uneducated."[3] In many ways, the changing relationship

EXHIBIT 3.1. INGHAM COMMUNITY VOICES GOALS: INCREASE HEALTH ACCESS AND ACCELERATE COMMUNITY IMPROVEMENT.

Goal 1

Increase access to health services for the uninsured by establishing an organized system of care—one in which every uninsured person in Ingham County has access to a health care coverage strategy that is non-stigmatizing, user-friendly, and affordable.

- *Coverage:* Create and sustain coverage strategies sufficient to give all residents access to an organized system of care by building on current successful innovations in Ingham County.
- *Zero disparity*: Eliminate all barriers to quality health care based on economic, cultural, ethnic, and racial differences.
- *Ownership*: Mobilize Capital Area leaders to create community ownership of the need for universal access to health care.
- *Oversight*: Engage the community in an ongoing process of analyzing health data and allocating health care resources in ways that will improve health status and health care access for uninsured people.
- *Outreach*: Enable both traditional and nontraditional providers of health information to connect people to a full range of services and health education resources.
- *Oral health*: Increase access to oral health services for residents of the Capital Area.
- *Mental health and substance abuse*: Increase access to mental health and substance abuse services for residents of the Capital Area.

Goal 2

Improve health by mobilizing neighborhoods and communities.

- *Capacity building*: Build the capacity of neighborhoods, organizations, and communities to measure health broadly and develop strategies for improving health (both policy change and new programming).
- *Networks:* Assist in establishing sustainable, positive working relationships among neighborhood and community stakeholders (including residents, associations, faith-based institutions, schools, businesses, providers, and funding entities) to improve health.
- *Communication*: Establish mechanisms and provide information for neighborhoods, communities, organizations, and resource holders to communicate about strategies for improving health and measuring progress.

Source: Adapted from *Ingham Community Voices: Phase III,* PO105791, Annual Report, July 1, 2003, to August 31, 2004.

of ICHD to the community it served directly illustrates both these ideas, and is a direct result of ICV's use of dialogue in the search for local solutions to the health care crisis.

Access to Health Dialogues

Facilitated dialogue unmistakably changed the tenor of Ingham County's approach to access to health care. Whereas at the start of the initiative, stakeholders were quick to point up all the reasons why caring for the uninsured was *not* a feasible proposition (too costly, turfism, corporate irresponsibility), sustained dialogue highlighted everyone's shared interest in supporting an organized system of care. Through dialogue, participants became increasingly aware of the viability of the Ingham Health Plan and the compelling firsthand accounts of the experiences of uninsured people. By the time the first Action Plan was completed in 2001, virtually all stakeholders were touting the county's success in covering the uninsured and their role in helping make it happen. Many were actively recruiting more uninsured people to enroll in the plan.

Community Health Summits

Through Community Voices, ICHD also funded seven "Community Health Summit" processes, each managed and implemented by community members. Three of these were neighborhood-based within the city of Lansing, two focused on rural towns in the county, and two focused on the county's African American and Hispanic/Latino residents, respectively. Because each process was driven by local residents who were part of the population whose needs were being identified, each was unique in terms of its approach. All, however, used facilitated dialogue as the principal means of assessment, planning, and mobilization.

The first phase of each of these summit processes involved local residents gathering data and perspectives on what constituted community health and what needed to be done to promote the health of the community. These "leadership institutes" variously consisted of interviews with residents and other key informants, workshops on ways to organize and gain influence in decision-making processes, and environmental scans of the geographic areas under analysis. Findings from this work were then presented to the local population in a half-day or full-day summit session that culminated in the identification of approximately seven to twelve goals. Local organizers then validated and refined these into action plans that guided community health activism for the affected area for the next several years.

Impressive, concrete improvements resulted from these community-driven initiatives, which inevitably defined *health* much more broadly than ICHD or any similar institution would have done. Issues such as home ownership, employment, and transportation were just as likely to show up in Action Plans as physical activity, access to food, and medical care. Six organizations came into being to serve as the "action arm" of their summit process—and continue to do so in 2010, with support from a wide variety of funding sources (Exhibit 3.2). Many of the health initiatives reported in the next two sections are in fact carried out by grassroots outreach workers organized by these new local entities.

Power of We Consortium

Perhaps the strongest evidence that dialogue has become a standard practice in Ingham County is the evolution of the Power of We Consortium (PWC) during the time of Ingham Community Voices. This body, which came into being in the early 1990s under a state directive to improve collaboration across public agencies at the local level through "multi-purpose collaborative bodies," has grown from its initial seven members to sixty-five public and private organizations, agencies, and community groups. Many of these were directly involved in the far-reaching dialogue processes of ICV at either the institutional or grassroots level, and subsequently approached the health department for assistance in facilitating new dialogues on a variety of community-building initiatives. The PWC itself also adopted dialogue as a standard methodology for its monthly meetings, and included it as one of its five essential community practices (Exhibit 3.3).

Whenever community concern about an issue or problem emerges, the PWC's first step is now to engage in community dialogue to assess its impact and identify strategic remedial actions. Recent issues in which PWC has invested time and energy exploring through dialogue have included the creation of a ten-year plan to end homelessness, resolving persistent transportation barriers experienced by the county's residents, improving coordination of services to Lansing's large and diverse refugee population, and developing community supports for ex-offenders returning to the community from incarceration.

Further evidence of the impact of ICV's dialogue orientation on the PWC can be found in its own conceptualization of the work of comprehensively improving the community and building its assets. Figure 3.4 illustrates one attempt to capture this concept visually.

In support of this concept, the PWC's Data Committee regularly produces a report on twenty-three indicators of community well-being grouped under the broad categories of health, safety, economy, intellectual and social development, environment, and community life. The evolution of the Community Indicators Project is advancing in its sophistication, and community ownership in the process is growing as the community engages in facilitated dialogue in many venues on the meaning and implications of data trends illuminated by the report. The fourth edition of "The

EXHIBIT 3.2. CENTERS FOR OUTREACH AND ACTIVISM.

Allen Neighborhood Center

NorthWest Initiative

Southside Community Coalition

South Lansing Community Development Association

Greater Lansing African American Health Institute (GLAAHI)

Lansing Latino Health Alliance

Allen Neighborhood Center's Health Outreach Team, 2004.

Source: Photo courtesy of Allen Neighborhood Center.

Creative Solutions: To protect a neighborhood fence from repeated collisions, ANC staff decided to make it beautiful.

Source: Photo courtesy of Allen Neighborhood Center.

EXHIBIT 3.3. FIVE ESSENTIAL COMMUNITY PRACTICES.

1. *Engaging and mobilizing community members* in the identification of issues and the development of solutions
2. *Facilitating dialogue and creating connections* across a diverse array of people to achieve breakthroughs in thought and action
3. *Identifying and supporting civic leadership* so that all community stakeholders—not just policymakers and resource holders—are involved in decision making
4. *Using all of the assets of the community for change* so that community-based groups view institutional resources as their assets and institutions view the community's assets as their greatest resource
5. *Sharing and using data and information to support and monitor progress* through data democratization, the full use of technology, and increasingly creative uses of communication techniques

Power of We" report on the well-being of the Capital Area, subtitled "Strengthening Community Connections for Action," is in development. In addition to updating the indicators and measures contained in the second edition of the report, the third edition contains several new indicators, including one on health equity.

FIGURE 3.4. HOW THE POWER OF WE CONSORTIUM RELATES TO AND BUILDS UPON COMMUNITY STRENGTHS.

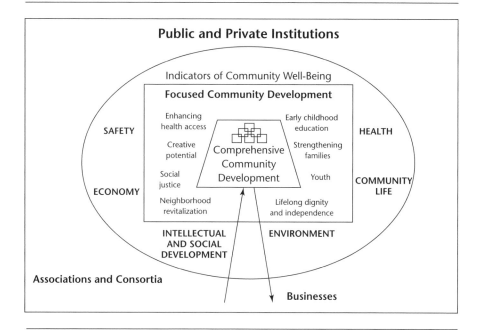

Much of the work begun by the ICV data democratization initiative is continuing through the Community Indicators Project. The driving force behind "data democratization" is to ensure that public information is accessible to and comprehensible by all members of the community so that they can understand community problems and the resources available to address them, plan effective strategies, and evaluate progress toward their goals.

For example, some of the data recently collected for the community indicators project were accomplished in such a way as to permit comparisons of Lansing's neighborhoods and communities of color with aggregate information for Ingham County and the Capital Region. The sampling methods for the Behavior Risk Factor and Social Capital Survey were appropriately weighted to yield reliable information for three of Lansing's neighborhoods and for African Americans. An in-depth analysis of this new data will assist ICHD's many partners with using this information to engage and mobilize residents in the creation of a shared vision and strategies to achieve a healthier, more inclusive community for all.

The Social Justice Project

Perhaps the most striking development in ICHD's use of facilitated dialogue as a vehicle for change is the Social Justice Project, which began in 2005 and continues to be emulated and replicated by local health departments around the country.[4] The project's objectives were to illuminate the ways in which the department's policies and practices had a bearing on the root causes of health inequity—the systematic and unjust differences in the distribution of illness and disease—in Ingham County, and to create and implement an Action Plan for improving the department's responsiveness to those root causes. The Social Justice Project was the department's first attempt to use facilitated dialogue to engage and mobilize its own employees around an initiative intended to change the department's internal practice.

Although the Social Justice Action Plan that resulted from the 2005 initial dialogue process did not immediately transform the department's practice, it did lead to the establishment of health equity as a core department value ("We improve the health of the entire community by working toward a fair and just distribution of the social opportunities needed to achieve well-being") and the discovery of the need for a much deeper intervention. Again, dialogue was seen as the most promising vehicle for meeting this need.

In 2008, ICHD recruited, selected, trained, assessed, and certified a team of twenty facilitators, about half of whom were department employees and half community members. Each step of this process was informed by dialogue. Rather than conduct conventional interviews with applicants, for example, project organizers facilitated interactions between four to six applicants at a time, encouraging each to ask relevant questions of the others. After completing twelve days of training with expert facilitators in 2008, the facilitator team then created a four-day workshop model, which it began providing in 2009. Over the course of two years, all three hundred of the ICHD's employees and more than a hundred community members will complete the workshop, which immerses participants in an in-depth, often uncomfortable exploration of modern forms of oppression based on race, class, gender, and other forms of difference, and its impact on the health of communities.

Early assessment of the workshop's impact on participants has been impressive. Participant understanding of core concepts (health disparity, health equity, social justice, and so on) increased by 30 to 40 percentage points for each concept. Even more heartening, whereas only 33 percent understood the relationship of social justice to their work prior to the workshop, 70 percent said they understood it after the four days. Another striking finding from pre- and post-workshop questionnaires was a decrease from 65 percent to 36 percent in those who believed community health was primarily determined by behaviors and lifestyle. The percentage of those who recognized housing, transportation, and living wage as determinants of health rose to 92 percent, while those who saw opportunity and power as determinants rose to 78 percent.

The Social Justice Project is the most recent example of ICV's reverberating impact on a local health department and the community it serves. As the project's dialogue-based approach to recognizing and responding to the health impacts of racism, classism, and gender discrimination is replicated in other departments around the nation, this legacy will continue.

Strategic Community Partnerships

From its inception, ICV intentionally was designed as a collaborative community improvement process with multiple partners, rather than as a distinguishable administrative structure or brand for one organization. ICV utilized existing organizational structures and encouraged their adaptation, connection, and improvement. When structures did not exist to address the specific needs and concerns of community members, grant dollars were strategically invested to support their development.

Minority Health

The Greater Lansing African American Health Institute (GLAAHI) formed as a result of a 2000 Community Health Summit focused on the health of African Americans. GLAAHI remains a principal grassroots forum and catalyst for discussion, research, and understanding of the inequalities of health for African Americans in Ingham County. Recognizing the leverage to be gained by working closely with the faith community, GLAAHI hosts annual "Pastors' Breakfasts" to educate the community about health disparities faced by African Americans. GLAAHI understands that theories and data must be tempered with practical information that will help people access the services they need to improve their health and well-being. The organization disseminates important information about health coverage and other community resources. GLAAHI has forged partnerships with other organizations to confront issues such as mental health concerns, chronic disease, AIDS, and homelessness. These strategic partnerships have helped to broaden GLAAHI's reach and ensure its sustainability.

ICV also made a concerted effort to address the needs and interests of Latino and Native American people. While initially the Mestizo Anishnabe Health Alliance represented Latino and Native American community members, it became clear that it was preferable to focus on the specific needs of each community. The Lansing Latino Health Alliance (LLHA) was formed to advocate for health-related issues, disseminate information about available health services, and promote access to English-as-a-second-language and interpreter services for Latinos. LLHA promotes access to quality, culturally sensitive health services and encourages youth education and accelerated professional development for Latino health professionals. The organization's vision is to become the premier advocacy organization for improving the health status of Lansing area Latinos.

To address the needs of Native Americans, ICHD established a permanent position for a Native American Outreach Advocate (NAOA) within its own infrastructure. The NAOA works with Native American families and individuals within Ingham County to ensure an overall strong and healthy community. Services include connection to a medical home, assistance in applying for medical coverage and other supportive programs, and education on health issues such as diabetes, heart disease, substance abuse, and tobacco use. Equally important, the NAOA strives to strengthen ties within the Native American community by actively engaging those who are served in activities such as Pow-Wows, lectures, conferences, Indigenous People's Day, Native American Heritage Month, feasts, and Anishinaabemowin language programs. The NAOA also facilitates presentations and workshops designed to improve the cultural competence of service providers. The workshops and presentations help to increase understanding of and appreciation for the unique strengths and insights Native Americans bring to the community.

Mental Health and Substance Abuse

Mental health and substance abuse were identified as priority issues in the original 2001 *Action Plan for an Organized System of Care in the Capital Area*. Community dialogues on substance abuse produced recommendations for improved access and were developed into an action plan in 2002. The dialogues revealed that multiple layers of stigma and denial form barriers to preventing and treating substance abuse in individuals and in the community as a whole. To overcome stigma and denial, a demonstration project funded by a Healthy Communities Access Program grant from the Department of Health and Human Services placed two substance abuse case managers in four primary care health centers operated by ICHD. Co-location of providers allowed patients to be introduced to the substance abuse case manager by someone they already trusted (the clinic staff) and in the context of helping the patient rather than gatekeeping for the system. Assessments were conducted immediately on site with all necessary referral paperwork expedited. Primary care staff and substance abuse staff pooled their expertise and resources, both formally and informally; each learned from the other how best to address patients' needs. The demonstration project showed the efficacy of linking these services with primary care. A second community dialogue in 2007 declared a "Unified Concept of Care" as a goal of future community efforts to improve access: "Assert and demonstrate the value of adopting a unified concept of health care—one that responds to the inter-relatedness of primary care, oral health, mental health, substance abuse, and pain management."

One of the community's most significant accomplishments was the establishment of the Ingham Substance Abuse Prevention Coalition (ISAPC), of which ICHD is a founding member. Developed in 2005, ISAPC has made progress in a number of areas related to substance abuse. After completing a needs analysis and resource scan, the members of ISAPC generated a report, "Substance Abuse in the Capital Area," that includes baseline data on a number of indicators of substance abuse in the community. The Coalition used baseline data to identify priority issues and developed discussion guides to spark conversations, raise awareness, and mobilize the community to address these issues. Each year the ISAPC selects evidence-based strategies to promote prevention and reduce substance abuse. The strategies form a comprehensive community plan that coalition members take responsibility for implementing.

Community dialogues on mental health, supported with CV funding, illuminated the many ways in which mental health is tied to so many other aspects of community life: meaningful work, spiritual grounding, social connection, harmonious relationships at home and in school, relief from stress, and a sense of one's value to others. The dialogues revealed that the strategic actions that can lift overall mental health need to be owned and led by a broad and diverse set of community partners, not merely those agencies that provide mental health services. The Mental Health Partnership Council (MHPC) grew directly out of the dialogues and convened community partners dedicated to eliminating the stigma experienced by persons with mental illness, emotional disturbances, developmental disabilities, or substance use disorders. The MHPC is dedicated to identifying community needs, identifying and bolstering community assets and strengths that foster mental health, understanding and improving mental health services, and taking action to improve mental health and mental health services. The MHPC has become a subcommittee of the Capital Area Health Alliance (CAHA), ensuring that important mental health issues will remain "on the front burner" in the community. CAHA is a coalition of organizations, businesses, health care professionals, and volunteers working together to improve community health. As a subcommittee of CAHA, the MHPC has increased access to influential community members who can assist with advancing its goals of promoting the mental health of the capital area and the quality and accessibility of mental health services within the community.

Community-Based Participatory Evaluation

A local firm, Public Sector Consultants (PSC), designed the evaluation of ICV using a collaborative research model that engaged all community partners in evaluation activities. PSC worked with primary stakeholders to develop a logic model reflecting ICV principles, goals, priority areas, and activities, and refined the model as ICV evolved. The ICV logic model was used as the basis for development of an evaluation design addressing both program activities and policy targets.

The evaluation design—including measures, data sources, and time frames—was developed in consultation with primary stakeholders and community partners. Quantitative data included activities of community health workers, enrollment in the Ingham Health Plan, and estimates of the proportion of population who would be without health coverage if the health plan did not exist. Qualitative data included identification and descriptions of ICV approaches and lessons learned, and perspectives of community partners on policy changes.

Methods to engage community partners in the evaluation included interviews, surveys, and study circles. Study circles are small, peer-led discussion groups that meet over time and involve community partners in dialogue and action on important issues. Study circles were used in the ICV evaluation to build the capacity of stakeholders to participate in evaluation and use evaluation data for continuous improvement; provide forums for local data analysis and interpretation; bring multiple perspectives together to enhance the community's understanding of the changes taking place; and support partnerships that strengthen all stakeholders and unify their efforts.

Evaluation reports chronicled the initial focus of ICV on community dialogues for the creation of an organized system of care, the later identification of effective community practices for community improvement, and ICV's movement toward action on the determinants of health and community capacity building. Two goals were originally identified for ICV through a series of stakeholder interviews, community dialogues, and neighborhood summits. The goals were to (1) increase access to health services for the uninsured by establishing an organized system of care; and (2) improve health, as experienced by residents, by mobilizing neighborhoods and communities (see Exhibit 3.1). During the early phases of ICV, the focus under the first goal was the creation and expansion of a viable funding strategy for the Ingham Health Plan (IHP), which provided health care coverage for the uninsured. The funding strategy did not include grant funds, which helped to ensure sustainability of the

IHP. The second goal led to a wide range of community and neighborhood development activities aimed at building capacity to measure and implement strategies to improve health. In the process, working relationships were established among stakeholders, and mechanisms for communication were created between community organizations and policymakers. As ICV evolved, the two goals and the strategies for each became increasingly intertwined. The local evaluation documented that strategies originally intended to engage and mobilize communities, such as community outreach workers, were effectively utilized to increase enrollment in IHP, and the availability of coverage through IHP served as an incentive to engage community members. As participation in community development and neighborhood activities grew, the community's role in needs assessment and planning was strengthened, leading key informants to observe that community institutions began to recognize the resources neighborhoods have to offer and work *with* the neighborhoods, rather than *for* them. The community-based participatory evaluation process helped institutional partners change the way they did business. They became more involved with the community and neighborhoods, relying on the ICV process for neighborhood needs assessment, using information from community summits and action plans in the development of strategic plans, and targeting funding to community priorities.

During the final evaluation of ICV, key informants most often used descriptors such as *a community engagement process, involvement of grassroots citizens, access to health care, a broad definition of health, collaboration, improving the health and well-being of the community,* and *raising the voices of those who traditionally have not been heard in the policymaking process* to describe what ICV meant to them. Discussions with community partners such as the Power of We Consortium to identify and define the methods and patterns of practice that led to ICV's accomplishments led to the identification of five catalytic community practices for accelerating community improvement: (1) engaging and mobilizing community members; (2) facilitating dialogue and creating connections; (3) identifying and supporting civic leadership; (4) using all the assets of the community for change; and (5) sharing and using data and information to support and monitor progress (see Exhibit 3.3).

Over the course of the initiative, evaluation documented that through ICV community partnerships and leveraging of funds, the community achieved results—health care coverage and access to oral health services has increased for the community's uninsured; thousands of community members have been engaged in facilitated dialogue on community health and neighborhood revitalization; institutional partners have modified planning and financing practices to support community improvement; and a grassroots network for engagement, planning, and action has been created. ICV evaluation documented that participation by residents in community development, and neighborhood activities aimed at improving health increased as did the participation of minority and rural populations. Information sharing among organizations and between organizations and neighborhood-based efforts improved, and cooperative efforts on community health goals increased across neighborhood organizations, agencies, and city and county governments.

Community involvement in ICV evaluation facilitated ongoing information sharing among institutions and neighborhood-based efforts and promoted shared accountability for community health improvements.

Ensuring Coverage and Access to Care

Health Care Coverage

The Ingham Health Plan was launched in the fall of 1998 but was not widely known until a year or two into its existence. Initially covering about six thousand people who had active medical records with the ICHD's health centers, the plan began to expand significantly after community awareness grew through public awareness campaigns, community dialogue processes, and grassroots outreach efforts. The plan reached an enrollment peak of more than seventeen thousand members in 2007, covering over 50 percent of the total uninsured in the county, including nearly all of the residents who were not eligible for another form of coverage such as Medicaid or MIChild (Michigan's health insurance program for children). The number of providers willing to see IHP patients also increased dramatically over the course of the initial years of ICV. Whereas in the beginning, members could only be seen at the health department's own community health centers (ten sites), by 2002 more than thirty different practices had agreed to take on a predetermined number of people enrolled in the plan. Currently there are forty-eight participating practices in the county.

The IHP is not health insurance, but rather a health coverage program providing primary care, specialty care, lab, radiology, and prescription drugs to its members. Members earning less than 35 percent of the Federal Poverty Level (FPL) have been eligible for a somewhat enhanced benefit during some of the plan's history, including in-patient and emergency room care.[5] Although the majority of the members who earn between 35 percent and 250 percent of the FPL did not receive this benefit, many were eligible for participating hospital systems' charity care programs. On two occasions, the IHPC has provided additional payments to the hospitals proportionate to the percentage of IHP members for which they had provided uncompensated care.

Enrollment in the plan is free. Copays for various services have varied over the eleven years of the plan's existence, ranging between $1 and $10 for specific visits, services, or prescriptions. The only copays for those earning less than 35 percent of FPL are $3 for office visits and urgent care, and $1 for prescription drugs. Through a separate program also managed by the IHPC, non-IHP members can also receive a discount on prescription drugs (usually around 25 percent) if they do not have and are not eligible for prescription coverage.

As indicated earlier, the IHP's success was predicated on the collaboration of all its public and private partners. To manage the many administrative functions of the plan, the Ingham County Health Department had to develop new capacities and new infrastructure, in the form of a Health Plan Management unit that grew from a staff of two to a staff of twenty-five within the first six years of its existence. ICHD successfully exported this capacity to more than fifty other counties in the state, handling various functions such as enrollment, training, and member services for similar but independently administered county plans.

Careful and strategic management of gathered health care resources for the uninsured has obviously been critical to the IHP's growth and stability. Throughout its existence, the plan has struggled to engage specialty care providers, usually identifying them on a case-by-case basis for patients. Redetermination of the eligibility of members has also been an issue, as the plan's board of directors seeks to provide coverage to as many uninsured residents as possible while not stretching enrollment beyond its financial capacity. In recent years, rising unemployment and Michigan's severe economic crisis (which began much earlier than the national crisis) have greatly taxed the IHPC's ability to meet the needs of the growing number of the uninsured people in the county. Financial modeling suggests that maintaining the current level of coverage will exhaust the plan's financial reserves within three years. Consequently, a new flurry of community activity is underway to explore new options to sustain care for the county's uninsured population, balancing the community value of a *right to health care* with new coverage options arising from national health care reform and the likelihood of several more years of severe economic stress.

Community Health Workers

ICV understood health broadly, and work consequently was focused both on increasing access to care for vulnerable populations and on improving the social determinants of health. Community health workers were enlisted to provide targeted outreach to enroll the uninsured in health coverage plans, provide information and linkages to health and social support services, and engage residents in community improvement efforts. Consistent with its view of community organizations as assets in the accomplishment of its work, ICHD contracted with community organizations that employed CHWs to support its grassroots outreach efforts to lower-income families with children who were uninsured and potentially eligible for enrollment in Medicaid or the Ingham Health Plan.

The CHW outreach teams proved to be excellent partners because they were organic (having developed in response to the needs in several discrete areas) and nimble (able to respond more quickly to emerging needs and challenges). The teams enabled ICHD to keep its finger on the pulse of the community and to respond more effectively to community needs. For example, outreach teams identified early on that many community members who were nominally enrolled in coverage programs did not seek the care they needed because they lacked a relationship with a primary care provider. ICHD then negotiated with the organizations employing the CHWs to add to their scope of services assisting residents with establishing a medical home. Consequently, the CHW outreach teams not only enrolled new members in health coverage plans, they also assisted them with making and keeping their initial appointments with their selected primary care provider, thereby helping them to establish a medical home.

ICHD staff developed an innovative "braided funding" strategy for leveraging dollars to support the work of CHW outreach teams. Braided funding combines several funding sources into one contract and uses a progressive Michigan Medicaid policy to support outreach activities to increase public awareness about Medicaid eligibility and benefits, assist with Medicaid applications, provide translation and transportation services, and promote utilization of preventive health services. The braided funding mechanism continues to fund CHW outreach in the community.

The outreach strategies employed by ICHD are distinct in that they integrate outreach for access to health care and effective utilization of services with engagement and mobilization of residents to improve community health. ICHD, through its community organization partners, deployed CHWs in a role significantly expanded beyond the usual one of addressing specific health concerns such as diabetes, asthma, or hypertension. CHWs helped enroll eligible people in health coverage plans and linked them to a broad array of services and resources ranging from smoking cessation to financial management and assistance with filing for earned income tax credits, depending on the individual's needs and situation. As they did their work, CHWs developed trusting relationships and were able to encourage community members to become actively engaged in community improvement, to move from being consumers and clients to being civic participants and problem solvers.

Men's Health

ICV worked with the Discharge Planning Aftercare and Community Support (DPACS) Committee, which was focused on assisting men who had been incarcerated to make a successful transition back into the community. Relationships were established with adult probation and parole offices, and information about Ingham Health Plan, Medicaid, and community supportive services was provided to probation and parole agents, who previously were largely unaware of these resources to benefit their clients. In addition, ICV actively participated in an ad hoc committee of the Power of We Consortium to gather information, compile data, and make recommendations to the community about ways to help parolees. When the work of the DPACS

Committee was subsumed under a broader umbrella of community organizations working to end homelessness in the community, NorthWest Initiative, one of the community partners supported by ICHD, developed a program to continue to provide support expressly for ex-offenders and their families.

Oral Health

For over forty years, at its Adult Dental Clinic at its Cedar Street Community Health Center, ICHD has provided dental services to adults who may not be able to access care through the private sector. The Oral Health Task Force (OHTF), convened by ICV, promoted the development of the Healthy Smiles Dental Clinic, a new dental care facility for children, most of them on Medicaid. The OHTF worked closely with ICV to increase access to oral health services in the community. It successfully sought grants from Volunteers in Health and the American Dental Association to stage specific events geared to providing services to the uninsured and to raising community awareness about the need for oral health services. Events included Give a Kid a Smile Day; a Baby Bottle Mouth Education Workshop with Early Head Start families; screening and sealant days; and "Perio-Bootcamp," which focused on offering continuing education credits in periodontics for those who volunteered their services during the boot camp. The OHTF became a permanent subcommittee of the Capital Area Health Alliance and, as such, continues its commitment to increase access to oral health care by exploring solutions to the lack of access.

In 2007, Adult Dental provided 4,321 service encounters to uninsured residents, and Healthy Smiles provided 6,726 service encounters to children on Medicaid. The two dental centers combined performed 29,529 oral health procedures. However, ICHD had difficulty filling vacant dentist positions due to Medicaid cuts and the shortage of dental providers in Ingham County who serve the underserved and uninsured. These dentist vacancies resulted in a dramatic decline in the number of patients that could be served, and in 2008, Adult Dental had only 3,748 patient encounters while Healthy Smiles had 7,496. The positions were subsequently filled, but, even with both dental centers fully staffed, the need for dental services continues to increase. Though ICHD expects to provide oral health care to an increased number of individuals, the needs are so great and resources so limited that the community's need for oral health care is not likely to be met in the foreseeable future.

Tobacco Prevention and Cessation

In its combined efforts of improving access to health care and services, ICV provided an opportunity to work with the American Legacy Foundation to reduce tobacco use in Ingham County. ICV chose low-income pregnant and parenting women as its focus. This important group remains the focus of *House Calls*, an innovative, home-based cessation program that has proven highly popular with participants. *House Calls* offers smoking cessation support as an enhancement to the home visiting services provided by ICHD. *House Calls* addresses disparities in cessation access for low-income pregnant and parenting women by addressing identified barriers to utilization. The project's three goals are (1) developing comprehensive, sustainable, and accountable smoking cessation services for low-income women who are pregnant and parenting and who seek services at ICHD; (2) engaging a greater number of pregnant and parenting women who smoke in cessation support and successfully stopping smoking; and (3) increasing the number of women who maintain abstinence from tobacco during the postpartum period.

House Calls has clearly demonstrated that utilization increases when barriers to services are effectively addressed. From January to May 2007, only twenty women participated in free cessation support services offered at ICHD. A medical resident developed a survey that elicited the reasons why women were not availing themselves of services. An intervention was developed to address the barriers that were identified. *House Calls* began in October 2008, and over 140 women enrolled during the first year. Like ICV, *House Calls* is an example of ICHD's model of integrating new projects and programs into existing services as a strategy for effectiveness and sustainability.

Lessons Learned

The many and varied components of Ingham Community Voices offer a number of lessons to other communities and policymakers seeking to improve health, expand health coverage, and eliminate health inequity.

- *The discipline of public health can play a dynamic and proactive role in mobilizing the community to improve access and equity.* In the United States, public health as a discipline has receded from its original commitment to human rights and equal opportunity as foundational to population health. Those values rose in response to the abuses of industrialization. In recent decades, local health departments have defined their purpose largely through regulatory functions, categorical programming, and a disease-based model for health. Ingham Community Voices demonstrated the efficacy of a return to community mobilization and health equity as cornerstones of public health practice.
- *All social policy is health policy.* This lesson was learned particularly by staff and administrators of the ICHD as they moved into new relationships with grassroots organizers who redefined *community health*. Community groups repeatedly demonstrated that health is about neighborhood safety, employment, education, and social connection, rather than strictly a matter of medical care and behaviors.

- *Facilitated dialogue can illuminate new collaborative pathways for social change and health care reform.* Dialogue methodology was a consistent area of exploration and growth for all of the partners in ICV. At different points in the initiative, the use of dialogue subverted the presumed polarization of stakeholders regarding health care reform, enabled institutional partners to perceive the very different realities of community partners and vice versa, and enabled the articulation of a vision for change that everyone could comfortably own.
- *Access to health care supports health equity, but can never guarantee it.* As ICHD moves into an intentional path toward changing its practice with a focus on health equity and social justice, the early lessons from community health workers and uninsured patients continually remind us that access is not an end in itself. Even with the coverage represented by an IHP membership card, an Ingham County resident may continue to experience unjust treatment in medical care, in housing, in employment, in education, and in law enforcement. To the degree that this treatment is systemic and patterned, it will ensure the continuation of persistent health disparities for people of color, women, people of low socioeconomic status, and members of other target groups. The ensuring of health equity therefore depends on an unending commitment to eliminating the modern forms of oppression, exploitation, and unearned privilege that reinforce these disparities.

Conclusions

ICV succeeded in spreading its coverage model and dialogue methodology to many other organizations, departments, and communities. The transformative effect of the CV initiative on ICHD in turn led the organization to intense self-examination and a commitment to the transformation of public health practice itself. It also led ICHD to support nontraditional grassroots partners in promoting a new idea of community health, one that placed community members in leadership roles. Through training and technical assistance to other departments in Michigan and elsewhere, ICHD continues to replicate its strategies for expanding coverage and eliminating health inequity.

ICV's insistence in engaging in facilitated dialogue about racism, exclusion, and other forms of oppression has been instrumental to achieving a better understanding of the social determinants of health and illness. These dialogues are driving a deeper excavation of root causes of inequity within institutions and in the community as a whole. Collaborative efforts to sustain and expand coverage for the uninsured, build strong social networks in economically challenged neighborhoods, and effectively organize diverse stakeholders to improve conditions are all now seen in the much larger context of social justice.

Notes

1. *Action Plan for an Organized System of Care in the Capital Area* (Lansing, Michigan: Capital Area Health Alliance, 2001).
2. Information on ICA's excellent training courses can be found at www.ica-usa.org.
3. P. Freire, *Pedagogy of the Oppressed* (New York: Herder and Herder, 1970).
4. R. Hofrichter (ed.), *Tackling Health Inequities Through Public Health Practice: A Handbook for Action* (Washington, D.C.: National Association of City and County Health Officials, 2006).
5. IHP members earning less than 35 percent of FPL would previously have been in Michigan's State Medical Plan (SMP). Part of the financial arrangement that financed the IHP included the county's agreement to assume responsibility for managing the care to this population, who were enrolled in a benefit commensurate with what they had received under the SMP.

CHAPTER FOUR

COMMUNITY VOICES MIAMI

Building Spaces and Relationships That Promote Promising Practices and Access to Health Care[1]

Leda M. Pérez and Elise M. Linder

This chapter discusses the manner in which Community Voices Miami developed as a collaborative focused on providing practical and policy recommendations to improve access to health care and social services for uninsured and underserved populations in Miami-Dade County. After reading this chapter, the reader will

- Learn about the elements involved in convening a successful multi-stakeholder process
- Learn about how research and data may be used strategically to improve decision making
- Learn about how resources can be leveraged through community relationships and partnerships
- Learn about promising practices and policies for connecting people with health and social services

Introduction

When the Kellogg Foundation first funded Community Voices Miami (CVM) at Camillus House, a long-standing community-based organization in the service of homeless people, two key factors drove this decision. The first was that supporting an organization with a focus on the homeless offered an opportunity to look carefully at the issues facing some of the most marginalized and vulnerable people in society. Funding Camillus would help to create awareness for the many faces of the underserved and shine a spotlight on their issues and needs. The other reason had much to do with the vision and leadership capacity at this organization. Camillus's chairman of the board in 1998 was a well-known physician, Dr. Pedro Jose "Joe" Greer Jr.,[2] who had spent the past twenty years working to raise awareness about the social, economic, and political determinants of health and the need to address these as a first step toward eradicating poverty and ill health in Miami. A locally and nationally known figure, Dr. Greer would be essential for his leadership in this work.

Onlookers might have guessed at the time that the scope of work would include a process for building consensus on the issues that the Miami-Dade County (MDC) community would have to address in relation to the uninsured and underserved, as well as the homeless. But no one really imagined that the process ultimately would look carefully inward. Prior to solving some of the practical issues facing those on the margins, an overriding concern surfaced regarding the very structures that allowed barriers to care to continue for some of the poorest in the community.

CVM developed over the years as a veritable multi-stakeholder process—which brought with it a convener, "dedicated staff" for health and social service providers as well as community-based organizations and the political leadership of Miami-Dade County—through which leaders could present their concerns about health care access and propose solutions to the same. In this context, CVM bore witness to and disseminated the best thinking of the Miami-Dade community regarding practical and political ways in which to improve health care access for all people living in the county. In the early years, much of the focus was placed on the governance structures related to health planning and spending. In later years, having successfully reformed the health planning governance model, CVM turned its attention to fortifying the collaboratives

> It occurred to me immediately that the driving force behind this work—the impetus which would create substantive change across the country in both practice and policy—was a commitment to participatory democracy in the way in which decisions *must* be taken about health care for some of our most vulnerable populations. This was work I could feel passionate about. The heart and soul of this initiative was entirely about "community voices" stepping up to the plate, saying, "We are here and will be seen and heard on the issues that affect the way we live our daily lives!"
>
> —Leda M. Pérez, Ph.D., Vice President, Health Initiatives, Collins Center for
> Public Policy and Director, Community Voices Miami

and partnerships that would ensure the continuation of some of the promising practices in health care access being experimented with throughout the country.

Today, all of the thinking and work developed through CVM is embedded throughout different health and social service organizations in MDC. The Collins Center for Public Policy, an independent, nonpartisan organization, where CVM devoted its last five years of programming, is now staffed with a Health Initiatives division, a notable accomplishment considering that it is the only think tank in Miami—whose tagline is "Thinking. Doing. For Florida."—that maintains health programming and policy activities.

Origins and Factors That Called for Change

Miami's particular social, economic, and political context at the time of its funding necessitated leadership that would take a broad approach in improving access to health care. In the late 1990s and into 2000, Miami, with a population of approximately 2.5 million, was considered the poorest city in the United States. The situation in this ethnically and racially diverse setting was exacerbated by neighborhoods segregated by economics and race, where at one point in the mid-1990s, the African American population was considered the poorest of that in any U.S. city. In this highly unequal context, where the country's lowest wage-earning zip code was separated from the country's highest income zip code only by Miami's Biscayne Bay, there also existed a fragmented system of health care and social services.

There is only one public hospital in Miami, and it operates as a result of extra revenues generated from a half-penny sales tax on all purchases in the county. This exclusive payment to Jackson Memorial Hospital, meant to help offset the costs of indigent care, created particular tension among other providers of health care who believed that they should also receive some support for their efforts in providing uncompensated care. As a result of this situation, as well as the competition for scarce resources, the collaboration among Miami's providers was poor, at best. Meanwhile, health disparities were on the rise, particularly for low-income people. In addition, there was a large immigrant population experiencing other serious access barriers due to immigration status, language, and culture that needed serious attention.

Organizing to Do the Work

Beyond the single public hospital, Jackson Memorial, which maintained thirteen primary care center sites throughout the county, a separate network, Health Choice Network, existed as an umbrella organization to seven federally qualified community health centers across Miami-Dade. In addition to this, a number of community-based organizations provided maternal and child health services as well as services targeting the needs of immigrants.

In this context, an important policy focus in the first five years of the work in Miami was on the serious concern among health care providers about the level of transparency related to the public dollars received through the Public Health Trust, the governing board of Jackson Memorial. In an environment with approximately half-a-million people uninsured in Miami, other providers of health were concerned that even though Jackson received county funding to treat the uninsured, it could not possibly meet the full demand for health services.

Early CVM responses to this situation can be seen through the way in which CVM organized itself. That is to say, in its first five years of existence, CVM functioned as a triumvirate, with the core "dedicated staff," administrative, and funding arm located at Camillus House, which, in turn, subcontracted two partners, Rand and the United Way of Miami-Dade County. By bringing together key actors and initiating a conversation about practical and policy concerns and solutions, CVM's Camillus House project team did three essential things: (1) organized two leadership bodies—an Oversight Team, composed of key health, social service, and political leadership in the county, and a Multi-Agency Consortium, comprising the county's administrators of health and social service organizations; (2) commissioned key policy analysis reports on indigent health care and the governance of public dollars in Miami-Dade County; and (3) led community-based dialogues about community needs and perceptions in relation to health care access for underserved populations.

Oversight Team: Leadership Through Power Brokers

The Oversight Team became the equivalent of CVM's board of directors. In effect, this was the highest authority of the project and the space at which all final decisions were made. Its chair was Dr. Joe Greer, and under his leadership some of the key decisions made by the Oversight Team included insisting on policy changes in the way that Jackson Memorial Hospital administered its funds and approving a county-wide plan for programmatic and policy-oriented recommendations that has continued to serve as a reference since its development, the Miami Action Plan (MAP) for Access to Healthcare.[3]

Multi-Agency Consortium: Leadership Through Spaces and Relationships

Meeting for the first time in April 1999 the Multi-Agency Consortium (MAC) brought together all of the leadership of Miami-Dade's diverse health and social service provider community. Under the guidance of two powerful leaders, then-director of the Miami-Dade County Health Department and then-chief of staff of Miami-Dade County, this body established itself as a formidable space for thinking and consensus-building in relation to Miami-Dade's most vexing programmatic and policy-oriented health care access issues. One of the important outcomes of this space was the commissioning of a few reports that would later be used for countywide recommendations for improved access to health care.

Rand Reports

As one of the three partners of the triumvirate, Rand's role in the project was two-fold: provide analysis of local policy issues of concern and provide an internal evaluation of CVM. On the first role, Rand was called upon by the MAC to develop an analysis regarding funds flow at Jackson Memorial Hospital. The end result of this work was a report titled "Hospital Care for the Uninsured in Miami-Dade County: Hospital Finance and Patient Travel Patterns," which provided analysis and recommendations for how to improve the public hospital's reporting on the level of uncompensated care it provided, and how to better collaborate with others to improve health care access for uninsured populations.[4] On the basis of this study, another report was requested of Rand, this one meant to provide specific recommendations for improved health policy structures in Miami-Dade health-governing bodies in general and governance structures of Jackson's governing board The Public Health Trust specifically.[5] The recommendations of these reports were included in the MAP and were ultimately considered in future decision-making bodies. One concrete result was the creation of the Office of Countywide Healthcare Planning (OCHP), described in more detail further on.

Community Dialogues

The third member of CVM's triumvirate, the United Way of Miami-Dade County, played an active role in bringing the community voice—to the extent possible, a direct consumer perspective—to the decision-making table. In this endeavor, United Way engaged in eighteen community dialogues across some of Miami-Dade's most "at risk" neighborhoods to glean a better understanding of the access issues facing different populations of this very diverse county. The result of this work culminated in a report titled "Community Dialogues About Health and Health Care."[6] This report, like Rand's work, became an important input to the final MAP.

Building Relationships, Creating the Possibilities for Planning and Action

The main pillar of CVM was its collaborative nature. The support received in Miami was not used to fortify existing infrastructure but to create the possibilities for dialogue, consensus-building, and viable recommendations. Thus the core of CVM's work was based in these spaces and the commitments, work, and products that would be derived from the same.

Mayor's Health Care Access Task Force

If the Oversight Team was the equivalent of CVM's board of directors, then the MAC was its engine! It is this body that produced the MAP, a highly political document that carved out a blueprint—or a "roadmap"—for improving access to health care in Miami-Dade County (Figure 4.1). Informed by the Rand and Community Dialogue reports as well as by the individual and collective expertise of Miami-Dade's health and social service leaders, the MAP was probably the most important product produced by CVM in its first phase of funding, 1998–2003. It was this work, combined with the ongoing leadership and pressure deriving from both the MAC and the Oversight Team, that ultimately prevailed on the County Mayor's Office to convene a Task Force on Health Care Access.

This fifty-two-member Task Force composed of the county's top health leadership met for one year and concluded in 2003 with a series of key recommendations derived from the MAP, one of which was the recommendation to create a separate health care planning body outside the purview of Jackson's Public Health Trust. Until this time, the hospital had been the recipient of both the half-penny sales tax and, through its board, the Public Health Trust, the sole decision maker on how these funds would be spent. However, the creation of the OCHP, resulted in the impetus for and establishment of an independent countywide agency charged with planning for how all public resources related to health might be best spent, including making recommendations for Jackson Memorial.

FIGURE 4.1. MAP GOALS.

Coverage for All	**Eliminate Insurance Barriers**	**Training, Education, and Outreach**	**Policy Planning and Sustainability**
To create and sustain coverage strategies sufficient to give all people in Miami-Dade County access to appropriate, convenient, quality health care services.	To remove barriers other than insurance coverage that prohibit people who are uninsured and underserved from accessing health care services.	To enable both traditional and nontraditional providers to link people with a full range of services while giving consumers the navigation tools to advocate.	To assure continuous quality of the health care system through policy planning and sustainability.

Under Goal 4 of the MAP, devoted to policy planning and sustainability, the first objective stated,

> Convene and empower an independent body to continuously monitor and evaluate the health care system for the uninsured and underserved in Miami-Dade County to determine if the policies and actions to increase access to health care are sufficient, effective, and efficient. The body will also be empowered to report results and recommendations to the County Commission, other funding and/or planning boards, health care providers and the community in order to implement necessary policy changes that are responsive to the community's needs.[7]

Though innocuous on the surface, it took many months of work and consensus building to have the MAC finally approve this objective and present it to the Oversight Team for final ratification. The same objective later found its way into the Mayor's Task Force final recommendations and was the basis for the creation of the Office of Countywide Healthcare Planning.

Community Access Program

Like other Community Voices sites, CVM participated in the federally funded Health Resources Services Administration (HRSA) Community Access Program (CAP). As in other instances, CVM played the role of community convener, setting the table for other providers and community-based organizations to develop a process for applying for these funds. The way in which this particular grant came to Miami was the result of a conversation.

CVM leaders knew that tensions existed between The Public Health Trust/ Jackson Health System and other community-based providers. Because CVM was not a provider, its leadership saw an important opportunity to bring together all of the county's providers in a coalition, as it were, to bring these funds to Miami. The first year of funding had already been lost because two providers in the county applied and disqualified the county as a viable site. Knowing this, CVM leaders approached the colleagues at Jackson to determine whether they would take leadership of this endeavor if CVM agreed to bring the other parties to the table. An agreement was struck, and at the end of a few months, Miami-Dade was awarded a $1 million CAP grant, with Jackson at the helm. However, what CVM had been able to negotiate was a full advisory committee composed of the other providers and community-based organization leadership. In addition, it was also agreed that the Alliance for Human Services, a government body empowered to make recommendations for the allocation of outreach dollars, would manage the outreach funds for the CAP grant, thus creating a structure in which both the decision making and financial leadership were equally shared. All decisions taken by Jackson Health System, CAP's fiscal leader, needed to be consulted with the grant's local advisory group.

Ultimately, a few million dollars later, CAP was funded in Miami for six years. In the first four years, the program succeeded in bringing additional support from local funders—including The Health Foundation of South Florida and the Jackson Foundation—and in strengthening coordination and integration of services within the community; enabling eligible patients to receive public services; linking more than ten thousand people to medical homes in their communities; avoiding costs of more than $1.4 million through disease management, decreasing emergency room visits, and hospitalizations while enrolling people into health insurance; and improving the health of five hundred chronically ill through disease management. In the final two years of the program, CVM participated directly, with an agreement to train community health workers (CHWs) and patient navigators for CAP, something that was useful not only in terms of capacity building but also in what was learned from CHWs and navigators in the field and what they were able to bring back and share about gaps in health services delivery with the advisory group.[8]

As in any effort involving a multi-stakeholder process, there were highs and lows; agreements and disagreements. From CVM's perspective, however, an important accomplishment for collaboration and relationship-building is that it changed the way in which providers and community-based organizations worked together. The CAP model in Miami created a transparent and democratic space in which neither the public hospital, nor the other hospitals and providers, nor the community-based organizations took decisions unilaterally. Instead, they met once or twice a month to check in and determine a course of action for health practices that ultimately had an impact on thousands of Miami-Dade residents.[9]

The Miami Coalition for School-Based Health

Sometimes it is the efforts thought least likely to succeed that really bear fruit. One example of this was CVM's work in convening the Miami Coalition for School-Based Health (MCSBH). School-based health had figured as one of the key recommendations made for Miami-Dade in the MAP. A group of providers and advocates who had years of experience working on the issue—among them, the John T. MacDonald Foundation, the Department of Health, and Dade County Public Schools—approached CVM to join forces.

As a result, CVM agreed to staff a process to help support the implementation of full-service schools. For approximately a year, CVM convened this group, which was ultimately successful in developing a much-needed inventory regarding what was available in the county with regard to school-based health. Not even two years later in 2003, the recently established Children's Trust, a private-public entity devoted to the health and well-being of all children in Miami-Dade County, prepared to develop its initial target areas by way of a process that was community-informed. One of the areas under their consideration was school-based health, and CVM was called upon to share the inventory of the services available in Dade County schools that it had helped develop in partnership with the MCSBH.

While it may have appeared that proceeding toward a path of school-based health would be an easy win, whether The Trust should invest initially in this area was not at all clear when work began.

Many community leaders testified on the value of The Trust developing a school health program. Among those leaders was CVM, prepared with the added benefit of having valuable information to impart on the level of readiness of each school in Miami-Dade's more-than-three-hundred-strong public schools system. CVM's report became immediately relevant.

Today, The Trust maintains programming in school health through its Health Connect program, which includes a portion dedicated to providing a team of nurses or nurse practitioners, social workers, and health aides to public schools for health and mental health services. While certainly CVM cannot be credited with the creation of this program, the commitment to spaces, relationships, and the development and dissemination of ideas ultimately served a purpose in helping to foster a critical access strategy.

Using Data to Inform Policy and Program Implementation

Beginning in 2003, project leaders across the country began to work more narrowly along distinct policy targets: men's health, case management, oral health, mental health and community health workers. CVM developed work related to all of these targets to some capacity and continued to use its methodology of convening, space creation, and collaboration to promote these. However, CVM also took a great interest in mining data to support strong practices and progressive policies. There were a few areas in which this approach was particularly successful: CHWs, men's health, and oral health.

Community Health Workers

Sometimes good ideas develop in the most unexpected ways. CVM's CHW work was one of those. Through Kellogg-sponsored international travel to Latin America in 2000 and 2001, CVM leaders had the opportunity to witness the CHW model in action in different parts of the region. One experience that especially caught the attention of one CVM leader was the work developed in Trujillo, Peru. On the basis of the notion that the entire family must be the center of concern for the CHW, the UNI-Trujillo model[10] demonstrated to CV leaders how the UNI-Trujillo CHWs kept files on entire families in order to better serve them. Given Miami's own diverse Latino population, many of which are concentrated in low-income and at-risk neighborhoods, CVM leaders saw direct applicability of this model in Miami's East Little Havana neighborhood (a misnomer in the past two decades since it has become more of a combination of Little Managua, San Salvador, and Tegucigalpa).

With the collaboration of a local community-based organization, Abriendo Puertas (Opening Doors), devoted to the service of immigrants in this neighborhood, CVM leaders launched a pilot to replicate the Trujillo-based model in Miami. The result of this was a trained cadre of CHWs based at this organization, better skilled in treating the whole family, connecting them to services, and relaying their issues to providers and policymakers. Moreover, the model spread to other parts of the county with high immigrant populations such as Sweetwater, composed also of a mix of Central American immigrants, mostly Nicaraguan. There they organized as the Grupo Bajo del Arbol (Under the Tree Group), composed of mostly mothers of children from one of the local public schools who typically waited for their children under a tree. It was in this context in which a local clinic leader who had been influenced by the work in East Little Havana began to organize this group of women to help connect other families to care using the principles of the UNI-Trujillo and to employ the same strategy to advocate for themselves and their families.

With the success of this pilot and its heightened visibility, so also grew the enthusiasm and vision for its application in different parts of the county. Soon project leaders were discussing with local funders and health providers how to best develop this as a best practice model for improving access to care in Miami. In 2002, CVM, in partnership with the United Way of Miami-Dade, commissioned a study that looked at the "state of the art" regarding CHWs in the county, while comparing the roles and efforts of CHWs throughout the nation. That study was the catalyst to convene a working group of providers, CHWs, funders, and other local leaders to consider how to advance a CHW program in Miami-Dade.

As discussions ensued, a core group of CHWs were organized to help lead thinking on what was needed. Formalized as the Curriculum Working Group, these CHWs met to define the work to be accomplished. What emerged from these discussions was an agreement to develop a standardized, basic training for CHWs. The power of this work came from the CHWs who led the way, and who provided the substance of what was required to make the lessons in the training real and relevant. The CHW Curriculum, with the support of CVM leaders, was their brainchild.

It was envisioned that the creation of the CHW Curriculum would accomplish three goals. First, it would provide needed training to paraprofessionals who were already doing the work in some voluntary capacity but perhaps lacked specific information or skills that would enable them to better inform clients and ultimately connect them to care. Second, it would offer a path to professionalization. This meant that the work would be raised to another level, with the expectation that CHWs might expect better recognition and compensation for their services. Finally, by helping to professionalize this work, CVM sought also to integrate the Miami-based efforts with the other national work already happening, helping to create momentum for supporting CHWs as part of the integrated system of health care delivery and as key members of this system who make a critical difference in helping people access health and social services (CHWs were recognized as part of the formal workforce in the U.S. Department of Labor in 2009).

CVM organized an initial funders' collaborative (including The Health Foundation of South Florida, The Women's Fund of Miami-Dade, the Annie E. Casey Foundation, the Alleghany Franciscan Ministries Foundation, the P.L. Dodge Foundation, and the Dade Community Foundation) to support the work of building the Curriculum (other partners who supported the work at later stages included The Children's Trust, the Community Access Program, and the Little Havana Community Partnership). This organization made possible the development of a basic, level I training manual for CHWs with a minimum prior educational requirement of a GED. A partnership was established with Miami-Dade College to offer the classes for a certificate of completion.

Conducting them first as a pilot, CVM tested the Curriculum with three different classes that took stock of Miami's diverse ethnic and linguistic composition: one offered in English; one in Spanish; and the final class, taught by a Haitian, Creole-speaking instructor, primarily in English but with references in Haitian Creole. With the successful completion of the three pilots, CVM hosted a graduation ceremony for the first class of CHWs. For many, it was the first formal educational recognition they had ever received in their lives!

With the success of the pilot classes and the recognition ascribed to CVM as a trainer of CHWs, other funding was made possible by The Children's Trust. Seeing the value in this model, The Trust pledged funding for CVM for three years to further develop the Curriculum and train their contracted CHWs throughout the county. With this support, CVM was able to develop the beginning of a level II training, adapted from Cornell University's Family Development Training and Credential (FDC) program.[11]

While the original vision for the CHW training was that it would develop into a three-level curriculum culminating in an Associate of Science degree in human services with a certification in community health work, at this writing, this has yet to happen. With the economic downturn of 2008, resources at The Trust declined, as with many other funders, and the decision was made to discontinue funding.

"Francoise" was facilitating an educational workshop on Florida KidCare at the North Miami-Dade Health Clinic. A young Haitian woman, who looked very concerned, approached her together with her two small children. She asked "Francoise" if she might help her. When "Francoise" asked the lady what was wrong, she explained that one of her children was sick and was in need of health insurance. She further explained that she had tried to apply for KidCare but had problems filling out the forms. "Francoise," who is also Haitian, told her that she had a computer with her and if she had the time, she could help fill out the forms right then and there. The lady happily agreed and proceeded to fill out the forms with "Francoise's" help. Within a month, the lady learned that her children were eligible for KidCare and soon thereafter, she called "Francoise" to let her know the news and thank her for her help. She informed "Francoise" that her children were healthy and seeing a pediatrician through the North Dade Clinic.

—www.collinscenter, Health Initiatives, Community Voices Miami

However, in the four years in which the Curriculum was developed, nearly two hundred CHWs were trained in the basic level I and numerous others were trained in the first module of level II, allowing these CHWs to receive their certification in FDC. Today, The Children's Trust and other health and social services agencies throughout Miami-Dade continue to employ CHWs, many of whom were directly trained through CVM's standardized training. Moreover many of these CHWs have coalesced to share their experiences in the field and continue to grow together. A few have become active participants in the ongoing efforts to develop a national association of CHWs.

Men's Health

With the move to the Collins Center for Public Policy in 2003, CVM gained access to other programs and colleagues with whom to partner. Indeed, one of the driving decisions to move CVM to Collins was that it would provide an environment that focused more narrowly on policy development. The previous five years of work had been focused on building the relationships that would create an environment propitious for improved practice and policies. Beyond making the space for these, some programmatic and policy changes were also achieved. However, at this stage of the work, what became most important was the space through which to lift both the practices on the ground and the voices of community directly into the discussion around several key policy areas. One of these areas was men's health.

With the other work happening across the country—Baltimore's critical role in developing and maintaining the nation's first full-time Men's Health Center; the Men's Health Report Card in North Carolina; Denver's work in having CHWs connect men to care; and the other activities happening elsewhere, CVM chose to support the work by bringing new data to bear.

At the Collins Center, CVM sought out an intra-organizational collaboration with the Growth Partnership and the Overtown Civic and Design Center. The end product was a critical report, the "Overtown Men's Health Study," which highlighted the dire health issues for men living in Overtown, one of the most impoverished communities of the United States.[12] The seminal study revealed that of 129 men, approximately two-thirds of them had had experiences with the criminal justice system. The report succeeded in highlighting a highly distressed community that bears many similar characteristics to other low-income and blighted communities of the United States (Exhibit 4.1).

The publication of this work raised several questions, the first being, "Why?" What is the common denominator of these distressed communities? Why is the health status of the men in these communities so poor? Why are so many men in prison? Why is it that the only place where some men are able to receive health services is in the correctional system? And, what are the repercussions of the dearth of services for men on their families and communities?

The report had ripple effects that no one foresaw. First, it served to galvanize a core group of men in Overtown to coalesce and consider their situation and options for advocacy. One important outcome was the extraordinary opportunity for one young Overtown man to testify before the Federal Medicaid Commission in Washington, D.C., in 2007 regarding the lack of services and overall dire situation for men, particularly those who, despite working one or two jobs, still fall into a low-income bracket and many of whom are fathers and have small children who depend on them. Later, two national conferences, "Saving Men's Lives I and II," were organized in Atlanta and Washington, D.C., respectively, to bring into one room many of the very men affected by the lack of health and social services and generations of poor policies that have done nothing to uplift them but have instead served only to punish. These conferences succeeded in convening the leadership of important national organizations and stakeholders, including the Congressional Black Caucus Health Brain Trust, the U.S. Department of Health and Human Services, Men's Health Network, National Council of La Raza, the national Urban League, Congress, the International Society of Men's Health, state and national departments of corrections, and university faculty. They came together to hear and discuss the personal stories, and to commit the political leadership to action. A continuation of this work has been driven through the National Center for Primary Care's Community Voices Freedom's Voice annual meeting, now having celebrated its second conference, which is developing into a formidable movement around the issues of men's health and community well-being.

EXHIBIT 4.1. OVERTOWN MEN'S HEALTH STUDY FACT SHEET.

Who are they? Demographic profile of men in sample (N = 129)
❑ 95% African American
❑ 55% have high school diploma
❑ 9% have college degrees
❑ 40% are employed
❑ 53% earn less than $10K per year

What are their experiences?

"Housing Arrangements"
❑ 28% have lived on the streets
❑ 1 in 4 has lived in a shelter
❑ Two-thirds have been in jail or prison

Physiological Health
❑ 1 in 5 received dental care in the previous year
❑ 60% live with bodily pain
❑ For 29%, the hospital ER is the primary health care facility
❑ 47% smoke cigarettes

Mental Health
❑ More than 1 in 4 is a victim of police violence
❑ 60% report restlessness
❑ 29% feel worthless
❑ 60% feel "everything is an effort"
❑ 55% feel disabled to some degree by their mental health state

What is to be done?
❑ Pre-release transition support and ex-offender community re-entry services
❑ Integrated case management, community health workers, "navigators"
❑ Supported housing
❑ Supported employment
❑ Integrated physiological, mental, and oral health services

Source: Adapted from A.M.W. Young, *Overtown Men's Health Study Fact Sheet* (Miami: The Collins Center for Public Policy, 2006). Retrieved July 23, 2010, from http://www.collinscenter.org/ resource/resmgr/Health_Care_Docs/Overtown_Summary_Stats.pdf.

Beyond the activist work, several other peer-reviewed articles came from the early men's health work and the "Men's Health Study." For example, a journal article produced as a result of this study was recognized as one of the top-ten most-read articles in a two-year period by the *International Journal of Men's Health*, indicating the significance of and rising global interest in men's health as a public and primary health and prevention issue. This in turn has paved the way for international linkages with the International Society of Men's Health and the World Congress on Men's Health, the latter just having celebrated its sixth biannual meeting and at which there is now a recognized agenda item on the social and economic determinants of men's health and a veritable movement toward ensuring that global attention is paid to men's health as an indicator for community health and well-being.[13]

Finally, the findings of the "Men's Health Study" have also been an important platform from which the Collins Center has developed specific work on Justice Reform, including alternative policy options around making reentry efforts more successful, reducing recidivism, and developing a model for restorative justice.[14]

Oral Health

CVM's work in oral health concentrated in three areas: (1) strategic planning, (2) research and analysis, and (3) advocacy and coalition-building. Though one of the policy targets of concern in the CV initiative was oral health, it was also an objective laid out in CVM's own community-developed MAP. As such, CVM's leadership was sought out locally to move forward a process on the issues.

Strategic Planning. Beyond the support that Kellogg provided throughout the years, CVM was successful in leveraging local funding from a number of agencies and foundations. On oral health issues, CVM found an enthusiastic partner in the Health Foundation of South Florida, which in 2004 provided support to CVM to convene providers and community stakeholders to develop a community-driven plan for increasing access to health care.

This process resulted in a "living document," *The Strategic Plan for Improving Oral Health for the Uninsured and Underserved in Miami-Dade County*, which was adapted from the statewide oral health strategic planning in which CVM participated, thus making this document a tool used beyond the county to build consensus for policy and programs to improve access to care. Part of the planning also included a study of dental providers in Miami-Dade as well as a national review of best practices to improve oral health access (Exhibit 4.2). These now constitute a report titled *Oral Healthcare Access for the Underserved and Uninsured in Miami-Dade County*.[15]

Research and Analysis. In the 2004 Florida legislative session, the legislature approved a managed care pilot for oral health services in Miami for two years under the provision of Medicaid. Evaluation reporting on the pilot from the Agency for Health Care Administration (AHCA), conducted through the University of Florida, was not available until the end of 2006, and the stated purpose of that evaluation was "to design and implement an evaluation model to examine providers' and families' satisfaction with the Medicaid prepaid dental health program in Miami-Dade County." The evaluation was funded at $65,530, while the annual program costs exceeded $12 million.

EXHIBIT 4.2. PROMISING PRACTICES IN ORAL HEALTH.

- Targeting primary preventive care to very young children and their families in order to limit overall disease burden
- Paying dental providers at "market rates" by contracting with commercial dental plans or managed care vendors
- Expanding engagement of the dental community through outreach and expanded case management
- Stimulating expansion of preventive efforts by primary medical providers
- With recent changes in federal law and regulations, the time is ripe for further experimentation that will lead to improved health of Florida's children at less cost to the state

Concerned about the comparatively small amount of funding ascribed to such a well-funded program, CVM sought out collaboration with researchers at Columbia University's School of Dental and Oral Surgery to conduct an independent analysis of the Medicaid Pre-paid Oral Health Pilot in Miami-Dade. By comparing utilization data from before the pilot's inception to data during the pilot, the analysis *Miami-Dade County Prepaid Dental Health Plan Demonstration: Less Value for State Dollars*,[16] found that Florida paid nearly the same for the pilot but utilization of services decreased so that overall value of state dollars decreased. Nearly all measures of quality declined, so Florida lost value by paying the same amount for less care and less quality. Fewer dentists were available to treat children, and fewer children had prevention checkups.

Advocacy and Coalition-Building. Using these findings, CVM joined with other local and state advocates to educate policymakers about the full impact of this pilot program. A policy brief, *Understanding the Impacts of Florida's Medicaid Pre-Paid Dental Pilot*[17] was produced, which provided background and outlined the findings from the analysis along with possible alternatives for Medicaid programs to increase access to care. With broader Medicaid reform having begun in July 2006 in Duval and Broward counties, CVM, along with other providers and advocates, was concerned about informing policymakers about the importance of a full, independent analysis of utilization and provider participation data.

An important result of CVM's work was that the Miami-Dade Department of Health's Consortium for a Healthier Miami-Dade added an Oral Health Committee as a result of CVM's independent analysis of the oral health pilot in Miami-Dade. CVM leadership participated regularly for the first two years as co-chair. Beyond the Health Department, in late 2006, Florida Community Health Action Information Network (CHAIN), a well-known health advocacy coalition, coordinated a dental work group to focus specifically on educating legislators. Much of this group's work was about helping to inform the Broward and Duval county Medicaid Reform pilots as a result of what was learned in Dade County with the oral health pilot.

An interesting campaign led by CHAIN released an action alert asking people to immediately and automatically send letters to key Florida officials, explaining that (1) the number of dental providers willing to treat Medicaid children in Miami-Dade had dramatically decreased, meaning that children have less access to dental care; (2) there must be incentives for dentists to treat these children and accurately report the care provided; (3) the state must slow down with renewing this contract and consider better ways to treat children and evaluate the outcomes; (4) AHCA and Atlantic Dental (the only HMO providing care in Miami-Dade) should develop specific solutions for increasing access to dental care and discuss them in a public forum; and (5) if the state wants Medicaid reform to be a success in Florida, policymakers must consider all evaluations—even critical ones—and respond accordingly before making any expansions.

Florida CHAIN would later report to the work group that "Due to the influx of calls and emails that have been sent as a result of our CHAIN Reaction Alert of the excellent Collins Center study as well as the media attention that has been brought, legislators have been prompted to call for more frequent and stringent reporting from AHCA. Florida Senator Rich has asked that advocates help her by getting the Miami Dade Delegation more involved."

Despite the best efforts of community leaders to have the state reevaluate the pilot, AHCA/Medicaid renewed the oral health pilot in Miami-Dade nonetheless. However, even though they also considered expanding the oral health pilot to other counties beyond Miami-Dade, in the end AHCA/Medicaid desisted. It may be possible that these plans were halted as a result of both the data provided by the University of Florida evaluation and CVM's own independent commissioned study, which suggested that there was insufficient information to determine whether the program had been successful enough to expand. As of this writing, advocates and health providers alike continue to bring attention to what appears to be insufficient analysis of the data.

In the past few years, statewide interest has continued to grow on oral health, including the continued independent leadership of the Florida Department of Health's Oral Health Consortium. Moreover, the Health Foundation of South Florida has maintained its commitment to the issue, pledging $7 million to these efforts beginning in 2008.

Lessons Learned

A ten-year initiative could only bring a wealth of euphoric epiphanies as well as bittersweet moments in which leaders wished they had not proceeded down a particular path. This dialectic, it would seem, is the formula of which learning is composed, and certainly CVM's experience was no less. Following are some of the lessons which most stand out:

- *Multi-stakeholder processes are effective tools for building consensus and advancing recommendations.* CVM's leadership of a truly multi-stakeholder process may have been unprecedented in Miami-Dade County. While other similar processes had been launched in the past, CVM's was unique because of the length of time in which it was successfully sustained as well as because of the consistent participation and commitment of leaders from different sectors.
- *Continuous steward-like guidance, facilitation, or both is essential.* Opening the "space" alone is insufficient. A key component toward success in Miami is that CVM was able to be the convener of the space as well as the "dedicated staff" to the community. However, the community led the way, and CVM facilitated its decisions.
- *Neutrality can help move the process.* The neutrality of the convener or facilitator may help in moving the process, as others will know that this entity has nothing to gain and can help be an arbiter for discussions among group members.
- *Group composition is of critical importance!* It is essential that the people at the table be able to perform different functions, such as making and implementing direct decisions, informing the process, and providing a reality check for the depth and breadth of community needs.
- *The process should also be multisectoral.* In addition to being multi-stakeholder, the process should also be multi*sectoral*. That is, it includes representation from every relevant layer of the community all the way from the mayor to the final consumer.
- *Institutionalize the work!* CVM, through its multisectoral process, was able to institutionalize the work by ensuring that other key stakeholders and sectors adopt the practices and policies. For example, the continued employment of CHWs by The Children's Trust—in some cases having CHW wages increased by local providers—as well as The Trust's development of a school health component; the Justice Initiative at Collins, which looks carefully at, among other things, men's health; and local funders' continued commitment to oral health might never have been possible had it not been for the work which began as early as in the MAC and evolved through the years.
- *Policy changes come with compromises.* For CVM, an important lesson was in learning when to compromise and when not to. While the creation of the Office of Countywide Health Care Planning (OCHP) was an important achievement in obtaining public recognition for the value of good governance, CVM might have done better in not rushing its creation. In order for the enabling legislation to pass, leaders agreed that OCHP would fall under the direction of the Board of County Commissioners (BCC). On one hand, it was true that this body might not have been approved had the legislation not delineated that it would report to the BCC. On the other, it might have been worth delaying the creation of the Office to ensure better clarity as to how the OCHP would interact with the BCC.

Conclusions

CVM leaders often felt the deep sensation of, "so much to do, so little time!" Despite the ten-year initiative and the accomplishment of so very much, an important lesson—and call to action—is that so much more remains to be done. In some ways, the success of the work has paved the way for more that must happen.

At this writing, even though CHWs have made initial headway into the systems of care as seen through the U.S. Department of Labor's recognition of them as part of the workforce, there is still considerable progress and integration that must be achieved to truly reap the full benefits of the efforts made by CHWs.

With so much revealing data about the health status of men, more must be done to promote this as an area for future state and national inquiry. In Florida, some recognition has begun through the establishment of the Council on the Social Status of Black Men and Boys, with which the Collins Center has collaborated. Along these lines, there is also the space to implement recommendations from the "Men's Health Study" around resources required for men in communities as well as advocating for the expansion of Medicaid to include poor men. At a minimum, the state of Florida has recently passed legislation that, it appears, will no longer terminate Medicaid benefits for incarcerated populations but merely suspend these. While at this writing this policy has yet to be formally put in practice, if the state of Florida succeeds in this it will ensure that many people leaving jail or prison—among these a large number of low-income men of color who suffer from chronic illness (such as diabetes, hypertension, and some infectious diseases; treatable mental illness; or substance abuse treatment issues) will have immediate access to Medicaid benefits upon release. The evidence is clear that health insurance coverage is a protective factor against recidivism.[18]

Florida will continue to need to pay careful attention to health care reform efforts, whether they are those currently being spearheaded by the Obama administration or those continuing into the future. In the meantime, as Medicaid reform continues in the State, policymakers will need to be open and transparent about what has functioned and what has not, and be ready for possible policy alternatives that might make a difference in health coverage and quality of life for many.

Finally, while CVM did not directly develop programming on mental health care access and policy, very good work in Florida was—and is—led through Judge Steven Leifman of the Eleventh Judicial Criminal Circuit Court, which has successfully promoted jail diversion as a best practice for providing care for mentally ill people as an alternative to incarceration. In like fashion, through its promotion of Crisis Intervention Training (CIT), a nationally recognized model, it has succeeded in diverting thousands from the county jail. Still, far too many people sit in the mental health ward of Miami-Dade's county jail, otherwise known to veterans as "the ninth floor." While excellent work in the county and state continues to push for changes that would effectively provide community-based treatment on demand, there remains road to travel. Through the Collins Center's current continued work in justice and health, the spotlight will remain on these issues in Florida and in the nation for some time to come.

Notes

1. *Space* here is used metaphorically. It is meant to signify not a physical location, but a point in time.
2. In 2009, Dr. Greer was honored with the Presidential Medal of Freedom.
3. Collins Center for Public Policy, *Community Voices Miami: Miami Action Plan (MAP)*, 2009. Retrieved July 23, 2010, from http://www.collinscenter.org/?page=CVMMiamiActionPlan.
4. *Hospital Care for the Uninsured in Miami-Dade County: Hospital Finance and Patient Travel Patterns*, "Summary," 2009. Retrieved July 23, 2010, from http://www.collinscenter.org/resource/resmgr/Health_Care_Docs/TravelPatternsSummary.pdf.
5. C. A. Jackson, K. P. Derose, and A. Beatty, "Governance for Whom and for What: Principles to Guide Health Policy in Miami-Dade County," *Rand Health* (Santa Monica, CA: Rand, 2003). Retrieved July 23, 2010, from http://www.collinscenter.org/resource/resmgr/Health_Care_Docs/RAND_GOVERNANCE_REPORT.pdf.
6. Community Voices Miami, *Community Dialogues About Health and Health Care*, 2002. Retrieved July 23, 2010, from http://www.collinscenter.org/resource/resmgr/Health_Care_Docs/Community_Dialogues_Part1.pdf.
7. Community Voices Miami, *The Miami Action Plan (MAP): For Access to Health Care*, 2009. Retrieved July 23, 2010, from http://www.collinscenter.org/resource/resmgr/Health_Care_Docs/Miami_Action_Plan.pdf.
8. Community Voices Miami, *Community Access Program of Miami-Dade County Highlights: A Collaborative Approach to Get People to Healthcare*, 2005. Retrieved July 23, 2010, from http://www.collinscenter.org/resource/resmgr/Health_Care_Docs/CAP_FACT6-13-2005.pdf.
9. K. P. Derose, A. Beatty, and C. A. Jackson, "Evaluation of Community Voices Miami: Affecting Health Policy for the Uninsured," *Rand Health* (Santa Monica, CA: Rand, 2004). Retrieved July 23, 2010, from http://www.rand.org/pubs/technical_reports/2004/RAND_TR177.sum.pdf.
10. M. Northridge, M. J. Ro, and H. M. Treadwell, *Community Health Workers and Community Voices: Promoting Good Health*. Retrieved July 23, 2010, from http://www.communityvoices.org/Uploads/CHW_FINAL_00108_00042.pdf .
11. The Center for Transformative Action, *Family Development Credential*, 2009. Retrieved July 23, 2010, from http://www.human.cornell.edu/HD/FDC.
12. A.M.W. Young, *Overtown Men's Health Study* (Miami: The Collins Center for Public Policy, May 2006). Retrieved July 23, 2010, from http://www.collinscenter.org/resource/resmgr/Health_Care_Docs/OvertownMensHealthPages.pdf.
13. Collins Center for Public Policy. (2009). *International Men's Health*. Retrieved July 23, 2010, from http://www.collinscenter.org/?page=HCIntlMens.
14. Collins Center for Public Policy, *Justice Reform*, 2009. Retrieved July 23, 2010, from http://www.collinscenter.org/?page=JusticeReformHome.

15. A. I. Balsa and P. Mercader, *Oral Healthcare Access for the Underserved and Uninsured in Miami-Dade County*, February 2005. Retrieved July 23, 2010, from http://www.collinscenter.org/resource/resmgr/Health_Care_Docs/Oral_Healthcare_Access_March.pdf.

16. B. L. Edelstein, *Miami-Dade County Prepaid Dental Health Plan Demonstration: Less Value for State Dollars*, August 2006. Retrieved July 23, 2010, from http://www.collinscenter.org/resource/resmgr/Health_Care_Docs/MDCoPrepdDentalAnalysis8-06.pdf.

17. Community Voices Miami, *Understanding the Impacts of Florida's Medicaid Pre-Paid Dental Pilot*, August 2006. Retrieved July 23, 2010, from http://www.collinscenter.org/resource/resmgr/Health_Care_Docs/Oral_Health_PilotPolicyBrief.pdf.

18. N. Freudenberg, J. Daniels, M. Crum, T. Perkins, and B. Richie, "Coming Home from Jail: The Social and Health Consequences of Community Reentry for Women, Male Adolescents, and Their Families and Communities," *American Journal of Public Health* 95, no. 10, 1725–1736, Retrieved July 23, 2010, from http://www.ncbi.nlm.nih.gov/pmc/articles/PMC1449427; J. Lee, D. Vlahov, and N. Freudenberg, "Primary Care and Health Insurance Among Women Released from New York City Jails," *Journal of Health Care for the Poor and Underserved* 17, no. 1, 200–217, Retrieved July 23, 2010, from http://muse.jhu.edu/login?uri=/journals/journal_of_health_care_for_the_poor_and_underserved/v017/17.1lee.html.

CHAPTER FIVE

COMMUNITY VOICES NEW MEXICO

Integrating Practice with Policy for Health and Well-Being

Wayne Powell and Daniel Derksen

This chapter focuses on Community Voices New Mexico, which promoted improved health care access and population well-being through an approach that integrated the development of strong practices with informing and *improving* public policy. After reading this chapter, the reader will

- Learn about the specific pathways for change created by Community Voices New Mexico in a complex social, economic, and political context
- Learn about the strategies that Community Voices New Mexico employed in working to improve access to health care and social services while informing public policy
- Learn about innovative models for creating pathways to health care and social services
- Learn how collaborative efforts across different sectors can help leverage key relationships and resources for continuing and future efforts in both practice and policy
- Learn about best practices for improving health care access and care management
- Learn about a combined case management and Community Health Workers model

Introduction

A focus on policy and its power in creating improvements in population health has been a most enduring contribution made by Community Voices New Mexico (CVNM). Through placement of a good amount of energy on policy reform, a number of long-term benefits have been derived. CVNM's partnering with forums that would contribute to the development of strategies that had programmatic, community, and political viability created the opportunities to sustain gains and programs beyond the Kellogg grant. By fostering ownership by policy stakeholders, CVNM ensured that the focus on their carved-out areas of concern would remain at the decision-making tables until the present.

CVNM was unique within New Mexico. Other programs in the state focused more narrowly on specific communities or areas of interest. With the broad parameters set forth by the Kellogg-funded initiative, CVNM eventually encompassed most of the areas of focus of other partners. It became a leader in areas such as oral health; supported efforts to institutionalize the roles of community health workers (CHWs) as integral members of the systems of care; promoted funding systems change and interventions; and created forums for in-depth policy formation. In the end, as a result of the partnerships formed by CVNM, the environments of access and coverage, health professional education, relationships among service providers, and sustainable resourcing for programs and services were positively altered.

Concretely, as CVNM considered the changing health care environment in New Mexico, there emerged several opportunities to inform policy:

- Integrating CVNM with other initiatives that shared similar objectives in order to further develop programs and services for the underserved
- Identifying and incorporating sustainable financing to support new service delivery models
- Informing policy on social determinants and reduction of health disparities

CVNM's focus on collaboration, financing, and policy development would become the cornerstones of its work and ultimate contributors to success in New Mexico.

Origins and Factors That Called for Change

New Mexico is the fifth largest state in size, with two-thirds of its population living in rural areas. It is culturally rich, including the second highest percentage of ethnic minorities (38 percent Hispanic, 8 percent Native American, and 2 percent African

American) in the country. New Mexico also leads the country in several disturbing health statistics.

In 1998, New Mexico was first in the percentage of its population that was uninsured (25.6 percent or 438,000 individuals) and first in poverty. It was among the top three states in rates of motor vehicle accidents as a cause of death (25.5 percent—more than half of this due to alcohol abuse), of births to teenage mothers (18.4 percent), of births to unmarried women (42.6 percent), and of low utilization of early prenatal care.

Despite its rural majority, two-thirds of its physicians practiced in urban areas. As a result, thirty of its thirty-three counties were designated as Health Professional Shortage Areas (HPSAs) or Medically Underserved Areas (MUAs) by federal standards. There was a moderate to critically severe shortage of primary care providers in all counties, limiting access for nearly one-third of all New Mexicans, but especially for the uninsured. Public health concerns also included high rates of domestic violence, substance abuse (including tobacco), suicide, homicide, and poor school outcomes. Tables 5.1 and 5.2 capture data on the eight targeted counties of the Community Voices (CV) Initiative. Table 5.1 reflects the age-adjusted mortality rate by cause of death as averaged over the three-year period 1993–1995. Table 5.2 reflects projected medically indigent profiles for the same eight counties, based on 1996 Census estimates. It lists the population, rankings, percentages below poverty, and percentage of population residing in HPSA-designated areas of New Mexico counties targeted for five-year phase-in of the CV project.

Unmet needs among uninsured populations included access to preventive primary care, oral health, and behavioral health. An example of this, historically, had been the under-enrollment of eligible children in Medicaid. In 1997–1998 there were over ninety thousand children eligible for Medicaid statewide who were not enrolled under the state's threshold of 185 percent of the federal poverty standard. In Bernalillo County (the largest and most urban, in which Albuquerque and the University of New Mexico are located) and Rio Arriba County (one of the poorest and most rural) it was anticipated that more than twenty-four thousand children were eligible in fiscal year 1999 as a result of the State Comprehensive Health Insurance Initiative for expanded Medicaid coverage up to 235 percent of poverty. For those children who were already enrolled in Medicaid, Early Periodic Screening Diagnostic and Treatment (EPSDT) compliance levels were dismal. Immunization levels for all children were only at 70 percent.

Uninsured women of child-bearing age were also underserved. Early prenatal care and family planning services were not widely accessed. Preventive and intervention services such as cancer screening, outreach diabetic screenings, and dental care were increasing, but not meeting projected need on the basis of population. Table 5.3, adapted from the Urban Institute, reflects New Mexico insurance coverage relative to U.S. rates for years 1994–1995.

TABLE 5.1. AGE-ADJUSTED MORTALITY RATE BY CAUSE OF DEATH (1993–1995 AVERAGE), RATE/100,000.

Gender County	Heart Disease		Malignant Neoplasms		Accidents		Diabetes Mellitus		Alcoholism		Homicides		All Causes	
	M	F	M	F	M	F	M	F	M	F	M	F	M	F
Bernalillo*	213.0	210.2	193.4	177.0	66.9	28.2	22.4	27.3	6.6	2.0	20.1	5.1	886.8	828.1
Chaves	228.0	250.1	207.3	177.2	63.1	32.1	19.6	34.7	4.6	4.4	23.2	10.6	875.9	888.9
Doña Ana	209.2	220.4	185.0	145.4	56.1	26.3	37.3	45.0	2.8	—	11.9	2.1	769.2	735.1
Otero	301.7	334.7	206.9	188.7	62.8	22.5	16.1	35.6	8.2	4.1	8.3	1.3	975.8	979.2
Rio Arriba*	175.8	167.8	136.9	123.7	149.6	48.1	48.0	55.1	19.9	7.6	40.6	16.6	995.4	718.9
Sandoval	210.3	160.9	187.4	148.4	68.4	31.6	23.0	33.4	6.5	1.9	14.8	2.1	843.4	741.4
Santa Fe	171.6	218.1	159.5	165.9	73.7	26.5	22.5	37.7	7.2	2.7	11.3	4.0	757.6	790.6
Torrance	211.4	239.4	230.6	184.7	99.0	22.4	22.0	11.8	—	5.2	10.8	5.3	824.6	828.0
New Mexico	217.3	222.5	187.6	163.6	75.3	29.3	24.8	33.5	6.4	2.3	16.7	4.7	859.7	802.6

Note: * Year 1 and 2 Community Voices Counties.

TABLE 5.2. PROJECTED MEDICALLY INDIGENT PROFILES, COMMUNITY VOICES PARTICIPANT COUNTY ESTIMATES (EIGHT TARGETED COUNTIES >60 PERCENT OF THE NM UNDERSERVED).

	Estimated 1996 Census	# Population Below 200% Poverty Level	% Population Below 200% Poverty Level	County Rank by Indigent Population	# County Population in HPSA	% County Population in HPSA
Bernalillo*	525,104	123,871	23%	1	57,761	11%
Chaves	62,532	18,317	29%	8	6,690	10.7%
Doña Ana	164,029	54,110	33%	2	45,108	27.5%
Otero	55,810	20,445	37%	7	5,134	9.2%
Rio Arriba*	37,612	15,989	42%	9	20,348	54.1%
Sandoval	83,185	33,179	40%	4	33,523	40.3%
Santa Fe	118,952	36,032	30%	3	27,597	23.2%
Torrance	13,715	4,818	35%	21	13,415	100%
Total	1,060,939 (62%)	306,561 (62%)			209,876 (20%)	
State	1,711,256 (100%)	494,160 (100%)			521,933	30.5%

Note: * Year 1 and 2 Community Voices Counties.

TABLE 5.3. NEW MEXICO INSURANCE COVERAGE RELATIVE
TO U.S. RATES (1994–1995).

	New Mexico	United States
Non-Elderly Population		
Percent uninsured[a]	25.6%	15.5%
Percent Medicaid[a]	16.0%	12.2%
Percent employer-sponsored[a]	49.9%	66.1%
Percent other health insurance[a,b]	8.5%	6.2%
19–64 Population		
Percent uninsured[a]	28.4%	17.9%
Percent Medicaid[a]	7.0%	7.1%
Percent employer-sponsored[a]	53.8%	67.8%
Percent other health insurance[a,b]	10.8%	7.2%
0–18 Population		
Percent uninsured[a]	20.9%	10.4%
Percent Medicaid[a]	31.1%	23.1%
Percent employer-sponsored[a]	43.4%	62.5%
Percent other health insurance[a,b]	4.6%	4.0%
<200 Percent of the Federal Poverty Level, Non-Elderly Population		
Percent uninsured[a]	37.4%	25.3%
Percent Medicaid[a]	31.7%	34.1%
Percent employer-sponsored[a]	21.9%	33.9%
Percent other health insurance[a,b]	9.0%	6.7%

Notes: [a]Two-year concatenated March CPS files, 1995 and 1996. Files are edited using the Urban Institute's TRIM2 micro-simulation model and exclude those in families with active military members.

[b]"Other" includes persons covered under CHAMPUS, VA, Medicare, military health programs, and privately purchased coverage.

The state had opted to pursue Medicaid Managed Care in 1996 and implemented the New Mexico ¡SALUD! Medicaid Program on July 1, 1997. The ¡SALUD! Program replaced a state-operated primary care network that began as a practice-based case management model to incentivize primary care practitioners to expand care management to their panels of Medicaid-eligible patients. Providers had been paid an additional $3 to $5 above the respective fee schedule per Medicaid patient per month to manage primary care, ensure access to needed service, and coordinate entry and discharge to needed and prior approved tertiary care.

At the onset of ¡SALUD!, behavioral and oral health services were carved out and separate behavior health organizations (BHOs) and oral health organizations (OHOs) were contracted for Medicaid-eligible patients. Immediately, advocates, providers, and consumers of behavioral health reacted, complaining that there was fragmentation and new limitations in the scope and availability of behavioral health. Oral health remained the smallest program in the new managed care environment, and the transition drew little attention, since the oral health Medicaid program had few providers and thus lower numbers of consumers to protest change.

For behavioral health programs, almost immediate massive reductions in patient volume and revenues threatened the University of New Mexico Health Sciences Center (UNMHSC) community residential treatment centers and other long-duration behavioral health programs. While safety net providers—medical and behavioral—struggled to adapt to the new environment, specific data on the uninsured were not readily available to guide effective responses.

Beyond the traditional public and primary health care needs, uninsured and economically disadvantaged populations were not accessing wellness and health promotion services within their communities. Morbidity and mortality from pulmonary disease, alcohol-related injuries, and other chronic diseases were more prevalent in New Mexico than in other states, perhaps related to the limited health choices available to this population. Public transportation was virtually absent in most areas, impeding access to care for vulnerable populations. As ¡SALUD! rolled out in the first few months of the fiscal year in 1997, utilization of programs dropped immediately as enrollees were reassigned providers—in some cases more than a hundred miles away from their home community—and, to the surprise of the new Medicaid Office of Managed Care, the portion of the Medicaid Program that provided resources for travel had not been included in the bid process! As a result, many patients missed appointments; others were lost from the rolls as communications regarding new providers, opting in or out of coverage, and lack of clarity on the relationships between MCOs and other systems such as Indian Health Services reduced the utilization rates.

Also during this period in 1997, the Department of Defense was revamping the Civilian Health and Medical Program of the Uniformed Services (CHAMPUS) as well as services to enlisted personnel within the United States. Not to be outdone, the UNMHSC had undertaken a revamping of its programs for indigent patients in Bernalillo County, the site of the UNMHSC. The county, by New Mexico home rule statute, provided property mill levy income to support the University of New Mexico (UNM) Teaching Hospital's care for indigent Bernalillo county residents.

UNM CARE was established, along with the Department of Defense TriWest Health Program (Arizona, New Mexico, and Colorado portion), a twenty-one-western-state network, and the New Mexico Medicaid ¡SALUD! in July 1997. At the center all the programs had shared targeted outcomes:

- Increasing efficiencies
- Increasing healthier outcomes
- Creating "best practices"
- Increasing access

It was in this context in 1998, as all of the changes to the major health financing systems, Medicaid, County Indigent Funds, and TriWest unfolded, that the W.K. Kellogg Foundation's Community Voices Health Care for the Underserved National Initiative was launched and New Mexico was selected as a "learning laboratory" along with twelve other sites. CVNM proposed several integrated priorities and strategies to address issues facing the state's underserved and to respond to the drastically altered public financing systems, Medicaid, county indigent funds, and the Federal Department of Defense (Exhibits 5.1 and 5.2). As a consequence of the changes in the financial systems and reductions in levels of support from Congress, it became apparent that the state's other large public system, the Indian Health Service and the Native Americans served by that system, would also be included within the scope of the CV National Initiative.

Collaborative Efforts: Integrating with Shared Mission Initiatives

As in other CV sites, CVNM knew the value of effective collaborations in improving access to health care by way of practice and policy. There were a number of opportunities that were present near or around the time of the launch of the initiative that helped to further the goals.

Robert Wood Johnson State Coverage Initiative

In 1999 the Robert Wood Johnson Foundation (RWJF) announced "Communities in Charge," a health coverage planning grant opportunity for states and local communities. CVNM partnered with the New Mexico Hospital Association, Chambers of Commerce, and others and submitted a successful application for development of a coverage plan for the uninsured in four counties in the center of the state. At the submission of that plan and the request for implementation funding for the next four years, the RWJF program staff suggested that the request be modified to include the

EXHIBIT 5.1. CVNM PATHWAYS TO CHANGE.

Health Systems Organization
- *Enhanced primary care:* Further develop an enhanced primary care interdisciplinary service/education model (integrating primary care, behavioral health, oral health, public health, case management, and community health workers) guided by the community served.

Seamless Medical-Behavioral-Social Service System
- *Facilitate linkage* between the health care system and a range of community health services via community health workers.

Health Services Workforce
- *Behavioral health and primary care:* Address scarcity of behavioral health professional services by training health professionals on the primary care team in basic mental health, alcohol and substance abuse skills.

Oral Health and Primary Care
- *Expand training* opportunities for dentists and dental hygienists who serve rural and indigent patients.
- *Pipeline development:* Recruit a health workforce representing the ethnic and geographic diversity of the state, starting with middle school students.

Access
- *Universal access to primary care:* Create a statewide twenty-four-hour nurse triage line for medical and social services. Enhance web-based information systems to assign individuals to a "primary care home." Expand the capacity of collaborating interdisciplinary primary care provider groups in the public and private sectors to accept an increased panel of the uninsured.

Outcomes and Dissemination
- *New Mexico Center for Primary Care and Rural Health:* Implement strategies for disseminating program models and outcomes throughout the state, nation, and world.
- *Evaluation:* Create a multilevel research design, evaluating programmatic impact on health care access, health status and disparities, interorganizational collaboration, CVNM plan sustainability, patient and provider satisfaction, and degree of dissemination (local, national, and international).

whole state and that the format for change include consideration of waivers and other financing sources such as employer participation for covering the uninsured. Acting on the Foundation's suggestions, the New Mexico partners agreed to pursue a grant under the joint submission of the Department of Human Services, the Legislature, and the New Mexico Hospital Association.

EXHIBIT 5.2. CVNM STRATEGIES.

Enhance existing partnerships with key collaborators, programs, and initiatives, including the New Mexico Department of Health, New Mexico Human Services Department, federally qualified health centers (such as Healthcare for the Homeless and First Choice Community Health, Inc., in Bernalillo County and Hidalgo Medical Services in Hidalgo County), health centers in inner city underserved areas (such as UNM Southeast Heights Multi-service Center), First Nations Urban Indian Health Center, Albuquerque Area Indian Health Service, New Mexico Hospitals and Health Systems Association, state legislators, governor's office and key health cabinet secretaries, city and county government, county health councils, and UNM Health Sciences Center.

Utilize community health workers (community health advocates, community health representatives, and *promotoras*) to reach out to uninsured individuals, especially men, and bring them into a seamless, enhanced, community-based system of primary care.

Incorporate the "Health Commons" model. Enhance the integrated network of systems between fragmented service, education and support services (primary care, behavioral health, oral health, case management).

Reduce health disparities utilizing a diverse health professions workforce. Build on the UNM School of Medicine and the Department of Family & Community Medicine's national and international experience in family practice residency training, undergraduate primary care problems and community-based learning, and rural medicine training.

Disseminate information about the models at local, state, national, and international venues, including print, radio, television, film, manuscripts, and web-based products. International dissemination will be facilitated through the Network: Towards Unity for Health, and UNM's World Health Organization (WHO) Collaborating Center through affiliation with the Pan American Health Organization (PAHO).

Utilize "Health Commons" Resource Team members to focus on each of the prioritized activities. Because the "Health Commons" involves different community stakeholders—public and private—and different sectors of society in addressing intractable health problems, no single provider group or sector can successfully address the problems alone.

Committees were formed, and as a kick-off CVNM sponsored a national conference on the uninsured. A task force comprising all stakeholders including unions and advocates was formed, and the process was begun. In a period of thirteen months the task force developed the "State Coverage Initiative" (SCI) that was modeled after the UNMCARE program operated by CVNM sponsor UNMHSC. A 1115 waiver was subsequently approved in 2002. Although enrollment expectations of forty-five thousand individuals have not yet been met, the program did have incremental increases to a projected seventeen thousand participants in 2007. A summary of benefits and cost-sharing limits for SCI participants appears in Table 5.4.

TABLE 5.4. BENEFITS AND COST-SHARING LIMITS FOR SCI PARTICIPANTS.

The benefit package is limited to $100,000 in benefits payable per member per benefit year.	Copay at 0%–100% FPL	Copay at 101%–150% FPL	Copay at 151%–200% FPL
Physician/Provider visits (no copay for preventive services)	$0	$5	$7
Pre- and post-natal care	$0	$0	$0
Preventive services	$0	$0	$0
Hospital inpatient medical and surgical**	$0/per admission	$25/per admission	$30/per admission
Hospital inpatient maternity**	$0/per admission	$25/per admission	$30/per admission
Hospital outpatient surgery and procedures	$0	$5	$7
Home health**	$0	$5	$7
Physical therapy, occupational therapy, and speech therapy	$0	$5	$7
Diagnostics (excluding routine lab and X-ray)	$0 (included in office visit)	$0 (included in office visit)	$0 (included in office visit)
Durable medical equipment and supplies	$0	$5	$7
Diabetes treatment, equipment, and support	$3	$3	$3
Diabetes management	$0	$5	$7
Emergency services	$0	$15 a visit, waived if administered within twenty-four hours	$20 per visit, waived if administered within twenty-four hours
Urgent care	$0	$5	$7
Prescription drugs: Generic Name brand	$3 per prescription	$3 per prescription	$3 per prescription
Behavioral Health and Substance Abuse: Outpatient office visit and outpatient substance abuse treatment Inpatient behavioral health detox	$0 $0	$5 $25	$7 $30
Limits on Out-of-Pocket Expenses	All participants will be limited to 5 percent of countable family income per benefit year. Pharmacy out-of-pocket charges for all participants will be limited to four (4) prescriptions per month.		

Notes: Data are as of July 2005.

* Subject to plan limitations and plan prior authorization requirements.

** Inpatient hospitalization coverage is limited to twenty-five days per benefit year. This twenty-five-day limitation is combined with home health services and inpatient physical health rehabilitation (10/19/05).

The SCI has also expanded the potential for indigent funds and other sources to support the enrollment of other resident populations not covered under the SCI guidelines and, most recently in 2008, the development of the Pathways program by the UNMHSC to case manage those who are not eligible for any of the current programs.

Health Resources Service Administration-Community Access Programs

CVNM, along with other CV sites, discussed the Health Resources Service Administration Community Access Programs (HRSA-CAP) program model and, with HRSA as the agency, began to roll out the initiative. Over the course of the program's existence, three CAP awards were made in New Mexico. While CVNM participated in the grant writing and provided support staff for implementation, only the Central New Mexico CAP program has developed sustainable systems change and programs to increase access for the underinsured and the uninsured.

The Central New Mexico CAP included the UNMHSC; Departments of Health and Human Services; Health Care for the Homeless; First Choice Health Care (area federally qualified health center—FQHC); Sandoval County; Indian Health Service Area Office; and First Nations Health, an urban Native American community clinic. Matching HRSA support with CVNM grant support for project management and consultant services produced several products utilizing technology to increase access for the uninsured. CAP's $950,000 grant from HRSA has resulted in the development of several significant models that have been sustained by various stakeholders long after the CVNM and HRSA CAP investment.

Nurse Advice Line. CVNM and CAP invested in the development of a twenty-four-hour nurse advice line, now supported by the Medicaid Managed Care Organizations, state appropriations, and individual contracts with rural and urban hospitals and practices. The only one of its kind in the nation, the line is available to the entire state and can be accessed regardless of coverage. Staffed by nurses operating with standard protocols, the line receives more than eleven thousand calls per month. Emergency room (ER) contacts and admissions are diverted on average at a rate of nearly 30 percent. The line is now being utilized to provide surveillance of public health status, including influenza, emerging infections from foodborne pathogens, and support for breast-feeding mothers. Twenty-four-hour access has brought relief to rural practices and, through a morning-after referral process, ensures continuity for those callers with providers, and referrals to accepting practices for those without a primary care home.

Primary Care Dispatch. ERs continue to be the point of access for many uninsured and those who are covered but do not utilize their primary care provider. As part of its commitment to technology development, the CVNM supported the staff of the Central New Mexico CAP in the development of a Primary Care Dispatch (PCD) system. Based in the public hospital (UNM Hospital), the system identifies individuals who are not in a primary care home and presenting at the ER for care. The PCD has a predetermined number of appointed slots for those without providers who are then appointed to those slots nearest their homes. The appointments usually are met within the week of the contact with the ER. This effort has reduced recurring ER admissions and linked the uninsured with providers or provider networks. The program is now under consideration for use by the county correction department to ensure continuity of behavioral and primary care for former detainees.

Identifying and Incorporating Sustainable Financing to Support New Service Delivery Models

Field Case Management

From the onset of the grant award, CVNM had focused on the value, clarification of roles, financing, and sustainability of the community health worker (CHW) within the context of health and social services systems. At the state level, as efforts moved forward in assessing policy goals, an important consideration was the capacity statewide for CHWs, as well as the health and social service criteria for contributing to the support of these workers. At this time, the Central New Mexico CAP and CVNM began a partnership with Molina Heath Care (an MCO) for field case management services for Molina's most noncompliant Medicaid program participants. Molina had taken the lead in identifying resources from its own budget, obtaining approval from the State Medicaid Program, and paneling referrals. CVNM financed the hiring of, training of, and six months of the initial salary for CHWs to manage the referrals.

While documented elsewhere in the archives of the CV initiative, the program has exceeded expectations and, at this writing, three of the four MCOs are participating, with services offered in six cities around the state. Utilizing corporate funds, MCOs are contracting for a rate of $321 per member per month for up to six months for members referred for field case management services. Nearing half a million dollars a year, the program has shown tremendous savings for the MCOs but, more important, it has linked more than four hundred individuals and their families in a meaningful and positive way with their primary provider and community resources.

It is anticipated that the program will take on increased significance for MCOs as bottom-line management becomes more and more difficult. Current plans call for a more intense investment in CHW training and expansion of their skills to include management of chronic conditions, behavioral health access facilitation, and outreach to populations such as pregnant women to increase prevention and intervention programming. As a footnote, though not incidental, CHWs employed in the program are covered for health insurance, and all are continuing certificate and education programs.

W.K. Kellogg Foundation/American Legacy Foundation Initiative

Seven of the national CV sites participated as grantee representatives of the CV effort to increase access to tobacco use prevention and access to care for cessation in minority communities. In CVNM, the efforts were coordinated with public clinics, public schools, the State Department of Health, the continuing medical education department of the UNMHSC, Eastern New Mexico University, and the State Medical Association. Projects were developed for adolescent cessation in high schools in the Albuquerque area; readiness to quit protocols for a rural community health dental clinic; smokeless tobacco intervention strategies in the rural ranch and farming areas of eastern New Mexico; CHW outreach and intervention in *colonias* in the southern border area; and a Clinical Prevention Initiative (CPI) focusing on all health providers in the state as part of a Continuing Medical Education (CME) credit initiative based on a readiness-to-quit protocol and motivational interviewing. Though all of the programs were moderately successful, the CPI succeeded in training more than 2,800 providers and has been incorporated into the New Mexico Medical Society Curricula data base.

Oral Health

Oral health access remains a major issue in New Mexico. While the efforts continue, including a renewed interest on behalf of the Kellogg Foundation, some extensive and valuable work has already been undertaken by CVNM and its partners. Most of the access and oral health workforce gains have been accomplished by UNMHSC, as a variety of programs and services have been developed that add to the service, educational, and eventually research underpinnings of a responsive oral health system.

The CVNM involvement with oral health issues got underway in a serious manner when CVNM began to share the costs for a UNMHSC chief dentist with the Department of Surgery. This financial relationship lasted for nearly seven years (1999–2006), during which the Dental Division took on the entire costs of the program efforts for dentistry at the UNMHSC. The partnership continues with joint efforts to address the development of oral health clinical services for the underserved

Out of the Mouths of Babes

A young lad attended one of our dental clinics. . . . [W]hen approached by the dentist he began to cry and became hysterical within seconds. It seems he was a "Medicaid child" who had been seen about a year before at one of the newly opened practices that primarily sees Medicaid and SCHIP kids. It appears the young boy had been "ground and filled" in one sitting. It became clear to our dentist that there would be little gained in pursuing treatment at this session; besides, he had seen three children already that month with the same behavior. In fact, the dentist's concern is that our program would see more and more children who not only were in need of having all of their teeth repaired at one time, but who had also come away from previous dental experiences with what appeared to be some variant of post-traumatic stress. Health care is sometimes filled with a variety of diametric opposites. Though no access may result in bad teeth, likewise access without quality and sensitive care may result in a loss of trust and a lifelong fear of the system.

Mother to Child

A young South Vietnamese mother eloquently expressed her gratitude for the opportunity to participate in the Kellogg Community Voices–sponsored DOULA training. Her firm, public commitment was demonstrated in front of a crowd from every segment of her community. She pledged that she would use her new skills to give back care and understanding, better access, and a healthier tomorrow. She pledged herself to serve, as her family looked on. At the end of her personal and touching testimony to community members, it was clear that her pledge for service was to the community, but the person who paid the most attention, hung on every word, was her daughter. For those of us who witnessed this in the crowded waiting room of the Southeast Heights Health Commons, what we saw was an intelligent, confident woman assume responsibility for making her community better. It was clear afterward that in her declaration of commitment, her powerful message was not for us. She had used perhaps the most important moment of her educational experience to teach her daughter a valuable life lesson. She had used her "community voice" for a very private conversation with her child.

—Wayne Powell, associate director, OVPCH

communities, expanding oral health services and education within the university and creating a base for informing oral health policy recommendations.

The Oral Health Program development by CVNM provides the most varied and sustained examples of policy-related successes. At every level—local, state, and federal—successes are noted. Many of these achievements are captured here as examples of not only the variety but also the level of resources committed to oral health care:

- An application was submitted, and approval for a residency program in advanced education in general dentistry began July 2003. This has included five residents per year; the Residency Center provides more than ten thousand visits per year to individuals who otherwise would not receive the level of care offered at the Center. The General Residency has expanded to ten residents and is establishing rural practice rotations in three areas of the state.
- An HRSA grant was received for $890,000 to cover Dental Residency startup costs.
- Appropriation was secured through Senator Jeff Bingaman for $380,000 for the development of the residency program and the study of dental education strategies for New Mexico.
- Dental specialty programs expanded through contracts between community partners and the UNM School of Medicine and now offer an average of three hundred days per month of coverage to rural and underserved areas at more than twenty different sites per year.
- Until privatization of juvenile justice system dental programs by the Children Youth and Families Department in 2003, dental services to 1,900 incarcerated juveniles were provided annually through the university program.
- The UNM Center for Community Partnerships' Specialty Extension Services provided temporary oral health professional staffing to community health centers in crisis, preventing closure of three facilities.
- The dental hygiene and dental divisions developed a dental clinic in the Van Buren middle school serving a very low-income neighborhood for 675 students and their siblings.
- Two counties funded new "health commons" centers and include oral health clinic spaces.
- The State Health Department and Sandoval County partnered with the Dental Hygiene Division of UNMHSC as a state model for the Women, Infant and Children's (WIC) oral health case management program for 220 participants.
- Atlanta Foundation funds five school-based sites to include oral health care in school-based health clinics. In total the coverage for oral health assessment, referral, and case management is being expanded to more than 2,700 middle school students.
- A contract was procured with the State Department of Health for oral health care for indigent adults.

- Congressional Appropriation was secured for the continuation of funding of the Indian Health Service Albuquerque Area Dental Clinic and First Nations Health Care for Urban Native Americans (The two clinics see an estimated 7,500 Native Americans per year who otherwise would have lost their dental program).
- Two consecutive state appropriations ($100,000) were made for expansion of the Dental Residency to a Program Graduate Year-2 Residency in Eastern New Mexico (Roswell-Chaves County) in 2008.
- A New Mexico State legislative appropriation ($1 million per year) was made for operations of the Residency Program in General Dentistry.
- The construction of a residency clinical education center received funding of $7.5 million.
- A National Josiah Macy Foundation Grant was received to develop a Bachelors of Arts/Doctor of Dental Surgery program in coordination with the Bachelor of Arts (B.A.), Medical Doctor (M.D.) program. (Recruitment focuses on minority and rural students for preadmission to medical school slots; at least twenty-five B.A., D.D.S. slots would be created.) The legislature is supportive of both initiatives.

Dental Residency Program: Direct Service Modeling

The Dental Residency Program has been a significant provider of care to the uninsured and the underserved. Utilizing two fixed clinic sites, one specialty clinic site, and the ER, the residency program is making a major contribution.

One clinic is located in the Southeast Heights quadrant of Albuquerque. Until 2006, this provider was the only dental clinic in that zip code. The population at the Southeast Height's clinic is 100 percent uninsured or on Medicaid. Treatment for those who are indigent is covered under a grant from the New Mexico Department of Health. Adult emergency services and more non-Medicaid comprehensive services for children are covered under this grant. This clinic also serves as the referral site for the students seen in the Van Buren School-Based Health Center. A dentist from this site also staffs the dental clinic at the middle school.

The other clinic is located in the Northeast Heights section of Albuquerque. At the Northeast Heights Clinic, 85 percent of the patients treated are on Medicaid. The remaining 15 percent are either cash-paying patients or patients with some type of indemnified insurance. During the 2005–2006 residency year, 10,069 patient visits occurred. In the first three-quarters of the 2006–2007 residency year, 11,636 patient visits have occurred.

If treatment were measured by dollar production, the 2005–2006 clinical production was $1,190,701, and after the first three-quarters of the 2006–2007 residency year, production stood at $1,034,676. Consequently, with either measurement, the amount of treatment being rendered to underserved populations has dramatically increased for the area in which dental residents provided care. The patient load for the current five residency slots has been maximized.

Increasing additional access through resident-provided care required more residency slots for New Mexico. In July of 2008, the residency expanded to ten slots and began a process to develop a dental pediatric residency program over the next four years. The residency program also provided treatment to patients with special needs. A full-time faculty member practices at Carrie Tingley Hospital, dedicated to special needs patients. The dental residents receive training and state Medicaid certification in this area of dentistry. In addition, the dental residents provide dental consultations at University Hospital for patients with complex medical needs. Finally, the residents cover the ER at University Hospital, a component that is greatly increasing in demand.

Patients throughout the state are increasingly showing up at the ER with severe dental infections that are treated by the dental residents. These infections could have been handled very simply and with much less expense if the patient would have had funded access to care outside the hospital ER. In this light, the dental residency program is truly functioning as a safety net.

Data for services provided by the UNM in the years 1998–2006 are summarized in Table 5.5. Service volume is estimated due to contractual services to other agencies and location on dental record information.

TABLE 5.5. SERVICES PROVIDED BY UNIVERSITY OF NEW MEXICO.

Demographics	
Urban	34,771 (58%)
Rural	25,179 (42%)
Visit Type	
General dentist/Emergency	35,970 (60%)
Hygiene student clinic	7,194 (12%)
Hygiene visits	9,542 (16%)
Developmentally disabled	4,916 (8.2%)
Orthodontic	2,278 (3.8%)
Distribution by Point of Service	
Community Site-Clinic	85.2%
Institution	14.8%
Total Dental Clients Served: 59,950	

Policy Development Through Systems Change in Addressing Social Determinants

Informing public policy has been a key component of CVNM activities in support of broader efforts to address social determinants of health. While some of the work has been noted previously, there are some outliers that exemplify the range and scope of the CVNM experience.

Health Commons Model

From the beginning of the CV grant, CVNM proposed a number of innovations to increase the access and efficiencies for programs serving the underserved. Intractable health problems in our society, such as health disparities between economic and ethnic groups, access to services for the uninsured, or epidemics of violence or of obesity, share their root causes in the social determinants of health. It was clear to CVNM leaders that these health problems and their social determinants cannot be addressed by "technical solutions" or by any one field of medicine alone, nor even by the entire curative and public health sector together, but require the collaboration of different community stakeholders and different sectors of society—a "health commons" approach.

The "health commons" idea is analogous to the town "commons" in colonial times, where citizens from all walks of life came to debate and plan for the common good—the building of roads, creation of public schools, removal of refuse, all things that were in the interest of the collective well-being (Figure 5.1). In the CVNM initiative, the "health commons" serves as a focal point for aspects of community assessment, determining and resolving systems barriers, promoting innovation, and allocating resources (Exhibit 5.3). While the objectives of the "commons" model are the same, the individual commons are as unique and reflective as the communities they serve. Contracting shared services and purchases, common intake processes, shared medical records, billing and exploration of financing, and, ultimately, the uniqueness of each community make each "common" one unto itself. Organizations that participate in a commons must clearly see a role for their organization within this model. Sharing both missions and values also will be of critical importance to the success of the venture.

Five health commons have been developed in New Mexico as part of the CVNM partnership initiative. During the 2008 legislative session, a bill was introduced that acknowledged the model as the health and social services delivery method for the future and directed state agencies to adapt and finance the model for future operations. As a model, the CVNM Health Commons has succeeded in evolving from theory to practice to public policy.

FIGURE 5.1. THE SHARED NEW MEXICO MODEL OF THE HEALTH COMMONS MEMBERSHIP.

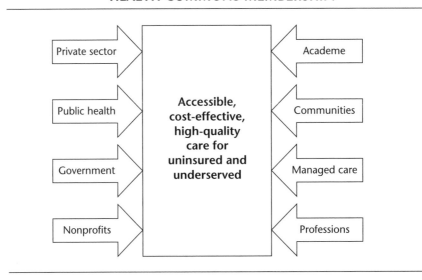

Poverty Workgroup and Policy Reform Recommendations

One of the more interesting CVNM efforts aimed at informing policy was the partnership that developed with the Poverty Workgroup of New Mexico Advocates for Children and Families (NMACF, now New Mexico Voices). As a result of the involvement with the NMACF, three policy briefs were developed.

The first brief addressed predatory lending on tribal lands by pawn shops, trading posts, tax preparers, and pay-day loan advance stores. The state continues to wrestle with this issue. Recommendations from the workgroup included the capping of interest charges for pay day and other loans or advances by nonregulated lending entities.

A second brief focused on the cumbersome eligibility process for financial assistance, food stamps, and Medicaid. The system has been broken for a number of years, and the eligibility process is not interrelated or interactive. Applicants are required to "enroll" for each program, although the programs have similar or same criteria for eligibility. In an analysis of state tax filings income, numbers in household and other reported data matches were made to the number of eligible participants in each of the public programs. On the basis of the data derived from the study, food stamps were under-enrolled by 30 percent of those eligible; Medicaid by 20 percent plus. One recommendation that required a policy shift was to use the state tax filing as

EXHIBIT 5.3. SHARED COMPONENTS FOR SUCCESS AMONG PARTICIPANT ORGANIZATIONS IN THE HEALTH COMMONS.

Shared resources: Agencies share common interests in shared populations. The "commons" requires a commitment to share resources for improved outcomes for those populations.

Shared responsibility: The operation of the "commons" requires the attention of the members and the shared responsibility for governance and operations, and shared expectations of the performance of the "commons."

Shared risks: Shared risks include those associated with financial viability of the "commons," individual program and agency sustainability to ensure resources, and support for the activities and programs conducted and the attitude and expectations of the community for which service is being provided.

Shared rewards: Increased efficiencies; reaching or exceeding program goals; healthier outcomes for communities; developing and securing new resources; and attribution of community and stakeholders are all shared as products of the "commons" with equal acknowledgment of the effort of all the agencies involved.

---

a statement of presumed eligibility based on household income, members in the household, and, for Medicaid, ages of children. All filers who were presumed to be eligible for programs based on criteria would be sent via data taping to the HSD, and that Department would then contact the filer by letter indicating the presumed eligibility and local contact information for the HSD Income Support Office for activation of the benefits. Another variant would be for the HSD to presume Medicaid eligibility and issue a letter to that effect. The letter could serve as the first notification of eligibility and be given to providers as services are required by the families.

A final area for which policy briefs were produced related to the New Mexico State Low Income Tax Rebate Program (LITR) and the adjustments to the LITR payment schedule. Research revealed that a revision to the LITR schedules upward would significantly reduce the numbers of children in poverty in the state. The study was conducted at a time a governor-sponsored tax refund and reduction of tax liability for high-income New Mexicans was under consideration.

While the studies mentioned above are by themselves valuable, the more important lessons came from the potential of local policy formation derived from locally based research models.

Community Health Worker Policy Development

A critical component of the CVNM proposal was the development of interdisciplinary teams that included the CHW (or *promotora*) as a key to increasing access to and benefit from services and programs for underserved communities. Historically the CHW has been called upon to increase effectiveness of programs, help researchers access the community, or translate for eligibility or financial participation purposes. Support for such activities has seldom been sustained. CVNM, along with other partner organizations, CHWs, and advocates, developed language for a Senate Memorial to formulate recommendations for support and incorporation of the CHW into the services networks in New Mexico.

During the Forty-Sixth Legislature, First Session 2003, the New Mexico Legislature adopted Senate Joint Memorial 076 (SJM 076). The Memorial requested that the New Mexico Department of Health (NMDOH) "lead a study on the development of a Community Health Advocacy Program in New Mexico, including the program's methods, structure, financing and implementation that utilizes various categories of community health advocates." As defined in SJM 076, Community Health Advocates included "community health workers, *promotoras*, community health promoters, community advocates, outreach educators, *doulas*, peer health promoters and community health representatives."

CVNM staffed and provided coordination for the work of the Task Force that was appointed by the NMDOH to conduct the study. The final report provided a comprehensive analysis of the contribution of CHWs to the health and stability of New Mexico communities and the potential for development of additional CHW programs in New Mexico. Included in the report were inventories of existing service delivery programs and sites and the supply and distribution of CHWs, as well as an assessment of the potential for CHWs to reduce health professional shortages.

The data, analysis, and findings of this report revealed that access to CHWs for many New Mexicans has the potential to improve public health outcomes, increase access to care, and reduce costs for health services. In a prescient move to provide the legislature with all the tools necessary to support CHWs, this report included recommendations for what was required to sustain CHWs and the ways in which a statewide CHW program, through public-private partnerships, might contribute to the economic and workforce development of New Mexico. Exhibit 5.4 provides a summary of the task force's major recommendations.

The NMDOH subsequently established an Office for Community Health Workers and an advisory committee for the Office of the Secretary. Currently, the Governor's Office is developing a list of nominees for the Advisory Committee, and an Executive Order is being prepared to elevate the Advisory Committee function to the level of the Governor's Office. The Advisory Committee will have direct policy access to the Executive Branch and to the various state agencies that will utilize and resource the CHW effort in the state.

EXHIBIT 5.4. SUMMARY OF TASK FORCE RECOMMENDATIONS ON CHWS.

Administration
- Establish a CHW Advisory Committee.
- Establish and fund a program in the New Mexico Department of Health to coordinate and facilitate development of the CHW program statewide.

Methods and Structures
- Recognize CHWs as generalists and specialists, depending on their training and field of work.
- Develop a certification process so that certification can be offered.
- Create a salary schedule and compensation plan based on regional parity and parity for practicing CHWs.
- Educate medical professionals on utilization of CHWs for health promotion and disease prevention and management.

Financing and Economic Development
- Increase and/or modify Rural Primary Health Care Act (RPHCA) funds to specifically provide resources for CHW services and incentives for recruitment and retention of CHWs.
- Leverage existing dollars from federal, state, tribal, and Indian health service programs for training and employment of CHWs.
- Investigate reimbursement for CHWs under Senate Bill 743, which requires third-party insurers to offer tobacco use and smoking cessation counseling services to their insured members.
- Establish a critical shortage area designation for CHWs providing care to the underserved.
- Develop criteria, designation, and expanded financial incentives for public-private partnerships that use CHWs to promote healthier communities.
- Use the Senior Employment Older Workers Program to provide subsidized job placement for adults age fifty and older wishing to serve as CHWs.
- Require organizations and facilities receiving state funds for clinic operations and services to, where feasible and appropriate, establish partnerships with private and/or other health providers for CHW services.
- Include CHW services in private health insurance plans through the State Insurance Commission.

Medicaid Best Practices
- Determine ways to maximize Medicaid funds through use of CHWs.
- Authorize the State Medicaid Program to develop, direct, and implement contractual modifications to current Medicaid Managed Care Contracts to assure a payment mechanism for support of the CHWs.

EXHIBIT 5.4. *(CONTINUED)*

Training, Curricula, and Career Ladder
- Create standards for core curricula based on core competencies established in this study.
- Develop a core training program with additional components on specialty areas of health.
- Enhance funding to New Mexico community colleges, technical schools, and universities to establish programs to promote a career ladder for CHWs.
- Use the Senior Employment Older Workers Program to provide training for adults age fifty and older who wish to serve as CHWs.

Evaluation and Effectiveness
- Create a statewide evaluation system and database for collecting and analyzing information about CHW programs and their effectiveness.

Center for Native American Health

CVNM recognized early in the formation of its workplan that policy gaps could widen if a specific area was not developed for sovereign tribes to inform the policy discussion with UNMHSC and the various interagency and tribal serving programs. As the CVNM initiative explored the options available, the UNMHSC began the process of developing closer relationships with tribal communities. In a joint effort between the UNMHSC School of Medicine, the Department of Family and Community Medicine, NMDOH Indian Health Services, tribes, and the Office of Indian Affairs, a summit with tribal leadership was held. From this summit came the request to establish a Center for Native American Health (CNAH) at the UNMHSC. The CNAH was formed, and initial startup support was provided by the School of Medicine and CVNM.

The CNAH Mission Statement is "To build and strengthen health alliances between the Native American and University communities and their partners to improve Native American Health in New Mexico." In accordance with its mission, the CNAH helps UNMHSC more effectively address health disparities in New Mexico Native American communities (Exhibit 5.5).

Yet another factor in the development of a policy and program forum for tribes within the UNMHSC was the resource shifts within Indian Health Service (IHS) under PL 93-638. In recent years, the trend toward self-determination in Native American health care has accelerated with the recent assumption of responsibility for health care services by various tribes exercising their self-determination option. These events have greatly changed the nature of Native American health care delivery, exacerbating problems with access to care and services in many Native American communities. While self-determination is meant to empower Native American communities to take charge

EXHIBIT 5.5. CENTER FOR NATIVE AMERICAN HEALTH GOAL.

To create measurable improvements in the health of Native Americans by

- Reducing the major health disparities in New Mexico's twenty-six Native American communities
- Creating a user-friendly clearinghouse for all UNMHSC activities relevant to Native American Health
- Creating sustainable partnerships with Indian Health Service, New Mexico Department of Health, and Native American communities to address the health concerns of Native American communities
- Increasing the number of Native American health professional faculty, with half of each member's time spent in Native American communities in service, education, patient care, or research-related activities
- Increasing by 20 percent the number of New Mexico Native American medical students and trainees entering health professions
- Recruiting and retaining Native American medical students by developing support services such as tutoring and medical board preparation courses
- Enhancing by 20 percent the practical translational research in support of Native American communities and coordinating UNMHSC research activities involving Native Americans
- Developing policy solutions to sustain financing of accessible, high-quality safety net health systems serving Native Americans living both on the reservation and in urban areas
- Incorporating the UNM Care Plan and "health commons" principles of enhanced, community-based primary care with medical, public health, dental, behavioral, and social services in Native American communities

of their own health care delivery system, it forces many tribes to assume a level of responsibility for which they are ill prepared. Whether tribes apply for PL 93-638 or remain dependent on an increasingly underfunded IHS, collaborative planning, new models of care, and policy development are nevertheless needed.

The Urban Native American Health Care Crisis. Access to care for urban Native Americans is more tenuous than for those who are reservation-based. As more Native Americans move to cities seeking jobs, reservation health resources do not follow them, and many of them, if not most, join the growing uninsured population. In New Mexico, just over half the state's Native Americans live in urban areas. IHS has a shrinking budget and recently reduced services. An urban Native American clinic, First Nation's Community Healthsource, is struggling to meet service demands under an extremely small budget. First Nations receives only $250,000 of its $1 million annual budget from the Albuquerque Area IHS office to subsidize urban Native American health care.

The collaboration of the UNMHSC, Central New Mexico CAP, and the Office of Community Partnerships was able to focus attention on the First Nation's Community Healthsource needs and developed a dental clinic, provided *locum tenens* (temporary physician coverage, in the absence of local providers), gave support for primary care, and developed board training for the community board of directors. After a number of years of struggle and effort to address the funding of the programs within First Nations, the clinic has now been designated a Federally Qualified Health Center and thus has become eligible for ongoing Health Resources Services Administration funding.

Fragmentation of University Resources for Native Americans. The rich resources in recruitment, education, service, and research at UNMHSC, which would be of great benefit to Native Americans, had been poorly coordinated and difficult to access. University programs were fragmented into different colleges, departments, divisions, and hospitals. These programs often responded to the demands of their funding agencies rather than to the needs of Native American communities. Few New Mexico Native Americans sought health professions education or careers. It is thus unsurprising that UNMHSC lacked sufficient Native American health professions faculty.

One promising line of work is that the CNAH will help recruit and retain Native American students to health professions careers in New Mexico. Most recently, nine Native American students were admitted to the School of Medicine Class of 2014. This represents the largest number of Native American students ever admitted to the program.

Collaboration. Tribal governments, NMDOH, the UNMHSC, and the IHS have collaborated in taking steps to develop more focused and beneficial working relationships around the health issues and concerns of Native Americans. UNMHSC partnered with IHS, First Nations Healthcare, and four other safety net provider groups to link all medical information systems and to provide universal access to integrated primary care systems through the HRSA Central Community Access Program matched by CVNM.

Behavioral and Mental Health

CVNM supported the development of the New Mexico First Town Hall, "Health Care in the 21st Century," in 1998. CVNM's principal investigator and the project director served as part of the writing and editing team for the background paper. Behavioral health programs and service parity were included in the paper and were recommended as a high legislative priority by the Town Hall attendees. A parity bill was passed and signed into law in the Spring legislative session following the town hall in 1999.

CVNM was also successful in altering the position of Health Care Finance and Administration (HCFA) with regard to the State Medicaid Plan's inclusion of behavioral health. Prompted by consumer and provider complaints during the first two years of the state Medicaid managed care contract, HCFA issued a letter of disapproval to the State Human Services Department (HSD) requiring a carve-out of behavioral health from the request for proposals, which was already public. The system reverted to a fee-for-service model, and consumers and the HSD were at odds over the reduced richness of the program. The legislative and the executive positions on mental health and Medicaid became more contentious. Lawsuits filed by the advocacy community led to increased reluctance of the HSD to participate in discussions with more than 250 organizations and individuals involved with Medicaid Mental Health Services.

At the receipt of the first letter of disapproval, CVNM offered to facilitate a mediation process with consumers, providers, and advocacy community representatives to move the discussions forward in planning for improving the Medicaid Behavioral Health program and answering the concerns of the department and the community. A facilitator was contacted by CVNM to facilitate two meetings, one in December 2000 and another in January 2001. Consumers, providers, and advocates met and decided upon criteria for creation and selection of representation on a Medicaid Behavioral Health Advisory Committee staffed and financed by the Human Services Department.

The resulting workplan for behavioral health was implemented, and consolidation of the state's various behavioral health budgets led to a purchasing cooperative and eventually to a comprehensive finance strategy for publicly funded behavioral health. The system, however, is still a carved-out behavioral health organization on the Medicaid side of financing, and providers continue to be overwhelmed with too many patients. Primary care practices have reported as much as 60 percent of their panels being made up of patients whose primary condition is substance abuse or other behavioral problems. At UNMHSC-operated clinics and health commons sites, the integration of primary care and behavioral health continues as a practice.

Lessons Learned

Over the years, numerous lessons surfaced, and the learning continues. As might be expected, much of the new knowledge was derived from the experiences with community, opportunities to have an impact on public policy, and leadership development.

- *First things first: the social determinants of health.* Communities are, all at once, resilient and fragile. The social determinants of health create fissures across the human landscape that can open at any time due to social, health, and economic variations.

Social determinants are the key factors that must be resolved first in order to address community and individual health concerns. Knowing this, communities must be heard in their own context, language, and time frame. Research is of little interest to communities unless they know that results will come that address what they seek and need. Ultimately, common approaches are possible within a defined, articulated, and community-backed model.

- *Establishing parity in community-campus partnerships is key!* Having been based at an academic institution, CVNM has learned that institutions, especially academic health centers, need to react to the community on a level of parity. Thus partnerships for the community as well as the academic institution must be structured in such a way that both gain from the relationships.
- *Public policy is a necessary but insufficient element for improving health and well-being.* Though CVNM made great strides and was a most prominent leader in the CV initiative where public policy was concerned, CVNM nonetheless recognizes that public policy is never a permanent fix. Sociopolitical realities need careful and consistent surveillance. Continual financial support for programs is a constant challenge to programs and services, as contrasting needs are continuously seeking resources.
- *Legislators must be approached with solutions!* At the legislative level, it must be understood at the outset that legislators seek and embrace answers to seemingly intractable problems that are thought out and carry support of the legislator's respective constituents.
- *Stewardship is a valuable style of leading and collaborating.* Sometimes leadership does not have to be "up front and center" but rather, subtle and indirect. CVNM learned that it could better support community needs by being a facilitator and equal partner in promoting the needs and communicating the changes that needed to be made. One of CVNM's greatest achievements has been its ability to translate the needs of the community and the responses of the system in a clearly understood way. CVNM's style of leadership was thus dynamic, following the needs of the community and the challenge of the moment. At the end of the initiative, a majority of the products, policies, programs, and participants have continued and in most cases have been improved upon. This is the transference of leadership that may be the true legacy of CVNM.

Conclusions

Most of the CVNM work has been in the development of systems responses to health care issues focused on the uninsured and at-risk populations. CVNM's goal from the beginning of the initiative was to obtain support for access to care for the state's 22 percent uninsured; fill program voids, such as enhancing oral health services where there was opportunity and influence; support health professional education as an extension of the mission of the host organization, UNMHSC, to the state's underserved communities; and inform policy when such action met the needs of the uninsured and the underserved. Within that construct, sustainability has been an objective from the start of the initiative. CVNM's acceptance of the dominant role of public financing of health services within the state and the acknowledgment that such dominance not only represented a number of the challenges but also the greatest opportunity for sustainable program development, has led to a number of favorable actions on the part of the legislative and executive branches of New Mexico's government.

The State Coverage Initiative (SCI), both state and federally funded, represents a public-private-partnership approach and has made significant inroads in expanding coverage for the uninsured, with expansion requests having been approved each year by the legislature. Of concern is the difficulty that the SCI is experiencing in enrollment into the program. The program challenge—to balance participation with access to care—may have a negative effect on its potential for sustainability. In all likelihood, the legislature will not continue to fund expansion of the program if enrollment goals are not met.

In the meantime, the future approach of the state to the health care system and financing of the same has been under study by Mathematica through a state contract. There are three recommendations from the study that were considered by the executive and the legislature during the 2008 legislative session. In brief, they are

1. A Health Security Act: 1.6 million New Mexicans (94 percent) of the non-institutionalized population under age sixty-five would enroll in a newly designed Health Security Plan.
2. New Mexico Health Choices: an expansion of Medicaid and SCHIP to a greater extent, accounting for 60 percent under version I and 64 percent under version II. This would require the creation of an "Alliance."
3. The Health Coverage Plan: would expand all current sources of coverage; it does not envision the creation of a new plan.

The common thread among the recommendations is the continuation of the SCI in either the current configuration or as a significant portion of expanded coverage. In the final days of the session, no action was taken on either of the comprehensive approaches. The SCI program continued to receive state support, and plans are underway to expand that program by another 7,500 participants.

Locally, the UNMCARE program continues to offer an alternative to Medicaid and the SCI. County funded, the program is an integrated component of the $63 million annual mill levy funding that supports the operations of the Health Sciences Center clinical and hospital programs. What has not occurred is that there does not appear to be any potential for major improvement in any coherent sustainability plan for integrated behavioral health programs. Although the CVNM investment in the behavioral system was minimal and the resulting "collaborative" was creative, represented the best thinking at the time, and had a great deal of consensus behind it, in the implementation it became yet another cost-management approach. Integration of behavioral health into primary care, along with oral health care and social services in the "health commons" model of service delivery, offers an approach that can yield improved overall health outcomes and may, in the near term, be a more sustainable approach.

CHAPTER SIX

FIRSTHEALTH COMMUNITY VOICES, NORTH CAROLINA

From Practice to Policy

Barbara Bennett, Lisa G. Hartsock, and Roxanne Leopper

This chapter highlights how a successful health care delivery system in the service of a large rural population affected local community issues while also influencing state and national decisions. By aligning with key stakeholders to design and deliver new services and products—many of which traditionally had been provided only by public health organizations and not-for-profit entities—this hospital system reorganized the manner in which it was providing care to underserved populations. Local practice and experiences served as the basis for critical state and national policy discussions, creating momentum for change. Upon completing this chapter, the reader will

- Learn about the work of FirstHealth of the Carolinas, a not-for-profit health care system and its coalition process aimed at addressing unmet needs
- Learn how a group of system leaders employed innovative strategies, while minimizing risk
- Learn how to raise awareness about needs that can lead to greater resource allocation for issues such as oral, mental, and men's health

- Learn about an innovative program that was able to improve oral health care for vulnerable populations by creating greater access to public programs and affordable health insurance
- Learn about tobacco use prevention and cessation efforts and appreciate the challenges confronted in addressing tobacco use cessation in North Carolina, a leading tobacco-dependent state
- Learn how a health care system capitalized on its strengths to have an impact on persons beyond those in its service area
- Learn about timing strategies in relation to policy advocacy, and how this health system shared data and stories with diverse audiences

Introduction

FirstHealth Community Voices (FHCV) in North Carolina came to life in tobacco country in a private, not-for-profit, nongovernmental health care delivery system, FirstHealth of the Carolinas. Its charge was to find new and innovative ways of serving a predominantly rural and increasingly diverse population with limited access to health insurance coverage and health care, a high rate of working uninsured, and a growing number of new immigrants in fifteen counties in the mid-Carolinas. The W.K. Kellogg Foundation and The Duke Endowment provided the impetus for this initiative with a combination of over $1 million in resources and, most important, a generous amount of time (five initial years with the possibility of five more for a total of a decade, depending on how well the first phase of the initiative progressed) to implement a model for change.

As the first initiative of its kind in North Carolina, Community Voices offered a unique opportunity to address numerous focus areas to increase access to care for the underserved through demonstration projects and policy change efforts. There had been several programs throughout North Carolina that addressed specific topic areas such as decreasing health disparities and addressing youth tobacco use rates; however, historically these projects had only worked on one focus area, as opposed to FHCV, which had a broader mission, ultimately leading efforts in a number of policy targets. The particular structure of Community Voices allowed FirstHealth to operate as a regional learning laboratory not only for policy change but also for grassroots outreach and pilot program implementation.

Over the years, FHCV met the challenges and exceeded its own expectations in both program and policy impact. Beyond working continuously to address the larger question of the uninsured in North Carolina, FHCV worked specifically along all of the policy targets that were established under the parameters of the Community

Voices initiative: men's health, oral health, access to care, case management, mental health, and community health workers (CHWs). Moreover, given its geographic location in the heart of tobacco country, FHCV led efforts to decrease tobacco use and change policy regarding the substance in the state.

At the end of a decade of work, FHCV continues programming in all of the original areas, has expanded collaborations in North Carolina with likely and unlikely partners, and has worked with its state legislature to introduce new items into an exciting policy agenda that would have otherwise not been considered. Consideration of unlikely issues such as the health of poor men and rethinking tobacco policy in a state well-known for its commitment to this industry would not have been possible without the tenacity of FHCV. FHCV has thus been a formidable force in North Carolina and remains so until this day.

Infrastructure and Demographics of the Service Area

FirstHealth of the Carolinas is a private, not-for-profit, nongovernmental integrated health care delivery system that is based in Pinehurst, North Carolina, and serves a predominantly rural population in the mid-Carolinas. It is a system composed of three hospitals, with 611 licensed beds, a rehabilitation center, three sleep disorders centers, three dental centers, seven family care centers, six fitness centers, a charitable foundation, a hospice program, home health services, and an insurance plan. FirstHealth serves as the regional referral center for the community and primary care hospitals in the region. In addition, critical care transport, emergency management services (EMS), and medical transport services are also part of FirstHealth. The system actively collaborates with local hospitals, public agencies, and private providers to ensure access and delivery of health care. FirstHealth, led by a community board of directors and board committees, established a Community Health Services division. Within this area operate programs related to disease prevention and early detection, as well as programs designed to facilitate access to health care for the underserved.

The concept of "community benefit" is a cornerstone of the FirstHealth mission. With a stated core purpose, "To Care For People," community benefit includes services to the underserved, including a mobile health van offering a variety of preventive screenings and education, dental clinics for children under age eighteen, school health services in Moore and Montgomery counties, a tobacco use prevention and cessation program, classes in healthy eating and active living, transportation services, medication assistance services, and a language interpreter program.

Leadership of FirstHealth is through the chief executive officer (CEO) and the FirstHealth board of directors. There are five presidents of FirstHealth entities reporting to the CEO—a chief operating officer (COO), a chief medical officer, a chief financial officer, a chief information officer—and two vice presidents. Community

Health Services is managed by an administrative director who reports directly to the chief medical officer. The Regional Health Services Board, comprising twenty community members representing the service area counties and the diversity of the population, provides oversight of Community Health Services, where FHCV is housed. The Regional Health Board reports directly to the FirstHealth Board.

FHCV was launched in the four primary counties in which the health system serves. The demographics of these communities are shown in Table 6.1.

Improving Community Health

Collaborative Efforts

It was evident from the start that relationships needed to be established at the state level in order to integrate Community Voices' priorities into the agendas of the state and of other collaboratives with potential for influencing policy. To this end, FHCV participated in a number of partnerships, including with the North Carolina Alliance for Health, Robert Wood Johnson's Oral Health Professional Grant Pipeline project, and others. Public-private partnerships and other less formal, though equally significant, relationships strengthened the resource base for ensuring care for the community.

To move an agenda, FHCV leaders first needed to understand the nuances of "how things get done" in North Carolina; they needed to take into consideration that each county has its own distinct community and style of communicating and directing resources. Ultimately, the informal network and power base within each county or community proved to be more influential in establishing collaborative partnerships and achieving results. In this setting, FHCV engaged the community in a number of ways.

For example, with the establishment of steering committees in each county, the health system's strategic plan, "2020 First-In-Health," created the opportunity for FHCV to prioritize and address health issues locally. In addition, the ethnically and geographically diverse Regional Health Services Board—a guide for community health efforts—is in effect a community collaborative with a significant influence in policy recommendations such as the creation of the tobacco-free campus and the adoption of a formal worksite wellness work group charged with assessing and modifying policies related to healthy eating and physical activity.

FHCV also worked to develop relationships within the business community to address the issue of the working uninsured. Efforts toward this end were made specifically in collaboration with the local businesses to design a portfolio of health plans to meet the needs of small businesses and their low-wage employees.

TABLE 1. DEMOGRAPHICS OF HOKE, MONTGOMERY, MOORE, AND RICHMOND COUNTIES COMPARED TO NORTH CAROLINA.

	Hoke	Montgomery	Moore	Richmond	Region	NC
Total population	42,303	27,638	83,162	46,555	199,658	8,856,505
Race						
White	44.5%	69.1%	80.2%	64.8%	67.6%	72.1%
African American	37.6%	21.8%	15.5%	30.5%	24.5%	21.6%
American Indian	11.4%	0.4%	0.7%	1.7%	3.1%	1.2%
Asian	0.8%	1.6%	0.4%	0.7%	0.7%	1.4%
Other	3.5%	5.7%	2.3%	1.1%	2.8%	2.3%
Two or more races	2.1%	1.3%	0.9%	1.2%	1.3%	1.1%
Hispanic or Latino	7.2%	10.4%	4.0%	2.8%	5.3%	4.7%
Age						
Under 18	29.8%	24.9%	22.1%	25.8%	25.0%	24.4%
18–64	62.5%	61.1%	56.1%	60.6%	59.2%	63.6%
65 and older	7.7%	14.0%	21.8%	13.6%	15.8%	12.0%
Sex						
Male	50.5%	50.6%	48.2%	49.1%	49.2%	49.0%
Female	49.5%	49.4%	51.8%	50.1%	50.8%	51.0%
Income						
Below poverty	17.7%	15.4%	11.4%	19.6%	15.2%	12.3%
Median household income	$33,230	$32,903	$41,240	$28,830	$35,461	$39,184
Median per capita income	$13,635	$16,504	$23,377	$14,485	$18,279	$20,307
Population per square mile	108	56	119	98	105	182

Reinforcing partnerships locally and at the state level through Healthy Carolinians chapters (Moore, Richmond, and Hoke counties), FHCV has also leveraged several million dollars in funding, resources, and expertise to address childhood obesity and a variety of other issues, with an emphasis on reaching disparate populations with these efforts.

Leadership. In addition to developing distinct collaboratives in different parts of the state, FHCV established within its core at FirstHealth strong dedicated leadership composed of a diverse group of talented community, business, and health care leaders with significant linkages to underserved populations. To this day, FirstHealth maintains successful models of cooperation, change-management techniques, extensive multidisciplinary approaches to management, strategic planning, and project management expertise.

A cultural norm within the organization is that the managers should have ongoing education about the knowledge and tools that are necessary to assist them in carrying out their jobs most effectively. They are held accountable and given the responsibility for their service area and the power to carry out those responsibilities.

Impact in Community. As a result of its community partnerships and leadership style, FHCV has successfully worked to raise the level of awareness regarding access to care issues and health policy at the organizational, local, regional, and state levels. A number of key areas have been developed. FHCV has

- Piloted a community-based insurance program, FirstPlan, which resulted in enrolling more than two hundred businesses that had at least 15 percent of their workforce uninsured
- Implemented Medicaid enrollment scholarships in each county, resulting in increased coverage through enrollment in government programs
- Established dental clinics to treat underserved children in three counties
- Established a gold standard smoke-free campus policy in health systems and school systems
- Increased the ability of the underserved and uninsured to access medication assistance, food stamps, interpretation and translation services, and health care navigation assistance as a result of the community health worker (CHW) model

FHCV furthermore brokered relationships between the health system and the state to produce key changes in health policy. Ultimately these linkages brought additional resources to the local area such as funds to expand one of the dental health clinics. The increased visibility at the state level has also led to many additional opportunities, including being called upon to testify for study commissions, participating in North Carolina's Institute of Medicine (IOM) committees, giving presentations at state-level meetings, and establishing the kinds of relationships with policymakers and state officials that positioned FirstHealth as a resource for information and lessons learned on access-to-care issues.

FHCV not only has changed the landscape of access to care at the local level but also has had a profound effect on the culture of FirstHealth. The level of awareness in the system regarding the benefits of community collaboration; the willingness to attempt pilot projects; and the ability to leverage additional funding for projects and program implementation have all increased as a result of CV. Today, FirstHealth and the state of North Carolina share

- A heightened awareness of health disparities, which has since resulted in formalized efforts to address health disparities through social marketing
- A better understanding of the "big picture" issues and challenges facing local organizations, which has served to coalesce for the common good, as was the case in designing a small business insurance product
- An openness to new projects such as FHCV's work related to men's health, and the publication of the first-ever North Carolina Men's Health Report Card (Figure 6.1).

Addressing Access to Care Through Practice and Policy

Lack of continuous insurance coverage was, and continues to be, an issue for many children and adults in North Carolina. For every person without health insurance coverage, there are as many as 2.3 persons without dental health insurance coverage. Mental health parity was only implemented as recently as July 2008. FirstHealth, in collaboration with FHCV, endeavored to address these issues in the development of a health insurance model.

FirstPlan. In 2001, in response to requests from small business owners for FirstHealth to assist them in providing affordable coverage for their employees, FirstHealth and independent surveyors collected and analyzed a variety of local data through interviews and formal surveys of area residents, business owners, and physicians to develop a keener understanding of the issue. Key findings of this assessment revealed the following:

- Seventeen percent of respondents aged eighteen to sixty-four reported having no health coverage; of those without coverage, 13.5 percent report said they had never had insurance coverage.
- Respondents with the lowest income levels reported the highest rate of uninsurance.
- Those without health coverage reported lower rates of preventive health screenings and dental care.
- Almost 17 percent of minorities reported needing routine health care but were unable to obtain it due to cost of insurance.

FIGURE 6.1. MEN'S HEALTH REPORT CARD.

In addition, FirstHealth learned through a telephone survey conducted during the same time period that 90 percent of the area's businesses were considered small businesses (fifty or fewer employees), and nearly half of their workforce was uninsured.

With the understanding that providing health insurance to the uninsured is a benefit to individuals, health care providers, and ultimately communities, FirstHealth developed an innovative, community-based approach to insuring the working uninsured through FirstCarolinaCare, the organization's wholly-owned, not-for-profit health management organization (HMO) subsidiary. FirstCarolinaCare's insurance portfolio, FirstPlan, is a result of efforts to identify efficient ways to pay for care, emphasize prevention, and develop a model of shared responsibility (Figure 6.2). FirstPlan offers interactive orientations for new enrollees to ensure a comprehensive understanding of benefits through health fairs, screenings, and disease management services. To ensure maximum participation and affordability, FirstHealth provides subsidies to employees earning less than $10 per hour and "CareCredits," which reduce employer premiums during the rating process within regulatory parameters. As the total financial benefit is realized, the subsidy funds have been "recycled" to expand the scope of the program by offering more subsidies to more employees. A number of factors contribute to the sustainability of FirstPlan, including 100 percent participation requirements, health care provider concessions, and moderate medical management.

FirstPlan enrolled nearly 2,500 workers and dependents from 180 local businesses, with 20 percent of those covered having been previously uninsured. To ensure affordability, more than 250 FirstPlan members received premium subsidies, and 90 businesses received CareCredits. In addition to providing health coverage to many in need, FirstPlan has also provided numerous insights into the feasibility of covering the uninsured through nongovernmental coverage.

FirstHealth and FirstCarolinaCare found that the uninsured do not seem to exhibit pent-up demand; utilization of services is similar among newly insured and previously insured individuals. This was consistent with FirstHealth's premise that the uninsured can be covered by a privately operated health plan, while maintaining financial solvency, and disproves participating physicians' initial fears that they would be "overwhelmed with previously uninsured patients."

The need for premium subsidies was also tested and, on the basis of FirstHealth's experience, it was determined that subsidies were not critical to enrolling the uninsured. This was due, primarily, to plan affordability, employer contributions, and the attainment of the "critical mass" of enrollees necessary to achieve a more balanced risk pool. Despite these findings, FirstHealth still considers that subsidies will likely be a necessary continuous requirement for certain populations. Though, subsidy costs are offset by premiums received and, through the 100 percent participation requirement linked to subsidy provision, larger pools of insured have led to stabilization of overall coverage.

In 2005, FirstHealth implemented another initiative, CoverMoore, to continue to expand coverage for the working uninsured. FirstHealth partnered with the Moore County Chamber of Commerce to develop the CoverMoore initiative, which targeted small businesses that were members of the Chamber of Commerce and that employed fifty people or fewer. The lessons learned from FirstPlan were applied in the

FIGURE 6.2. HEALTH INSURANCE AT FIRSTHEALTH.

FIRSTHEALTH COMMUNITY VOICES
FACT SHEET

 A Community-Based Model To
Cover The Working Uninsured

Working
Uninsured

FirstHealth of the Carolinas (FirstHealth) is a not-for-profit health care system serving a largely rural 15-county area in the mid-Carolinas. In 2001, FirstHealth conducted a survey of small businesses and determined that nearly 50 percent of small business employees surveyed did not have health coverage, primarily due to high cost. In response, FirstHealth through its wholly owned subsidiary FirstCarolinaCare Inc., developed FirstPlan, a health coverage product designed to be more affordable for small business employers and employees. FirstCarolinaCare is fully licensed by the N.C. Department of Insurance.

SHARED RESPONSIBILITY MODEL

FirstPlan is a special health care coverage product for businesses with 50 or fewer employees. FirstPlan is a community-based model, which consists of the following partners:
*   Health system – which accepts reduced reimbursement, grants and subsidy funding
*   Physician network – which agrees to reduced reimbursement and medical management model
*   Insurer – which provides infrastructure and education component to implement the product
*   Small businesses – which provide premium contributions and plan participation

FirstPlan offers incentives and final premium adjustments called CareCredits to employers currently without coverage. In order to balance the risk pool, FirstPlan requires all small businesses to have 100 percent coverage for eligible employees to qualify for the CareCredits. The employee must be covered through a spouse's plan, by government insurance or by FirstPlan.

Employees earning $10/hour or less may qualify for financial assistance with a portion of their premium costs subsidized.

PROGRESS TO DATE

As of September 2005, FirstPlan's enrollment covered 160 businesses with 2,400 members. Items of note include:
*   Close to 20 percent of FirstPlan membership was previously uninsured
*   Almost 11 percent of members are subsidized
*   Virtually 100 percent of network physicians agreed to accept the reduced reimbursement arrangement

BLUEPRINT FOR SUCCESS

FirstPlan is an innovative small business insurance model that provides increased access and affordability for the working uninsured. We encourage other organizations to implement a local solution for their communities. Through implementation of the product several lessons have been learned that should be taken into consideration when implementing a plan:
*   The community should be engaged to include brokers, businesses, leaders and physicians
*   Shared responsibility for the community works
*   The 100 percent participation requirement mirrored universal coverage on a private sector level
*   Subsidy is not always needed for participation
*   Initial health screenings assisted in early diagnosis and relationship building
*   There was lower pent up demand than initially expected
*   Continued education for small business owners and employees a must

FirstHealth believes if everyone is covered, everyone wins.

For more information, contact FirstHealth Community Voices at (877) 342-2255.   944-174-5

development of CoverMoore to include balancing the risk and eliminating adverse selection through the 100 percent participation requirement. CoverMoore offered four coverage options: a tiered network plan (HMO), a health savings account (HSA), a deductible plan with copays, and a copay plan.

In order to offer reduced premiums, 400 previously uninsured individuals were needed to fund the initiative and offset the costs. After an aggressive marketing campaign, CoverMoore was able to enroll only 130 previously uninsured individuals, and ultimately CoverMoore was not launched. However, valuable lessons were learned:

- The plan might have been more successful had it been more simple and affordable.
- There was confusion about whether the product was only meant for the uninsured.
- The target of four hundred created a "wait and see" attitude.
- There was uncertainty regarding plan sustainability.
- There was a lack of trust and understanding regarding the value of insurance coverage.
- The plan was not profitable for brokers to promote due to low interest.
- Small business owners hesitated to add the expense to their personal income.
- Similar to FirstPlan, there was no pent-up demand from the community for coverage.

But, most important, as became the norm for FHCV and FirstHealth, the previous work in practice led to important policy decisions at the state level. Due to FirstHealth's local experience, policymakers invited FirstHealth to educate state legislators on the need for further investigation of health care coverage issues, which in turn played a role in the development of a new North Carolina Health Care Study Committee that met prior to the start of the short legislative session in May 2006. The study committee, which had six subcommittees (Medicaid, Cost of Insurance for Employees and Employers, Patient Safety & Accountability, Health Care Workforce, Access to Health Care, and State Health Plan), provided recommendations that were debated and voted on during the 2007 legislative session. As a result, the North Carolina House of Representatives Health Care Committee championed legislation to develop a High Risk Health Insurance Pool to assist with coverage for North Carolina citizens.

Oral Health. In 1997, FirstHealth school nurses based in Moore County working in collaboration with a local school system identified dental care as the most pressing health need among low-income students. When a local task force composed of dental care providers, public health officials, educators, parents, and community representatives convened and assessed local data, this premise was confirmed.

In recognition that a local solution needed to be developed, particularly in light of the existing strains on the public oral health infrastructure in North Carolina and the lack of providers willing to accept Medicaid or Health Choice (North Carolina's Children's Health Insurance Program—CHIP) given low reimbursement rates, the task force recommended that FirstHealth lead efforts to address unmet dental needs of the estimated twelve thousand underserved children in the region.

The initial reaction of FirstHealth's leadership to this suggestion was a simple statement—"We don't do dental." But after further evaluation of both the need and the potential viability of numerous service delivery models, FirstHealth's leaders reassessed their position and determined that, unless FirstHealth acted, thousands of children in the region would remain without dental care (Figure 6.3).

Given this, FirstHealth and its partners determined that the establishment of a "public health" center that maintained a "private practice" setting offered the greatest opportunity for meeting the unique needs of the region while developing a sustainable model of dental care delivery. With this model identified, FirstHealth worked with unwavering commitment to ensure not only that a state-of-the-art dental care center was established in Moore County, where the need had initially been identified, but that two additional centers were established in neighboring counties to further expand access and meet local needs.

The result has been that Dental Care Centers which focus on education, prevention, treatment, and emergent care have been established in three counties where eligible patients up to age eighteen are treated. For very young children requiring complex treatment, referrals are made to pediatric dentists. Eligibility for free or reduced school lunches, based on a scale of 200 percent of the poverty line or below, makes many of these children eligible for treatment with public dollars, whereas patients with private insurance are referred to private practices.

The program is designed to provide cutting-edge health materials, implement preventive programs, and reduce access barriers to dental care, such as lack of health care coverage, transportation problems, and the relative less importance afforded to dental health. FirstHealth adopted an institutional policy to ensure that those eligible for publicly funded health care, including both dental and medical coverage, obtain it. Staff members personally assist families in completing financial assistance applications. Patients who remain uninsured are asked to make a low per-visit copayment, which may be waived in cases of financial hardship, establishing value for the services rendered.

The impact of this work has been significant. In fiscal year 2005, 4,500 (44 percent) of the region's Medicaid-eligible children were served by the FirstHealth Dental Care Centers, approximately one-third of whom had never seen a dentist before. According to random chart reviews, 61 percent of the children for which care was provided demonstrated improvements in overall dental health; 51 percent improved gingivitis scores; and, 62 percent improved calculus scores. Due to continued enforcement of patient appointment policies, the centers' no-show appointment rate is a mere 16 percent, a figure far below the national average of 30 percent.

FirstHealth continues to offer services to underserved children through the FirstHealth Dental Health Centers. In the meantime, there is still a need in the FirstHealth communities regarding access to oral health care for adults. Through its

FIGURE 6.3. FIRSTHEALTH FACT SHEET ON ORAL HEALTH.

FIRSTHEALTH COMMUNITY VOICES
FACT SHEET

Shortage of Dental Health Professionals
Heightens Disparities in Care

Dental

BACKGROUND

FirstHealth of the Carolinas (FirstHealth) is a not-for-profit health system serving a largely rural 15-county area in the mid-Carolinas. FirstHealth is concerned by the evidence that the burden of oral diseases and disorders is falling disproportionately on lower-income families and individuals, particularly in rural areas. One of the reasons for this disparity is the overall shortage of dental professionals in rural areas of North Carolina, as well as the shortage of dental professionals willing to serve Medicaid patients. That is why FirstHealth established three dental care centers for low-income and Medicaid-eligible children, serving an average of 1,000 children a month. However, the situation remains serious for low-income and uninsured adults and children in many areas of the state.

STATE AND LOCAL FACTS

- Only one in five North Carolina dentists treats 10 or more Medicaid patients per quarter.
- 2001-2002 statistics indicate that 24 percent of North Carolina children entering kindergarten have untreated tooth decay, a percentage that has remained stable over the last several years.
- North Carolina has 41 dentists per 100,000 persons, compared to a national average of 60 per 100,000.
- According to a professionally conducted community health survey performed for FirstHealth, only 43 percent of low-income adults visited a dentist or dental clinic within the last year.
- Within the FirstHealth service area, Anson, Hoke, Montgomery, Richmond and Robeson counties are federally designated dental professional shortage areas for services to low-income groups.

OTHER KEY FACTS

- Statistics indicate that since 1990 the number of dentists per 100,000 persons has been in decline nationally.
- Minority racial and ethnic groups are severely underrepresented in the dental profession as compared to their representation in the general population.
- An estimated 22.5 million Americans need and cannot obtain dental care.
- Preventable dental disease costs the United States billions of dollars in productivity due to time lost at work and school.

POLICY RECOMMENDATIONS

- Increase the diversity, capacity and flexibility of the dental health workforce by increasing dental school enrollment and more effectively utilizing "dentist extenders." One proposal by the American Dental Hygienists Association is to create an advanced dental hygiene practitioner position to expand the role of the dental hygienist as an important provider of preventive dental care.
- Encourage current dentists to open their practices to more Medicaid patients by improving Medicaid reimbursement for dental services.
- At the state and national level, provide development funds and grants for community health care providers to establish preventive care centers along the model of the FirstHealth Dental Care Centers.

For more information, contact Community Voices Project Director Lisa Hartsock at (877) 342-2255 or lhartsock@firsthealth.org

relationship with the University of North Carolina (UNC) Dental School, FirstHealth has organized adult oral health screening events in the community. One success in this area was FirstHealth's implementation of a voucher program for dental care needs in Montgomery County. Other plans include expanding the scope of services of the FirstHealth Montgomery Dental Care Center to include afternoon hours, targeting treatment services for the adult Medicaid population.

Men's Health. Men's health in North Carolina pales in comparison to national averages for men, and numerous health indicators point in worrisome directions. North Carolina men have higher mortality rates for heart disease, stroke, cancers, and diabetes. The disparity for men of color in North Carolina is even greater. In response to these issues, FHCV worked to increase awareness of men's health issues at both local and state levels as well as to implement specifically targeted programs through FirstHealth.

One of the ways in which FHCV sought to educate local and state leaders was by improving upon the dearth of data that existed regarding men's health in North Carolina, the result of which was the first North Carolina Men's Health Report Card (Figure 6.4).

The report card compares North Carolina men past to present and North Carolina men present to U.S. men present. The men's health report card trended data from past to current to determine the movement of indicators with letter grades assigned to each. Health categories that were graded include chronic disease, infectious disease, substance abuse and mental health, violence or injuries, barriers to health, and preventive health practices. The intent of this data was to raise awareness about men's health issues and begin the discussion at the state level on how to establish health care safety nets for men, secure funding for men's health initiatives, and establish datasets that could be monitored for improvement in trends.

The first report card of 2007 indicated that North Carolina men had higher mortality rates than U.S. men due to strokes, chronic lower respiratory disease, prostate cancer, and diabetes, the latter especially prevalent in men of color, though diabetes is on the rise in general for men of this state. Even though the rates of tobacco use showed a decline from past to present, North Carolina men still exhibited higher rates of tobacco use than U.S. men, and they were uninsured at higher rates than uninsured U.S. men. Finally, although the data also revealed that North Carolina men were participating at an average rate for preventive health screenings, they had higher rates of mortality due to chronic diseases.

In programming, FHCV developed a safety net initiative for formerly incarcerated men, men's health week activities, and a grassroots outreach program. These initial activities culminated in FirstHealth's organization of the first Statewide Men's Health Summit, held in January 2007. Local, state, and national partner organizations were represented on the summit planning committee, including the American Heart Association, the American Cancer Society, the North Carolina Office of Minority Health and Health Disparities, the North Carolina Institute of Minority Economic Development, the North Carolina Comprehensive Cancer Program, and the Men's Health Network. The goals of the summit were

- To define and increase overall awareness of North Carolina men's health issues
- To share what is happening at the national level with men's health issues

FIGURE 6.4. MEN'S HEALTH REPORT CARD DATA.

North Carolina Men's Health

Chronic Disease

	NC Men 1999-2000	NC Men 2000-2004	Trend	US Men 2003	Grade
Heart disease deaths per 100,000					
All	314.4	294.5	C	286.6	C
White	307.3	285.2	C	282.9	C
Minority	343.4	336.5	C	301.4	D
Cerebrovascular disease deaths per 100,000					
All	74.6	68.6	C	54.1	F
White	69.2	63.0	C	51.7	F
Minority	99.2	94.9	C	64.1	F
Lung cancer deaths per 100,000					
All	88.9	86.6	C	71.7	F
White	86.8	84.3	C	71.1	D
Minority	97.9	96.6	C	75.1	F
Chronic lower respiratory disease deaths per 100,000					
All	63.1	60.9	C	52.3	D
White	64.7	62.6	C	53.8	D
Minority	54.7	51.6	C	39.1	F
Diabetes deaths per 100,000					
All	27.8	30.0	C	28.9	C
White	22.9	24.9	C	27.0	C
Minority	50.2	54.6	C	42.0	F
Colorectal cancer deaths per 100,000					
All	23.2	22.8	C	22.9	C
White	21.9	21.4	C	22.4	C
Minority	29.2	29.0	C	26.2	D
Prostate cancer deaths per 100,000					
All	33.5	31.6	C	26.5	D
White	26.5	24.8	C	24.4	C
Minority	68.4	67.2	C	43.2	F

	2002	2005		2005	
Percentage aged 18+ with diabetes					
All	6.4%	8.5%	F	8.0%	C
White	6.0%	8.2%	F	7.7%	C
African American	9.9%	12.8%	F	11.0%	D
Percentage aged 18+ who are obese (BMI 30.0+)					
All	23.5%	25.3%	C	24.8%	C
White	21.7%	24.7%	D	24.5%	C
African American	28.4%	31.0%	C	29.9%	C
Percentage told by a doctor that they have asthma					
All	9.3%	8.3%	B	10.5%	A
White	9.8%	8.5%	B	10.7%	A
African American	10.3%	10.3%	C	10.9%	C

	2003	2005		2005	
Percentage aged 18+ with high blood pressure					
All	27.2%	28.0%	C	26.2%	C
White	26.1%	28.1%	C	26.8%	C
African American	35.4%	36.7%	C	31.2%	D
Percentage aged 18+ with high cholesterol					
All	33.2%	36.0%	C	37.2%	C
White	34.6%	36.8%	C	38.2%	C
African American	32.6%	36.7%	D	31.5%	D

- To start the conversation on establishing safety nets for North Carolina men
- To define what is currently available to men and determine what programs are successful at the local level to further refine initiatives that may work at the state level

With a target audience that included public health officials, state-level public health leaders, grassroots organizations, policymakers, legislators, and health professionals, the summit was the first statewide effort to broaden the discussion of men's

When challenged to work in the area of men's health, we immediately began researching the policies and available data as well as seeking out other advocates interested in the issue. However, the search turned up empty as there was little attention, interest, and momentum at the local and state levels for men's health. We noticed, by contrast, that there were plenty of data on women and resources and programs abounded for the same. The state had published report cards benchmarking various health indicators and formulating policy agendas in accordance with data indicators and access to care barriers for women, children, and minorities. Seeing this, we determined that the only way to begin to place men's health on the "map" was to produce a report card to determine the health issues and barriers to care for men in North Carolina.

We realized that to obtain the level of data needed to complete such a project, assistance would be needed from a state data source. As such, FHCV approached the University of North Carolina Shep Center to determine its interest in assisting with the project. In the initial meeting, we were told that there was no need for such a report card, and that it would only place people on the defensive if policy recommendations were made for men's health. We persisted, stressing that the purpose of the report card was to determine the status of men's health in North Carolina and to utilize the data to define the health issues and share with policymakers to determine how best to address these. Following the meeting, staff at the Shep Center "googled" "men's health report cards" and got zero hits; they then googled "women's health report cards" and got more than a thousand hits. After this realization, the Shep Center provided in-kind services to assist FHCV with data analysis. In addition to the Shep Center, we sought feedback on the report card methodology from the North Carolina Office of Minority Health and Health Disparities and the North Carolina Department of Health and Human Services.

The 2007 North Carolina Men's Health Report Card placed men's health as a priority issue at the state level. During the long legislative session of 2009, an Office of Men's Health bill was introduced at the state level. When the bill was in drafting, the state contacted FHCV for input on best-practice language for such an office. The state budget crisis took hold during the session, and the bill did not pass committee. However, it can still be addressed in short session 2010. In addition, the North Carolina Office of Minority Health and Health Disparities is considering publishing pull-out sections of the major chronic diseases to compare minority women to minority men. This would continue to steer resources and programs to the population with the greatest need.

—Roxanne Leopper, policy director, FirstHealth of the Carolinas health issues across North Carolina. In addition, FirstHealth used the summit as a platform at which to unveil the Men's Health Report Card.

The decision to time the release of the first Men's Health Report Card together with the inaugural Men's Health Summit was by design. Knowing that the there was an upcoming long North Carolina legislative session in 2007, this provided an opportunity to educate and inform policymakers about the issues of men's health in the state prior to the beginning of the session. It was decisions such as these that would mark FHCV as an astute strategist in placing unlikely concerns such as men's health and tobacco at the center of discussions in the state's Congress.

FHCV was also keen about inserting itself into nongovernment communities such as academia, understanding the power of education as a force of its own in dissemination of knowledge about the issues. So in addition to the report card and the men's health summit, FHCV accepted an invitation to serve as a preceptor for the North Carolina School of Public Health Action-Oriented Community Diagnosis course. Because of the strong work that FHCV had developed in unveiling men's health issues, it was determined that the topic for Moore County would be men of color in Moore County.

In leading the course, FHCV was assigned a team of five public health masters students to develop the work during two semesters. The students were responsible for assimilating into the Moore County community and for conducting one-on-one interviews and focus group meetings, culminating in a final report of the findings presented at a community meeting. FHCV worked closely with the students and community both during the study and after in order to implement program recommendations in Moore County.

A key result of these efforts was that a formal group of African American men from Moore County—*Coming Together for Moore*—assembled and meet on a regular basis to tackle five core community issues: health care, employment, family and youth, education, and race relations. FHCV continues to serve as a resource to the group on health care initiatives.

Reentry. Through a special partnership with JobLink, a part of the Employment Security Commission, FHCV has been able to provide resources to formerly incarcerated people (FIP) in a community environment. Services provided via a resource coordinator include medication assistance, health system navigation, and linkages to community resources; all FIP are referred to local JobLink programs upon reentry.

FHCV has been an effective partner for JobLink by contributing to outreach and branding needs for the organization. Other partners at the JobLink include the Chamber of Commerce, the School System, the Community College, and the local Vocational Rehabilitation program, the Housing Authority, Partners in Progress, the

Literacy Council, and Communities in Schools. The collaborative functions as a partnership and works to meet individual program goals as well as overall program goals for the JobLink.

On a more individual level, FHCV began working with a small core group of previously incarcerated men who volunteered to establish themselves as mentors to assist young at-risk men. Working from the premise that positive role models are a protective factor for at-risk youth, the mentors recruited a small cohort of young men facing challenges with education, the justice system, and employment. To date, the young men brought to the program are aiming to earn their GEDs and moving forward with new employment possibilities.

Mental Health. The climate of mental health care in North Carolina has been in transition for some time. The entire North Carolina Division of Mental Health/Developmental Disabilities/Substance Abuse Services is undergoing a transformation referred to in the state as Mental Health Reform.

The state is broken into several regions for mental health care, with each region categorized as a Local Management Entity (LME). Previously, the LMEs were responsible for providing mental health care and services to the uninsured and underserved. Upon the implementation of statewide reform, however, all LMEs were ordered to divest of services and become management entities by contracting work to local mental health professionals to include social workers. This process has resulted in program budget cuts, access issues, and a reduction of state hospital beds and facilities. As a result, state legislators have convened a study commission on Mental Health to analyze the effects of reform and provide state-level budget and program recommendations to ensure the success of the same. Nonconcurrent funds have been designated to pilot programs in the state; however, reform remains a challenge, and barriers to care are increasing for the uninsured (Figure 6.5).

Given this context, FHCV focused on two strategies related to access to mental health care. FHCV knew through its ongoing assessment within the community that mental health needs were underserved, with access to care as a primary barrier for local residents. Mental health screenings with appropriate providers are limited, and services are often inaccessible or not available. In the expansion of the services for the mobile health van operated by FirstHealth's Community Health Services division, mental health screenings became an important consideration, and the organization sought to provide additional services in partnership with other community partners.

An additional possibility for providing mental health screenings for the underserved was a joint venture with FirstHealth of the Carolinas and the Moore County "Free Clinic." This "Free Clinic" is operated through private grants and staffed with

FIGURE 6.5. MENTAL HEALTH FACT SHEET.

FIRSTHEALTH COMMUNITY VOICES FACT SHEET
Mental Health Reform Efforts Pose Challenges

Mental Health

BACKGROUND

FirstHealth of the Carolinas (FirstHealth) is a not-for-profit health system serving a largely rural 15-county area in the mid-Carolinas. In 2003, FirstHealth commissioned a survey of adult residents in its service area to determine health status, behaviors and needs in a defined region. The survey area included Moore, Hoke, Montgomery and Richmond counties, as well as the Pembroke area of Robeson County. As described below, responses to questions about mental health status suggest that providing adequate access to mental health services should be a high priority for local and state policy makers and health agencies.

LOCAL FACTS

- Almost one quarter of those surveyed reported three or more days in the past month when their mental health was not good (national rate is 18.7 percent).
- Nearly 30 percent reported two or more years in their lives when they have felt depressed or sad on most days (national rate is 22 percent).
- Forty-two percent reported that they have experienced feeling worried, tense or anxious for three or more days in the past month.
- Eleven percent report indulging in binge drinking (five or more drinks on a single occasion).

STATE FACTS

In 2002, the N.C. legislature mandated that the state's public mental health system undergo reform requiring divestiture of most state-run mental health services while imposing responsibility for provision of services on community-based private providers. However, many communities do not have sufficient mental health resources to provide adequate services.

- The United States Bureau of Primary Healthcare has designated 97 out of 100 counties in North Carolina as underserved for mental health services (at least in part).
- Studies indicate a severe maldistribution of physicians providing psychiatric services in the state, with rural areas in particular being chronically underserved.
- Results of a joint Division of Mental Health, Developmental Disabilities and Substance Abuse/ North Carolina Hospital Association task force indicate that many community hospitals lack sufficient resources to take on inpatient psychiatric services that were previously provided by state facilities.

POLICY RECOMMENDATIONS

- Ensure that state budgets allocate sufficient funds to the local communities to support local providers' efforts to provide needed mental health services.
- Develop a long-range strategy for increasing the range of services available in communities.
- Carefully monitor reform implementation to ensure that the burden of providing services is not shifted to private providers before an adequate community care delivery system is in place.
- Ensure that local management entities collaborate with key community providers.
- Provide incentives to community hospitals to add or expand inpatient services.

For more information, contact Community Voices Project Director Lisa Hartsock at (877) 342-2255 or lhartsock@firsthealth.org   1056-174-4

---

local volunteers. Current services provided at the clinic are based on a primary care model with non-acute emergency services available on a limited basis. Mental health services were not originally included in this clinic but recently have been added. With the commitment of FirstHealth's Behavioral Services and the skills and availability of the Behavioral Services Assessment Team, a skilled nurse clinician was employed at this site to conduct mental health screenings in this venue.

Changing Policy

A key to FHCV's success was the understanding that local communities have the ability to address policy at the organizational level, which can, in turn, influence statewide policy. Capitalizing on this knowledge, FHCV worked slowly and steadily, first with local community groups, showcasing promising practices regularly as these arose. Through its persistent efforts in both practice and collaboration, FHCV is now a role model for policy change in tobacco policy and oral health.

Tobacco Policy

FirstHealth of the Carolinas was the first health care system in North Carolina to adopt a tobacco-free-campus policy. As a leader in this work, FirstHealth has developed resource materials and implementation guidelines to assist other health systems and organizations to establish the same. It has assisted three out of four counties in their adoption of a gold standard tobacco-free school campus policy. FHCV has also worked at the state level to educate policymakers about the dangers of secondhand smoke and the benefits of the tobacco-free policy in all public places. Becoming a role model for other organizations, this work developed into a statewide initiative led by North Carolina Prevention Partners, a formal statewide organization dedicated to improving health prevention practices and access throughout North Carolina, with FirstHealth in an advisory capacity (Figure 6.6).

However, change did not come easily. Influencing policy takes time, particularly at multiple levels including local, state, and federal policy. But influencing tobacco policy in a state notorious for its tobacco production and consumption was trailblazing!

In 2005, as other states around the country adopted smoke-free policies, North Carolina still had rules on the books that designated 25 percent of every state building for smoking. In state legislative buildings, smoking was still allowed; citizens and employees were permitted to smoke at health departments; and a law referred to as "preemption" deemed that local governments could not make stronger policy than state government, hence eliminating any option for local control. In addition, North Carolina had the second-to-lowest excise tax on cigarettes in the country at 5 cents per pack despite scientific evidence proving that for every 10 percent increase in product pricing, the percentage of youth decrease in smoking was even greater.

In the context of FHCV's work—and in great measure because of it—the landscape on tobacco policy in North Carolina has changed dramatically over the past few years. Several initiatives have been implemented statewide by individual systems, such as hospitals and schools adopting tobacco-free policies. The establishment of a "gold standard" has become equivalent with no smoking on campus grounds, in vehicles, or

FIGURE 6.6. INCREASING THE COSTS OF CIGARETTES: TOBACCO PREVENTION POLICY BRIEF.

FIRSTHEALTH COMMUNITY VOICES FACT SHEET

 Increasing the Cost of Cigarettes
A Barrier to Start, a Motivator to Quit

Tobacco Statistics

DEFINING THE ISSUE – NORTH CAROLINA TOBACCO STATISTICS

Tobacco products cause a wide range of health problems, including heart disease, stroke, lung cancer, emphysema and asthma. According to the Centers for Disease Control (CDC), tobacco-related health care expenses cost North Carolina $1.9 billion per year, including more than $600 million in Medicaid costs. North Carolina counties spent $30 million in 2003 on smoking-related costs for Medicaid patients.

Almost 25 percent of North Carolinians smoke tobacco products regularly. Every day, 3,000 teens start smoking in the United States – which translates to 24,000 North Carolina children per year. Thirty-four percent of North Carolina's high school students use tobacco products; 27.3 percent smoke cigarettes. Of those students, half of those who continue to smoke will die prematurely of tobacco-related illness.

WHAT CAN BE DONE?

Numerous studies by the CDC and other professional health organizations have shown that there is a significant decrease in smoking overall and an even larger percentage decrease in youth smoking for every 10 percent increase in the price of cigarettes. One of the most effective ways to prevent and reduce tobacco use by youth is to substantially raise the cost of cigarettes.

HEALTH EFFECTS OF RAISING THE COST OF TOBACCO

Increase the cost by	Reduce Youth Smoking	Fewer Adult Smokers	Fewer Future Youth Smokers	Prevent Premature Deaths	Fewer Smoking Harmed Births	Save In Long-term Health Care Costs
45-cents	9.4 percent	33,900	60,900	28,300	1,580	$282.2 million
70-cents	16.1 percent	70,000	105,750	47,700	2,630	$1.15 billion

IN SUMMARY

North Carolina is not the first state to face the issue of raising the cost of tobacco products. In the past two years, 37 other states have raised the costs of cigarettes. All other tobacco-producing states in the Southeast have either already raised the cost of cigarettes or are seeking to do so in 2005. Evidence-based research supports the fact that increasing the cost of cigarettes can be a barrier to youth smoking and a motivator for smokers to quit.

For more information, contact the FirstHealth Community Voices Project at (877) 342-2255.   522-174-5

---

at organizational events. Through a number of campaigns FHCV made inroads in changing attitudes toward tobacco. For example, working with Teens Against Tobacco Use and Tobacco Reality Unfiltered youth groups, FHCV trained youth regarding the dangers of tobacco, the addiction patterns, and the harmful effects of secondhand smoke. Having developed their own organic leadership, youths hold events in their communities to further educate other youths on tobacco realities.

FHCV also took the lead in launching a smoke-free dining campaign to educate local restaurant and business owners on the dangers of secondhand smoke and the advantages of a smoke-free policy. Products including receipt stickers, fact sheets, window decals, and certificates of recognition were developed (Figure 6.7). As a result of FHCV's campaign, a number of local restaurants adopted a tobacco-free policy.

At the state level, FirstHealth has worked diligently in collaboration with the North Carolina Alliance for Health to change state-level environmental tobacco policy. This, in combination with FHCV's local level successes, yielded significant results. Between 2005 and 2007, several policy changes were implemented at the state level:

1. Health departments can adopt smoke-free policy to extend fifty feet beyond the door.
2. The state government legislative building declared smoke-free policy in 2006.
3. The state prison adopted smoke-free policy effective 2008; five prisons piloted smoking cessation programs in 2007.
4. A statewide quit line was established.

FIGURE 6.7. MOORE COUNTY SMOKE-FREE DINING CERTIFICATE.

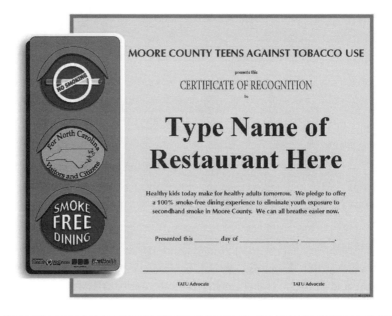

5. Two bills were introduced proposing a statewide smoking ban in restaurants. Both failed by narrow margins, though the bills made history in North Carolina nonetheless.
6. All state government buildings became smoke-free effective 2007.
7. All University of North Carolina campuses adopted smoke-free policies effective 2007.
8. All community colleges have been given the right to adopt campuswide tobacco-free policy.
9. North Carolina's excise tax increased from $.05 per pack to $.35 per pack.

In North Carolina, the "chipping away" method proved an effective technique in changing environmental tobacco policy one step at a time. Continued efforts were focused on overturning "preemption" and establishing a statewide smoking ban in all public places. Persistence paid off at the state level. North Carolina passed a law in 2009 (effective January 2010) stating that all restaurants and bars that serve food and are inspected by health departments will be smoke-free. In addition, the law provides a provision for local governments to make stronger smoke-free policy to further protect workers from exposure to secondhand smoke. Though real heroic efforts made change possible, further reform on tobacco policy in tobacco country remains a challenge, with a continued need for additional education for both the public and the policymakers to implement best practices to protect all workers and public places from secondhand smoke.

Oral Health Policy

In addition to the preventive and educational programs directly targeting its local population of underserved children, FHCV led a policy initiative with state partners to inform decision makers on the need for oral health reform.

On May 25, 2000, the U.S. Surgeon General, David Satcher, M.D., released the nation's first comprehensive review of scientific literature on the state of oral health. The national attention given to this report was a significant step in addressing the severity of dental disease and inaccessibility of dental care for uninsured and underserved populations across the nation.

The Surgeon General's report succeeded in redefining the traditional concept of oral health, with the study not only addressing problems such as tooth decay and the disproportionate suffering of some groups but also highlighting the association between oral health problems and general health, and the need to view oral health as a component of total wellness. FHCV was present at the release of this report and served as a topic expert for a call-in program following the presentation.

FHCV also continued to provide leadership in national efforts to improve access to dental care for the underserved by serving on the Robert Wood Johnson (RWJ) Advisory Board at the University of North Carolina for the Pipeline, Profession and Practice: Community Based Dental Education Grant 2002–2007. This program was designed to help increase access to dental care by increasing the recruitment and retention of low-income and underrepresented minority students in dental schools.

FHCV moreover is an active member of the North Institute of Medicine Dental Health Task Force. This task force meets periodically to update goals and objectives from a 1999 report, which includes recommendations for expanding care to rural areas, increasing the number of minority professionals, and increasing quality care. As a participant in this Task Force, FHCV has worked on key policy issues at the state level to include increased Medicaid reimbursement and implementation of licensure by credentials. Both policy changes have been fully implemented.

Of continuing interest is the dental school at Eastern Carolina University (ECU), which has a first graduating class target date of 2010. This dental school's focus is on training students who are interested in establishing rural-setting practices. The ECU dental school will establish rural dental clinics throughout the state for students to complete practical rotations. FHCV continues to watch this carefully, as the establishment of the program could provide opportunities to further focus on adult oral health care for the uninsured.

Informing National Policy

While FHCV's policy work was primarily at the state level, FHCV realized the importance of bringing the lessons learned to bear in national terms. One area in which this was critical was men's health. Working with national network agencies such as the Men's Health Network, FHCV worked with the Network to further outreach efforts in North Carolina, culminating in the first statewide summit on men's health in January 2007, discussed earlier. The Men's Health Network assisted with online registration technology, marketing efforts, and speaker recruitment. In return, FirstHealth provided the Men's Health Network with the opportunity to present to a statewide audience on national health issues pertaining to men, such as the establishment of a national Office of Men's Health. The Men's Health Network was able to provide best-practice models for states that have established commissions and committees on men's health.

In another national collaboration, FHCV worked with The Trust for America's Health (TFAH), a national organization that works on policy issues pertaining to obesity rates in America and is a resource for data and policy recommendations. FirstHealth has developed a working relationship with TFAH to address obesity in North Carolina. TFAH participated in keynote addresses at several meetings in North Carolina to lend guidance on policy recommendations and next steps for addressing this epidemic in the state.

Finally, FirstHealth has experienced the benefits of developing a certification course of study with a local community college for CHWs (called patient navigators) and then employing those CHWs /patient navigators at the local level. Through its work with Community Voices, an opportunity was presented to collaborate with a national network of CHWs to assist in establishing a National Association of Community Health Workers. This national association is working to professionalize the work of CHWs and is developing a code of ethics, bylaws, and guidelines, which will contribute to the institutionalization of the profession (Exhibit 6.1). FirstHealth specifically served on the policy subcommittee.

EXHIBIT 6.1. PROMISING PRACTICES.

"Bridging the Gap: Partnerships Between Dental Schools and Colleges to Produce a Workforce to Fully Serve American's Diverse Communities." "Bridging the Gap" was a policy brief developed by FHCV to showcase a model partnership between the University of North Carolina Dental School, the Robert Wood Johnson Dental Pipeline grant team, and the future East Carolina University Dental School program. The brief succeeded in bringing awareness not only to the partnership as a best practice but also to the health disparities in oral health care experienced by uninsured and underserved populations. Since then, this brief and other descriptive material regarding this model have been widely disseminated as a best-practice model for future curriculum development in North Carolina.

FirstQuit. FirstQuit is the tobacco-cessation program offered through FirstHealth. It is open to employees of the health system, volunteers, and community members. During the formation of the program, Community Health Services, a program of FirstHealth, researched best-practice models regarding nicotine replacement therapy methods and quit rates. The program currently offers one-on-one counseling, support groups, and group classes to assist with behavioral change. In addition, the nicotine replacement therapy offered includes patches, gum, and lozenges. Being sensitive to the issues of replacement therapy, physician referrals into the program are required if any replacement therapy is utilized by the patient. As a result of implementing evidenced-based quit techniques, the FirstQuit program six-month quit rate is 30 percent compared to the national average of 25 percent.

Community Health Workers. Because of the success of other community health worker (CHW) programs within the Community Voices initiative, FirstHealth developed a model certification program with a local community college. This course of study is a semester-long program offered through the Continuing Education department of the community college with administrators and superintendents of local health care and community agencies serving as the faculty for the program. The end result is currently twenty graduated CHWs, called patient navigators, who serve as "bridges" connecting their communities to health care and community resources.

Lessons Learned

Following a decade of work in the Community Voices initiative that resulted in en-hanced relationships and cutting-edge policy shifts, FHCV amassed a number of lessons that continue to inform its decisions and practices to this day.

- *Health insurance is a necessary but insufficient condition for access.* In FHCV's experience, it is clear that health insurance alone will not make health care accessible to the uninsured in North Carolina. Coverage strategies must be balanced with commu-nity-based access through primary care homes as well as case management for both private- and public-sector programs.
- *Mental health coverage and parity of services has road to travel.* Despite FHCV's best efforts, much more needs to be done regarding the deficit of knowledge regarding the concept of parity for mental health coverage.
- *Minority professionals are key to improving health care access and reducing health disparities for vulnerable populations.* In terms of continuing efforts to improve access to care in an increasingly diverse state, more efforts must be made to recruit and train minority health professionals. Through the work in North Carolina and other places it is well-documented that this practice has a local effect on access to care and is a key factor that may help curb health disparities in rural regions.
- *State and federal funding alike must be part of the formula for sustainability.* Despite the best community-driven efforts and successes in obtaining and providing health cover-age, both state and federal funding programs and partnerships must provide support.
- *Data are essential for policy change!* Data can, and did, drive the changes that occurred in North Carolina on the initial successes with tobacco as well as with oral health. Data collection, analysis, and evaluation are thus imperative in assessing needs, defining goals, targeting and effectively implementing programs, and establishing program successes. While much has been accomplished regarding men's health in the state of North Carolina, continuing to collect data regarding men's health in relation to health status, health care safety nets, health coverage, and access to care at both the state and federal levels will be critical in order to justify the funding of pilot programs at the local level and to establish a safety net for men. Public data and the dissemination of the same will be essential toward feeding the movement for men's health at the state and federal levels.
- *The power of collaboratives and partnerships must not be underestimated.* Working with local communities, collaboratives, and coalitions proved to be a beneficial strategy for advancing policy. FHCV learned quickly that individuals in collaboratives bring diverse skills to the table, which, when utilized efficiently, can play a key role

in stimulating policy changes. Partnering with local organizations such as the Department of Social Services, the Health Department, and provider offices to embed CHWs in those settings proved to be an efficient contribution in defining the integrated system of care.

Conclusion

FirstHealth's years of testing programs and new ways of working with community have resulted in a number of innovative programs and policies that have been adopted by the state of North Carolina. In addition, through its work with Community Voices, the perspectives and concerns of many layers of community, including the grassroots, are now regularly included in the mix of information considered by the health system as well as in the recommendations presented to local and state policymakers. As the work of FirstHealth of the Carolinas continues, FHCV's efforts have cemented its legacy, ensuring that the practice of caring for the community while educating policymakers about the gaps in coverage and access continues to be a part of the organization's work.

CHAPTER SEVEN

NORTHERN MANHATTAN COMMUNITY VOICES COLLABORATIVE

Forging Partnerships to Advance Social and Political Change and Drive Improvements in Health Care Access

Jacqueline Martinez and Allan J. Formicola

This chapter recounts the process through which the Northern Manhattan Community Voices Collaborative coalesced into a potent force devoted to improving access to health and social services for one of New York's poorest communities, while bringing attention to the underlying social and economic determinants of the public's health. After reading this chapter, the reader will

- Learn about how a highly diverse and dynamic collaborative was formed and sustained
- Learn about how to embed the valuable role of Community Health Workers to address underlying determinants of poor health outcomes
- Learn how to develop and integrate community outreach efforts to increase enrollment in public benefits and address other barriers to health care access
- Learn about promising practices in delivering difficult-to-cover services and informing policy to increase access to these services, specifically for dental and behavioral health services
- Learn about an insurance product to enroll uninsured people
- Learn about using a technology tool built to help navigate the health care system

Introduction

Northern Manhattan Community Voices was born within a larger movement toward reclaiming a hopeful vision for change and a rising wave of dissatisfaction with the status quo. Even though the economic upturn of the late 1990s had not reached the enclaves of northern Manhattan, the potential for change had nonetheless created an environment of high expectations for positive change and a restored vision for hope. Northern Manhattan, comprising two diverse neighborhoods, Harlem and Washington Heights, was slowly healing from a decade or more of community breakdown. Injured by the tumultuous years of the illicit drug industry and the associated violence of the crack cocaine epidemic, these two communities had reemerged determined and expectant of a new era for a future generation.

The resilience of the people, the families, the organizations, and the institutions became the foundation for a cadre of leaders to fight for—and demand—social and political action for change. And while this was all coupled by great financial need, what finally served as a platform for the success of the Community Voices initiative was the grounds of hope and determination and leadership on which the program began to spread its seeds. In an environment where so much need existed, an investment of $4.5 million could not have possibly served to permeate a far-reaching spread for program development and policy changes, yet the will superseded the need, and the investment became the backbone of a vision that had already been set forth by several community leaders and members.

The Northern Manhattan Community Voices Collaborative (NMCVC) was formed within this social dynamic. The real question was how to give a "voice" to this emerging movement for change and how to ensure that the voice would lead to action and action would lead to change. The first step was to identify individuals from the institutions and the community committed to improving the overall health of the community while strengthening the existing safety net providers. The initial collaborating forces that served as the lead organizations were Columbia University's College of Dental Medicine (formerly know as the School of Dental and Oral Surgery); Alianza Dominicana, a local community-based organization in the primary service of northern Manhattan's Dominican community; and Harlem Hospital.

A precursor to Community Voices, the Community DentCare initiative at Columbia University College of Dental Medicine had already begun to bear fruit and became the foundational concept for a wide-ranging partnership to address health concerns in the community. With a deeper understanding of its call to social responsibility and community engagement, Columbia was ready to take on bigger issues. Alianza Dominicana had already acquired fifteen years of experience as a social change agent. Having established respected programs in the community, Alianza had become a trusted and integral component of the fabric of Washington Heights. Harlem Hospital, a long-standing and historical medical facility, was under new leadership, and there was a willingness to raise the bar in the health care delivery for the neighborhood's residents.

After the initial and core partnership was agreed upon, the next important question was how this local partnership would respond to the overall goals and objectives of the call to action from the W.K. Kellogg Foundation's Community Voices initiative. Though in retrospect it may appear that the consensus process led to a clearly defined set of local goals and strategy, the reality was that this would prove to be one of the first strains on this newly formed partnership. But in the end there were four major systems changes that the NMCVC strove to initiate and sustain. They were

1. Enhance community-based primary care network services to include neighborhood-by-neighborhood health promotion and disease prevention efforts
2. Extend outreach to increase enrollment in Medicaid and Child Health Plus
3. Improve the provider network's capacity to offer targeted services for difficult-to-cover services, including dental services and behavioral and mental health services
4. Develop and implement an insurance product to enroll more of the uninsured

The overall mission for the collaboration was to promote systems change to focus on disease prevention and create a system shift toward wellness-in-health care delivery.

A Look into the "Community"

Northern Manhattan is an area of 7.3 square miles with a population of approximately 452,000. Though the area is largely composed of low-income, working class families, the racial and ethnic populations of the two neighborhoods that make up northern Manhattan are quite different. Harlem historically has been an African American community with clusters of Puerto Rican families situated in East Harlem, which was affectionately known to its residents as "El Barrio." Washington Heights, on the other hand, historically has been populated mostly by Latino immigrants, hailing from the Dominican Republic, Puerto Rico, Cuba, and most recently Central America. As of the 2000 Census, the demographic breakdown of these two neighborhoods is 51 percent Latino, 36 percent African American, and another 4 percent who report two or more racial or ethnic identities.

If northern Manhattan were considered a city it would be the twenty-second largest in the country, just ahead of Seattle. As a city within a city, northern Manhattan boasts significant assets—most of which are founded in the historically diverse populations that have called this community home. These range from a strong reputation in setting cultural and artistic trends, especially in music, fashion, and dance; a "gateway" location at the hub of multiple transportation systems and an intersecting point for the neighboring state of New Jersey; and a diverse labor pool, 27 percent of which is bilingual, reflecting the diversity of New York City and the country's future consumer and labor markets.

Yet even with this rich, diverse history, northern Manhattan has also experienced its share of social unrest, political neglect, and economic woes—all of which have contributed, in part, to a public health crisis. Rates of asthma, diabetes, obesity, mental illness, and infant mortality are the highest in the city. In 2002, one in four children living in Harlem was diagnosed with asthma. In 2001, the New York City Department of Health reported that the rates of diabetes were 85 percent higher than the rest of New York City. Despite this community being home to a handful of prestigious, nationally recognized health care institutions, the outcomes of these diseases were glaringly poor—with rates of preventable death and hospitalizations related to these conditions being far worse than the national figures. In fact, a study that looked at health outcomes in Harlem concluded that a Harlem man's chances of living past the age of forty were less than those of the average male resident of Bangladesh—one of the poorest countries in the world.[1] The disturbing trends pointed to underlying causes that cut across issues of access to care and the social determinants of health. In addition, the poor outcomes in health juxtaposed against the existence of the large health care providers in the northern Manhattan community further fueled a longstanding distrust between community members, local grassroots organizations, and these institutions.

This tug between the underlying—mostly socioeconomic and political— factors and the existing health crisis they had led to were at play throughout the ten years of the NMCVC. Where to focus the attention of the leaders of the community— tackle issues related to poverty *or* take on initiatives to address the myriad chronic disease-specific problems that were plaguing the community—was a constant strain that staff needed to negotiate. However, the strain challenged all the players that eventually constituted the collaborative—health care institutions, community-based organizations, faith-based leaders, and legislative representatives—to acknowledge the interconnectedness of the social, political, and economic factors and health outcomes. If the community was going to move from a place of frustration with the status quo to one of positive changes, then everyone needed to take responsibility for the outcomes and move from blame to action. Hence the establishment of the

Collaborative moved northern Manhattan closer to addressing the socioeconomic determinants of health, one of the most outstanding barriers to healing this community.

Guiding Principles for Setting the Infrastructure

Northern Manhattan Community Voices built much of its infrastructure through its utilization of collaborative models and working groups. Moreover, it developed and formalized a strategy in which the University would engage and partner with the community for forming grant programs, writing papers, and co-presenting ideas to policymakers. Health promotion programs were embedded into existing organizations, thus transforming how social services were delivered and investing in the development of opportunities to promote health and health care through "unlikely venues," such as Alianza Dominicana, Northern Manhattan Improvement Corporation, and Fort George Community Life Center.

The development of the Collaborative was guided by two operational principles. Project leaders knew that at some point NMCVC would no longer be funded by the W.K. Kellogg Foundation. Thus the first principle was that the Collaborative should only deal in *stimulating* change through initiatives that had a "home" capable of institutionalizing the effort. This recognized that the existing institutions and community-based organizations could develop the capacity to adopt the various projects and that the main idea behind Community Voices was to build the capacity in the community rather than to create a large new infrastructure that could not sustain itself. The second principle was that the Collaborative would have to become known in the institutions and the community in order to get its goals and objectives achieved, but that the "credit" for the success of its individual initiatives would accrue to others. NMCVC would have to be satisfied in knowing that it helped plant the seeds for efforts to improve the health safety net in northern Manhattan!

In addition, NMCVC was committed to distributing the funds awarded by the Kellogg Foundation in a way that would support the collaborative objectives rather than divide the funds to appease any past or political tensions—a practice which, unfortunately, happens more often than not. Alianza received a five-year budget of $1.5 million to increase the enrollment of residents into Medicaid and Child Health Plus and to provide leadership in developing and embedding community health workers (CHWs) into the work of partner organizations and institutions. The Community Premier Plus, the Medicaid Managed Care Company of three safety net hospitals at the time (New York Presbyterian, the Harlem, and North General Hospitals), received $650,000 to develop insurance plans for those ineligible for existing insurance.

The remainder ($2.4 million) was received by the dental school to administer the grant and to lead the processes of building capacity for local organizations to deliver health promotion and disease prevention programs and informing policies to expand access to mental and dental health services. Some of these latter funds were provided to the School of Public Health for a Community Voices scholars program. NMCVC was committed to serving as an educational hub and providing a "learning" environment for upcoming public health students to become social change agents.

Policy Factors That Influenced Change

A key factor in the public policy success of Northern Manhattan Community Voices was the existing political connections that the individual partnering organizations brought to the table. As a result, project leaders invested time, energy, and resources in informing policymakers from the outset of the project. With this approach, NMCVC helped frame the most pressing health issues; stacked them into categories (Community Health Workers, Access to Care, Mental and Oral Health, and so on) in which project leaders could leverage the existing resources and relationships; and then identified a strategy that combined program development, policy advocacy, and a carefully structured communication strategy to elevate the urgency of these issues among key leaders throughout the state.

These efforts were helped by a number of different policy opportunities looming as the CV initiative began in New York. New York State had struggled for decades with reducing its number of uninsured and containing costs for caring for the un- and underinsured. More than 2.4 million New Yorkers lacked health insurance, 900,000 of whom were eligible for public health insurance coverage. The reasons behind uninsurance were many: some did not know about the programs; others did not know they were eligible; and still others were reluctant to accept public benefits or had difficulty completing the enrollment paperwork.

The cost of delivering care in New York State historically has surpassed the national average. At $125 billion, total annual health care spending in New York exceeded every state except California. The state's Medicaid program, at more than $49 billion per year, continues to be the single largest spending area in its budget, and per-enrollee spending is more than twice the national average. Despite higher spending, New York has not achieved demonstrably better health outcomes compared to states where spending is lower.

In 1999, this situation drove state leaders to reconfigure how services were delivered and accessed. One of the major shifts to address this problem included the shifting of Medicaid to managed care. The emerging partners of the NMCVC were well-positioned to assist the community (its members, its institutions, and organizations) in leveraging this change to bring about positive outcomes in access to care and to work toward a seamless transition for the Medicaid population, the uninsured, and underinsured.

This statewide trend allowed for "access to health insurance coverage" to become one of the cornerstones of the NMCVC. In the pages that follow, a synopsis is provided of several of the milestones that were accomplished in the ten years of this Collaborative. And, of course, the milestones would be incomplete if it were not for the unintended consequences and lessons that we stumbled on throughout the duration of this journey, an important part of the story.

A Collaborative in Action: Stimulating Change to Deliver Results

During the early months of the Collaborative, the first step toward organizing a strategic effort was prioritizing the energy, leadership, and financial investment. Developing the strategic priorities of the Collaborative required a sound needs assessment. The purpose of the needs assessment was threefold: (1) gather data to set a common ground among partners; (2) establish an objective and neutral starting point for prioritizing the focus of the Collaborative's efforts; and (3) begin to engage the target populations, which included the residents of northern Manhattan, the medically underserved, and the institutional and community leaders.

The needs assessment was completed in two parts. First, a population-based survey was conducted by faculty of the Columbia University School of Public Health, and second, a series of interviews were held with community leaders, providers, and institutional executives. The results of both parts of the assessment confirmed several assumptions held by the initial partners of the Collaborative, as well as revealed some new insights about what people perceived as the most pressing health issues affecting the community. Among two of the most salient health issues identified by the residents of northern Manhattan were asthma among children and obesity and diabetes among adolescents and adults. For the providers and institutional leaders, costs related to caring for the uninsured was among one of the most pressing concerns. Hence, during the initial months of Community Voices, Collaborative leaders organized the work to address several of these immediate concerns and tackle some of the long-standing issues that were driving the costs of health care. The following four working groups were developed to execute the goals of Community Voices and respond to the pressing needs of the community:

1. Health Promotion and Disease Prevention
2. Difficult-to-Cover Services: Mental Health and Oral Health

3. Increasing Access to Health Insurance
4. Expanding Coverage: HealthGap

The following is a synopsis of the major accomplishments of these working groups and the lessons that were learned.

Health Promotion and Disease Prevention

Under the Health Promotion and Disease Prevention Workgroup, a core set of the partners focused on devising strategies to address five of the major health concerns: obesity and diabetes prevention and management, asthma prevention and management, tobacco use, childhood immunizations, and emergency room reduction. The Collaborative partners agreed that improving the prevention and management of two of the most pressing health concerns—increasing the number of children adhering to the recommended vaccinations and working to intervene with the frequent users of the emergency room—could potentially yield to better health outcomes and, more important, help the Collaborative address some of the systemic problems in the health care system (such as lack of coordination and access to primary and preventive care). The goal was to reduce the burden of chronic illnesses by developing sustainable community-based prevention programs and tackling policies that could advance or stymie progress in these areas.

Community health workers became an integral component of the core initiatives developed by this working group. CHWs share common racial and ethnic backgrounds, cultures, languages, and life experiences with the communities in which they live and serve, and therefore are better equipped to build the necessary trust to help people improve their health and well-being. CHWs have a unique ability to break down real and perceived barriers and help people receive the care they need, when they need it. The evidence of the role of CHWs in improving health outcomes, increasing access to care, and reducing overutilization of costly health services (such as the emergency room) has been well documented.[2] This was enough to convince the leadership of NMCVC to invest in the model and develop strategies to replicate, scale up, and sustain CHW-led efforts. In addition, as part of the national CV initiative, NMCVC partners and staff had spent a considerable amount of time learning from CHW-led initiatives in other countries. CHWs in remote parts of the world were tackling social, political, and economic contributors to poor health outcomes in poverty-stricken cities and towns in other countries. Where others saw hopelessness, CHWs were organizing community residents and seeking solutions to problems such as lack of sanitation and a clean water supply, lobbying for resources to build new health centers, and increasing vaccinations among children. The model had worked in cities across the United States and the world, and it was time to develop the workforce in the front lines of the northern Manhattan community.

Following is a brief outline of the various initiatives that were developed as part of the Health Promotion and Disease Prevention working group. For several of these initiatives the role of CHWs was carved out and supported not only to address several of the immediate health concerns but also as an opportunity to create a network of the powerful leaders sprinkled throughout the neighborhoods of Washington Heights and Harlem. CHWs in turn became a collective and resounding voice of wisdom and experience that helped shape the programs and, more important, formalize a voice for community residents to inform the underlying policies that had an impact on their health.

Obesity and Diabetes Prevention and Management: The Healthy Choices Initiative

The obesity and diabetes epidemics are among the most serious public health threats facing communities across the United States. Efforts to reverse the rising trends of these two related health problems will require multiple levels of interventions. Over the past four decades obesity rates have nearly quadrupled, and type II diabetes rates have grown from 5.2 percent of the population in 1980 to more than 8 percent. Today, more than 33 percent of children and adolescents are overweight or obese— that's nearly twenty-five million kids and young people! Approximately twenty million Americans have type II diabetes, and another fifty-four million have pre-diabetes, putting them at high risk for developing the disease. In cities like New York, one in eight persons has diabetes. And rates are not declining in any state. Experts estimate that given the present trajectory, 75 percent of Americans will be overweight or obese by 2015.

The strain on the economy, in terms of health care costs and loss of productivity associated with these two conditions, is already a severe crisis. Diabetes and obesity are causing a severe financial drain in the health care system: childhood obesity alone is estimated to cost the nation up to $14 billion each year in direct health care costs to treat kids. New York State spends $6.1 billion yearly in obesity-related medical expenditures.

The United States arrived at this juncture because of a nexus of environmental and social trends. In short, the U.S. culture has fueled this epidemic: nearly a third of children and teens eat fast food at least once a day; adults consume larger portions of more unhealthy, processed foods; school-aged kids spend more than four nonschool hours a day in front of a screen; and nine out of ten kids are driven to school versus biking or walking. But it is clear that the underlying causes of these behavioral trends are rooted in factors beyond individual control. Several of the main contributing factors to obesity include high cost of healthful foods, location, lack of grocery stores, disproportionate numbers of fast-food restaurants located in low-income neighborhoods, poor access to safe places to exercise, and the unavailability of preventive health care services. Therefore, reversing the diabetes and obesity epidemics will call for multiple community- and policy-level interventions to affect change in the physical and social environment, including making healthy eating options more accessible and restoring or introducing physical activities as a routine part of life.

The Community Voices Healthy Choices Committee formed to address several of these major problems. The Committee comprised several key leaders and stakeholders that were invested in addressing these problems. This consisted of a representative of the Superintendent's office and the Department of Fitness and Physical Development of Region 10 in northern Manhattan, Isabella Geriatric Center, Cornell Cooperative Extension, and a physician and leader that had initiated several programs at the New York Presbyterian Hospital. The Workgroup had the following three objectives over a three-year time line:

- To develop a Healthy Choices Curriculum for high school students
- To create a formal liaison between Community Voices and the Superintendent of Schools Office for the purpose of developing and implementing a "Healthy Choices" program in middle schools and high schools in northern Manhattan that targeted children, families, and community leaders
- To organize community residents and organizations as part of New York's "City Lives in Moving Bodies" (CLIMB) initiative to improve the parks and make them more accessible for the Walking Groups component of Healthy Choices (Figure 7.1).

With the collaboration of Cornell Cooperative Extension, New York Presbyterian Hospital's Women, Infants and Children (WIC) program, and George Washington High School (GWHS), NMCVC developed a curriculum for ninth and eleventh graders at the GWHS. The curriculum focused on the short- and long-term impact of nutrition and exercise on the body and mind. Age- and culturally relevant topics were identified after a series of interviews with teachers and students. Topics such as weight and self-image, media and eating disorders, exercise, and mental health were among the areas covered in the curriculum. More important, activities such as "community mapping and organizing for youth and by youth" were embedded into the curriculum. The interactive approach was developed to engage youth in developing solutions to the obvious inequities in healthy food access and safe recreational spaces that existed in northern Manhattan, compared to the more affluent neighborhoods south of 96th Street. The youths involved in these programs became a cadre of informal CHWs. Though they were not formally trained as CHWs, the youths, as natural leaders in their communities and among their peers, learned how to take their experiences, document them, and use them to create innovative solutions to the social and

FIGURE 7.1. CLIMB.

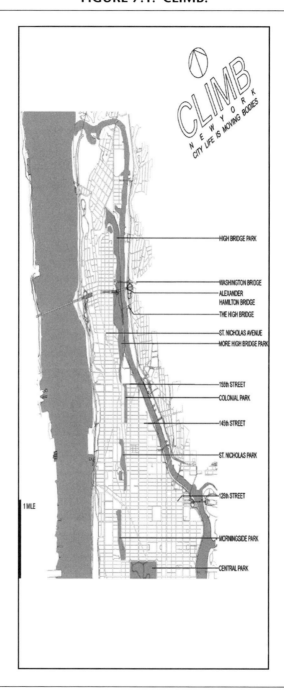

political concerns they faced. Several youths began a letter-writing campaign to local representatives urging them to address the inequities in access to healthy foods and safe recreational space in their neighborhood. Though this story does not end with concrete results, the training of these community leaders yielded a stronger network of solution-focused residents determined to fight for a healthier northern Manhattan.

The second component of the Healthy Choices program involved the faculty of the school and parents of the students. The Healthy Choices committee implemented an eight-week nutrition course for parents and staff of the school. By June 2004, the program had enlisted fifty parents and staff—forty of them completed the course and received a certificate of completion from Cornell Cooperative Extension, the organization that facilitated the classes.

On the basis of the experience with this pilot program, Collaborative leaders testified at a New York State Assembly Hearing on Health Education in New York City (NYC) Schools. The recommendations included the incorporation of culturally effective nutrition and fitness education for New York's youth as part of the high school health curriculum.

The health curriculum in NYC had not been updated since 1989. Considering the staggering rate of obesity and childhood type II diabetes in the community, the curriculum developed by NMCVC offered an accurate and present-day health education tool that is interactive and family oriented. In addition, informal interviews with program participants in the Healthy Choices intervention suggest that partnering with youth-centered education and parent education yields better results for behavioral changes in dieting and exercise in the household. As a result, the recommendations to the Assembly members included the integration of community-based health intervention programs for the parents and guardians of students in the public school system.

NMCVC was able to create and embed the tools necessary to broadly implement a program to combat the obesity epidemic throughout the public school system.

Asthma Prevention and Management: The Asthma Basics for Children (ABC) Initiative

Several studies pointed to a childhood asthma epidemic in northern Manhattan, estimating that nearly one in four children living in Harlem had been diagnosed with the disease. The rate of asthma hospitalizations per hundred thousand children between the ages of ten and seventeen years was 2.2 times higher in northern Manhattan than in the city at large. To address this crisis, the Collaborative developed and established the Asthma Basics for Children (ABC) initiative. The initiative brought together a cohort of community-based organizations, including housing groups, day care centers, faith-based organizations, health care providers, and the New York

City Department of Health Childhood Asthma Initiative, to devise a strategy for a communitywide asthma intervention initiative that would focus on helping parents and caretakers implement asthma care programs and build a coalition that would inform environmental and organizational policies to tackle the asthma epidemic in northern Manhattan.

The goal of the coalition was to embed key activities, mostly led by CHWs, within a core set of organizations that would lead to the improved management of child asthma and reduction of asthma emergency visits and school absences. The lead organizations of this effort that continues as of this writing are the Mailman School of Public Health, Northern Manhattan Perinatal Partnership (NMPP), and the Northern Manhattan Improvement Corporation. The ABC initiative is now fully supported by the Centers for Disease Control and Prevention. As of 2006, several Early Childhood programs had agreed to participate in the ABC program: Columbia University Head Start programs; Community Life—Taino Towers; NMPP Center for Preschool & Family Learning; and Pleasant Avenue. In total, there are seven organizations and three health care provider networks. The coalition provides asthma education and support first to staff within the partnering organizations and then to each of the organization's members and participants, specifically the parents and children. The coalition developed a handbook that guides each phase of these activities. The ABC program also works to connect families to primary care providers through referrals to providers who have been identified as well trained to address asthma in the environment in which the families live. The coalition strives to provide services to at least 1,700 children per year.

Over the course of the first five years of existence (2000–2005), the ABC initiative trained 1,504 workers throughout the key agencies. These trained individuals also received core competency training as CHWs, thus strengthening the network of CHWs that NMCVC was committed to building (Exhibit 7.1).

Addressing Tobacco Use

The American Legacy Foundation joined with the Community Voices program to assist local underserved communities in combating high rates of smoking. The NMCVC was one of the sites to receive an $800,000 grant to develop collaborations to help prevent smoking in children and to develop smoking cessation programs. Two major programs were initiated. The first was directed toward children and adolescents, who were guided into understanding the hazards of smoking through short plays that the children wrote. A cadre of youth leaders developed a series of community-wide activities that brought antismoking messages to the masses, from youth-led performances to letter-writing campaigns to legislators to demonstrations to counteract smoking advertisements that were placed in the community. The second program sought to integrate smoking cessation programs at the Ambulatory Care Network of

EXHIBIT 7.1. TRAINING A CADRE OF CHANGE AGENTS: THE TRAINING AND DEVELOPMENT OF COMMUNITY HEALTH WORKERS IN NORTHERN MANHATTAN.

The conceptual basis for the Community Voices CHW training program is the Paolo Freire model for community education and mobilization, which situates self-identified priorities of community residents at the center of a curriculum. Through a training program comprising interactive, culturally relevant, and experiential modules, CHWs built their capacity to assist families and their communities. The core competencies of the curriculum developed by several of the partners, and led by Alianza Dominicana and Columbia University, included a set of holistic, health-promoting skills related to community organizing, outreach, intake and assessment, referrals and case management, social support, informal counseling, provision of specialized education, follow-up, and system navigation.

The NMCVC CHW training program built the foundation for a highly integrated model in which CHWs and CHW-led activities were interwoven in the culture of the organizations, and they became a cornerstone of all the health promotion activities of the NMCVC partners.

---

the New York Presbyterian Hospital. The successful Smoking Cessation Clinic in the School of Dental and Oral Surgery, known now as the College of Dental Medicine, served as the model to replicate in the hospital's network of primary care facilities in Washington Heights. In the process of establishing the smoking cessation programs, more than one hundred physicians, nurse practitioners, and ancillary staff were educated on how to utilize effective antismoking measures. An easy-to-use guide titled *Columbia University Pocket Guide to Tobacco Cessation* was produced. The communitywide effort included training CHWs with the resources to refer their clients for services.

Childhood Immunization: The Start Right Initiative

One of the most well-known markers of adequate primary care for children, childhood immunization rate, was only 57 percent for children in northern Manhattan in 2000, compared to 66 percent for the city and 72 percent for the nation. The statistics, like the ones related to asthma, pointed to a need to reorient primary care strategies in ways that would more effectively engage families and the larger community to improve the health of children. Again, adopting the CHW approach, the Collaborative established the Start Right Immunization Program in 2000. The immunization program received a grant from the Centers for Disease Control and was developed by a coalition led by the Mailman School of Public Health of Columbia University, Alianza Dominicana, and Harlem Congregation for Community Improvement. The coalition has twenty-three member programs, including early childhood education programs, parenting programs, faith-based organizations, housing advocacy groups, health care providers, and the New York City Department of Health Bureau of Immunizations.

During the planning phase, the coalition identified programs and staff from each organization that could serve as vehicles to embed immunization promotion activities. The cornerstone of the initiative is the integration of immunization promotion activities into the ongoing social service programs within its network of community social service organizations. Each organization had established an annual recruitment target of bringing two thousand children up to date with immunizations per year. The program mission was to increase child immunization rates to 90 percent. The immunizations are tracked through two immunization registries and review of the immunization cards by the partnering organizations. Over the course of five years, 792 workers were trained as "immunization experts" within the organizations. These workers, as with the asthma initiative, also received training in CHW core competencies. In 2005, the evaluation of the community-based immunization Start Right program revealed that the immunization rates within the African American community in Harlem had surpassed the national average for all African American children and equaled the national average.

Reducing Emergency Room Visits

Salud A Su Alcance[3] (SASA) was developed by the NMCVC health promotion and disease prevention working group and was supported by a grant from the Health Resources and Services Administration (HRSA) Healthy Community Access Project (HCAP). The initiative was implemented at and spearheaded by the leadership of NewYork Presbyterian (NYP). The initiative was composed of three major elements: the Emergency Department Diversion Program, the Pharmacy Assistant Program, and the Referral Program.

The SASA care management team consisted of health priority specialists (HPSs) that provided telephone case management; a network of community health workers and parish nurses situated in local organizations that facilitated access to social services (such as behavioral health, housing, employment services); and a proprietary software program called the "Event Monitor" that identified frequent ER users and prompted an email to the health priority specialist.

NMCVC worked diligently with NYP to evaluate the outcome of this three-year initiative. The evaluation focused on data collected from the ER diversion program between January 2003 and December 2004 and examined the interventions delivered by the HPS and CHW. The primary objective of the evaluation was to explore ways in which ER utilization may have been positively affected by HPS interventions.

Employing a Health Priority Survey Form, developed by NYP and NMCVC staff for use in this program, data on the demographic, ER treatment history, level of severity, health insurance, primary care access, health awareness, education and satisfaction, and intervention were collected. The three-month and six-month instruments also included outcome assessments that reviewed emergency and non-emergency department visits as reported by the patient and tracked through the institution's event data tracking system.

Between January 2003 and December 2004, 711 patients were identified as frequent flyers through the electronic event monitoring system (called WEBCIS) and were referred to the HPS for further assessment and intervention. The HPS conducted each of the patient assessments. Of the 711 patients initially identified, 539 (75.8 percent) were reached and interviewed for "baseline" assessments. At three months following baseline, 537 (75.5 percent) patients were reassessed (September 2003–June 2004) and at six months following baseline, 177 (24.9 percent) were assessed again (December 2003 and September 2004).

Key findings of the evaluation showed that in the sample of patients seen at three assessment points, a significant decrease in number of ER visits was observed. The patients in this sample were economically and culturally representative of the urban poor (in other words, nonwhite, Hispanic or other minorities, and low income). The interventions of the HPS and CHW staff were examined in relationship to ER usage. At the three-month assessment, referral to a primary care provider was significantly associated with ER use. At the six-month assessment, more interactive interventions were associated with decreases in ER use, namely, the provision of health education, teaching the patient how to use the health care system, and providing the patient with counseling on social or emotional issues.

NMCVC worked arduously to present and disseminate the positive impact and return on the investment of the initiative in order to secure the sustainability and replication of this program. To date, not only have several of the components been sustained as part of New York Presbyterian, but the Pharmacy Assistant Program also became the backbone of a city-wide initiative to implement pharmacy assistant services throughout community health centers in New York City.

Furthermore, the results of the evaluation were used by key leaders to work with the leadership of New York City Health and Hospitals Corporation (HHC), an integrated health care delivery system known as the largest municipal health care organization in the country. HHC serves 1.3 million New Yorkers every year, and more than 450,000 are uninsured. In September 2004, the SASA program was replicated at the Lincoln Medical Center in the South Bronx, part of the Generations+/ Northern Manhattan Health Network of HHC. The fact that this program was replicated within the largest public hospital systems that provides care to a highly underserved community is one of the major success stories of the NMCVC initiative.

Cross-Cutting Lessons and Outcomes from the Health Promotion and Disease Prevention Working Group

Community health workers were the key to driving change among the various initiatives developed by the Health Promotion and Disease Prevention Working Group. They drove our programs forward, reached out to individuals and families that had been marginalized, advocated for necessary change, and used their knowledge and experience to achieve a wide range of positive health outcomes. We did not label them all "community health workers" when we began. Some were youth leaders, referral specialists, health priority specialists, outreach workers, or peer educators. Neither did we anticipate the critical role CHWs would play not just in developing programs but also in sustaining the improvements that were accomplished by their work. The NMCVC leaders at the time perhaps did not fully comprehend the extent of the impact of the work of CHWs (Exhibit 7.2). During the initial years, CHWs were part of a team of community members who came from the same class and culture as the people they were trying to reach. They were "ordinary people" who were intricately woven into the fabric of community, and they were soldiers that sought to create a healthier environment, address social issues, improve community leadership, and reclaim hope for future generations.

Between 2000 and 2005, these CHWs facilitated access to health improvements for over forty thousand people. The immunization program brought enrolled children's immunization rate up to 80 percent, closing the gap of national rates.[4]

At the end of eight years, the programs developed as part of this working group accounted for over an additional $25 million that was leveraged from federal, state, and local resources. The programs described above became the backbone of initiatives supported by state grants, federal grants (specifically from Health Resources and Services Administration and the Centers for Disease Control and Prevention), and part of operating budgets from several of the key partners. To date, several of these programs continue to exist and flourish. More importantly, the network of CHWs that was trained and developed as part of these programs remain a vibrant voice for the residents of northern Manhattan. Today many of them are part of ongoing efforts in the state to formalize and sustain the role of this workforce as an integral component to a health care system that promotes health, prevents illness, and addresses the public health needs of a community.

EXHIBIT 7.2. UNINTENDED RESULTS: CHW INITIATIVE YIELDS SEVERAL KEY CHANGES IN ORGANIZATIONAL POLICIES AMONG NMCVC PARTNERS.

NMCVC's Community Health Worker (CHW) initiative has produced a number of organizational policy changes that have resulted in the effective integration of CHWs as key members of the health care workforce of several of the NMCVC health provider affiliates. The executive leadership at New York Presbyterian (NYP) worked closely with Alianza Dominicana to develop institutional protocols to include CHWs as an integral part of the hospital delivery of services on diabetes and asthma education to underserved and uninsured residents, primarily persons of Dominican descent. NYP wanted to effectively reach out to patients of the hospital who were suffering with diabetes or asthma to help improve their self-care or help them navigate the health care system. Through the partnership facilitated by NMCVC, the hospital and Alianza also worked to integrate training for the medical doctors and other professionals, such as social workers, on the role of CHWs in improving the health outcomes of the residents of northern Manhattan. The commitment of Alianza and NYP's executive leadership led to internal policy changes that further led to acceptance of CHWs as important members of the health care workforce of the hospital. Through several of the NMCVC initiatives, CHWs had clearly contributed to improved outcomes for persons with diabetes, including reduced hemoglobin A1Cs and reduced ER visits, through appropriately diverted admissions.

The utilization of CHWs by Columbia University (CU) and NYP as part of the integration of smoking cessation services in the outpatient clinics had required changes in job descriptions that included CHWs as key players in the workforce. One of the key outcomes of the smoking cessation program was that both CU and NYP needed to reach out to Medicaid- and Medicare-eligible persons and make them aware of these services. The integration of CHWs led to an increase in the number of persons participating in smoking cessation services and reporting smoking cessation at three months. As the result of this success, the hospital is now paying for 100 percent of the smoking cessation program and the CHWs who work in this program.

After learning of the successes of several of these NMCVC initiatives, another of NMCVC's partners began to develop employment opportunities for CHWs. Community Premier Plus, a Medicaid-managed care plan serving residents in northern Manhattan, began to integrate CHWs to help persons access and retain insurance. CHWs were sent into the community to enroll clients into Community Premier Plus and inform them of services provided through managed care organizations.

NMCVC became increasingly invested in replicating the role of CHWs among its partners. More so, NMCVC staff began to develop relationships with key stakeholders in the city, the state, and the nation to identify opportunities in sustaining the critical role CHWs played in health care. To date, NMCVC is working with organizations such as the CHW Network of NYC, New York State Department of Health, NYC Department of Health and Mental Hygiene, and Office of Medicaid to secure the role of CHWs in New York State. Efforts are under way to standardize core competencies for CHWs and establish a reimbursable scope of practice for this workforce.

Difficult-to-Cover Services: Oral and Mental Health Care

Oral Health Care

Because NMCVC lead partners included the College of Dental Medicine (CDM) and the Harlem Hospital Dental Service, major advances were made in improving access to oral health care. The NMCVC was based on a program instituted by CDM, Community DentCare, which was established to combat the high caries (decay) rate in northern Manhattan. A study by CDM showed that the children in Harlem and Washington Heights experienced much higher dental disease rates with comparatively less treatment than national groups. The CDM, working with community groups and in collaboration with the Harlem Hospital and the Mailman School of Public Health, established prevention and treatment programs in eight public schools in northern Manhattan. In addition, the network of school-based care was enhanced with a mobile van program that visited Head Start and elderly centers. The CDM affiliated with community-based clinics to help staff their dental clinics and served as the hub for specialty care. The DentCare program provides approximately forty-five thousand patient visits in the northern Manhattan community each year.

The DentCare program was featured during the rollout of the Surgeon General's Report on the Oral Health of the Nation in 2000.[5] It became the inspiration for the largest initiative in dentistry ever undertaken by foundations (the Robert Wood Johnson Foundation, the California Endowment, and the W.K. Kellogg Foundation). The $30 million program was designed to address access to care and was titled *Pipeline, Profession & Practice: Community-Based Dental Education (Dental Pipeline) Program*. It funded twenty-three dental schools, almost half of all U.S. dental schools, to educate students in the problems of the underserved, including cultural competency training through community service in their senior year, and to increase the enrollment of underrepresented minority students. According to many experts, the lack of minority practitioners is an important reason why the worst oral health is seen in racial and ethnic minorities. With a careful focus on policy change, further work was carried out by NMCVC in collaboration with the Community Voices National Program Office at the Morehouse School of Medicine to address the lack of minority practitioners.

As part of the policy initiative, NMCVC explored how to make more progress in improving access to oral health care in underserved population groups through a new approach to enrolling underrepresented minority students in dental schools. In this context, the Bridging the Gap (BTG) study was designed to uncover nontraditional means to increase the recruitment and enrollment of underrepresented minority (URM) students in dental schools.

The BTG study (competed in May 2006) noted that there were efforts underway to increase recruitment and enrollment of URM students into the traditional track from college into dental school. The Dental Pipeline program cited earlier was well underway and was proving successful in increasing the representation of underrepresented minority students in the majority dental schools. However, the gap between the number of minority practitioners and the ever-growing minority population in the United States is so great, the BTG study group found that another track into dental school needed to be identified.

The BTG study group learned about a unique program in medicine that had been developed in the 1980s to recruit talented minority high school students who were prepared to enter into a coordinated seven-year college-medical-school program. Students admitted must have a strong commitment to practice in underserved communities. The Sophie Davis School of Biomedical Education, City College of New York, operated this unique program. It had an excellent track record of graduates who practiced in underserved communities.

Following a five-year college and pre-medical curriculum that included service-oriented projects at the Sophie Davis School, students completed the last two clinical years at six cooperating medical schools. The BTG study committee believed this to be a model program that dentistry could follow. It would recruit a different pool of students. Rather than pursuing the traditional path of recruiting students already in professional school, it was decided to begin earlier in the pipeline, at the high school level. The study committee suggested that there were areas of the country that had the right conditions in which to consider coordinating a high-school-to-dental-school program. The necessary conditions were collaboration between dental schools and minority-serving colleges and universities that had established pipelines into high schools. In addition, high-priority states for the program would be those with large underserved minority populations.

As a result of the BTG study report, the Josiah Macy Jr. Foundation funded three sites to plan and implement unique programs based on the Sophie Davis principles. The sites were in New Mexico, Georgia, and New York. The American Dental Education Association was the recipient of the Macy grant. In 2007, the College of Dental Medicine at Columbia University with the Sophie Davis School of Biomedical Education at the City College of New York became one of the three sites funded. In Georgia, The Medical College of Georgia School of Dentistry, another funded school, planned to develop a BTG program with Morehouse School of Medicine and schools within the Atlanta University Center (Morehouse College, Spellman College, and Clark Atlanta University). The third site was the University of New Mexico, through the Division of Dental Services at the Health Science Center. It should be noted that New Mexico does not have a dental school but had developed a strong dental residency program to help the state deal with a woefully trained dental workforce that was to treat a large number of underserved.

These three sites completed a thorough analysis of how they could adapt a Sophie Davis–type model of education to recruit a new pool of students who would be committed to serving the underserved. In June of 2009, each site indicated its plans to implement the model, albeit Georgia and New Mexico modified the plan considerably while Columbia was able to build upon the Sophie Davis model by designing an additional pool of dental candidates into the existing Sophie Davis School of Biomedical Education. Both New York and Georgia appear ready to implement programs once they receive funding. New Mexico appears to be considering opening a dental school; however, it did design a coordinated Bachelor of Science-Doctorate of Dental Science (BS-DDS) program.

The important lesson that comes out of the BTG initiative is that there are ways to approach various issues related to the dental access problem. It is a complex problem that has many dimensions. The underserved live in crowded urban communities and sparsely populated rural areas. Few dentists—only 16 percent, according to the Surgeon General's Report—will treat Medicaid patients. Dental services under Medicaid are mandated for children, but are optional for adults. Unless there are many national efforts to provide dental insurance for the population, to increase minority practitioners, and to make it attractive for graduates to practice in underserved areas, the United States will not address oral health care access in an adequate manner. The BTG project became an offshoot of the national Community Voices initiative because it recognized that it needed to seed many different efforts to meet its overall goal of improving health care for the underserved. As a result, a new pathway for minority students to become dentists will open.[6]

Mental Health Care

The first step in determining the course of action and strategy for change in the area of mental health care was to undertake an assessment of the mental health needs, community challenges, and resources available to address access to care for mental health. A stakeholder advisory group was formed, consisting of local psychiatrists that were part of the safety net system in northern Manhattan, the New York State Psychiatric Institute—a major institution and part of the Columbia University Medical Center—community-based providers of mental health, community advocates for improved mental health, and faculty from the Mailman School of Public Health. As the group evolved, clergy members, especially in Harlem, became deeply invested and committed to participating in this newly formed advisory group. These community leaders had become the frontline responders to what had become a growing, and silent, crisis in the African American and Latino communities of Harlem and Washington Heights.

Through this advisory group, NMCVC had set the platform for a far-reaching assessment that would become a community-wide landmark study of the mental health needs and barriers to care for the residents of northern Manhattan. The policy report that emerged from the weekly meetings of this cadre of dedicated leaders was titled *Mental Health: The Neglected Epidemic*. The report included a comprehensive inventory of the services available in the community and the perceptions of providers and community residents on seeking mental health services. Four major challenges to improving the mental health system were identified: the manner in which funds and resources were allocated, the limited capacity of the system to meet the existing need for services, the dearth of culturally responsive mental health providers, and the barriers related to the lack of mental health parity in New York State.

The findings of this report were widely discussed with local, city, and state mental health groups, and recommendations were agreed upon regarding the ways to build the capacity of the existing mental health safety net, strategies for community approaches to prevention and awareness of mental health problems, and approaches for coordination of services. The report also included recommendations regarding the need for greater cultural competence on the part of providers in managing the mental health problems in the racially and culturally diverse northern Manhattan community.

During the final development of the report, new relationships with city- and state-wide advocacy groups had crystallized. The leadership of NMCVC was using the report as a tool to convene meetings with key decision makers throughout the state to devise solutions that would address the needs for mental health services for northern Manhattan and other communities that were identifying with findings of the report. Among the decision makers were key leaders of the New York City Department of Health and Mental Hygiene. Eventually the report had become a blueprint for many improvements in the mental health safety net in northern Manhattan.

Among the programs that were developed was the integration of mental health services within the outpatient clinics of New York Presbyterian and the creation of one of Harlem's now well-established, free-standing primary care community health centers with integrated mental health services. To date, the center has been merged into a network of Federally Qualified Health Centers in New York City and continues to provide culturally responsive mental health services to residents of Harlem, especially the elderly population. The work of this task force also led to the evaluation of best practices that were meeting the needs of the surrounding communities. One of these evaluations was of a community practice in the South Bronx, Full Circle Health (FCH), which sought to improve compliance in treatment by African American men. Through a collaborative evaluation, it was determined that this practice provided a doctor-patient cultural and spiritual concordance, and a cultural environment in harmony with the community. It was shown that there was response-significant correlation between number of visits and improvement in mental health status, with those men remaining in treatment for eleven or more visits having the greatest improvement. One of the most important outcomes of this effort was identifying best practices and raising their visibility among institutional providers such as faculty at the Columbia University Medical Center and community providers. The strategy for NMCVC was to identify these special gems in the community, assess their impact, and work with partners to replicate the models that were yielding results. This is one of the greatest legacies of NMCVC. That is, to set into motion initiatives that would improve the health of the community through capacity building.

Finally, one of the most rewarding contributions of NMCVC was to be part of a larger network of mental health advocacy organizations seeking to increase access to mental health services across New York State. The NMCVC mental health report had been the first of its kind. The report made visible the concerns of the people, providers, academic leaders, and community leaders of northern Manhattan—raising the collective "voice" of a people determined to fight for solutions to this crisis. More so, the report and the inclusive process to gather the information gave local ammunition to a statewide battle cry led by mental health advocacy groups seeking to establish equitable coverage for mental health services. The report and the members of the stakeholder advisory group became part of a larger advocacy effort that sought to put an end to the discriminatory laws that got in the way of people receiving the mental health services they needed. After the tragic loss of a young child whose mental health needs went untreated because of the coverage limitations, Timothy's Law, the mental health parity law for New York State, passed on December 16, 2006. After six arduous years of campaigning and advocacy, the Law mandated that insurance providers covering any health care services must also provide coverage for mental health and that coverage must be "on par" with all other health care services covered by the policy. The law placed New York among a group of leadership states and helped build a foundation for the national parity law—The Paul Wellstone and Pete Domenici Mental Health Parity and Addiction Equity Act—signed into law in 2008.

The work of NMCVC simply set the stage for local leaders to be part of a collective, statewide effort that led to mental health parity in New York State. There is still much to accomplish in the area of mental health care in northern Manhattan and throughout the state of New York—the good news is that advocacy groups across the state, including the NMCVC partners, have maintained a strong presence and continue to fight for improved access to mental health services.

Increasing Access to Insurance and Expanding Coverage

In 1998, approximately 1.5 million low-income New Yorkers lacked health coverage. However, there were significant opportunities to decrease this number. It was estimated that nearly 900,000 of them were eligible for federal and state health insurance.[7] Of those eligible but not enrolled, a quarter of them were children and two-thirds were working adults. According to a report from the New York Forum for Child Health, nearly three-quarters of uninsured children in New York City were eligible but not enrolled in Medicaid or Child Health Plus.[8]

NMCVC had several approaches to increasing and expanding access to insurance coverage. The first was an effort led by one of NMCVC's partners, Community Premier Plus (CPP), a managed care company. CPP was tasked with the challenge of developing a new affordable insurance plan for working people and small businesses. The second was a major initiative carried out by Alianza Dominicana, one of NMCVC's founding partners. Alianza led several successful strategies to increase enrollment into Medicaid. As a multiservice, community-based agency with a solid history of serving the Dominican population in Washington Heights and Inwood, Alianza was also well poised to leverage emerging opportunities to increase access to newly developed public insurance products that were in the making in New York State during the initial years of Community Voices. Finally, on the basis of the success rate of facilitating enrollment to the residents of northern Manhattan, NMCVC was approached in its later years to help develop and pilot an online tool to further facilitate access to public insurance products and services available to the uninsured and underinsured. The vision for HITE—Health Information Tool for Empowerment— evolved from leaders of the Greater New York Hospital Association and became a highly valued tool for many of the social service agencies and their respective professionals, including community health workers and social workers, that had partnered with NMCVC to tackle the challenges of increasing access to care to the un- and underinsured in northern Manhattan.

What follows is a brief description of these initiatives.

Expanding Coverage for Small Businesses: HealthGap, Family Health Plus, and Healthy New York

Washington Heights historically has been an enclave of thriving small business, largely owned by the dominant groups that had immigrated from various parts of the world into the northern tip of this island—known to many as the Capital of the World. As far back as the 1940s, many of these small businesses (bakeries, fish markets, and many more) were built by Jews that had settled in New York after Word War II. In the 1960s a largely Cuban cadre of business leaders settled and further built their niche of small businesses (dry cleaners, restaurants, flower shops, and so on). The Cuban immigrants then began to pass along ownership to a small but rapidly growing group of Dominican entrepreneurs that began to settle in Washington Heights in the early and mid-1970s. Slowly the proportion began to shift, and an increasing number of Dominicans began to establish small businesses throughout the community. Currently, many of the small grocery stores (aka bodegas), hair salons, dry cleaners, livery cab companies, and so on are owned, operated, and employed by Dominican-born immigrants. This rich history of entrepreneurial spirit has survived waves of economic upswings and downturns. During the initial years of NMCVC, these business were experiencing a stable period in sales and profit. However, the downside of this seemingly positive scenario was the large number of store owners and employees that were not able to afford health insurance nor qualify for Medicaid. One of the goals of the NMCVC was to develop a health insurance package that would meet the needs of this critical target population—after all, the businesses represented a glimpse of sustained prosperity and hope to the residents of northern Manhattan.

The proposed NMCVC strategy was to develop HealthGap, a managed care model for providing insurance coverage to small businesses and the self-employed. The effort was led by Community Premier Plus, a nonprofit health plan founded by the leading safety net providers in northern Manhattan and serving northern Manhattan and the Bronx. A market survey and an actuarial analysis were conducted to determine the product scope and feasibility. A full HealthGap plan was designed in the first three years of NMCVC; however, as the plan emerged, it was obvious that it required a state subsidy to keep the costs reasonable for individuals or small businesses. Unfortunately, the climate in the state was not such that such a subsidy was forthcoming, and ultimately HealthGap could not be implemented even as a pilot project. However, NMCVC partners stood the course and used their collaborative approach to join other forces and advocate for statewide initiatives that would expand coverage to the hard-working residents of New York State. Leaders in Albany were receptive and, more important, willing to change the rules and expand coverage for this population. The State of New York delivered on its promises, and two major health insurance initiatives were developed to address the coverage needs of the uninsured: Family Health Plus (FHP) and Healthy New York (HNY).

The more significant of these two plans was FHP. FHP is a comprehensive, publicly funded New York State coverage program for low-income working adults aged nineteen to sixty-four years who earn too much for Medicaid but do not have access to employer-sponsored coverage or cannot afford the private coverage. Enrollees must meet certain income requirements and be legal immigrants or residents, including those who would otherwise be excluded under federal rules (that is, arrival in the United States after August 1996). More than a quarter-million adults were enrolled in this comprehensive managed care program as of June 2003. A major limitation of FHP is that its income limitation requirement still excluded a portion of people who could also not qualify for Medicaid. The other major limitation is the exclusion of undocumented immigrants (Figure 7.2).

Another initiative implemented was Healthy New York, a state program designed to make commercial coverage more affordable for small businesses and individuals by

FIGURE 7.2. FACILITATED ENROLLMENT.

requiring that health maintenance organizations offer fairly comprehensive coverage with state subsidies used to fund a layer of reinsurance to reduce premiums. The program had just fewer than forty thousand enrollees at the end of 2003. When this coverage was initially offered, premiums were indeed lower than those in comparable individual and small-group markets, by as much as 30 to 50 percent less than in the individual market and 15 to 30 percent less than small-group premiums. However, even with recent program changes aimed at lowering costs further, premiums in Manhattan average $193 per month for individual coverage with a pharmacy benefit. This still prices the product out of the reach of most of the low-income uninsured residents of northern Manhattan.

Although these products have had an impact in reducing the number of uninsured, a sizeable gap still remained. To that end, NMCVC project leaders continued to explore mechanisms for expanding coverage. In March 2004, NMCVC conducted a legislative analysis to determine what mechanisms to pursue. Although there were a number of proposals in both the State Assembly and the Senate, none were likely to pass, due largely to budgetary constraints. Project leaders interviewed key informants regarding coverage expansion opportunities—all of whom indicated that significant expansions were not likely during the fiscal climate or the administration of the time. During that fiscal year, the governor had also proposed cuts to Family Health Plus and the elimination of facilitated enrollment, the highly successful process that enrolls families in public programs. At the same time, the governor did award a $2 million grant to subsidize the premiums for child care workers purchasing insurance through Healthy New York. Although this was a small grant with no guarantee of continuation, it did set the precedent for subsidized coverage.

Given the situation, NMCVC focused on two key efforts:

First, NMCVC and Community Premier Plus incorporated the information gathered for the HealthGap product to develop a policy marketing document titled "The Health Gap in Northern Manhattan and the Bronx." This document highlighted the issues of access to health care and insurance coverage in northern Manhattan and the Bronx and illustrated the demographics, disparities, assets, and needs of these communities. It showcased the efforts of local partners both in communities and within the health care system. Targeting policymakers, government agencies, health care leaders, funders, community leaders, and community members, the document was used to draw attention to the needs of northern Manhattan and the Bronx and garner support and resources for our efforts.

Second, in the midst of threatening financial setbacks, NMCVC partners joined together to advocate for sustaining existing public health coverage programs. Community Premier Plus and Alianza Dominicana led a coalition of advocacy organizations to educate policymakers on the importance of maintaining Family Health Plus and the facilitated enrollment initiative. Using the outcome of the facilitated enrollment initiative (described further on), Alianza Dominicana was successful in rallying local and state support for the continuation of this model. The document "An Experience with Outreach and Facilitated Enrollment," prepared by Alianza and NMCVC, was used to inform policymakers of the impact of the outreach and facilitated enrollment model in reducing the gap of racial or ethnic disparities in accessing health care and increasing insurance coverage for eligible populations.

To date, the facilitated enrollment initiative and Family Health Plus have weathered the latest changes to the state budget on health care, although Family Health Plus will have copays.

Reducing the Number of the Uninsured: Facilitating Access to Coverage for the Eligible but Not Enrolled

The statewide opportunities that arose from the political and social movements to expand coverage for New Yorkers also brought along new challenges that demanded local approaches to leverage these positive changes in the state. One of the main challenges was reaching out to people who were now eligible for coverage and enrolling them into Medicaid and the new products that had been recently developed by New York State government. Interwoven into a complex web of barriers were issues of mistrust and fear experienced by immigrant communities throughout New York. The fears and mistrust were caused by historical and recent policies that had restricted public services for immigrants—including those that were "lawfully present."[9] Fears such as "what if recent changes were just a ploy by government to further strip 'us' of other things, like a job, an apartment, and so on?" were prevalent among community residents. The concerns, though some were perceived and not based on facts, were real and ran deep into the heart and soul of the community. More so, the concerns were not shared just by first generation immigrants; the fear and mistrust were also prevalent among their American-born children and grandchildren. And these weren't the only concerns; there were also issues of shame and guilt associated with attaining any government-sponsored benefits. Many had already refused to sign up for programs such as WIC or Welfare because they did not want to be labeled as dependent on the government. The other layer of barriers had to do with complexity of the enrollment process, including paperwork and documentation to prove eligibility. The enrollment forms were not just a barrier to enroll but also to staying enrolled after one year of coverage.

These and other "social" concerns were getting in the way of thousands of residents attaining necessary and timely health care. The impact was being felt in the emergency rooms and contributing to some of the highest rates of preventable mortality among children and adults in northern Manhattan.

Alianza was well poised to address several of the underlying barriers to care for residents of northern Manhattan. A multiservice, community-based organization that provides comprehensive and integrated services for children, youth, and families in New York City, Alianza had evolved into a critical resource for the northern Manhattan community for over fourteen years. Alianza had developed a strong leadership and advocacy role in the community and had become one of the leading authorities in the nation on the Dominican community. From child care to employment and community development, Alianza's strategy was to deliver comprehensive and integrated services and promote economic and social development for the community at large. This long-standing history of Alianza and the trust that people had in it as a resource for their families became the backdrop to what became an effective model to enroll people—and keep them enrolled!

Two of the core ingredients to the success of this program were the recruitment of community residents as enrollers and comprehensive training of staff. Building on the model of CHW described in earlier sections, recruitment of workers began in the community. As word of the program and new services offered at Alianza spread through the agency and the community, an extensive network of volunteer and paid outreach workers began to grow quickly, referring insurance inquiries to the trained enrollment staff. More and more satisfied users of the Alianza services became informal recruiters in the neighborhood. The training comprised health insurance products 101, enrollment procedures, cultural sensitivity, and empowering of participants to advocate for themselves.

The enrollment workers were also trained to not only assist participants in their application for health insurance, but also follow up throughout the process until the health insurance card was in the hands of the consumer—making sure that participants scheduled an initial visit to the doctor's office, assisting them with any problems they might have, and reminding them of the need for recertification.

Alianza fully embraced the challenge of health care expansion with the creation of the Center for Health Promotion and Education. Located in the heart of the Washington Heights-Inwood community, the Center became a safe haven for community residents. The Center, decorated with traditional artifacts representing the Dominican culture, offered a warm and inviting "at home" atmosphere for area residents.

The Center for Health Promotion and Education eventually became known as the community hub for insurance outreach and enrollment services. In addition to insurance enrollment, education, and training, the Center also became the home for other NMCVC and non-NMCVC health care initiatives, including the Healthy Heart Project, the Asthma Project, Teens Against Tobacco Use, the Child Immunization Project, and nutrition and wellness education.

The HITE Network: Using Technology to Navigate the System

The NMCVC became well-known as an advocate for improving the health care system in northern Manhattan. Project leaders were approached often to work on one initiative or another. During the final years of the program NMCVC collaborated with the Greater New York Hospital Association on the development of the Health Information Tool for Empowerment (HITE), an easy-to-use tool to help health and social service professionals and their clients navigate the maze of health care resources available to low-income, uninsured New Yorkers. HITE has two components: a resource directory and an eligibility calculator.

The resource directory was developed as a comprehensive directory of national, state, and local organizations and programs available to low-income, uninsured people, as well as links to dozens of websites that provide information on everything from how to sign up for clinical trials to where you can get free or low-cost medications. The eligibility calculator was sponsored by the Office of the Mayor of the City of New York. It allows users to determine whether they meet the basic eligibility requirements for one of New York's publicly funded health insurance programs: Medicaid, Child Health Plus, and Family Health Plus.

In addition to NMCVC, the HITE tool was being developed and piloted with two other organizations in New York State: a social service organization in Brooklyn, New York, and a coalition serving a seven-county region in the Binghamton area. To date, the Collaborative has gathered information on more than three hundred resources for un- and underinsured residents in northern Manhattan. The resources project leaders concentrated on the geographic location of Washington Heights-Inwood and Harlem, the assigned neighborhood for the development of HITE. Within the HITE tool, there are more than a thousand resources captured by the three HITE pilot sites in New York State. NMCVC also worked with the New York Academy of Medicine to develop the evaluation instruments and strategy to measure the impact and outcome of integrating the HITE network in community-based health care systems. It was found that 93 percent of the frequent users—social service professionals and community health workers—of HITE reported that the system allowed them to be more efficient in helping clients and that almost half of the users were using HITE as their main source of information for social services and low-cost care. Increasing the efficiency of those on the front line of helping community residents to improve their health and social needs continued to be a priority for NMCVC, and HITE was a means to that end.

Lessons Learned

Today, the initiatives developed by NMCVC have established roots and have led to a more coordinated system of care, improved coverage, and increased access for the uninsured. A number of lessons are shared here.

- *Transformational change is possible!* One of NMCVC's legacies and lessons learned is the demonstration that institutions and community can overcome mistrust and come together to create transformational change.

- *Building a solid infrastructure to operate a collaborative and leverage the strengths of individual partners is critical to initiating and sustaining improvements.* Through NMCVC's collaborative structure, myriad partners and interests were brought to the decision-making tables, creating a change in the way that decisions were taken and leading the way toward the creation of much needed new service programs, building upon the strengths and resources of those who invest themselves in the community.

- *Committed leadership is necessary.* Changes depend on the committed leadership of a cohort of men and women who will not waver in their vision for a healthier and more prosperous future. At the end of ten years, it was NMCVC's constant and tenacious "voices" that pressed forward beyond the clutter of "nay-sayers" and opponents, effectively securing the successes that were developed and expanded throughout the life of Community Voices. The energy and outlook of these leaders became the foundation of the Collaborative's success.

- *Health care concerns must be addressed on multiple fronts.* Over a decade, NMCVC developed a far-reaching collaborative structure linking community-based, faith-based organizations, medical and academic institutions, and safety net providers in northern Manhattan. Recognizing that individuals and communities are affected by multiple social, economic, and political factors, NMCVC strived to address health care concerns on multiple fronts. The strategy was not innovative but it was consistent. It involved mobilizing existing resources from diverse sectors to focus on northern Manhattan's most vulnerable, medically underserved residents. Despite the availability of resources, there were many challenges, including the fragmentation of the health services coupled with unstable job security; deteriorating housing conditions; cuts in education funding; and growing economic hardship threatening the quality of life for residents, especially for racial and ethnic minorities and undocumented immigrants in northern Manhattan. By bridging existing agencies that served the various complex needs of these communities, NMCVC was able to pool resources to create and strengthen programs that serve the unmet needs of community residents.

- *NMCVC was seen as a leading force to raise financial support to replicate and sustain programs developed by the partners.* One of the key successes of NMCVC was to identify opportunities to leverage additional state and federal dollars to support the expansion of best practices that emerged from the efforts of the Collaborative. This role was not only important to secure the continuation and expansion of programs, it also helped facilitate NMCVC relationships among partners. By bringing additional resources to the community, NMCVC could maintain its role as a neutral convener of the Collaborative—serving as a conduit to raise support for programs and equitably distributing resources among partners of the Collaborative.

Conclusion

By the fifth year of the Community Voices initiative, NMCVC had trained a cadre of 1,504 CHWs, and established three model programs addressing health and health care needs of the community. The CHWs facilitated health insurance enrollment for nearly thirty thousand individuals, helped eight thousand children to become completely immunized, and supported four thousand families in improving asthma management.

Furthermore, these and other efforts fostered sustainable community-wide promotion programs for the most threatening and prevalent diseases in northern Manhattan. By bridging existing agencies that have been serving the needs of the community, the NMCVC has been able to pool resources to create effective programs that serve the unmet needs of community residents. In effect, the work of the Collaborative leveraged more than $45 million in additional funding to support and expand the initiatives that were established throughout its ten years of existence. The result has been a stronger network of comprehensive health services upon which community residents can rely.[10]

Notes

1. M. Marmot, "Inequalities in Health," *New England Journal of Medicine*, 2001, 345(2), 134–136.
2. National Community Health Advisor Study, Annie E. Casey Foundation, and University of Artizona. Health Science Center, *Weaving the Future: Final Report of the National Community Health Advisor Study* (Baltimore: Annie E. Casey Foundation, 1998); B. E. Weber and B. M. Reilly, "Enhancing Mammography Use in the Inner City: A Randomized Trial of Intensive Case Management," *Archives of Internal Medicine*, November 10, 1997, 157(20), 2345–2349; E. M. Howell, B. Devaney, M. McCormick, et al., "Back to the Future: Community Involvement in the Healthy Start Program," *Journal of Health Politics, Policy and Law*, April 1998, 23(2), 291–317; S. M. Swider, "Outcome Effectiveness of Community Health Workers: An Integrative Literature Review," *Public Health Nursing*, January-February 2002, 19(1), 11–20; A. Witmer, S. Seifer, L. Finocchio, et al., "Community Health Workers: Integral Members of the Health Care Work Force," *American Journal of Public Health*, August 1995, 85(8 Pt 1), 1055–1058.
3. *Salud a Su Alcance* means "health care within your reach."
4. S. E. Findley, M. Irigoyen, M. Sanchez, L. Guzman, M. Mejia, M. Sajous, D. Levine, F. Chimkin, and S. Chen, "Community Empowerment to Reduce Childhood Immunization Disparities in New York City," *Ethnicity and Disease*, Summer 2004, 13(3).
5. U.S. Department of Health and Human Services, *Oral Health in America: Report of the Surgeon General* (Rockville, MD: U.S. Department of Health and Human Services, National Institute of Dental and Craniofacial Research, National Institutes of Health, 2000).

6. A. Formicola, H. Bailit, K. D'Abreu, J. Stavisky, I. Bau, G. Zamora, and H. Treadwell, "The Dental Pipeline Program's Impact on Access Disparities and Student Diversity," *Journal of the American Dental Association*, 2009, 140, 346–353.

7. Ref: New York City Department of Health data on uninsured.

8. Dennis Andrulis et al., *Strategies to Increase Enrollment in Children's Health Insurance Programs: A Guide to Outreach, Marketing and Enrollment in New York and Other States* (New York: New York Forum for Child Health, January 1999).

9. The Illegal Immigration Reform and Immigrant Responsibility Act in 1996 restricted the access of recent immigrants to federally subsidized welfare or health insurance. Any person arriving after August 22, 1996, was barred from federally subsidized insurance programs, and any person whose immigration status was not regularized was denied access, regardless of date of entry. The 1996 laws left thousands of immigrants stripped of any public aid. This included migrants with legal visa status who were employed and paying their share of Social Security and Medicare taxes. Thousands of eligible immigrants, and their children, forfeited the benefits they had a legal right to attain. Children were the ones most affected by this surmounting fear. Although Medicaid continued to be available to any pregnant woman and her infant child, not all eligible infants were enrolled in the program. In 2001, a court decision eliminated the five-year ban imposed by the 1996 Act and made all "lawfully present" immigrants eligible for Medicaid, Family Health Plus, or Child Health Plus if they met all other eligibility criteria.

10. The Northern Manhattan Community Voices Collaborative is the subject of a book to be published by the Columbia University Press in 2010. The book is titled *Mobilizing the Community for Better Health: What the Rest of America Can Learn from Northern Manhattan*. It is a detailed account of the summaries of the various initiatives taken in the Community Voices site in New York City from 1999 though 2009.

CHAPTER EIGHT

OAKLAND COMMUNITY VOICES

A Case Study in the Power of Advocacy in Providing "Sanctuary" and Pathways to Health Care

Luella J. Penserga, Sherry Hirota, Jane Garcia, and Ralph Silber

This chapter examines Oakland Community Voices' efforts toward improving access to health care for vulnerable populations by developing collaboratives and coalitions and streamlining advocacy efforts aimed at producing policy change in Alameda County. After reading this chapter, the reader will

- Learn about how the combination of sustained leadership with unlikely partnerships can help drive policy change
- Learn how to build and sustain a multi-stakeholder coalition
- Learn how data—both through original research and other sources—can help to influence public policy
- Learn how the Alameda County Access to Care Collaborative raised awareness about the uninsured and underserved, and succeeded in improving access along these lines through policy change
- Learn how community health workers helped to raise awareness about hard-to-reach communities
- Learn about innovative tools and media through which to reach communities and policymakers alike
- Learn about how oral health efforts spearheaded by national foundations and implemented through local universities and dental students reached into underserved communities

Introduction

Oakland Community Voices (OCV) is located in Alameda County, California, east of the San Francisco Bay and the home to approximately 1.4 million people. One-third of the county's population resides in Oakland, a city that is one of the most racially and ethnically diverse in the nation.

The health care delivery system for the uninsured in Oakland and Alameda County is decentralized, and consists primarily of eight nonprofit community health centers and the county public hospital. Together, these health care providers offer services at more than seventy locations throughout the county. The community health centers and the public hospital work closely with the local Medi-Cal managed care health plan, as well as with the county government agencies (health services, public health, behavioral health, social services). Financial pressures on the safety net system have been constant—California ranks almost last in the country in terms of state health program reimbursements—making OCV's work to build collaborations to address health care access and associated issues even more critical.

OCV came to life in this context as a partnership of three nonprofit organizations seeking to provide "sanctuary" to low-income, working immigrant families in need of health services in the city of Oakland and in Alameda County. Asian Health Services and La Clínica de la Raza—two federally qualified community health centers with strong histories of advocacy and community mobilization—partnered with a third group, the Alameda Health Consortium, a regional clinic association, to create the "Sanctuary Project," later renamed Oakland Community Voices.

As in the case of many of the other Community Voices (CV) sites, collaboration was central to the success in Oakland and Alameda County. Early in the process, OCV leaders—well-known nationally for their work on minority health and community health center issues—knew that influencing health care policy and immigrant eligibility for public services would require broad participation by other local actors. In recognition of this need, OCV built alliances with powerful stakeholders, bringing together a coalition of government agencies (county health services, public health, social services); the local Medi-Cal managed care plan; the public hospital system; and community health centers. This coalition, the Alameda County Access to Care Collaborative, promised to be a powerful and unrelenting force.

OCV served as both the convener of the Alameda County Access to Care Collaborative and a participant in numerous coalitions focusing on immigrant rights, community health workers, men's health, and local elected officials' task forces (such as City of Oakland Mayor Dellums's Health Task Force).

Compared to other advocacy groups and efforts, OCV focused specifically on bringing together health care provider leadership, namely that of the community health centers and the public hospital. Because OCV was led by health care providers, efforts equally prioritized the local health care delivery system as much as broad policy changes. Using this kind of dynamic, OCV worked to help increase the advocacy capacity of community leaders while also strengthening the relationship between the community health centers and the county safety net (Exhibit 8.1).

The "sanctuaries" created by OCV were as much about creating safe havens—physical and temporal—for vulnerable populations as they were about ensuring the development of collaborations and strong policies that would contribute to improved access to health and social services for numerous populations that might have otherwise gone without. OCV's most lasting legacy was indeed its ability to change policy and to do so through the extensive power of organized advocacy on the issues.

EXHIBIT 8.1. A PROTOCOL FOR REPLICATION.

Because health care systems are so fragmented, building relationships among health care safety net institutions is a critical step in increasing access to care. As often stated during the Community Voices Initiative, "Relationships are primary; all else is derivative." In the experience of OCV, this work requires several key ingredients:

- Develop a shared mission or purpose (for example, ensuring access to care for all uninsured in a community).
- Ensure that decision makers are "at the table" by limiting group membership to executive leadership (that is, CEO-level participation).
- Identify and convene at least one or two "internal" CEO champions who can continuously strategize to keep the collaboration moving forward.
- Dedicate at least one or two staff to the group. Though the staff may be "housed" at one institution, there should be flexibility in work scope to be responsive to the various needs of member institutions.
- Pay attention to formal process (for example, develop group identity, logo, letterhead, and materials; agree on representation, regularity of meetings, rotating chairs).
- Pay attention to informal processes to develop trust (create opportunities for information interactions, such as dinners, and keep the group small).
- Recognize that a collaboration comprising CEOs requires careful management and cannot be treated in the same way as most coalitions (for example, factor in limited availability and hectic scheduling, competing demands, wearing of multiple hats and shifting institutional agendas based on political and financial pressures).
- Recognize that building collaboration takes time, and that many lessons will be learned from many mistakes along the way.

Social, Structural, and Political Factors That Called for Change

At the time OCV was created, there were tremendous economic, social, and political pressures on local health care safety net providers and their patients. In California, the existing system of health care was rocked by federal welfare reform policies, an unprecedented move by the State of California to shift Medicaid populations into private managed care plans, and new anti-immigrant policies passed by California voters to limit access to public services.

Working against the tide of anti-immigrant sentiment, community health centers such as Asian Health Services and La Clínica de La Raza struggled to keep their doors open for immigrant families and other stigmatized groups. Both community health centers offered—and continue to offer—language- and cultural-appropriate health services, using bicultural and bilingual health care providers and staff who reflect the demographic composition of the patients they serve.

The community health centers also recognized the importance of wrap-around, non-medical services in improving patients' health; like many community health centers, they went beyond the traditional "medical model." Wrap-around services such as community health education, health coverage enrollment assistance, interpreter services, and case management services are a critical part of the community health center health care delivery model.

Around the time in which OCV was funded, health policy advocates in California had been promoting a federal waiver for California to extend its SCHIP (State Children's Health Insurance Program) to provide health coverage to parents. The State of California, under Governor Gray Davis's administration, applied for the federal SCHIP waiver, and most observers and advocates were certain that the "parental waiver," as it was called, would be approved.

Among the many who were convinced that the waiver request would be approved was the Alameda County Access to Care Collaborative. The Collaborative moved ahead with local health coverage expansion plans for parents, working with the local Medi-Cal managed health care plan to create a new insurance program in 2001 called "Family Care." Family Care was subsidized by health plan revenues, local county government funds, private foundation funds, and premiums charged to members. Used as "bridge funding," it was believed that these sources would no longer be needed once federal funds became available through the "parental waiver."

Family Care was open to low-income working adults and parents, regardless of immigration status. More than seven thousand uninsured individuals enrolled in the first three years. Even though no formal health plan marketing was conducted, the enrollment skyrocketed nonetheless, due in part to the great need, as well as to community health workers (CHWs)—particularly those working at Asian Health Services and La Clínica de La Raza— who worked to enroll people into the program.

The California policy environment became turbulent when state Governor Gray Davis was recalled by California voters in 2003 and was replaced by Governor Arnold Schwarzenegger. Shortly thereafter, the economy began its downward decline. By the time the Bush Administration approved California's request to extend SCHIP to parents, it was too late. Because SCHIP requires states to provide matching funds in order to draw down federal funds, when the approval came, California faced severe budget problems and had run out of its share of matching funds.

Despite this setback, the response to the state budget shortfall was both local and statewide. In 2004 California and Alameda County voters passed several state propositions that created new revenue streams for services. On the state level, a new income tax was imposed on millionaires to fund mental health services; locally in Alameda County, voters approved a five-cent increase in the local sales tax to fund services for the uninsured.

The Power of Data and Collaboratives

Beyond OCV's efforts aimed at improving access to health care for the uninsured and underserved, it was understood that to create and sustain an environment in which access to health care was possible for all, OCV would need to bring forth the data that would confirm the anecdotal experiences. As a result, OCV placed a high premium on research and data analysis for consumption by the policy and advocacy community alike. It was clear that policy would not change unless the facts made the case for it.

County of Alameda Uninsured Survey

The large number of uninsured in Alameda County was a key reason for the creation of OCV, although the exact number of uninsured and the demographic makeup of the same in Alameda County were unknown at the time. The community health centers, public hospital system, and other safety net providers estimated from anecdotal experience that the uninsured numbered in the hundreds of thousands. The need for an accurate count of the uninsured to determine the extent of the issue could not be overstated. Surveys documenting the uninsured were either nonexistent, conducted only in English, or not representative of Alameda County's racially and ethnically diverse population.

To fill this data gap, one of OCV's major endeavors was its work with the University of California—Los Angeles (UCLA) Center for Health Policy Research and other Alameda County safety net providers to conduct the "County of Alameda Uninsured Survey." The County of Alameda Uninsured Survey (CAUS) was a household, countywide telephone survey conducted in seven languages: English, Spanish, Cantonese, Vietnamese, Mandarin, Korean, and Dari (Afghan Farsi). OCV also later worked with other community partners to gather data on the uninsured who are not traditionally reached through household telephone surveys, such as the homeless.

In 2001, OCV, UCLA, and Alameda County released the results of the survey in the report *Advancing Universal Health Insurance Coverage in Alameda County: Results of the County of Alameda Uninsured Survey* (Figure 8.1). Confirming health care advocates' longtime suspicion, the survey revealed that more than 147,000 adults in Alameda County were uninsured, the majority were working, and more than half of uninsured adults were immigrants. Analysis of the data was published as "Uninsured Working Immigrants: A View from a California County" in the *Journal of Immigrant Health*.[1]

Alameda County Access to Care Collaborative

With the knowledge that data would be critical to identifying the problems and framing the solutions, OCV leaders moved quickly with the new information yielded by the CAUS, allowing this to become the main impetus driving the convocation of major stakeholders in the county to strategize around covering the uninsured and underserved. OCV convened multiple sectors of the health care safety net to form what exists to this day as the Alameda County Access to Care Collaborative. Members include county government agencies (health services, public health, behavioral health, social services), county public hospital system, the locally developed Medi-Cal managed care health plan, and community health centers. Together, the group created the "Proposal for Universal Health Coverage for Alameda County" and presented it to local elected officials. The proposal was a key planning document for the development of future local health coverage programs such as Alliance Family Care.

The local Medi-Cal managed care plan (Alameda Alliance for Health) responded to the need by creating Alliance Family Care, a health insurance program for low-income adults not eligible for any other public program. Through its work in the Collaborative, OCV worked closely with the Alameda Alliance for Health to provide community feedback and to evaluate Alliance Family Care. Most significantly, OCV's CHWs launched a significant outreach effort to enroll families into the new program. More than 7,500 people enrolled with no formal health plan marketing. Lessons from the creation of Alliance Family Care were later published in the editorial "Valuing Families and Meeting Them Where They Are" in the *American Journal of Public Health* and in the article "Inclusion of Immigrant Families in U.S. Health Coverage Expansions" in the *Journal of Health Care for the Poor and Underserved*.[2]

FIGURE 8.1: ADVANCING UNIVERSAL HEALTH INSURANCE COVERAGE IN ALAMEDA COUNTY, SAMPLE PAGE.

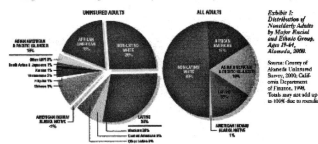

Over the life of its work, OCV continuously engaged community members on access to health care and other issues of concern to the uninsured. In 2002, OCV organized a town hall meeting in Oakland on immigrant health issues with policymakers, foundation representatives, and more than four hundred community members attending. One of the results of this gathering was the launching of a postcard campaign in 2003 that highlighted the personal stories of immigrants regarding their challenges in accessing health care (Figure 8.2). More than ten thousand postcards were distributed to community-based organizations and then sent to policymakers in Sacramento. The specific policy target was the State Legislature, which was considering the use of immigration status as a criterion for cutting health care services. Through this campaign, which was educational in nature and consistent with foundation restrictions on lobbying, OCV was able to raise state

FIGURE 8.2. DATA DISSEMINATION THROUGH PERSONAL STORIES.

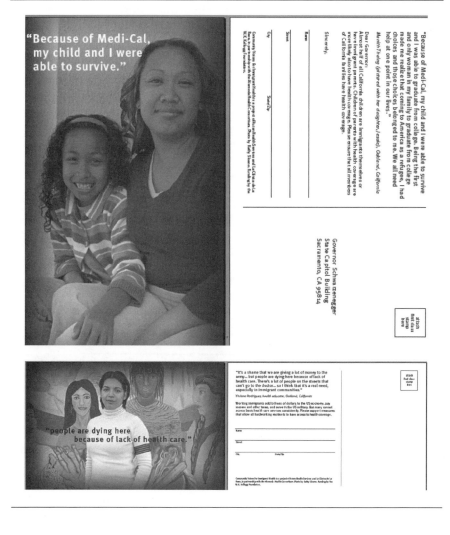

legislators' awareness about the issues facing the uninsured and access to care for immigrants.

Increasing Access to Care

Access to health care, as OCV leaders insisted, is not a simple equation or a problem whose mere solution is based on insurance coverage alone. Rather, access to quality health care is a complicated matter, often exacerbated by context. In a country as complex and diverse as the United States, the issue must often be seen on a community-by-community basis, with the understanding that each community is different and the barriers that impede care for some may not be the same for others. This was certainly the case in Oakland as a result of both the language and cultural diversity prevalent in different communities, but also because of the way in which issues were experienced by different populations and subpopulations.

Eliminating Cultural and Language Barriers

Beyond health insurance coverage, OCV was also concerned with non-economic barriers to health care, such as language and culture. In 2003, OCV worked with local elected officials (Alameda County Board of Supervisors) to survey fourteen hospitals in Alameda County on the language accessibility of services. The results of the hospital survey were released in the report, *The State of Hospital Language Assistance Services in Alameda County.*

OCV worked with the Alameda County Board of Supervisors to organize a press conference in 2004 highlighting the results, which gained widespread media coverage. Later OCV and the Board of Supervisors organized the 2005 Alameda County Language Access Summit, bringing together local hospital CEOs and medical leadership to commit to improving the language accessibility of services.

Community Health Workers

Supporting CHWs to provide services in a culturally competent health care system was another area of concern for OCV. While other CV sites did much to document the value of CHWs as part of the integrated system of care, in Oakland, beyond the recognition and support for this stance, CHWs were essential to reaching immigrant and hard-to-reach communities. Mostly indigenous to the neighborhoods they served, CHWs became not only the navigators who would open doors previously locked for non-English-speaking immigrants, mentally ill clients, or men who had been incarcerated, but also the "eyes and ears" for the issues facing different communities. CHWs in Oakland were the foot soldiers for health.

Reaching Asian Communities

Understanding that the needs in different communities are specific and sometimes unique, as part of OCV, Asian Health Services developed a specialized CHW curriculum to train CHWs working in the highly diverse Asian communities. One of the outcomes of this training is that it developed "ripple effects" in the community, with the CHWs organizing patients into "patient leadership groups" in the Chinese, Vietnamese, and Korean communities.

Reaching Men

Meanwhile, CHWs at La Clínica de La Raza organized the first men's health *promotora* (CHW) group in the Fruitvale District of Oakland, in addition to La Clínica de La Raza's ongoing commitment to organizing *promotoras* statewide. Staff and CHWs at La Clínica also continued to convene a weekly Latino men's support group. Committed to providing data in different forms to move policy, this group provided the basis for the production of a digital story (a "digital story" refers to the use of Web 2.0 technology to share relevant experiences or lessons).[3] Staff later secured a grant to support CHW training on the production of digital stories.

Through the participation of Asian Health Services' CEO in Oakland Mayor Dellums's Commission on Men's Health, an opportunity was created to inform policies on the basis of local experiences. The Commission released its findings in November 2006 and was used to inform OCV's continued work with the City of Oakland and then Mayor-Elect Dellums's plans to expand health access to Oakland residents.

Finally, the Alameda County Access to Care Collaborative also examined how to further expand and transform Alameda County's health care system such that it would be sensitive to men's health and the health of other vulnerable populations. Through dialogue among local elected officials, safety net providers, and community organizations, there was a distinct recognition that certain residents (for example, men, people who have been incarcerated, undocumented immigrant workers) were not accessing primary care services.

Through OCV's efforts devoted to highlighting the particular barriers to health care issues experienced by men, other important collaboratives became possible. In June 2006, La Clínica's leaders participated in the 2nd Annual Colloquium of Studies on Men and Masculinities in Guadalajara, Mexico, presenting two of the digital

> The Community Voices Initiative was integral to our planning here at La Clínica de La Raza. Because of the national leadership of Community Voices, and the increasing recognition of men's health locally, we decided to take a good look at how accessible our clinic services were to the men in the community. We are now expanding our programming in the area of men's health.
>
> —Jane Garcia, CEO, La Clínica de La Raza

stories that had emerged from their men's health group. International exchanges such as this were only possible because of La Clínica's earlier work through a health educator who helped to put the issue of Latino men's health on the policy map both in the United States and in neighboring Mexico, of great relevance because of the interdependence between many California residents and Mexico.

Mental Health

The Alameda Health Consortium was appointed a seat on the Alameda County stakeholders' steering committee for Proposition 63 (Mental Health Services Act) funds. Priority had been placed on mental health services for the homeless, as well as on expansion of services for immigrant populations. In 2005, OCV worked to promote an integrated model with a case management component and co-location of mental health professionals with medical staff on-site at OCV's community health centers. Furthermore, through the work of the Alameda County Access to Care Collaborative, mental health services for the homeless as well as an expansion of services for immigrant populations continue to receive priority to this day.

From a survey that OCV supported in 2003, OCV knew that approximately six thousand residents in Alameda County were homeless. A significant number of these had histories of incarceration, and a majority had a history with the foster care system. As in many parts of the country, the majority of the homeless in Oakland are men of color; moreover, most of the people provided with case management services at Highland Hospital have extreme housing needs, as well as mental health issues.

OCV worked with Proposition 63 stakeholders to expand the number of bilingual and bicultural mental health service providers in Alameda County. The largest and only providers of community-based bilingual and bicultural mental health services are La Familia, Asian Community Health Services (which works closely with Asian Health Services), and La Clínica de La Raza. Both Asian Health services and La Clínica conduct case management for patients, particularly those patients with mental health issues.

Oral Health Services

On the national scene, the importance of oral health services was gaining visibility. In 2000, Surgeon General David Satcher, M.D., Ph.D., released the first Surgeon General's report on oral health and disparities. The CV Initiative issued several reports on oral health, and the U.S. Department of Health and Human Services began requiring federally qualified community health centers to ensure access to dental services through direct provision of services or through referral arrangements.

In Oakland, oral health services for low-income residents expanded. Asian Health Services successfully raised enough government and private funds to open the first dental clinic in Oakland's Chinatown; the dental clinic was also notable because it was the first "paperless" dental clinic in the area, using dental practice management software that eliminated the need for paper files. In the same year, La Clínica de La Raza partnered with Children's Hospital-Oakland to become the provider of pediatric dental care on-site at the hospital campus.

Bolstering the efforts to expand oral health services was the community-based dental education Pipeline initiative of the Robert Wood Johnson Foundation, in collaboration with The California Endowment and The W.K. Kellogg Foundation. The initiative fostered partnerships between local dental schools and community health centers in the San Francisco Bay Area, including OCV clinics Asian Health Services and La Clínica de La Raza.

As a result of the initiative, local dental students from University of the Pacific and the University of California at San Francisco began completing dental externships at Asian Health Services, La Clínica de La Raza, and other nearby community health centers, thereby gaining experience in providing care in a community clinic environment. Prior to the initiative, most dental students drifted into private practice or toward practices that emphasized cosmetic dentistry. Few students were given the opportunity to experience the rewards of providing community-based care to patients in need. Through the Pipeline program, students were exposed to the needs of low-income patients in a community-based setting, and the importance of dental services as part of the overall provision of primary medical care and chronic disease management.

Health Care Delivery System Reform

Throughout the years, OCV developed a role as a convener of major health care stakeholders in the area. Covering the uninsured, naturally, continued to be a major policy priority. Gradually, however, OCV expanded beyond the issues of immigrant health and into broader issues of health care system delivery reform.

In 2004, OCV organized "The Power of Community in Health Conference: A Showcase of Community Health Center Advances," attended by more than 250 people and featuring keynote speaker George Halvorson, CEO of Kaiser Permanente.

The conference focused on quality improvement, cultural competency, and the elimination of health disparities. The conference proceedings of "The Power of Community in Health" conference were distributed to more than two thousand organizations across the country. A tangible result of the conference was that Kaiser donated $1 million to the community health centers to provide services to the uninsured.

OCV with the Alameda County Access to Care Collaborative also conducted a monumental study, *Increasing Access to Health Care for Low-Income Uninsured Residents of Alameda County, California: Baseline Assessment 2007*. The baseline was the first of its kind in Alameda County, and finally equipped stakeholders with not only the number of uninsured but *the number of uninsured who were actually receiving low-cost and free services through community health centers and the county public hospital*. The report provided safety net providers with a measure of their success in reaching the uninsured, absent a universal health coverage program. The report is now cited widely by county government officials as part of local planning efforts to expand access to care for the uninsured.

Last, the work of OCV led to opportunities to leverage new funds to continue working on access-to-care issues. The organizations involved in OCV went on to apply for funds for several important projects. Projects included the case management of frequent ER users at the local public hospital and partnerships with community colleges to train the health care workforce. Most notable was the work of the Access to Care Collaborative with the Alameda County government health agency to secure a multimillion dollar Medicaid waiver "Coverage Initiative" award from the State of California for chronic disease management of uninsured patients with diabetes, heart failure, or asthma. The State of California provided more than $8 million annually for three years. The program is now considered a model in California, and the lessons from Alameda County's work has contributed to the growing consensus among California policymakers that the state's use of Medicaid waiver dollars to expand access to uninsured patients with chronic disease is a success and should be continued.

Lessons Learned

Convening the Alameda County Access to Care Collaborative allowed the community health centers to work more closely with the local public hospital and the Medi-Cal managed care plan. From this dynamic a number of lessons emerged.

- *A multi-stakeholder process may allow for unlikely partners to sit at the same decision-making table.* This arrangement permitted an equal space for activists at the same table with county officials, making it possible for OCV leaders to be part of the bigger county planning process. As a result, OCV played a critical role in helping to strengthen the local safety net and leverage funding. In doing this it helped to create a foundation for the sustainability of local health plans.

- *Innovations, data, and promising practices must be showcased!* OCV knew the value of making its local innovations visible. Efforts toward promoting the good work of CHWs created a better understanding for the value of these para-professionals in connecting people to care. In like fashion, OCV's ability to gather different kinds of data—ranging from the numbers of uninsured to the health access issues experienced by men of color—was key in mounting the evidence that would showcase that policies needed change and barriers needed lifting.
- *Systems change can only happen through strong leadership that is willing to take risks.* The unequivocal leadership of OCV and its partners in forging a path toward system change must be recognized. Through their continued development of deep relationships among local partners, policymakers, and power brokers alike, they created the space not only for innovative work but for real policy change that would make the difference in the daily lives of many. Though OCV did organize some grassroots events, most efforts throughout the years were strategically focused on bringing together the executive leadership of community health centers, the public hospital, health plans, and county government and officials to create real change on health care issues.

Conclusions

Today, the Alameda County Access to Care Collaborative continues to be recognized as a convener of important discussions among stakeholders on timely topics such as men's health, the primary care "medical home," specialty care access, and elimination of racial disparities in health through "place-based" interventions. While the work is not finished, the collaborative structures that are in place, the promising practices that are being employed, and the lessons that have been learned from the successes in improving policy have created a visible pathway for other needed improvements. OCV certainly helped to forge the road ahead.

Notes

1. N. Ponce, R. J. Nordyke, and S. Hirota, "Uninsured Working Immigrants: A View from a California County," *Journal of Immigrant Health*, 2005, 7(1), 45–53.
2. D. Zahn, S. Hirota, J. Garcia, and M. J. Ro, "Valuing Families and Meeting Them Where They Are," *American Journal of Public Health*, 2008, 98(1), 62–64; S. Hirota, J. Garcia, R. Silber, I. Lamirault, L. J. Penserga, and M. B. Hall, "Inclusion of Immigrant Families in U.S. Health Coverage Expansions," *Journal of Health Care for the Poor and Underserved*, 2006, 17(1), 81–94.
3. "Not Just a Number," *Oakland Tribune* and InsideBayArea.com, accessed August 25, 2010, from http://www.bayareanewsgroup.com/multimedia/iba/njn/#/communityvoices.

PART TWO

COMMUNICATING THE CHANGE

The Role of the Community Voice in Building the Policy and Intellectual Basis for Community-Based Access to Care

Henrie M. Treadwell and Melva Robertson

The "community voice" has not been widely acknowledged as a viable guide for the work that must be done to achieve health justice in the United States. To broadcast this "voice" more directly, the Community Voices initiative explicitly required that the learning laboratories document their practice and inform policy efforts in the form of publications for peer-reviewed publications; for public media as op-eds; in the form of policy briefs and fact sheets; and through use of report cards and coffee-table books that tell the story of those who work to improve health care access. Part of what made Community Voices unique was its ability to communicate to others the gaps in care and the changes that were being accomplished in order to maximize the message and thereby ensure that attention would be given to a particular subject.

To accomplish this kind of communication, the initiative chose the expansion of knowledge as a strategy to undergird action. One key result of this strategy was the publication of a number of special theme issues in *The American Journal of Public Health* (race, poverty, and the invisible man of color, May 2003; oral health, May 2004; prison and reentry health, October 2005; mental health, October 2006; and a special Community Voices legacy issue in September 2008). Moreover, issues on a variety of topics related to community-based efforts to inform policy while serving the people may be found in the *Journal of Health Care for the Poor and Underserved* and the *American Journal of Health Studies*. Many other journals were the target for publications as well, including the *Journal of Correctional Health Care*. Though these publications are too numerous to list in this volume, they can be found easily through a search of the literature, and in some cases via www.communityvoices.org.

Because of this strategy of disseminating information as widely as possible about the necessary changes and promising practices, the learning laboratories succeeded in paving the way to new services; new insights; changes in marketplace practice and policy; and deliberations by policymakers, both in their own communities and states, and across the nation. Topics included the health of poor men of color; the power of providing "sanctuary" in some communities; oral health care for adults and for children; the importance of community health workers and community outreach; models for improved service delivery; building the workforce; the impact of racism; and more.

Where the policy barriers were just too high, the learning laboratories and the Community Voices Program Office wrote about public policy and how it contributes to the gender and age disparities; the impact of the criminal justice system on community health and well-being; the problems of reentry from prison and its impact on the health of the men returning home and on their families; and the collateral damage inflicted on those with a non-felony drug conviction. Our work on men's health has grown larger as time has progressed and resulted in men's health report cards in Denver and North Carolina to accompany the special theme issue in journals and the policy brief "Where Are the Men?" Our work took us to prison, as we found too few men in our clinics and on the streets of some neighborhoods. Population-based health care required that we be accountable for who was served and for who was not served because they could not access care. But our focus remains on the entire community because of our conviction that strengthening any part of the family dynamic will build family, community, health, and ultimately wealth. In all of our writing, we call out the weakest links in order to use these as levers to wedge the system closer to social justice.

The manuscripts and briefs shared in Part Two are only a small component of the repertoire but serve to put to rest old ideas that community efforts are fragile, yield too few results, and offer little to no insight. Most of the authors you will read here had never written for the public before becoming a part of the Community Voices family. They continue to share their learnings as their work grows and dispels the harsh reality of life in America for the poor, marginalized individuals who have no regular access to primary and preventive health care.

CHAPTER NINE

HEALTH DISPARITY AND VULNERABLE POPULATIONS CONFRONTING RACISM AND SEXISM TO IMPROVE MEN'S HEALTH

Henrie M. Treadwell, Mary E. Northridge, and Traci N. Bethea

Two fundamental determinants of men's health are confronted—racism and sexism—that the authors believe underlie many of the health disparities documented between women and men and place men of color at particular disadvantage in U.S. society. In doing so, the authors contend that race and gender, as well as racism and sexism, are social constructs and, therefore, amenable to change. They hope to allay concerns that gains in the health of men will come at the expense of continued advances in the health of women. Instead, by better understanding how the harsh intersections of racism and sexism have contorted roles for men of color and damaged their social ties, a healing process in intimate relationships, extended families, and entire communities may be fostered. Only by reforming historical injustices and reuniting men with their partners, families, and communities will sustained improvements in their health and well-being be realized.

A column revised for *American Journal of Men's Health* by invitation of Demetrius J. Porche, DNS, APRN, Editor, Professor and Associate Dean for Nursing Research and Evaluation, Louisiana State University Health Sciences Center, New Orleans (e-mail: dporch@lsuhsc.edu). From the National Center for Primary Care, Morehouse School of Medicine, Atlanta, Georgia (HMT); the Mailman School of Public Health, New York, New York (MEN); and Boston University School of Public Health, Massachusetts (TNB).

Keywords: men's health; health disparities; race; racism; gender; sexism

Gender differences in adult health are well documented, but only recently has research begun to investigate how race conditions gendered health disparities (Read and Gorman, 2006). Our long-term interest has been in a better understanding of the core determinants of excess mortality among African American men (McCord and Freeman, 1990), with a particular focus on the ways communities have developed strategies to mitigate, resist, and undo the adverse effects of discrimination on their health and well-being (Geronimus, 2000). In May 2003, *American Journal of Public Health* published a theme issue devoted to men's health that two of us (HMT and MEN) had edited closely together for more than a year. In his introductory remarks to that issue, Georges C. Benjamin, MD, FACP, the executive director of the American Public Health Association, explained,

> As we work to improve the health of our communities, we must address the root causes of such filtering. The reason for unhealthy behaviors is not that the public does not fully understand healthy ones; it is something more deeply rooted in the ills of our society. Unhealthy behaviors start in part as a response to a social environment that fosters no alternatives. To change that environment is the real challenge. (Benjamin, 2003, p. 704)

It is thus deeply rewarding for us to not only witness but be a part of the naissance of *American Journal of Men's Health* (AJMH*)*. We believe that focused attention on men's health is essential to fill the gaps in research, practice, and policy that were sorely evident to us more than four years ago when we first worked together on this topic. Furthermore, we honor the mission of AJMH to "disseminate scholarly multidisciplinary state of the science information regarding men's health" (see http://www.sagepub.co.uk/journalsProdManSub.nav?prodId=Journal201776&currTree=Subjects&level1=E00 for AJMH author guidelines, mission, aims, and scope). It is only through the interaction of committed scientists and scholars across sectors that we will make progress on answering societies' big questions and solving the world's big problems, including what is causing health disparities between women and men and what we need to do to eliminate them (Northridge, Sclar, Feighery, Fiebach, and Karpel Kurtz, 2008; Rieker and Bird, 2005; Satcher and Rust, 2006).

Rather than shy away from contentious issues, we have elected to confront two fundamental determinants of men's health—racism and sexism—that we believe underlie many of the health disparities documented between women and men and place men of color at particular disadvantage in U.S. society. In "A Glossary for Social Epidemiology," Nancy Krieger (2001) provided explicit descriptors of constructs of interest we then build on for nuanced understanding in the context of this particular article on men's health. We deal with our first fundamental determinant of men's health—racism—in the next section and our second fundamental determinant of men's health—sexism—in the subsequent section. Then we posit that the cruel intersection of racism and sexism has contorted men's roles as partners, husbands, fathers, brothers, uncles, nephews, sons, teachers, mentors, coaches, and heroes in the following three sections through examples at various levels of influence. The first example of this intersection deals with intimate relationships at the interpersonal level (White racism as a stressor within Black relationships), the second example is devoted to safety at the neighborhood level (the code of the street and recurrent trauma among young Black men), and the final example involves discrimination at the community and societal levels (disproportionate effects of incarceration on communities of color). We seek to reunite men with their partners, families, and communities by reimagining a society in which we can all reach our full potential.

Race and Racism

Krieger (2001) defined race as a social, not biological, category, referring to social groups, often sharing cultural heritage and ancestry, that are forged by oppressive systems of race relations, justified by ideology, in which one group benefits from dominating other groups, and defines itself and others through this domination and the possession of selective and arbitrary physical characteristics (for example, skin color) (p. 696).

Accordingly, racism, in her view, "refers to institutional and individual practices that create and reinforce oppressive systems of race relations" (p. 696).

In an earlier editorial titled "Poverty, Race, and the Invisible Men," one of us (HMT) asserted that "poor men and men of color live with a tremendous amount of pain, are demeaned and devalued in a system that rewards wealth and values some people over others, and die early" (Treadwell and Ro, 2003, p. 706). Over the past decade especially, the egregious effects of racism on the health and health care of African American populations have been ever more rigorously documented in the scientific literature, particularly in relation to mental health (Snowden, 2003; Whaley, 2004; Williams, Neighbors, and Jackson, 2003).

Nonetheless, most of the published studies we were able to find regarding racism and men's health focused on health care service delivery (Becker and Newsome, 2003; Chow, Jaffe, and Snowden, 2003; Ekundayo, Bronner, Johnson-Taylor, Dambita, and Squire, 2003; Meyer, 2003; Smith, 2003; van Ryn, Burgess, Malat, and Griffin, 2003) or compared morbidity and mortality rates for minority men to those of minority women (Rhoades, 2003; Satcher, 2003). Two reports, however, were of particular interest to us with respect to this article and are summarized below.

In his review article titled "The Health of Men: Structured Inequalities and Opportunities," David R. Williams (2003) reviewed data on the magnitude of health challenges faced by men in the United States and concluded that the forces that adversely affect men's health are interrelated, unfold over the life course, and are amenable to change. According to Williams, these forces include economic marginality, adverse working conditions, and gendered coping responses to stress, each of which can lead to high levels of substance use, other health-damaging behaviors, and an aversion to health-protective behaviors.

In their qualitative study titled "African-American Men's Perceptions of Health: A Focus Group Study," Ravenell, Johnson, and Whitaker (2006) conducted eight focus group interviews with select subgroups of African American men, including adolescents, trauma survivors, HIV-positive men, homeless men, men who have sex with men, substance users, church-affiliated men, and a mixed group of men (N = 71). Participants were queried regarding their definitions of health, beliefs about health maintenance, and influences on their health. African American men's definitions of health included physical, mental, emotional, economic, and spiritual well-being, as well as fulfilling social roles, such as having a job and providing for one's family. Health maintenance strategies included spirituality and self-empowerment. Stress was cited as a dominant negative influence on health and was attributed to lack of income, racism, unhealthy neighborhoods, and conflict in relationships. Positive influences included a supportive social network and feeling valued by loved ones.

Gender and Sexism

In seeking to examine gender and sexism in relation to men's health, we begin again with Krieger's (2001) definitions of these terms. She characterized gender as a "social construct regarding culture-bound conventions, roles, and behaviors for, as well as relationships between and among, women and men and boys and girls" (p. 694). Sexism, according to her glossary,

> involves inequitable gender relationships and refers to institutional and interpersonal practices whereby members of dominant groups (typically men) accrue privileges by subordinating other gender groups (typically women) and justify these practices via ideologies of innate superiority, difference, or deviance. (p. 694)

Although helpful as starting points, these definitions of gender and sexism are too often equated with women and harm suffered by women, respectively. Of course, to ignore the need for a womanist perspective (see Walker, 1983) or the abuse suffered by women at the hands of men would be negligent, at best. Rather, we strive here to fully understand the root causes of grave health disparities for men of color who have suffered historically from discriminatory policies and practices (see, for example, Kaufman, 1997). To do so, we turn next to qualitative studies for insights regarding the intersection of racism and sexism on the lives of African American women and men.

In "Through Black Eyes: African American Women's Constructions of Their Experiences with Intimate Male Partner Violence," Shondrah Tarrezz Nash interviewed nine former physically, emotionally, and sexually abused African American wives. Her findings suggest that participants' observations on Black men's social marginalization, educational and economic disparities between Black partners, Black women's role in safeguarding Black men, and gendered scripts on traditions of resistance influenced their perspectives on the causes of and responses to abuse (Nash, 2005).

White Racism as a Stressor Within Black Relationships

Among her many contributions to exposing the particularities and social structures undergirding some Black women's constructions of intimate male partner violence, Nash (2005) identified White racism as an external irritant that is both historically relevant and a present-day, ongoing site of stress within Black relationships. The following quotation from one of her participants (Kenya, a fifty-six-year-old, separated, emotional-abuse survivor and mother of two children) underscores this theme:

> It goes way back to slavery, and it's still here. A Black woman will be treated with more respect than a Black man by a White man. [For example,] if I want to get a job working in the house for this White woman, and my husband, this Black man, wants to be their yard man? Well, that White man would "talk down" to him, whereas, he wouldn't dare with me, because he would want to flirt with me. That still happens! [*laughs*]. . . . [That White man] doesn't want that Black man to feel secure. He wants to always make him feel that he has his foot on his neck. . . . How do you think [that that Black man] is going to act when he gets home? (p. 1433)

Nash also reported that academic and economic disparities were perceived by certain participants as additional systems of exclusion for Black men. Maxine, fifty-one, a police officer in a large Midwestern city during her three years as an emotionally and physically abused wife, attributed much of this tension to discriminatory work practices:

> It makes me angry, but not at [Black men] so much, but because of why they are like that. . . . [Black women] were brought in places so [Black men] wouldn't be brought in places, because we are the less threatening of the two. . . . So [Black men] *did* take some of the punishment around the assertiveness of that. And I think that they think they deserve a lot of reward around that. But they can't see the punishment [Black women] took and the sacrifices we made. And in the midst of this, it's like: "*You* can go to school. *You* all have opportunities to do this. *You* all have this and that—and [Black men] don't." (p. 1435)

Next, we examine the experiences of violence suffered by young Black men through their own words and perspectives.

The Code of the Street and Recurrent Trauma Among Young Black Men

John A. Rich and Courtney M. Grey (2005) interviewed young Black men between the ages of eighteen and thirty years who had been hospitalized after being shot, stabbed, or physically assaulted by another individual to better understand their experiences of violence. In doing so, they employed the framework of ethnographer Elijah Anderson (1999), who first identified respect as a central component of the code of the street whereby urban young Black men protect themselves physically while also safeguarding their fragile personal identities. The code of the street dictates that when someone disrespects you, whether physically, emotionally, or materially, you must respond aggressively to regain your respect.

This idea is especially salient for victims of violence because an act of violence committed against them is viewed as extreme disrespect. In the following two quotations from young Black men who were both shooting victims, they expressed the view that being seen as a sucker or punk might lead not only to physical harm but also to a damaged identity.

> A sucker is a person that if someone says something to them or does something to them they just sit there and take it and don't retaliate. If you're living in the inner city, you wouldn't want to be a sucker 'cause everybody will take advantage of you. (Rich and Grey, 2005, p. 818)

> Like, you're a punk if you let somebody come up in your face and disrespect you. If you let somebody hit you, and you don't hit 'em back, if you let somebody take what belongs to you without you saying anything about them taking what belongs to you, it means you're a punk. If they take your self-esteem away from you, then you're a punk. (Rich and Grey, 2005, p. 818)

Another aspect of the code of the street that emerged from these narratives was a profound lack of faith in the police. According to Anderson (1999),

> the code of the street is actually a cultural adaptation to a profound lack of faith in the police and the judicial system—and in others who would champion one's personal security. The police, for instance, are most often viewed as representing the dominant White society and not caring to protect inner-city residents. (p. 34)

Disproportionate Effects of Incarceration on Communities of Color

Public policies, including social welfare legislation, have been shaped by discriminatory practices that serve to devalue and stigmatize African American men (see especially Skocpol, 1992), but nowhere have racism and sexism been more influential than in the mass migration of generations of African American men and boys into U.S. correctional systems (Treadwell and Nottingham, 2005). Iguchi, Bell, Ramchand, and Fain (2005) have thoughtfully outlined how the disproportionate entry of people of color into prison for felony drug offenses may exacerbate the impact of disparities already evident in communities of color, above and beyond the clear adverse effects on the health and well-being of the offender, the family of the offender, and the community at large. Specifically, a felony drug conviction significantly decreases access to jobs and related health benefits; public housing; economic and health benefits such as food stamps; licenses, permits, and military service; financial support for higher education; and the right to vote while incarcerated (forty-eight states and the District of Columbia), while on parole (thirty-six states), and even to ex-offenders who have completed their sentences (three states; Iguchi et al., 2005). Opponents to felon disenfranchisement laws argue that "while facially neutral, they are actually thinly veiled attempts to disenfranchise Blacks without violating the Fifteenth Amendment" (Newman, 2006, p. 526).

Structural factors such as racism and sexism have been identified to affect the way Blacks are processed through juvenile courts, with biased outcomes noted in formal petitioning, predisposition detention, and out-of-home placement decisions (Sampson and Laub, 1993). At the interpersonal level, Bridges and Steen (1998) reported that probation officers' recommendations to courts were significantly more likely to attribute Black offenders' behavior to internal causes (that is, emotional state or intention) and White offenders' behavior to external causes (that is, mitigating environmental factor or events), even when controlling for criminal act and prior record. How do these external factors translate into unhealthy behaviors that affect the well-being of entire communities?

Social Disintegration and Unhealthy Lifestyles

One of us (MEN) was involved in analyzing results from an in-person survey conducted among 695 adults living in Central Harlem, New York City, from 1992 to 1994. Strikingly higher frequencies of self-reported licit and illicit substance use and most forms of trauma were documented between Central Harlem respondents and participants in U.S. national health surveys, as well as important differences in risk factors for excess mortality between women and men in Central Harlem (Fullilove et al., 1999). Furthermore, Central Harlem adults were more likely than were adults in other U.S. communities to report high rates of unemployment and homelessness and low rates of marriage.

The latter figures are viewed as markers of social engagement. At levels as high as those reported in Central Harlem a decade ago, the root causes of these figures move beyond any notion of poor individual choices to indicators of widespread declines in the social ties that hold communities together (Leighton, 1959). High rates of substance use and trauma often follow in the wake of community disintegration, leading to further instability. Indeed, social disintegration undermines the capacity of groups to support individuals in their efforts to create and maintain healthy lifestyles (Fullilove et al., 1999). If Benjamin (2003) was correct in arguing that unhealthy behaviors start in part as a response to a social environment that fosters no alternatives, we need to change the status quo.

Conclusion

According to Fainstein and Servon (2005), "gender has to do with socially constructed notions about appropriate roles and behaviors, but these roles change over time" (p. 3). We contend that systems of inequalities in the United States, especially with regard to race and gender, have contributed to egregious health disparities documented between women and men and have placed men of color at particular disadvantage.

It would be wrong, however, to view focused attention on improving men's health as meaning less attention for women's health. This is not a war between the genders, or a zero-sum enterprise, in which any change in one direction results in a loss from somewhere else (Fainstein and Servon, 2005). Rather, reuniting men with their partners, families, and communities, for example, through more humanistic and community-centered approaches to incarceration and rehabilitation (Freudenberg, Daniels, Crum, Perkins, and Richie, 2005; Golembeski and Fullilove, 2005), will lead to sustained improvements in the health and well-being of U.S. society as a whole. Men's invaluable roles as partners, husbands, fathers, brothers, uncles, nephews, sons, teachers, mentors, coaches, and heroes need to be reshaped and reimagined in full recognition of the historical oppressions they have suffered but with renewed hope that the American dream of life, liberty, and the pursuit of happiness might be available to all of us rather than remain the province of a privileged few. In a reimagined society without racism and sexism, dignity, intimacy, and joy would abound for everyone, and diversity would be celebrated rather than be used as a tool of oppression.

Acknowledgment

The authors thank Natasha Williams, M.P.H., J.D., Ph.D., senior researcher and health policy analyst, Community Voices at the National Center for Primary Care at the Morehouse School of Medicine, for research related to the discriminatory impact of social welfare legislation on African American men, as well as information on the provisions of the Voting Rights Act of 1965, felon disenfranchisement, and the Fourteenth and Fifteenth Amendments to the U.S. Constitution.

References

Anderson, E. *Code of the Street: Decency, Violence and the Moral Life of the Inner City*. New York: Norton, 1999.

Becker, G., and Newsome, E. "Socioeconomic Status and Dissatisfaction with Health Care Among Chronically Ill African Americans." *American Journal of Public Health*, 2003, 93(5), 742–748.

Benjamin, G. C. "Reducing Unhealthy Behaviors: Where Do We Start? *American Journal of Public Health*, 2003, 93(5), 704.

Bridges, G. S., and Steen, S. "Racial Disparities in Official Assessments of Juvenile Offenders: Attributional Stereotypes as Mediating Mechanisms." *American Sociological Review*, 1998, 63(4), 554–570.

Chow, J. C., Jaffe, K., and Snowden, L. "Racial/Ethnic Disparities in the Use of Mental Health Services in Poverty Areas." *American Journal of Public Health*, 2003, 93(5), 792–797.

Ekundayo, O. T., Bronner, Y., Johnson-Taylor, W. L., Dambita, N., and Squire, S. "Formative Evaluation of a Men's Health Center." *American Journal of Public Health*, 2003, 93(5), 717–719.

Fainstein, S. S., and Servon, L. J. *Gender and Planning: A Reader*. Piscataway, NJ: Rutgers University Press, 2005.

Freudenberg, N., Daniels, J., Crum, M., Perkins, T., and Richie, B. E. "Coming Home from Jail: The Social and Health Consequences of Community Reentry for Women, Male Adolescents, and Their Families and Communities." *American Journal of Public Health*, 2005, 95(10), 1725–1736.

Fullilove, R. E., Fullilove, M. T., Northridge, M. E., Ganz, M. L., Bassett, M. T., McLean, D. E., et al. "Risk Factors for Excess Mortality in Harlem: Findings from the Harlem Household Survey. *American Journal of Preventive Medicine*, 1999, 16(3, Suppl.), 22–28.

Geronimus, A. T. "To Mitigate, Resist, or Undo: Addressing Structural Influences on the Health of Urban Populations." *American Journal of Public Health*, 2000, 90(6), 867–872.

Golembeski, C., and Fullilove, R. "Criminal (in)justice in the City and Its Associated Health Consequences." *American Journal of Public Health*, 2005, 95(10), 1701–1706.

Iguchi, M. Y., Bell, B., Ramchand, R. N., and Fain, T. "How Criminal System Racial Disparities May Translate into Health Disparities." *Journal of Health Care for the Poor and Underserved*, 2005, 16, 48–56.

Kaufman, R. E. "The Cultural Meaning of the 'Welfare Queen': Using State Constitutions to Challenge Child Exclusion Provisions." *New York University Review of Law and Social Change*, 1997, 23, 301–328.

Krieger, N. "A Glossary for Social Epidemiology." *Journal of Epidemiology and Community Health*, 2001, 55, 693–700.

Leighton, A. H. *My Name Is Legion: Foundations for a Theory of Man in Relation to Culture: The Stirling County Study of Psychiatric Disorder and Sociocultural Environment* (Vol. 1). New York: Basic Books, 1959.

McCord, C., and Freeman, H. "Excess Mortality in Harlem." *New England Journal of Medicine*, 1990, 322, 173–179.

Meyer, J. A. "Improving Men's Health: Developing a Long-Term Strategy." *American Journal of Public Health*, 2003, 93(5), 709–711.

Nash, S. T. "Through Black Eyes: African American Women's Constructions of Their Experiences with Intimate Male Partner Violence." *Violence Against Women*, 2005, 11(11), 1420–1440.

Newman, C. A. "Constitutional Problems with Challenging State Felon Disenfranchisement Laws Under the Voting Rights Act of 1965." *Connecticut Law Review*, 2006, 38, 525–564.

Northridge, M. E., Sclar, E. D., Feighery, A., Fiebach, M. Z., and Karpel Kurtz, E. "Reinventing Healthy and Sustainable Communities: Reconnecting Public Health and Urban Planning." In *Pitt International Conference on Inequality, Health, and Society* (Bristol, U.K.: The Policy Press, Beacon House, 2008).

Ravenell, J. E., Johnson, W. E. Jr., and Whitaker, E. E. "African-American Men's Perceptions of Health: A Focus Group Study." *Journal of the National Medical Association*, 2006, 98(4), 544–550.

Read, J. G., and Gorman, B. K. "Gender Inequalities in U.S. Adult Health: The Interplay of Race and Ethnicity." *Social Science & Medicine*, 2006, 62(12), 3197–3198.

Rhoades, E. R. "The Health Status of American Indian and Alaska Native Males." *American Journal of Public Health*, 2003, 93(5), 774–778.

Rich, J. A., and Grey, C. M. "Pathways to Recurrent Trauma Among Young Black Men: Traumatic Stress, Substance Use, and the 'Code of the Street.'" *American Journal of Public Health*, 2005, 95(5), 816–824.

Rieker, P. P., and Bird, C. E. "Rethinking Gender Differences in Health: Why We Need to Integrate Social and Biological Perspectives." *Journals of Gerontology*, 2005, 60B, 40–47.

Sampson, R., and Laub, J. "Structural Variations in Juvenile Court Processing: Inequality, and Underclass, and Social Control." *Law Society Review*, 1993, 27, 285–311.

Satcher, D. "Overlooked and Underserved: Improving the Health of Men of Color." *American Journal of Public Health*, 2003, 93(5), 707–709.

Satcher, D., and Rust, G. "Achieving Health Equity in America." *Ethnicity & Disease*, 2006, 16(2, Suppl. 3), S3-8-13.

Skocpol, T. *Protecting Soldiers and Mothers: The Political Origins of Social Policy in the United States.* Cambridge, MA: Belknap, 1992.

Smith, A. L. "Health Policy and the Coloring of an American Male Crisis: A Perspective on Community-Based Health Services." *American Journal of Public Health*, 2003, 93(5), 749–752.

Snowden, L. R. "Bias in Mental Health Assessment and Intervention: Theory and Evidence." *American Journal of Public Health*, 2003, 93(2), 239–243.

Treadwell, H. M., and Nottingham, J. H. "Standing in the Gap." *American Journal of Public Health*, 2005, 95(10), 1676.

Treadwell, H. M., and Ro, M. "Poverty, Race, and the Invisible Men." *American Journal of Public Health*, 2003, 93(5), 705–707.

van Ryn, M., Burgess, D., Malat, J., and Griffin, J. "Physicians' Perceptions of Patients' Social and Behavioral Characteristics and Race Disparities in Treatment Recommendations for Men with Coronary Artery Disease." *American Journal of Public Health*, 2003, 96(2), 351–357.

Walker, A. *In Search of Our Mother's Garden.* San Diego, CA: Harcourt Brace Jovanovich, 1983.

Whaley, A. L. "Ethnicity/Race, Paranoia, and Hospitalization for Mental Health Problems Among Men." *American Journal of Public Health*, 93(5), 724–730.

Williams, D. R. "The Health of Men: Structured Inequalities and Opportunities." *American Journal of Public Health*, 2003, 93(5), 724–731.

Williams, D. R., Neighbors, H. W., and Jackson, J. S. "Racial/Ethnic Discrimination and Health: Findings from Community Studies." *American Journal of Public Health*, 93(2), 200–208.

CHAPTER TEN

DETERMINING WHAT WE STAND FOR WILL GUIDE WHAT WE DO

Community Priorities, Ethical Research Paradigms, and Research with Vulnerable Populations

Leda M. Pérez and Henrie M. Treadwell

Prisoners, ex-offenders, and the communities they belong to constitute a distinct and highly vulnerable population, and research must be sensitive to their priorities. In light of recent suggestions that scientific experimentation involving prisoners be reconsidered, community-based participatory research can be a valuable tool for determining the immediate concerns of prisoners, such as the receipt of high-quality and dignified health care inside and outside prisons. In building research agendas, more must be done to ensure the participation of communities affected by the resulting policies.

American Journal of Public Health, 2009, 99, 201–204. doi:10.2105/ AJPH.2007.125617.

Given recent proposals to reexamine federal regulations pertaining to human experimentation in prisons,[1-4] it is important that more be done to ensure that the viewpoints and life experiences of prisoners, ex-offenders, and their communities be considered. There has been recent debate about what constitutes ethical research in prisons and about the possible expansion of the scope of what is allowable. These questions arise because biomedical researchers are having difficulty in recruiting volunteers for clinical trials[5] in the United States and because a number of private companies are increasingly seeking volunteers in other countries in which the costs of these experiments are less expensive, protocols are less complex, and compliance standards are less onerous.[6-9]

Some U.S. researchers suggest that current regulations guiding prison research may be too strict and outdated,[1,4] and arguments have been made in favor of reassessing the current norms.[3,4] It has been noted, for example, that with the existence of institutional research boards, prisoners may actually benefit from this research if protocols are strengthened.[1,3,4] At least one researcher has argued that prisoners have a constitutional right to choose to participate in a study, clinical or otherwise.[2] Other work has suggested that prisoners ought to have the same access to experimental drugs as people who are not in prison and that there are ways to erect safeguards to ensure that the abuses committed in the past are not repeated.[2-4]

We argue that until the question of adequate health care for prisoners is resolved, human experimentation should not be allowed. Why are so many people from low-income, minority communities incarcerated? Why do these populations appear to be a convenient and natural source for social research? And, given that prisons do exist, why is it that a stronger focus is not placed on appropriate and dignified care for confined populations, such as those inside prisons as well as for ex-offenders and their communities? Why is not greater precedence being given to finding the best methods for ensuring one single standard for all?

We know, for example, that prisoners tend to be sicker than the rest of the population, bearing significantly higher rates of infectious diseases such as hepatitis C, tuberculosis, and HIV as well as chronic conditions including asthma, hypertension, diabetes, and oral illnesses. High rates of mental illness are also prevalent,[10-12] as well as the co-occurrence of substance abuse and mental illness. How these illnesses are treated in prison, and how much care is provided to ex-offenders after they leave prison, have direct implications for whether an ex-offender will reintegrate into society successfully.[13]

For research in prisons to be ethical, it must be interested in upholding prisoners' constitutional right to appropriate quality care while in prison and ensuring a stronger and more effective safety net for them when they return home. It must focus first on ensuring that the health of all is protected. It must ask what safeguards are in place for those who have engaged in clinical trials while in prison should they later become ill or infected.

Communities and Prison Populations

In 2007, the prison population of the United States stood at nearly 2.3 million.[6,14] This figure has quadrupled in the past thirty years,[6] caused in part by strict sentencing policies for drug offenses. During this period, African American men were arrested, convicted, and incarcerated at higher rates and for longer periods than were other racial and ethnic groups.[12] In the year 2000, Latinos in the United States made up 20 percent of the prison population.[15] Poor communities of color are particularly affected by this high incarceration rate on numerous levels, with women and children losing the active presence of partners and fathers and their income and support.[15,16] Women are presently the fastest-growing segment of the U.S. prison population.[17] Similar to male prisoners, female prisoners tend to have lower incomes, lower educational levels, and higher rates of mental illness and substance abuse than does the non-prison population.[17,18] Women also often leave behind children and families.

For many ex-offenders coming home, the resources are not there to support them.[12,16] In many cases, those returning to their communities may be living with a newly diagnosed mental illness or chronic disease.[19,20] Research clearly shows that health conditions and access to quality care are especially substandard for ethnic and racial minorities, both in general[21] and inside prisons, which house inmates mostly belonging to racial and ethnic minorities.[11, 22–24] The Eighth Amendment to the U.S. Constitution prohibits "cruel and unusual punishments," and although prisoners have a constitutional right to receive medical care,[2] far too often its availability and quality are limited. The recent situation in California's prison medical system, currently under federal receivership as a result of a number of prisoners who died of preventable causes, is one example of the challenges that prison health care providers are experiencing.[25] Furthermore, the efforts of prison providers may be hampered as a result of poor policies, limited resources, and prison infrastructure.

The problem extends beyond prison walls. Many U.S. communities—too often, communities of color—lack the bare minimum of health care. Should not research be concerned with the need for better health care for the most vulnerable communities, both inside and outside prisons?

Pathways Toward Ethical Research

Community-based participatory research (CBPR) offers one pathway to ethical research that includes the perspectives of prisoners, ex-offenders, and their communities. CBPR is increasingly recognized as an approach that includes the voices, knowledge, leadership, and thinking of community members in research and decision making.[26–29] This marks an important epistemological shift toward greater appreciation of knowledge from untraditional sources, as well as an opportunity for hearing and including the real concerns of communities. In pursuing CBPR, we are also confronted with critical ethical questions regarding how to proceed equitably on the basis of principles and values of partnership and how to ensure that those engaged truly benefit from this process—not because of what has been given to them but because of what they, through their own agency, have determined is valuable and constructive for themselves.

Communities can be defined in a number of ways. There are geographical communities as well as communities based on common conditions of existence.[27] Seen in this way, prisoners, ex-offenders, and the neighborhoods that they leave behind and return to may be viewed as a distinct, highly vulnerable community.[12,23,30] In trying to engage this community as partners in research through CBPR, researchers must first ask what its priority concerns are. The answer is clear: quality and dignified care for both those in prison and those outside and the resources and infrastructure to help ex-offenders resume their lives when they come back home.

More must be done to ensure that prisoners, ex-offenders, and their communities have a say in building a research agenda that will affect them and the manner in which they and, ultimately, all live in this nation. A first step toward building a stronger base for CBPR would be to work directly with affected groups and ensure that their recommendations are upheld. We explore how some of the possible applications of CBPR may help to shed light on the current health status of vulnerable communities, both inside and outside of prisons.

The Need to Improve Health Care

The data on the need to improve access to health care and its quality for everyone in the nation, but particularly for vulnerable populations, are irrefutable.[21,31,32] In one particularly strongly worded report, the Institute of Medicine noted,

> The U.S. health care delivery system does not provide consistent, high-quality medical care to all people. Americans should be able to count on receiving care that meets their needs and is based on the best scientific knowledge—yet there is strong evidence that this frequently is not the case. Health care harms patients too frequently and routinely fails to deliver its potential benefits. Indeed, between the health care that we now have and the health care that we could have lies not just a gap, but a chasm.[31(p1)]

In addition, research has shown how best to train public health practitioners and researchers to engage communities equitably.[33,34] CBPR holds promise as a way of working with vulnerable communities as equal partners, particularly because it underscores the ethical responsibilities that the scientific community has toward the public.[33,35] The National Institutes of Health has devoted attention to CBPR projects that seek to promote the use of partnership approaches in studying and addressing health issues.[27] These advances come at a time when there is increased recognition of the efficacy of community-driven approaches in health research, particularly where racial and ethnic disparities are concerned.[27]

Improving Community Research and Health for All Vulnerable Populations

CBPR offers an important pathway toward enabling communities to tell their story from their perspective. Israel et al. define CBPR as

> A partnership approach to research that equitably involves, for example, community members, organizational representatives, and researchers in all aspects of the research process and in which all partners contribute expertise and share decision making and ownership.[27(p5)]

Because it regards research as a collaborative process, CBPR offers opportunities for communities affected by social, economic, political, and environmental policies to be heard on equitable terms. This approach becomes particularly relevant for low-income communities—often communities of color—who have historic reasons to distrust research and researchers.[27] As Israel et al. have said, CBPR offers the space to create a climate of "cultural humility" and "cultural safety."[27] In the former, expertise is shared with the community in question; in the latter, the responsibility is on the researcher to ensure that community partners feel safe in the process.

Regarding prison research, CBPR may be an important vehicle for engaging affected communities on such pressing research questions as the following: What kinds of health care are prisoners receiving, and what kinds of chronic illnesses are they faced with in prison? How has the absence of appropriate care in prison contributed to ex-offenders' health outside of prison? What aggregate impact is this having on their communities? How might communities help to shape the research agenda? How might both prisoners and their communities be prepared for prisoners' return to these communities? What are the costs and benefits of clinical trials on entire communities? What happens to people who have undergone "voluntary" clinical trials in prison once they come home? Are there resources for follow-up care once they leave prison? What kinds of mechanisms might be developed to ensure that those who do undergo trials can deal with possible adverse reactions?

Research on the conditions in prison suggests that incarcerated people have no guarantee of health care when they leave prison.[24] There is evidence that those who have undergone clinical trials in prison have little or no follow-up care for potential secondary effects after they are released.[36] CBPR can further play a role here by bringing together those affected communities and prison health care providers to forge new and improved solutions.

Promising Practices

The principles laid out in the 1979 Belmont Report, *Ethical Principles and Guidelines for the Protection of Human Subjects of Research*,[37] continue to be relevant today, especially regarding research with vulnerable populations. Respect for persons, beneficence, and justice must still be considered touchstones that guide the work of ethical research. Through CBPR, respect for persons can be expanded to respect for communities, "do no harm" can be expanded to "do the right thing," and community empowerment can be promoted.[38] Finally, for there to be meaningful community collaboration and leadership in bringing about change, justice must be considered in terms of equitable access to decision making and the impact of policies on the community.[38]

Of further concern is the need to acquire information based on the real-life experiences of communities. For at-risk populations targeted for clinical trials, participatory research practices must work consistently toward strengthening communities, building social capital for those within the communities, and developing relationships with others doing advocacy work in similar areas to ensure that community concerns are also weighed in the research process (C. Caceres, M.D., Ph.D., Public Health and Administration Division, Universidad Cayetano Heredia, Lima, Peru, oral communication, April 2007). In this way, the issues that concern communities and the communities' thoughts on these issues inform research and subsequent policies.

Recent work has demonstrated the efficacy of CBPR in working with people returning to their communities from prison.[30,39] Beyond partnering with communities to inform city policies, some research designs have been able to uncover participants' experiences and their perceptions regarding prison's ability to prepare inmates for release and a return to the community.[30] The short-term effects of this research have been the drafting of policies that, at a minimum, begin to reflect the concerns of those affected.[30] Participatory research work in Miami, Florida, with men from the impoverished community of Overtown, revealed concerns about time spent in prison and the need for better policies aimed at reintegration and support for community well-being.[20] As this kind of research moves forward, providers of care must also be partners, because they too hold the keys for improved outcomes.

Conclusion

A recent report by a working group devoted to developing an action plan for prisoners reentering the community made two overarching recommendations: end the invisibility of prisoners and ex-offenders and end their isolation.[40] CBPR can be an effective tool for ensuring that prisoners and ex-offenders have a say in policies that affect them and for preventing their being marginalized by policies that do not reflect their needs.

Regarding human experimentation in prisons, a number of questions remain unresolved that would benefit from community input. Why, for example, has the prison population been singled out for this experimentation? Historically, the federal government's regulation of research involving vulnerable populations has also included nursing homes, hospitals, and mental institutions.[41,42] Why is there no review of appropriate ethical regulations where these populations are concerned? In effect, why not consider the ethical concerns of all vulnerable populations? Why single out one particular group, one that is so clearly populated by ethnic and racial minorities?

In the final analysis, research can best contribute to the improvement of the health of vulnerable populations by stressing ethics and the primary principles and practices that are the foundations of a civilized society. This would mean a concern for the immediate needs of the most marginalized, including access to health care and well-being. It would mean listening and giving fair time to those most affected. In the quest for knowledge and social evolution, determining what we stand for as a nation will guide what we do.

Notes

1. D. L. Moore, "An IRB Member's Perspective on Access to Innovative Therapy," *Albany Law Review*, 1994, 57(3), 559–581.
2. S. Hoffman, "Beneficial and Unusual Punishment: An Argument in Support of Prisoner Participation in Clinical Trials," *Indiana Law Review*, 2000, 33, 475–513.
3. Institute of Medicine, *Ethical Considerations for Research Involving Prisoners* (Washington, DC: National Academies Press, 2006). Available at: http://www.iom.edu/Object.File/Master/35/796/Prisoners.pdf. Accessed June 18, 2007.
4. B. H. Lerner, "Subjects or Objects? Prisoners and Human Experimentation," *New England Journal of Medicine*, 2007, 356, 1806–1807.
5. MedicineNet.com. *Definition of Clinical Trials*. Available at: http://www. medterms.com/script/main/art.asp?articlekey=2752. Accessed July 10, 2007.
6. I. Urbina, "Panel Suggests Using Inmates in Drug Trials," *New York Times*, August 13, 2006. Available at: http://www.nytimes.com/2006/08/13/us/13inmates.html. Accessed November 17, 2008.
7. K. Barnes, *Prisoners May Be Used to Fill Clinical Trial Patient Shortage*, August 17, 2006. Available at: http://www.drugresearcher.com/news/ng.asp? n=69892-clinical-trial-patient-recruitment-prisoner. Accessed July 3, 2007.

8. *Arrowhead Publishers' New Study Reveals Trends in Clinical Trial Outsourcing to Emerging Markets* [press release], May 18, 2007. Available at: http://www.pharmiweb.com/pressreleases/ pressrel.asp?ROW_ID = 2287. Accessed July 3, 2007.

9. A. Petryna, "Clinical Trials Offshored: On Private Sector Science and Public Health," *BioSocieties*, 2007, 2, 21–40.

10. C. Golembeski and R. Fullilove, "Criminal (In)justice in the City and Its Associated Health Consequences," *American Journal of Public Health*, 2005, 95, 1701–1706.

11. H. M. Treadwell, and A. J. Formicola, "Improving the Oral Health of Prisoners to Improve Overall Health and Well-Being," *American Journal of Public Health*, 2005, 95, 1677–1678.

12. N. Williams, *Where Are the Men? The Impact of Incarceration and Reentry on African American Men and Their Children and Families*, 2006. Available at: http://www.communityvoices.org/ Uploads/wherearethemen2_00108_ 00144.pdf. Accessed August 1, 2007.

13. K. Mallik-Kane and C. A. Visher, *Health and Prisoner Reentry: How Physical, Mental and Substance Abuse Conditions Shape the Process of Reintegration* (Washington, DC: Urban Institute; 2008). Available at: http://www.urban.org/UploadedPDF/ 411617_health_prisoner_ reentry.pdf. Accessed March 10, 2008.

14. Join Together Advancing Effective Alcohol and Drug Policy and Treatment. *2006 Saw Leap in U.S. Prison Population* (Boston, MA: Boston University School of Public Health; June 28, 2007). Available at: http://www.jointogether.org/news/ headlines/inthenews/ 2007/2006sawleap- in-us-prison.html. Accessed July 9, 2007.

15. Families Against Mandatory Minimums, *Latinos and the Prison System*. Available at: http:// www.famm.org/PressRoom/PressKit/FactSheets/Latinosandtheprisonsystem.aspx. AccessedMarch 10, 2008.

16. L. M. Pérez, H. M. Treadwell, A.M.W. Young, and N. Williams, "A Call to Action from the Grassroots: Men on What a Nation Must Do to Reverse a Legacy of Separation and Segregation," *American Journal of Health Studies*, 2007, 22(2), 67–72.

17. M. Mauer, C. Potler, and R. Wolf, *Gender and Justice: Women, Drugs and Sentencing Policy* (Washington, DC: The Sentencing Project, 1999). Available at: http://www.sentencing project.org/Admin/Documents/publications/dp_genderandjustice.pdf. Accessed March 10, 2008.

18. M. W. Byrnes, "Conducting Research as a Visiting Scientist in a Women's Prison," *Journal of Professional Nursing*, 2005, 21(4), 223–230.

19. V. Heines, "Speaking Out to Improve the Health of Inmates," *American Journal of Public Health*, 2005, 95, 1685–1688.

20. A.M.W. Young, *The Overtown Men's Health Study, 2006*. The Collins Center for Public Policy. Available at: http://www.collinscenter.org/usr_doc/OvertownMensHealthPages.pdf. Accessed July 14, 2008.

21. Institute of Medicine, *Unequal Treatment: Confronting Ethnic and Racial Disparities in Health Care* (Washington, DC: National Academies Press, 2002).

22. Z. G. Restum, "Public Implications of Substandard Correctional Health Care," *American Journal of Public Health*, 2005, 95, 1689–1691.

23. H. M. Treadwell, and J. Nottingham, "Standing in the Gap," *American Journal of Public Health*, 2008, 98, S170.

24. "Prisons and Health" [issue]. *American Journal of Public Health*, 2005, 95(10).

25. California Progress Report. *California's Desperate Need for Prison and Sentencing Reform*. Available at: http://www.californiaprogressreport.com/2006/12/californias_des.html. Accessed March 10, 2008.

26. F. Ansley, and J. Gaventa, "Researching for Democracy and Democratizing Research," *Change*, 1997, 1, 46–53.

27. B. A. Israel, E. Eng, A. J. Schulz, and E. A. Parker (eds.), *Methods in Community-Based Participatory Research for Health* (San Francisco: Jossey-Bass, July 2006).

28. M. W. Leung, I. H. Yen, and M. Minkler, "Community-Based Participatory Research: A Promising Approach for Increasing Epidemiology's Relevance in the 21st Century," *International Journal of Epidemiology*, 2004, 33(3), 506–507.

29. S. Flicker, R. Travers, A. Guta, S. McDonald, and A. Meagher, "Ethical Dilemmas in Community-Based Participatory Research: Recommendations for Institutional Review Boards," *Journal of Urban Health*, 2007, 84, 478–493.

30. J. Van Olphen, N. Freudenberg, P. Fortin, S. Galea, "Community Reentry: Perceptions of People with Substance Use Problems Returning Home from New York City Jails, *Journal of Urban Health*, 2006, 83, 72–81.

31. Institute of Medicine, *Crossing the Quality Chasm: A New Health System for the 21st Century* (Washington, DC: National Academies Press; 2001). Available at: http://www.iom.edu/Object.File/Master/27/184/Chasm-8pager.pdf. Accessed July 3, 2007.

32. R. L. Braithwaite, H. M. Treadwell, M. Ro, and K. Braithwaite, "Community Voices: Healthcare for the Underserved," *Journal of Health Care for the Poor and Underserved*, 2006, 17(1), v–xi.

33. K. Gebbie, L. Rosenstock, and L. M. Hernandez, *Who Will Keep the Public Healthy? Educating Public Health Professionals for the 21st Century* (Washington, DC: National Academies Press; 2002). Available at: http://www.iom.edu/Object.File/ Master/24/562/EducatingPHFINAL.pdf. Accessed June 18, 2007.

34. *Community Voices: Health Care for the Underserved*. Available at: http://www.communityvoices.org. Accessed July 14, 2008.

35. American Public Health Association, *APHA Policy Statement 2004-12: Support for Community-Based Participatory Research in Public Health*, 2004. Available at: http://www.apha.org/advocacy/policy/policysearch/default.htm?id =1298. Accessed July 14, 2008.

36. B. P. Wyman, "Biomedical and Behavioral Research on Juvenile Inmates: Uninformed Choices and Coerced Participation," *Journal of Law and Health*, 2000, 15, 77–104.

37. National Institutes of Health, *The Belmont Report: Ethical Principles and Guidelines for the Protection of Human Subjects of Research*, April 18, 1979. Available at: http://ohsr.od.nih.gov/guidelines/belmont.html. Accessed July 9, 2007.

38. N. Shore, *Conference Call Series on Institutional Review Boards and Ethical Issues in Research*. Co-sponsored by Community–Campus Partnerships for Health & Tuskegee University National Center for Bioethics in Research and Health Care, June 25, 2007. Available at: http://depts.washington.edu/ccph/pdf_files/Shore_presentation.pdf. Accessed July 14, 2008.

39. N. Freudenberg, J. Daniels, M. Crum, T. Perkins, and B. E. Richie, "Coming Home from Jail: The Social and Health Consequences of Community Reentry for Women, Male Adolescents, and Their Families and Communities," *American Journal of Public Health*, 2005, 95, 1725–1736.

40. M. B. Cohen, *Developing an Action Agenda for Prisoners Reentering the Community: Reconnecting to Health Services*, Community Voices: Healthcare for the Underserved and the National Academy for State Health Policy. Available at: http://www.communityvoices.org/ Article.aspx?ID =401. Accessed July 14, 2008.

41. *Institutional Review Board Guidebook*, "Chapter VI: Special Classes of Subjects." Available at: http://www.hhs.gov/ohrp/irb/irb_chapter6.htm. Accessed June 18, 2007.

42. *Institutional Review Board Guidebook*.

CHAPTER ELEVEN

"ORAL HEALTH IS THE MEASURE OF A JUST SOCIETY"

Henrie M. Treadwell and Mary E. Northridge

Abstract: Former Surgeon General David Satcher's report *Oral Health in America* documents the higher burden of oral diseases and conditions borne by those with relatively low social standing at each stage of life. When an entire community suffers from a health concern, that concern becomes a social justice issue. Racial and ethnic minorities, prisoners, and seniors suffer disproportionately from oral diseases and conditions due to societal prejudices that place them at risk over and above any risk associated with their economic means. Community-based delivery models that involve the community in planning and implementation, build upon the existing health safety net to link oral health services with primary care, and change public or institutional policy to support the financing and delivery of oral health care have proven successful. Here we champion the need for a national health plan that includes oral health care to promote social justice and oral health for all.

This article is reprinted with the permission of Meharry Medical College from the *Journal of Health Care for the Poor and Underserved*, Volume 18, Number 1, 12–20 (February 2007), Johns Hopkins University Press, publisher.

Key words: Oral health; dental health; health policy; social justice; medically un-derserved areas; racial and ethnic minorities; prisoners; seniors; community health services; health care reform

Introduction

In the United States today, there are those who would have us believe that class lines are blurred: we eat increasingly similar food at all-too-familiar national chains, dress up and dress down in fashions that cross traditional class lines, and listen to music from rap stars regardless of our income or wealth (or at least our children and grand-children do). Yet for those of us in the health care field, when we want to know a person's social class, we look that person not in the eye, but in the mouth.

Our purpose in this Guest Editorial is to use former Surgeon General David Satcher's ground-breaking report, *Oral Health in America*,[1] as the basis for reinvigorat-ing the quest for a national health care plan that includes oral health care. When entire communities suffer from a health concern such as poor oral health, that con-cern becomes a social justice issue that demands attention from elected officials, fund-ing institutions, and the larger public.

Oral Health in America: A Report of the Surgeon General

On May 25, 2000, David Satcher released the first-ever Surgeon General's report on oral health.[1] Among its incontrovertible findings were that the burden of oral diseases and conditions is disproportionately borne by those with relatively low social standing at each stage of life. Poor nutrition, lack of preventive oral health care, violence lead-ing to face trauma, and tobacco and alcohol use harm teeth and their supporting structures during various periods of the life course. In particular, such exposures may lead to dental caries (beginning in early childhood and continuing throughout life), periodontal diseases and tooth loss (especially in adults), and oral and pharyngeal cancers (predominantly disorders of the elderly).[2] Furthermore, research is currently underway to understand the relationship between periodontal infections in mothers and pre-term low birth weights of their babies,[3] which suggests that there may be intergenerational effects of oral diseases.

In addition, the Surgeon General's report went beyond health to document the pervasive effects of oral diseases and conditions on the well-being of disadvantaged members of our society. That is, oral diseases and their treatments may undermine self-image and self-esteem, discourage family and other social interactions, and lead to chronic stress and depression—all at great emotional and financial costs. They also interfere with vital functions of daily living such as breathing, eating, swallowing, and speaking.[1] Targeted initiatives for vulnerable populations including racial and ethnic minorities, seniors, and prisoners are key priorities in eliminating oral health disparities in the United States. Also deserving of increased public health attention and funding are proven population-based prevention measures, such as community water fluoridation; school-based sealant programs, and tobacco prevention and control programs.[4]

Inequalities in Oral Health Is a Global Concern

Of course, social inequalities in oral health and health care are not limited to the United States. A national survey in Australia found that significant social differentials in perceived oral health exist among dentate adults, and that inequalities span the socioeconomic hierarchy.[5] A Brazilian ecological study reported a significant negative correlation between dental caries and the proportion of the population that received fluoridated water, principally in the municipalities with the worst income inequality indicators.[6] The authors concluded that these results underscore the importance of fluoridation for the reduction of caries rates as well as to attenuate the impact of socioeconomic inequalities on the prevalence of dental caries.[5]

Thompson and colleagues[7] examined New Zealand's structural changes to the welfare state in the early 1990s and determined that the oral health of Maori children deteriorated over a five-year period in comparison with their European counterparts. They therefore cautioned policymakers to consider the health implications of major social and economic policy changes before they are implemented.[7]

It Takes a Community

From 1992 to 1994, an in-person, community-based survey was conducted among 695 adults aged eighteen through sixty-five years in Central Harlem, the largely African American community located in northern Manhattan, New York City.[8] Of more than fifty health complaints that were part of the survey, problems with teeth or gums were the most frequently cited among respondents (30 percent), a greater proportion than those reporting suffering from hypertension, asthma, or diabetes.[9] In contrast, only 10 percent of the participants surveyed in a 1989 special supplement on oral health in the National Health Interview Survey (NHIS) reported fair or poor oral health.[10] [Note: The NHIS is the largest source of self-reported data for the civilian, non-institutionalized household population of the United States related to (1) health and illness status; (2) general health attitudes, behaviors, and knowledge; and (3) health care utilization.[11] Prior to a survey redesign in 1997, the NHIS questionnaire consisted of two parts: a set of basic health and demographic items contained within a core component and one or more sets of questions on current health topics contained within a supplement component, for example, the 1989 oral health special supplement that contained questions on oral health care utilization.[11]]

Rural communities also suffer oral health disparities, due in part to fewer practicing dentists in these medically underserved areas.[12,13,14] When an entire community suffers from a health concern, that concern becomes a social justice issue. As Allukian and Horowitz[4] argue, "Just as it takes a village to raise a child, it will take a village to resolve the neglected epidemic of oral diseases, especially for vulnerable populations" (p. 370).

The Mouth Is a Reflection of Overall Health and Well-Being

As it is put in the Surgeon General's report, the mouth is the gateway of the body.[1] It not only senses and responds to the external world, it also reflects what is happening deep inside the body. The mouth signals nutritional deficiencies and serves as an early warning system for diseases such as HIV/AIDS, other immune system problems, general infections, and stress.[1] Poor oral health is associated with diabetes, heart disease, and stroke.[4] The cultural values and symbolism attached to facial appearance and teeth are underscored in the anthropological and ethnographic literature.[1] Moreover, the stigma associated with facial disfigurements due to craniofacial diseases and conditions and their treatments limit educational, career, and marital opportunities and affect most other social relations.[1]

Conversely, good oral health allows us to eat, chew, talk, smile, kiss, sleep, read, think, study, and work without oral pain, discomfort, or embarrassment. In other words, "Oral health is having a smile that helps you feel good about yourself and gives others a healthy and positive image of you" (p. 358).[4]

How the Mouth Became Disconnected from the Rest of the Body

Beginning with the establishment of the first dental school in 1840, the medical and dental professions developed separately in the United States. Today, U.S. medical schools teach very little, if anything, about oral health.[4] Moreover, since medicine has played a dominant role in the development of health policy and practice in the United States, oral health is usually excluded or not considered part of primary health care.[4] As Allukian[15] marveled, "It makes no sense that children, diabetic patients, or senior citizens with an abscess on their leg can receive care through their health insurance or a health program, but if the abscess is in their mouth, they may not be covered" (p. 843).

Only 4 percent of dental care is financed with public funds, compared with 32 percent of medical care.[1] But what does this coverage mean in terms of access to quality oral health care? Consider New York State, for instance. In New York, Medicaid includes comprehensive primary oral health care coverage, Medicare has no dental component, and private insurance may or may not cover oral health services.

In the Central Harlem survey previously cited,[9] the oral health assessment consisted of the question, "During the past twelve months, have you had problems with your teeth or gums?" Those who answered *yes* to this question were then asked, "Did you see a dentist for problems with your teeth or gums?" Among participants reporting oral health complaints ($N = 209$), two thirds (66 percent) reported having seen a dentist for the complaint. People who had private insurance were more likely to have sought treatment from a dentist (87 percent) than those who had public insurance (62 percent) or were uninsured (48 percent). In the authors' view, "It is disturbing that a third of those who suffer from dental problems did not seek care. Among those who did, having insurance coverage was significantly associated with receipt of care. Those with private coverage were less likely to report having dental problems and more likely to report seeking treatment when problems existed than were those with public coverage or no coverage" (p. 51).[9]

Zabos et al.[9] then speculated that "receipt of oral health services for people in need may be improved if those services can be integrated into comprehensive primary care programs. This problem is particularly vexing because the New York State Medicaid program has one of the most comprehensive dental benefit packages among the 50 states, providing coverage for people of all ages. This suggests that there are other barriers to care that must be examined (e.g., geographic accessibility and availability of dentists who both accept Medicaid and provide culturally competent care)" (p. 51).

Addressing Oral Health Disparities and Increasing Workforce Diversity

According to the Sullivan Commission[16] report titled *Missing Persons: Minorities in the Health Professions*, African Americans, Hispanic Americans, and American Indians together make up more than 25 percent of the U.S. population but only 9 percent of the nation's nurses, 6 percent of its physicians, and 5 percent of its dentists. Evidence of the direct link between poorer health outcomes for racial and ethnic minorities and the shortage of racial and ethnic minorities in the health care professions was compiled by the Institute of Medicine[17] in its landmark report, *Unequal Treatment: Confronting Racial and Ethnic Disparities in Health Care*.

Mitchell and Lassiter[18] recently reviewed the literature concerning health care disparities and workforce diversity issues, particularly within the oral health field. They then synthesized the recommendations intended to address identified needs, with a focus on the role of academic dental institutions (ADIs).[16] They believe that, first and foremost, ADIs must develop a culture conducive to change and must reflect diversity considerations. This will require consistent support from the leadership within ADIs, including a formal declaration of each institution's commitment to diversity, cultural competency, and the elimination of oral health care disparities.[18]

In the coming decades, the racial and ethnic composition of the United States is expected to shift to include more people of color, particularly Hispanics.[19] The need for ADIs to enroll and support more applicants from underserved minority groups is crucial to the elimination of disparities in oral health care. Two other underserved groups with respect to oral health care are prisoners and seniors, both of whom face considerable societal hurdles in accessing and receiving respectful oral health care.

Ensuring the Oral Health of Prisoners

Dental care is listed as an essential health service by the National Commission on Correctional Health Care.[20] Nonetheless, the oral health status of prisoners is overridingly poor. As with other individuals of low social standing in the U.S. population from which prisoners disproportionately come, adults who are incarcerated in either federal or state prison systems are more likely to (1) have extensive caries and periodontal disease; (2) be missing teeth at every age; and (3) endure a higher percentage of unmet dental needs than employed U.S. adults.[21,22] Even taking these differences into account, racial differences remain. At the United States Penitentiary in Leavenworth, Kansas, White inmates had significantly fewer decayed teeth than did Black inmates, and the number of decayed teeth increased significantly with inmate age.[21]

The empirical evidence to date indicates that prisoners deem oral health a priority, and that access to oral health services improves the conditions of their mouths. For instance, among prisoners in Maine, smoking and dental health were the most commonly reported health problems after mental health and substance abuse.[23] A recent study of continuously incarcerated individuals in the North Carolina prison system found that the prison dental care system was able to improve markedly the oral health of a sample of inmates,[24] confirming the idea that dental health improves when access to services is provided.

The Crisis in Oral Health Care for Seniors

McNally[25] and Lamster[26] have recently called attention to the disproportionate effect on the elderly of oral and dental diseases. After years of exposure of the teeth and related structures to microbial assault, oral cavities show evidence of wear and tear as a result of normal use (chewing and talking) and destructive oral habits such as bruxism (habitual grinding of the teeth). The elderly also suffer from chronic disorders that can directly or indirectly affect oral health, including autoimmune disorders, and often require multiple medications, which commonly reduce salivary flow.[26] Several societal changes have left many of our seniors unable to afford any dental services whatsoever, let alone the most appropriate treatments.[2,26] Among the changes responsible for the lack of oral health care for older adults are (1) rapid population shifts and the resulting larger numbers of older adults in the United States; (2) lack of routine dental service coverage under Medicare; (3) willful neglect; and (4) ageism.

Disparities in oral health and health care accumulate and intensify throughout the life course, yet it is never too early or too late to intervene to improve the oral health status of disadvantaged groups.[2] McNally[25] believes that determining the extent to which elders endure an unreasonable burden of illness and disability, or are underserved with respect to illness or disability, is an important first step toward understanding the meaning of justice in the context of caring for elders. Lamster[26] perceives the need for a coordinated effort to address the oral health care needs of the elderly.

With adequate attention and focus, a variety of national initiatives with implementation on the state and local levels will serve to improve access to oral care for older Americans who are currently most in need, including the poor and disabled. According to McNally,[25] "A clearer understanding of justice will allow the oral health community to begin to recognize appropriate levels of responsibility to address the issue of just and respectful caring for these vulnerable populations" (p. 56).

Community Voices Delivery Models to Improve Access to Oral Health Care

One size does not fit all when it comes to improving access to oral health care for uninsured and underserved populations. Three Community Voices programs—Northern Manhattan's Community DentCare, New Mexico's Health Commons, and North Carolina's FirstHealth—were recently presented as innovative partnership models that seek to address the unmet oral health needs of diverse populations.[27] Even given this diversity, however, three common core elements were identified that made these models successful: (1) involving the community in planning and implementation; (2) building upon the existing health safety net to link dental services with primary care; and (3) changing public or institutional policy to support the financing and delivery of dental care.

Such delivery models, which offer basic oral health services in connection with community-based primary care services, may help ensure holistic, comprehensive health care for our nation's most vulnerable and underserved populations. Unfortunately, state governments, desperate to get their budget deficits under control, are cutting adult dental benefits from their Medicaid programs.[27] Rather than having made progress since the Surgeon General's report on the neglected epidemic of oral diseases, there are indications that we are losing ground on hard-won gains and that oral health disparities are widening between the haves and the have nots.

Oral Health Is the Measure of a Just Society

The Surgeon General's report on oral health describes the mouth as a mirror of health or disease, as a sentinel or early warning system, as an accessible model for the study of other tissues and organs, and as a potential source of pathology affecting other systems and organs.[1] While improved nutrition and living standards after World War II have enabled certain population groups to enjoy far better oral health than their forebears did a century ago, not all Americans have achieved the same level of oral health and well-being.[18] According to Allukian and Horowitz,[4] people are much more likely to have poor oral health if they are low-income, uninsured, developmentally disabled, homebound, homeless, medically compromised, and/or members of minority groups or other high-risk populations who do not have access to oral health services.

A Framework for Action for developing a National Oral Health Plan to improve quality of life and eliminate health disparities was set forth in the Surgeon General's report on oral health.[1] Without funding or legislation, however, no national impact was or is expected. Allukian and Horowitz[4] offer the following five recommendations:

1. A national health program should be made available for all U.S. residents, with a meaningful comprehensive oral health component that stresses prevention and primary care.
2. A much higher priority should be given to oral health by federal, state, and local government agencies and by nongovernmental organizations and institutions.
3. All public schools should provide (a) comprehensive health education, with an oral health component, for all children in grades K through 12, and (b) dental care services in all school health clinics and centers for high-risk children.
4. Effective prevention programs, initiatives, and services, such as water fluoridation, must be the foundation for all dental programs at the local, state, and national levels.
5. Responsible parties must promote, in the oral health workforce, greater diversity, flexibility, sensitivity, and expertise in population-based oral health prevention programs and services for vulnerable populations. (p. 374)

Social justice, meaning equity and fairness, has been envisioned by Krieger and Birn as the foundation of public health.[28] Levy and Sidel have recently reviewed definitions and concepts of social justice,[29] endorsing the view of Braveman and Gruskin that social justice is an ethical concept grounded in principles of distributive justice.[30] In order to achieve true social justice in U.S. society, we must summon the popular and political will to address the root causes of current inequities, notably poverty and the increasing gap between the rich and the poor; maldistribution of resources within society; racism and other forms of discrimination; weak laws or enforcement of laws protecting human rights and other rights; and disenfranchisement of individuals and groups from the political process.[29] Further, we must reconnect the mouth to the body of public health and convince funding and legislative institutions to prioritize oral health and health care needs.[1,31] If and when we are able to ensure respectful and accessible health care that includes comprehensive oral health care to everyone regardless of race/ethnicity, socioeconomic position, age, gender, sexuality, or immigration status, then the United States will have achieved the measure of a just society: oral health for all.[19]

Acknowledgments

The authors thank the editors of the *Journal of Health Care for the Poor and Underserved* and three anonymous peer reviewers for their thoughtful and explicit comments that clarified the ideas expressed in this Guest Editorial.

Notes

1. U.S. Department of Health and Human Services (DHHS), *Oral Health in America: A Report of the Surgeon General* (Rockville, MD: DHHS, National Institutes of Health, National Institute of Dental and Craniofacial Research, 2000).
2. M. E. Northridge and I. B. Lamster, "A Life Course Approach to Preventing and Treating Oral Disease," *Soz Praventivmed*, 2004, 49(5), 299–300.
3. D. Mitchell-Lewis, S. P. Engebretson, J. Chen, et al., "Periodontal Infections and Pre-Term Birth: Early Findings from a Cohort of Young Minority Women in New York, *European Journal of Oral Science*, February 2001, 109(1), 34–39.
4. M. Allukian, and A. M. Horowitz, "Oral Health," in B. S. Levy, and V. W. Sidel (eds.), *Social Injustice and Public Health* (New York: Oxford University Press, 2006).
5. A. E. Sanders and A. J. Spencer, "Social Inequality in Perceived Oral Health Among Adults in Australia," *Australian and New Zealand Journal of Public Health*, April 2004, 28(2), 159–166.
6. M. H. Baldini, A. G. Vasconcelos, J. L. Antunes, [Association of the DMFT Index with Socioeconomic and Dental Services Indicators in the State of Parana, Brazil], *Cad Saude Publica*, January–February 204, 20(1), 143–152.
7. W. M. Thompson, S. M. Williams, P. J. Dennison, et al. "Were NZ's Structural Changes to the Welfare State in the Early 1990s Associated with a Measurable Increase in Oral

Health Inequalities Among Children? *Australian and New Zealand Journal of Public Health*, December 2002, 26(6), 525–530.

8. R. E. Fullilove, M. T. Fullilove, M. E. Northridge, et al., "Risk Factors for Excess Mortality in Harlem: Findings from the Harlem Household Survey," *American Journal of Preventive Medicine*, April 1999, 16(3Suppl), 22–28.

9. G. P. Zabos, M. E. Northridge, M. J. Ro, et al., "Lack of Oral Health Care for Adults in Harlem: A Hidden Crisis," *American Journal of Public Health*, January 2002, 92(1), 49–52.

10. B. Bloom, H. C. Gift, and S. S. Jack, "Dental Services and Oral Health," *Vital Health Statistics* 10, December 1992 (183), 1–95.

11. J. T. Massey, T. F. Moore, V. L. Parsons, et al. "Design and Estimation for the National Health Interview Survey, 1985–1994," National Center for Health Statistics, *Vital Health Statistics* 2, 1989 (110).

12. S. Beetstra, D. Derksen, M. Ro, et al. "A 'Health Commons' Approach to Oral Health for Low-Income Populations in a Rural State," *American Journal of Public Health*, January 2002, 92(1), 12–13.

13. W. Powell, C. Hollis, and M. de la Rosa, et al. "New Mexico Community Voices: Policy Reform to Reduce Oral Health Disparities," *Journal of Health Care for the Poor and Underserved*, February 2006, 17(1 Suppl), 95–110.

14. L. G. Hartsock, M. B. Hall, and A. M. Connor, "Informing the Policy Agenda: The Community Voices Experience on Dental Health for Children in North Carolina's Rural Communities," *Journal of Health Care for the Poor and Underserved*, February 2006, 17(1 Suppl), 111–123.

15. M. Allukian Jr., "The Neglected Epidemic and the Surgeon General's Report: A Call to Action for Better Oral Health," *American Journal of Public Health*, June 2000, 90(6), 843–845.

16. The Sullivan Commission, *Missing Persons: Minorities in the Health Profession: A Report of the Sullivan Commission on Diversity in the Healthcare Workforce.* The Sullivan Commission, 2004. Available at http://www.aacn.nche.edu/Media/pdf/ SullivanReport.pdf.

17. B. D. Smedley, A. Y. Stith, A. R. Nelson, et al. (eds.), Institute of Medicine, Committee on Understanding and Eliminating Racial and Ethnic Disparities in Health Care, *Unequal Treatment: Confronting Racial and Ethnic Disparities in Healthcare* (Washington, DC: The National Academies Press, 2002).

18. D. A. Mitchell, and S. L. Lassiter, "Addressing Health Care Disparities and Increasing Workforce Diversity: The Next Step for the Dental, Medical, and Public Health Professions," *American Journal of Public Health*, October 2006, 31 (Epub ahead of print).

19. U.S. Census Bureau, *Projected Population of the United States, by Race and Hispanic Origin: 2000 to 2050* (Washington, DC: U.S. Department of Commerce, Economics and Statistics Administration, U.S. Census Bureau, March 2004). Available at http://www.census .gov/ipc/www/usinterimproj/natprojtab01a.pdf.

20. H. M. Treadwell, and A. J. Formicola, "Improving the Oral Health of Prisoners to Improve Overall Health and Well-Being," *American Journal of Public Health*, October 2005, 95(10), 1677–1678.

21. J. M. Mixson, H. C. Eplee, P. H. Feil, et al., "Oral Health Status of a Federal Prison Population," *Journal of Public Health Dentistry*, Summer 1990, 50(4), 257–261.

22. M. E. Salive, J. M. Carolla, and T. F. Brewer, "Dental Health of Male Inmates in a State Prison System," *Journal of Public Health Dentistry*, Spring 1989, 49(2), 83–86.

23. Maine Civil Liberties Union, *The Health Status of Maine's Prison Population: Results of a Survey of Inmates Incarcerated by the Maine Department of Corrections* (Portland, ME: Maine Civil Liberties Union, 2003).

24. J. J. Clare, "Dental Health Status, Unmet Needs, and Utilization of Services in a Cohort of Adult Felons at Admission and After Three Years Incarceration," *Journal of Correctional Health Care*, 2002, 9(1), 65–75.

25. M. McNally, "Rights Access and Justice in Oral Health Care: Justice Toward Underserved Patient Populations—The Elderly," Journal of the American College of Dentists, Fall 2003, 70(4), 56–60.

26. I. B. Lamster, "Oral Health Care Services for Older Adults: A Looming Crisis," *American Journal of Public Health*, May 2004, 94(5), 699–702.

27. A. J. Formicola, M. Ro, S. Marshall, et al. "Strengthening the Oral Health Safety Net: Delivery Models That Improve Access to Oral Health Care for Uninsured and Underserved Populations," *American Journal of Public Health*, May 2004, 94(5), 702–704.

28. N. Krieger, and A. E. Birn, "A Vision of Social Justice as the Foundation of Public Health: Commemorating 150 Years of the Spirit of 1848," *American Journal of Public Health*, November 1998, 88(11), 1603–1606.

29. B. S. Levy and V. W. Sidel, "The Nature of Social Injustice and Its Impact on Public Health," in B. S. Levy and V. W. Sidel (eds.), *Social Injustice and Public Health* (New York: Oxford University Press, 2006).

30. P. Braveman, and S. Gruskin, "Defining Equity in Health," *Journal of Epidemiology & Community Health*, April 2003, 57(4), 254–258.

31. M. E. Northridge, "Reconnecting the Mouth to the Body of Public Health," *American Journal of Public Health*, January 2002, 92(1), 9.

CHAPTER TWELVE

POVERTY, RACE,
AND THE INVISIBLE MEN

Henrie M. Treadwell and Marguerite J. Ro

Improving access to primary health care by the poor, the underserved, and those living at the economic and social margins of this nation's social construct has been work that the W.K. Kellogg Foundation has pursued rigorously and with deep commitment. We have worked to lead and serve as we supported health clinics, as well as to define, refine, and implement pathways to improve health for many. But like most, we have neglected a significant part of the population most in need of health care. We were blind to the fact that when we visited clinics and worked with communities to address their health needs, there were few men in the waiting rooms of the clinics where primary health and prevention services were being provided. Virtually no health efforts were directed toward men. Poor men had become invisible and their health needs neglected.

Why a Focus on Men's Health

Ultimately, we confronted the brutal reality: poor men and men of color live with a tremendous amount of pain, are demeaned and devalued in a system that rewards wealth and values some people over others, and die early. When social determinants

Treadwell, H. M., and Ro, M. "Poverty, Race, and the Invisible Men." *American Journal of Public Health,* 2003, 93(5), 705–707.

of health—such as poverty, poor education and educational opportunities, underemployment and unemployment, confrontations with law enforcement, the sequelae of incarceration, and social and racial discrimination—are factored into the health status of men, the scope and depth of the health crisis is even more evident and poignant. Poor men are less likely to have health insurance, less likely to seek needed health services, and less likely to receive adequate care when they do.

Even among the poor, some men are less than equal. The generally abysmal health status of men of African descent best demonstrates the great peril that poor men have to face. Life expectancy for African American men is 7.1 years shorter than that for all men.[1] Forty percent of African American men die prematurely from cardiovascular disease, compared with 21 percent of White men.[2] And death rates for HIV/AIDS are nearly five times higher for African American men than for White men.[3] African American men also have the highest incidence rates of oral cancer.[4] Sadly, the health status of African American men may serve as the proverbial canary in the coal mine for other poor men in this nation and in our global village, and it is a clarion call to health care providers and policymakers charged with defending the nation's health.

This society has no system in place to support the health and health-seeking behaviors of men who work at the lowest wage levels or of those who are unable to work as a result of poor education, absence of jobs, mismatch in skills, or other reasons. Those in the faith-based community and in community-based organizations tell us that men are so concerned about their daily survival, caring for their families, and having a good job that they do not make their health a priority. Recent articles in major U.S. newspapers have shown how poor men jeopardize their health as they seek to support their families and themselves.[5-9] Working conditions are frequently hazardous, and policies designed to protect these employees are often grossly inadequate. Most often, low-paid and low-skilled workers are not offered health insurance coverage through work. Low-income men who are childless are excluded from publicly funded insurance programs. The only exceptions are for those who qualify for insurance because of disability or who find coverage through very limited state or local programs for the indigent.

Sadly, the penal system is the only place where men have the right to health care, under the U.S. Constitution's protection from "cruel and unusual punishment." There are currently more than 1.4 million inmates in federal and state prisons, and more than 600,000 inmates are to be released during the year.[10] A recent report funded by the U.S. Department of Justice highlights the great need for health care by this population.[11] The report demonstrates the high rates of communicable disease, chronic disease, and mental illness of inmates (93 percent of whom are male and 44 percent of whom are people of color). The report acknowledges that these men are a largely underserved population. It recommends federal support for the provision of services for these "captive" men, in part to reduce the threat to the public's health upon their release. Clearly there is a need to treat inmates, but what are we doing for these men before they enter the penal system, and if we are not doing anything, what is the cost to them and to society?

While access to care is theoretically available through prisons, there are no clear data that suggest that the care provided results in improved health status. Studies have clearly indicated that mental health and oral health access in prisons is extremely curtailed despite the high need.[11,12] In addition, the health care that is provided is expensive. Wisconsin alone spent $37.2 million to provide health care to approximately 14,900 inmates in fiscal year 1999–2000.[13] A rough comparison reveals that federal and state health care expenditures per inmate approximate or exceed expenditures for a Medicaid enrollee. The average cost for health care in prison was $3,242 in 1999, while the average cost for health care for a Medicaid enrollee was $3,822 in 1998.[14,15] However, if we exclude the elderly, blind, and disabled, the average cost for an adult Medicaid enrollee was $1,892. We must ask whether the federal and state money being spent on inmate health care could be better spent, both within and outside prison walls.

One of the major challenges we face in addressing the health status of poor men and men of color is a lack of data. Existing research, while important, focuses on issues related to reproductive organs, illnesses resulting from sexual practices or contagious disease (such as HIV/AIDS), violence, substance abuse, behavioral health, and other conditions that characterize these men, by inference, as not having the same illnesses and concerns that women and well-to-do men face. Does this lack of research reflect society's "isms" that perpetuate disparities in health and well-being? Or does it reflect limited interest by a cadre of health policy researchers who may need more diversity in their ranks to broaden the research agenda and fill in the gaps? How else to explain this epidemic of poor health among men of color and poor men and lack of proven intervention and prevention strategies?

In the numerous documents on access to care and quality of care that we examined, little mention was made of poor men. Seminal reports such as those produced by the Institute of Medicine have yet to examine the availability and quality of prison care. Nor is there adequate documentation on the accessibility or quality of preventive and primary health care for the diverse population of poor men. We were not able to identify benchmarks for access to or quality of care that apply universally to all men, women, and children.

Despite our efforts, we did not find the intellectual underpinnings that would guide our actions or affirm our strategies. Ultimately, we were left to decide that our responsibility was to act now, even though the practice and policy pathways were not apparent.

A Men's Health Initiative

As part of Kellogg's Community Voices initiative (http:// www.communityvoices. org), we began the process of teaching ourselves about the issues. We developed three publications, designed for a variety of audiences, that highlight the disparity in health outcomes and the barriers to care experienced by men, particularly men of color.[16, 17] (Additional information is available from the authors upon request.) Included in each publication are policy strategies and recommendations for improving the health of men.

The Kellogg Foundation's trustees authorized $3 million for a men's health initiative. The use of these funds in specific markets (Atlanta; Baltimore; Boston; Clarksdale, Mississippi; Denver; and Miami) will provide focused care for men and education for health care providers, as well as inform policy on shaping health services and providing health care coverage for poor men. An equally important goal of this initiative is to engage men in shaping the delivery of care for themselves. Social and educational programs will be included as integral components of comprehensive primary care. Strategies will include extensive use of community outreach, use of focus groups, case management, and identification of service gaps. Proposed coalitions including men, health and human services providers, family members, and concerned community members will work across state lines to build a policy program that informs decision makers and promotes inclusion of poor men as beneficiaries of publicly supported coverage programs (such as Medicaid and the Children's Health Insurance Program).

While many in the policy arena tell us that the time may not be right for a discussion of coverage for poor men, we know that it is not acceptable for any human beings to be left out, included incrementally only when convenient. Regardless of whether the nation's budget is running a surplus or a deficit, our nation's leaders have never declared it the right time for providing coverage to poor adults, specifically poor men. Yet the financial, physical, and emotional devastation that is experienced by poor men who have no health care is too harsh a price for all of us to pay.[18,19] Emphasizing treatment rather than prevention creates a system that is impossible to sustain and perpetuates disparity. We know how to improve the public health of our nation. We simply have yet to do what is best for our nation's families, and particularly its sons.

Sustaining Change in a Time of Competing Priorities

The opportunity we have with this issue of the *Journal* is to begin to change the paradigm that treats poor men and men of color as undeserving of routine primary health care. The articles in this issue begin the process of revealing men's needs, the services that exist, and the changes in services, systems, and policies that are required to improve the situation. We wish we could tell you more about what men want, their priorities, and their aspirations with regard to health and well-being. We wish that more voices could have been raised in this issue. We wanted to gain more understanding about men's social contexts and be provided clues as to how to support them. And we wanted to discuss how good primary health care providers take into account all contextual variables (educational level, employment, housing, enfranchisement) when they treat the body so that they might also heal the spirit. We are at the beginning. We are so very proud to be able to help guide comprehensive efforts to include men in the realm of health and health care services so that they and their families can live with more dignity, respect, and freedom. We hope that these efforts will also serve as a platform for health and human rights, reminding us that inclusiveness in the health care setting and good health cannot exist in a world where priorities are based on wealth, social status, race, or creed. We hope that all who read this issue of the *Journal* will join us in our mission: "Leave no poor father, brother, uncle, nephew, or son behind, as they too have a right to the tree of life."

We trust that we at the Kellogg Foundation have done no harm as we have stepped forward to claim this public health issue and to initiate this review of what we know, what we do not know, what we must do—and why we cannot wait.

Notes

1. R. N. Anderson, and P. B. DeTurk, "United States Life Tables, 1999," *National Vital Statistics Report*, 2002, 50(6), 33.
2. E. Barnett, M. L. Casper, J. A. Halverson, et al., *Men and Heart Disease: An Atlas of Racial and Ethnic Disparities in Mortality* (Morgantown, WV: Office for Social Environment and Health Research, West Virginia University, June, 2001). Also available at: http://oseahr.hsc.wvu.edu/hdm.html (PDF file). Accessed March 17, 2003.
3. R. N. Anderson, "Deaths: Leading Causes for 2000, *National Vital Statistics Report*, 2002, 50(16), 1–85.
4. U.S. Department of Health and Human Services (DHHS), *Oral Health in America: A Report of the Surgeon General* (Rockville, MD: DHHS, National Institutes of Health, National Institute of Dental and Craniofacial Research, 2000).
5. S. Hudak and J. F. Hagan, "Asbestos: The Lethal Legacy; Families of Workers Blame Deaths on Plant's Use of Asbestos," *Plain Dealer* [Cleveland, Ohio], November 4, 2002, A1.
6. K. Miniclier, "Coal Miners Dig for Pay, Perks: Workers at Rangley Site Brush Aside Issue of Danger," *Denver Post*, August 25, 2002, B01.
7. D. Parker, "Hazardous-Job Workers Learn to Live with Fear," *Corpus Christi Caller-Times*, August 11, 2002, H1.
8. S. Roman and S. Carroll, "Migrant Farmworkers Live Their Lives in the Shadows: Housing for Migrants in Manatee County Among Worst in State," *Sarasota Herald-Tribune*, January 16, 2003, AI.
9. D. Barstow and L. Bergman, "At a Tax Foundry, an Indifference to Life," *New York Times*, January 8, 2003, A1.

10. P. M. Harrison and A. J. Beck, *Prisoners in 2001* (Washington, DC: U.S. Department of Justice, Bureau of Justice Statistics Bulletin, 2002).

11. *The Health Status of Soon-to-Be-Released Inmates: A Report to Congress.* 2 vols. (Chicago: National Commission on Correctional Health Care, 2002). Also available at: http://wwwncchc. org/pubs/pubs_stbr.html. Accessed March 17, 2003.

12. M. E. Salive, J. M. Carolla, and T. F. Brewer, "Dental Health of Male Inmates in a State Prison System," *Journal of Public Health Dentistry,* Spring 1989, 49(2), 83-86.

13. Wisconsin Legislative Audit Bureau, *Prison Health Care* [press release], May 2001. Available at: http://www.wispolitics.com/freeser/pr/pr0105/May%2015/pr01051510.htm. Accessed March 17, 2003.

14. B. Bruen and J. Holahan, *Medicaid Spending Growth Remained Modest in 1998, But Likely Headed Upward* (Washington, DC: The Henry J. Kaiser Family Foundation, February 2001), Publication 2230.

15. R. M. Stana, *Federal Prisons: Containing Health Care Costs for an Increasing Inmate Population* (Washington, DC: General Accounting Office, 2000).

16. J. A. Rich and M. Ro, *A Poor Man's Plight: Uncovering the Disparity in Men's Health* (Battle Creek, MI: The W.K. Kellogg Foundation, February 2002).

17. *What About Men? Exploring the Inequities in Minority Men's Health* (Battle Creek, MI: The W.K. Kellogg Foundation, 2001).

18. Committee on the Consequences of Uninsurance, Board of Health Care Services, Institute of Medicine, *Coverage Matters: Insurance and Health Care* (Washington, DC: National Academy Press, 2001).

19. J. Hadley, *Sicker and Poorer: The Consequences of Being Uninsured* (Washington, DC: The Urban Institute and the Kaiser Commission on Medicaid and the Uninsured, 2002).

CHAPTER THIRTEEN

REDUCING UNHEALTHY BEHAVIORS

Where Do We Start?

Georges C. Benjamin

I remember sitting in the office of the chairman of the Human Services Committee of the District of Columbia City Council. The Queen of England had recently completed a visit to the city, and a contingent of schoolchildren was preparing to go to London to visit the Queen. The chairman noted how excited the children were about the trip, and I commented that I too would be excited if I were one of those children and were going to London. The chairman looked at me with the expression of an experienced legislator who was about to give the health officer a lesson in cultural competency. "London!" he exclaimed. "These kids are excited because they are going to the airport. These children," he pointed out, "live in a part of the city where they see airplanes fly up from the horizon and over their homes, but they have never seen where they came from." I suddenly understood that these children had had experiences vastly different from those of most Washingtonians. This in a city less than ten miles square!

Days later the chief medical officer came to see me. She had just left a room full of elementary school children. Our department was holding forums around the city to talk to children about public health and prevention. This was part of our effort to address the needs of the city's children and ingrain healthy behaviors in them at an early age. We discovered that these children had seen and heard our many

Benjamin, G. C. "Reducing Unhealthy Behaviors: Where Do We Start? *American Journal of Public Health*, 2003, 93(5), 704.

prevention messages on television and radio and had seen some of our written materials. They knew that avoiding drugs and cigarettes was an important health behavior. They knew about "the birds and bees." They even knew that condoms would prevent sexually transmitted diseases.

But they also had a frightening and intimate knowledge of handguns. Their knowledge of the various types of illegal drugs, their side effects, and techniques to get the "best high" was also of great concern. These were bright kids who had a concept of finances and a knowledge of the "business of the street" that would make the chair of any M.B.A. program take note.

These kids had heard our messages but when they put them through the filters that they used every day, they found our messages tough to reconcile with their reality. The world these kids lived in was one where health care disparities were accepted as a way of life, secondary to issues of poor housing, poverty, and the tasks of everyday existence. For some, an acceptance of hopelessness and helplessness defined the filters through which they heard our prevention messages. In short, our messages simply were not relevant to them.

As we work to improve the health of our communities, we must address the root causes of such filtering. The reason for unhealthy behaviors is not that the public does not fully understand healthy ones; it is something more deeply rooted in the ills of our society. Unhealthy behaviors start in part as a response to a social environment that fosters no alternatives. To change that environment is the real challenge.

Where do we start? We start at the beginning.

CHAPTER FOURTEEN

COMMUNITY HEALTH WORKERS

Social Justice and Policy Advocates for Community Health and Well-Being

Leda M. Pérez and Jacqueline Martinez

Community health workers are resources to their communities and to the advocacy and policy world on several levels. Community health workers can connect people to health care and collect information relevant to policy. They are natural researchers who, as a result of direct interaction with the populations they serve, can recount the realities of exclusion and propose remedies for it. As natural researchers, they contribute to best practices while informing public policy with the information they can share. In this light, community health workers may also be advocates for social justice.

Reprinted from *American Journal of Public Health*, January 2008, 98(1), 11–14.

Community health workers are the integral link that connects disenfranchised and medically underserved populations to the health and social service systems intended to serve them.[1-3] Worldwide, community health workers—also known as *promotoras*, natural helpers, *doulas*, lay health advisers, and frontline workers—increase access to care and provide health services ranging from health education and immunization to complex clinical procedures in remote areas where they are often the only source of health care.[4] Community health workers have appeared repeatedly throughout history as those who heal others and help communities thrive.[5,6] Although the central role of community health workers is to be outreach workers who help clients access health or social services, they do more than merely link individuals to a doctor's office.

Community health workers play a paramount role in connecting people to vital services and helping to address the economic, social, environmental, and political rights of individuals and communities. They are also "natural researchers"—they can observe and relay community realities to outsiders—placing them in a position to influence policies that affect public health. Their history and the breadth and scope of the roles they serve distinguish them as social justice and policy advocates for underserved communities across the world. Their work is linked to social justice precisely because it focuses on ensuring that individuals and communities share equally in the benefits society has to offer.[7] Likewise, as policy advocates with close relationships with the communities they serve, community health workers are in the position to inform policies based in reality. This role as social justice and policy advocates must be upheld in community health workers' development and as they become critical figures in the integrated system of health care.

Public health literature has examined the relationship between community health workers, community health work in general, and social justice.[8-10] Farmer et al.[11] espoused the value of community health workers as advocates for patients' health. Their discussion focuses on the history and importance of community-based participation in health care and on the broader vision of health and human rights. Specifically they see a practical benefit in community health work, not only in the connection of patients to care and services but also in community health workers demonstrating how the issues that people face in their lives, both those directly related to health and those that result from social, economic, cultural, or political exclusions, impact their life conditions, which may be the more relevant unit of analysis for an illness than illness itself.

Others look at the subject from a broader community health lens, focusing on how community health work and partnerships in the community succeed in promoting better community health outcomes, including more-equitable environments and personal economies.[9] Politzer et al.[10] have discussed the importance of community health centers, specifically their efforts to reduce racial and ethnic health disparities in low-income communities.

Along this theoretical construct of defining health and assessing outcomes in health is the following question: Are diseases to blame for illness, or are established health and social policies and structures the more germane unit of analysis?[12,13] In other words, what are the perceptions, decisions, policies, and structures that determine one's health before the disease? Considering this body of work and its significance in pointing to some of the root causes of poverty and ill health (broadly defined), we also ask what else is required to fill the gaps. Who else is necessary to raise consciousness about those most excluded and their needs and rights? In this context, the work of community health workers must be understood on two levels, as those who can connect people to care and as advocates who can attest to the realities of marginalization and how it must be remedied. The natural research component of community health work activities is critical to contributing to best practices in the field and also to influencing thoughts and paradigms. Those working on the front lines in the community are concerned about changing the social ills, institutions, and policies that contribute to disease. In this light, community health workers are natural helpers and researchers and advocates for social justice. Here, we share our thoughts about the importance of recognizing community health workers' function and about their historical and current role as advocates for health, social justice, and human rights.

Origins of Community Health Workers

The history of community health work can be traced to the early seventeenth century. During a shortage of doctors in Russia, laypeople known as *feldshers* received training in the field to provide basic medical care to military personnel.[5,13a] Also known as "barber-surgeons," the *feldshers* provided low-cost health care to a marginalized population. The formalization of these healers became the foundation of the training of "barefoot doctors" in China.[6,13a] The barefoot doctors were laypersons, many of whom could not afford shoes, and were educated in setting broken bones, delivering babies, treating wounds, and meeting other basic medical needs. Their mission was to take primary health care to remote rural areas that were without doctors.

Promotores became a powerful force in Latin America in the 1950s, when labor rights and liberation theology—a Catholic dissident movement that sought to empower the poor against their oppressors[14]—were on the rise. Community health workers thrived throughout the region, their role being to help remedy an unequal distribution of health resources and to bring health care to the poor. They employed popular education theory, which seeks to help people organize their knowledge and use it to benefit their communities.[15] Community health workers played an essential role in connecting people to needed services and in transferring the advocacy capacity to their constituencies.

In the 1960s, community health workers began to emerge in the United States as part of the Great Society domestic programs. The mission of the Great Society efforts was to end poverty, promote equality, improve education, rejuvenate cities, and protect the environment.[16] As part of the Great Society's new careers program, the government created and promoted community health work jobs as entry-level positions for career development. In the early 1960s, the federal government began to formally support community healthwork programs through the Federal Migrant Health Act of 1962[17] and the Economic Opportunity Act of 1964.[18] Both pieces of legislation mandated outreach efforts to low-income neighborhoods and migrant worker camps. The first community health work programs established under the Economic Opportunity Act of 1964 were part of neighborhood community health centers such as the Columbia Point Housing Project in Dorchester, Massachusetts.[19]

In 1968, the Indian Health Service founded its community health representative program to work with tribal managers in the federally recognized American Indian and Alaska Native communities. Since then, the Indian Health Service has maintained the only categorical community health work programs in predominantly American Indian communities in the United States.[20]

The rising prominence of community health work programs began to wane in the 1970s and early 1980s. In the late 1980s and early 1990s, community health work programs resurged in migrant and seasonal farmworking communities. Programs established during this period include the Camp Health Aide Program, sponsored by the Midwest Migrant Health Information Office; the Border Vision Fronteriza Program, based at the University of Arizona; and Nuestra Comunidad Sana, based in Hood River, Oregon. All of these programs remain an integral component to the health care delivery system of their respective states. Throughout history, community health workers have emerged and reemerged as a critical response to a health care crisis—a crisis that was identified during a social or political upheaval that sought to redress social injustice and inequity. In the United States, as witnessed in the 1960s and later in the 1980s and 1990s, community health workers became vehicles for social justice in socially and politically charged contexts. For example, the health and social challenges of marginalized migrant communities, and the legislation that recognized them as well as other civil rights-influenced policies, helped to create a role for community health workers as those who link vulnerable populations to needed services and information.

On health outcomes, research has suggested that the reliance on community health workers and techniques that are part of a cultural competency model could theoretically improve the ability of health care providers to deliver appropriate services to diverse populations, helping to improve health outcomes and reducing health disparities.[21] Moreover, there is evidence that the efforts of community health workers have improved pregnancy and birth outcomes as well as health- and screening-related behaviors.[22] A growing body of evidence documents the effectiveness of community health workers in diabetes care and education efforts.[23]

Community health workers play the role of the trusted adviser and health navigator in the community, but at the same time they share their communities' issues with different policymakers. They are people who influence health outcomes both through their ability to connect people to care and through their participation in public policymaking.[24] The course of history, as it relates to the rising role of community health workers, continues to define the impact and scope of the influence of these workers on the health system of the United States. The need for these types of workers has also defined the characteristics and qualifications of the community health work role. The auxiliary responsibilities to improve social, environmental, and economic conditions to affect health are essential to the role of a community health worker.

Community health workers in different parts of the United States work for the rights of inclusion of the most marginalized. In communities densely populated with new immigrants, for example, community health workers play a critical role in helping to advise communities of their rights on immigration laws and, in some cases, helping their clients navigate highly bureaucratic systems.[24] They also help people register to vote, and they help victims of domestic abuse find shelter and counsel their clients as to their rights under the law. Working in an economically and socially oppressed neighborhood in Miami, Florida, one community health worker recounted, "Ninety-five percent of my work is helping people get basic needs [met] like food, shelter, employment, and [a] safe and decent environment, even before we begin to talk about diabetes or asthma" (K. Joseph, Human Services Coalition of Dade County, oral communication, July 2006). When asked to explain her work in one sentence, she said, "It is about getting people from poverty to prosperity and doing whatever it takes to get there." Social, environmental, and political issues affect the communities community health workers serve, so they must approach health in a holistic manner. If there is not a good quality of life in the social, environmental, or political spheres of individual or community existence, it will affect individual and community health.

Community health workers' translation of these complex cases for policy advocacy is as important as their ability to connect a client to care. As one public policy director expressed (A. Colon, Human Services Coalition of Dade County, oral communication, July 2006):

> Public opinion shapes public policy and community health workers are the gatekeepers of the public's opinion. They are in the field living the stories with the people. They create the case and convey the message; they rally the troops and add credibility to policy changes we advocate for.

The role of community health workers is vital as this advocacy group "engages the people who are really in crisis." As the director explains, "the most profound stories, these are the ones the community health workers come back and share with us, these are the ones that enact change for the greater good." Community health workers are powerful and credible because they emerge from contexts in which there is a need for connection to the mainstream precisely because of conditions of health, social, economic, environmental, or political exclusion. The role has flourished, historically and presently, because there is a community need for an ombudsman, an advocate.

Community health workers are powerful and credible because they emerge from contexts in which there is a need for connection to the mainstream precisely because of conditions of health, social, economic, environmental, or political exclusion. The role has flourished, historically and presently, because there is a community need for an ombudsman, an advocate. Community health workers understand the complexity of the needs and are able to translate the issues to others in decision-making positions.

Conclusions

We support the current definitions and multiple functions elaborated in the literature on the role and functions of community health workers as part of the U.S. health care system. However, we strongly caution that the history and underlying purposes of these workers should not be lost in translation in the midst of efforts to institutionalize their role. Our nation *will* equally benefit from a cost-efficient health care system as much as it would from working to change the root causes of illness.

As we continue to uncover the inequities that limit access to social, economic, political, and environmental well-being, the foundation and history of community health workers as advocates for social justice becomes increasingly relevant. Although health care access and quality care remain laudable goals, the fact is that, day to day, too many people still do not have access to these benefits. Community health workers play a critical role in responding to and voicing the call for inclusion. They must be understood as a critical component of integrated systems of health care and as advocates for the myriad issues that keep people outside of the grasp of life, liberty, and the pursuit of happiness.

From a health policy perspective, the practical role of community health workers and the information that they have access to can inform how health practitioners and policymakers define health and well-being and how they can improve these areas.

Their knowledge can improve system structures and inform how resources are allocated. Community health workers have the ability to serve as connectors and navigators of the health system, which is critical, but their work and firsthand knowledge must also be harnessed and expanded to ensure their capacity to affect policies and inform decision makers. Community health workers are resources to not only their communities as connectors to care but also to advocates and policymakers, for the information they bring and the potential to create change.

Acknowledgments

We acknowledge Elaine Ruda, who was at the time an undergraduate at the University of Miami, Coral Gables, Florida, and Sara Timen, who was at the time an M.P.H. candidate at the Columbia University School of Public Health, New York, who contributed to this work as research assistants. We also thank the Human Services Coalition of Dade County, Florida, for the expertise shared with us and for their valuable contributions to improving the health of residents of Miami-Dade County. Finally, we thank our reviewers and colleagues for their insightful comments.

Notes

1. H. Mahler, "Promotion of Primary Health Care in Member Countries of WHO," *Public Health Report*, 1978, 93, 107–113.
2. G. Walt (ed.), *Community Health Workers in National Programmes: Just Another Pair of Hands?* (Philadelphia: Open University Press, 1990).
3. R. W. Richter, B. Bengen, P. A. Alsup, B. Bruun, M. M. Kilcoyne, and B. D. Challenor, "The Community Health Worker," *American Journal of Public Health*, 1974, 64, 1056–1061.
4. S. M. Swider, "Outcome Effectiveness of Community Health Workers: An Integrative Literature Review," *Public Health Nursing*, 2002, 19(1), 11–20.
5. V. A. Kenyon, "Feldshers and Health Promotion in the USSR," *Physician Assistance*, 1985, 9(7), 25–26, 29.
6. *A Historical Overview of Lay Health Worker Programs* (Hood River, OR: La Familia Sana Program, 1992).
7. Center for Economic and Social Justice, *Defining Economic Justice and Social Justice*. Available at: http://www.cesj.org/thirdway/economicjustice-defined.htm. Accessed October 18, 2007.
8. G. Farmer and N. Gastineau, "Rethinking Health and Human Rights: Time for a Paradigm Shift," *Journal of Law and Medical Ethics*, 2002, 30(4), 655–668.
9. P. V. McAvoy, M. B. Driscoll, and B. J. Gramling, "Integrating the Environment, the Economy, and Community Health: A Community Health Center's Initiative to Link Health Benefits to Smart Growth, *American Journal of Public Health*, 2004, 94, 525–528.

10. R. Politzer, J. Yoon, L. Shi, R. Hughes, J. Regan, and M. Gaston, "Inequality in America: The Contribution of Health Centers in Reducing and Eliminating Disparities in Access to Care," *Medical Care Research and Review*, 2001, 58, 234–248.

11. P. E. Farmer, F. Léandre, J. S. Mukherjee, et al. "Community-Based Approaches to HIV Treatment in Resource-Poor Settings," *Lancet*, 2001, 358, 404–409.

12. N. Kreiger, "Theories for Social Epidemiology in the 21st Century: An Ecosocial Perspective," *International Journal of Epidemiology*, 2001, 30, 668–677.

13. P. Farmer, *Pathologies of Power: Health, Human Rights, and the New War on the Poor* (Berkeley: University of California Press, 2005).

13a. N. Wiggins and A Borbón, "Core Roles and Competencies of Community Health Advisors," in E. L. Rosenthal, N. Wiggins, J. N. Brownstein, et al. (eds.), *The Final Report of the National Community Health Advisor Study: Weaving the Future* (Tucson: Mel and Enid Zuckerman College of Public Health, University of Arizona, 1998), 15–49.

14. L. Boff and C. Boff, *A Concise History of Liberation Theology*. Available at http://www.landreform.org/boff2.htm. Accessed December 1, 2006.

15. P. Freire, *Pedagogy of the Oppressed* (New York: Continuum, 1972).

16. L. B. Johnson, Great Society speech. Available at http://coursesa.matrix.msu.edu/~hst306/documents/great.html. Accessed July 1, 2006.

17. Pub L No. 87-692; 76 Stat 592.

18. Pub L No. 88-452, 78 Stat 508, 42 USC § 2701.

19. *Community Health Workers: Essential to Improving Health in Massachusetts*. Available at: http://www.mass.gov/Eeohhs2/docs/dph/com_health/comm_health_workers_narrative.pdf. Accessed September 8, 2006.

20. A. Witmer, S. Seifer, L. Finocchio, J. Leslie, and E. O'Neil, "Community Health Workers: Integral Members of the Healthcare Work Force," *American Journal of Public Health*, 1995, 85, 1055–1058.

21. C. Brach and I. Fraser, "Can Cultural Competency Reduce Racial and Ethnic Health Disparities? A Review and Conceptual Model," *Medical Care Research and Review*, 2000, 57(suppl 1), 181–217.

22. J. N. Brownstein and E. L. Rosenthal, "The Challenge of Evaluating CHA Services," in E. L. Rosenthal, N. Wiggins, J. N. Brownstein, et al. (eds.), *The Final Report of the National Community Health Advisor Study: Weaving the Future* (Tucson: Mel and Enid Zuckerman College of Public Health, University of Arizona, 1998), 50–74.

23. Centers for Disease Control and Prevention, *Community Health Workers/Promotores de Salud: Critical Connections in Communities*. Available at: http://www.cdc.gov/diabetes/projects/comm.htm. Accessed July 31, 2006.

24. A. Cornwall and J. Gaventa, *From Users and Choosers to Makers and Shapers: Repositioning Participation in Social Policy* (Brighton, England: Institute of Development Studies, 2001), IDS Working Paper 127.

CHAPTER FIFTEEN

STANDING IN THE GAP

Henrie M. Treadwell and Joyce H. Nottingham

The United States is undergoing what has been provocatively
described as one of the largest mass migrations in our nation's
history. Every year, 630,000 residents will cross the border
between the community and the correctional system, and they
will make the journey virtually unseen and unheard. Many of these
voiceless migrants might have stayed at home if they had only
had access to comprehensive primary health care services,
including substance use prevention and treatment services. While
U.S. prisons have traditionally held poor men, disproportionate
numbers of whom have been African American, and increasing
numbers of whom are Latino, the numbers of women in prison
are rising exponentially. The demographics of women prisoners
are tellingly similar to those of their male counterparts.

Treadwell, H. M., and Nottingham, J. H. "Standing in the Gap." *American Journal of Public Health*, 2005,
95(10), 1676.

One out of every five African American men born between 1965 and 1969 served time in prison by the time he reached his early thirties. Nearly 60 percent of African American high school dropouts born during this period served time in state or federal prison by their early thirties. Formative research in the Overtown community of Miami, Florida—a community of nine thousand mostly African American residents, whose wages are among the lowest in the country—revealed that 66 percent of the 129 men interviewed had been incarcerated at some point in their lives, 17 percent had experienced homelessness in the thirty days before the interview, and 53 percent earned less than $10,000 per year at the time of the interview (Community Voices, unpublished survey, May 2005).

In effect, individuals like these now live with the residual effects of imprisonment. Their chances of remaining in their communities have been compromised by poor health insurance coverage, gaps in social services, and public policy limitations that make it difficult for them to apply for education loans or secure public housing. Inadequately funded public health clinics cannot provide this population with needed culturally competent mental health services or adult oral health care.

When we began work on this special theme issue, we knew we faced a challenge, but we had no idea how truly monumental the task was that we had set for ourselves. We had hoped to construct a compendium of best practices on prisons and health to fast-forward effective partnerships between public health and social services with the goal of healing people while rapidly reducing recidivism. Instead, we learned that although we as a nation are very good epidemiologists and can tell what is wrong and how many are affected, we do a very poor job of moving beyond simply quantifying or describing the problem.

The loss of so many people to prison is felt not only by those behind bars, but by their families, potential employers, and entire communities. Many leave home for prison far too young. Some grow old in prison, where they develop chronic conditions in the absence of primary care. Was it our intention to replace the old mental health system with a prison industrial complex to stimulate economic development? Was it our goal to eliminate services for prisoners reentering our communities to ensure that they would repopulate the prisons when their health care needs were not addressed? Did we intend for unmet health and educational needs to drive investment in prison construction? With this issue, we "stand in the gap" on behalf of the land (Ezekiel 22:30). We hope to find supporters who will stand with us.

CHAPTER SIXTEEN

STRENGTHENING THE ORAL HEALTH SAFETY NET

Delivery Models That Improve Access to Oral Health Care for Uninsured and Underserved Populations

Allan J. Formicola, Marguerite J. Ro, Stephen Marshall, Daniel Derksen, Wayne Powell, Lisa G. Hartsock, and Henrie M. Treadwell

The mission of the W.K. Kellogg Foundation's Community Voices initiative is to improve access to primary, behavioral, and oral health care for uninsured and underserved populations. Poor access to dental services and growing racial/ethnic disparities in oral health demand new interventions and models of delivery.[1] Oral health is a core component of all thirteen Community Voices "learning laboratories." Three of these programs—northern Manhattan's Community DentCare, New Mexico's Health Commons, and North Carolina's FirstHealth— provide innovative partnership models that seek to address some of our nation's most pressing oral health care needs.

Formicola, A. J., Ro, M., Marshall, S., et al. "Strengthening the Oral Health Safety Net: Delivery Models That Improve Access to Oral Health Care for Uninsured and Underserved Populations." *American Journal of Public Health*, May 2004, 94(5), 702–704.

Northern Manhattan Community DentCare Model

Poor oral health was identified as the number one health complaint in a 1992–1994 population-based survey of Central Harlem adults.[2] In response, the Columbia University School of Dental and Oral Surgery, working in partnership with community-based organizations, devised and implemented the Community DentCare Network.[3] Three linked community-based dental programs provide oral health care access to residents of northern Manhattan across the life span, from children in the Head Start program to the elderly. The Community DentCare delivery system provides preventive and comprehensive treatment from fixed and mobile facilities, regardless of patients' ability to pay for services. The three major components of the Community DentCare Network are seven public middle-school-based dental programs; one mobile dental clinic to reach the Head Start population during the school year and the elderly population during the summer; and four community health center sites offering comprehensive dental services.

Dental examinations revealed higher rates of dental caries in northern Manhattan schoolchildren than in African American and Hispanic schoolchildren nationwide.[4] The Community DentCare Network recorded fifty thousand patient visits last year and provided seven thousand school children with critical preventive dental services (including sealants) and dental treatment. Follow-up studies are needed to determine how effective Community DentCare has been in reducing oral health disparities for northern Manhattan residents.

New Mexico: The "Health Commons" Model

Access to oral health services in New Mexico is poor and getting worse. Nationally, New Mexico ranks forty-ninth in dentists per capita, fiftieth in child poverty, and first in the percentage of its population that is uninsured. In response to this oral health crisis, New Mexico Community Voices has been piloting and disseminating its "health commons" model.[5]

This community partnership model of enhanced primary care includes medical, behavioral, social, public health, and oral health services. It focuses on improving access to and quality of care for New Mexico's underserved populations. Many of the intractable health problems in New Mexico's communities are the consequences of historic, social, and economic factors. Such issues cannot be addressed adequately by a single health provider group or even by the health sector as a whole. Better solutions emerge when different sectors of society, including government agencies, educational institutions, businesses, and public and private stakeholders, collaborate rather than compete. Integrating key health services and community resources results in improved quality, efficiency, and capacity.

The cornerstones of the health commons model are the neighborhood care sites that serve as the safety net for the uninsured and underinsured. At these centers, medical, behavioral, social, public health, and oral health services are co-located. But co-locating services is only the initial step in implementing an interdisciplinary, holistic approach to health care delivery. Many oral health patients have comorbidities such as diabetes and depression, in addition to social, language, and economic barriers to care. Each component of health care delivery (medical, behavioral, and dental) improves with better coordination of services and information.

In the health commons model, patient-centered oral health care is delivered by an interdisciplinary team. Depending on the client's needs, the service providers may include a primary care physician or provider, a dentist or dental hygienist, a nurse or nurse's assistant, a social worker, or a community health worker. The health commons safety net sites receive reengineering training enabling all members to function as a patient-centered, interdisciplinary team. The health commons model embraces health professions students and resident trainees as integral members of these interdisciplinary teams.

The University of New Mexico (UNM) Health Sciences Center is the state's only academic health center. It provides critical safety net services and trains future health providers. For example, 40 percent of the state's actively practicing physicians were trained at UNM during medical school or residency. While New Mexico lacks a dental school, UNM already trains dental hygienists and just received approval to begin a dental residency program. With support from the W.K. Kellogg Foundation's Community Voices Initiative, the UNM School of Medicine's Department of Surgery greatly expanded the capacity of the Division of Dental Services. While the institution had no dentists on the faculty at the start of the program, it now has eight. Its capacity has grown to include a four-chair dental clinic at UNM, a referral system for dental emergencies arriving at the emergency department, the newly approved dental residency program, and outreach dental services throughout the state. Over the past year, UNM dentists and dental hygienists have provided care to more than 23,600 adults and children at community-based health clinics, federally qualified health centers, and university-operated sites.

The First Health Model

Hoke, Montgomery, and Moore counties in North Carolina have twelve thousand medically underserved children without health care coverage or access to dental care. FirstHealth of the Carolinas, a private, not-for-profit health care network, strives to meet the comprehensive health care and dental needs of all residents of the mid-Carolinas. In a dental needs assessment, oral health care was cited as the number one unmet need for low-income children in the region, but only 10 percent of dentists participated in publicly assisted programs. Few Medicaid patients were being seen, yet dental care providers were already working at capacity. The shortage of providers was especially acute for pediatric dental services.

Accordingly, FirstHealth developed an integrated model of dental service delivery. An oral health task force was created to identify strategies to address the oral health crisis. The task force prioritized improving access for children through a public model based on a private practice setting. With support from the W.K. Kellogg Foundation and local philanthropies, including the Duke Endowment and the Kate B. Reynolds Charitable Trust, FirstHealth opened a community-based dental care center in each of the three counties in the region.

Two of the three dental care centers use existing medical centers as their home sites, and the third operates in a newly constructed facility. These dental care centers provide comprehensive dental care for more than seven thousand children, or nearly 60 percent of the targeted underserved population. By ensuring that all children who are eligible for insurance coverage are enrolled in Medicaid or other programs, FirstHealth proactively assists the financial sustainability of its dental care centers. In addition, children and their families can access other health benefits through the program and delivery sites.

Crucial Elements for Strengthening the Oral Health Safety Net

The common core elements of these three successful models are (1) involving the community in planning and implementation, (2) building upon the existing health safety net to link dental services with primary care, and (3) changing public or institutional policy to support the financing and delivery of dental care.

At all three sites, community support and involvement have been critical to building the political will and resources for the development of these dental programs. In each region (northern Manhattan, New Mexico, mid-Carolinas), a committee, council, or task force was created to build consensus on the problems and potential solutions. Because they involve providers, educators, community members, and policymakers, these three models are community-based, linked to primary care, and integrated with needed social services. In building upon the existing infrastructure safety net services, information and data systems, and health provider capacities (both medical and dental), each model integrates oral health into primary care services, thus improving the efficiency of both medical and dental services.

These collaborative efforts are helping to sustain the delivery of critical services while longer-term strategies are developed to improve access to oral health care and reduce oral health disparities. These longer-term strategies include surmounting the shortage of dental providers in underserved communities, increasing the diversity of the health professions workforce, and balancing the financing of health care to cover early prevention and health promotion as well as treatment of existing disease.

Improving access to oral health care and reducing disparities in oral health requires both institutional and health policy changes. Health service fragmentation creates formidable barriers. Using existing health care providers—pediatricians, family physicians, emergency room physicians, dental hygienists—where there are dental provider shortages can help strengthen the oral health safety net. While forty-four million Americans have no health insurance, one hundred million have no dental coverage. Most uninsured and underserved populations rely on Medicaid, yet states are cutting budgets and eliminating dental benefits. Thus, collaborative models such as those presented here may be the most cost-efficient and high-quality way to ensure access to oral health services. Coverage of dental services and adequate reimbursement rates will help improve access to care for underserved and uninsured populations.

Scaling Up Community-Based Dental Care Models

A perplexing dichotomy currently exists. *A National Call to Action to Promote Oral Health* exhorts the dental profession and community-based clinics to take action to improve access to dental care in the United States.[6] On the other hand, state governments—desperate to get their budget deficits under control—are cutting adult dental benefits from their Medicaid programs. Models offering basic oral health services in connection with community-based primary care services may ensure holistic, comprehensive health care for our most vulnerable and underserved populations.

Notes

1. U.S. Department of Health and Human Services (DHHS), *Oral Health in America: A Report of the Surgeon General* (Rockville, MD: DHHS, National Institutes of Health, National Institute of Dental and Craniofacial Research, 2000).
2. G. P. Zabos, M. E. Northridge, M. J. Ro, et al. "Lack of Oral Health Care for Adults in Harlem: A Hidden Crisis," *American Journal of Public Health*, 2002, 92, 49–52.
3. S. Marshall, A. Formicola, and J. McIntosh, "Columbia University's Community Dental Program as a Framework for Education," *Journal of Dental Education*, 1999, 6312, 944–947.
4. D. A. Mitchell, K. P. Ahluwalia, D. A. Albert, et al., "Dental Caries Experience in Northern Manhattan Adolescents," *Journal of Public Health Dentistry*, 2003, 63, 189–194.
5. S. Beetstra, D. Derksen, M. Ro, W. Powell, D. E. Fry, and A. Kaufman, "A 'Health Commons' Approach to Oral Health for Low-Income Populations in a Rural State," *American Journal of Public Health*, 2002, 92, 12–13.
6. *A National Call to Action to Promote Oral Health* (Rockville, MD: National Institute of Dental and Craniofacial Research, May 2003. NIH 03-5303.

CHAPTER SEVENTEEN

VULNERABLE POPULATIONS, PRISON, AND FEDERAL AND STATE MEDICAID POLICIES

Avoiding the Loss of a Right to Care

Leda M. Pérez, Marguerite J. Ro, and Henrie M. Treadwell

Unknown numbers of incarcerated people are losing public benefits. Instead of suspending these until the prisoner or detainee is released into society, some states are simply terminating benefits upon incarceration. Although there is evidence to suggest that this policy is having negative consequences for those who are reentering society and on their communities and systems of care, the precise impact is not clear because a systematic monitoring of these actions is nonexistent. A more efficient system would (a) suspend benefits and automatically reinstate the same to those eligible upon release and (b) establish a monitoring mechanism that would provide an accurate accounting of how these benefits are being applied.

L. M. Pérez, M. J. Ro, and H. M Treadwell, "Vulnerable Populations, Prison, and Federal and State Medicaid Policies: Avoiding the Loss of a Right to Care," *Journal of Correctional Health Care*, 2009, 15(2), 142–149.

Keywords: inmates; releasees; Medicaid; health care systems; quality assurance

Statement of the Problem

One in every one hundred adults in the United States today is imprisoned (Warren, 2008). As former prisoners and detainees are released into their communities—seven hundred thousand people a year—a concern of health policy and criminal justice advocates and researchers is that many prisoners are automatically losing health and social supports because of state policies that terminate, rather than suspend, Medicaid (Gupta, Kelleher, Pajer, Stevens, and Cuellar, 2005; Koyanagi and Blasingame, 2006; Rosen, 2003). Moreover, the federal government does not track and monitor who is terminated versus suspended from benefits, despite its monitoring of systems in other areas.[1] Such inaction makes it exceedingly difficult for policymakers and providers to have accurate information regarding how—or if—care is being provided to those who are eligible.

To be wholly efficient in financing care and monitoring the provision of the same, the Centers for Medicare and Medicaid Services (CMS) and/or other government entities must amplify their scope of auditing to safeguard the rights of vulnerable populations. Policies that promote suspension of benefits coupled with a tracking system would have the dual benefit of supporting a continuum of care for eligible former prisoners and monitoring how benefits are being applied. Without such a system, it is impossible for researchers, policy analysts, and, most important, the providers of care to protect the rights of this population effectively.

Who Is Paying the Price?

Communities

More often than not, prisoners hail from poor, underserved communities (Johnson, 2007). Many enter the system in need of both physical and mental health services; many more leave prison or jail in need of care for acute illnesses developed while in custody (Miller, 2007; Williams, 2006; Young, 2006). African American men carry much of the incarceration burden of the U.S. prison system. In 2006, 1 in every 33 Black men was a sentenced prisoner, compared to 1 in every 205 White men and 1 in every 79 Hispanic men (Sabol, Couture, and Harrison, 2007). Presently, 1 in 30 men, aged between twenty and thirty-four years, are in prison; for Black men in this age group the proportion is 1 in 9 (Warren, 2008). At the same time, the number of female prisoners rose at a faster rate than the number of male prisoners (Williams, 2007).

As decided by the Supreme Court in *Estelle* v. *Gamble* (1976), inmates are entitled to access health care and to see an appropriate health care professional while in prison.[2] Once outside of prison, former prisoners, like everyone else, have no particular right to health care. With no mechanism in place to systematically track and monitor incarcerated populations as they enter and leave prison, it is impossible to determine the degree of immediate support that is available for former prisoners and detainees. Because of disparate applications of policies in each state, many may have been disenrolled from Medicaid and other social supports and must reenroll upon release, leaving these individuals highly vulnerable due to lengthy postapplication waits.

For men and women whose Medicaid benefits have been terminated, this may have disastrous effects on their personal health as well as that of their children, who may also lose coverage (Miller, 2007). Former prisoners are mostly people who were residents of, or who have spent time in, distressed communities before their incarceration (Young, 2006). The process of returning to a community that is already depressed creates a vicious cycle for former prisoners who return, and for their communities.

Systems

People who are eligible for health and social service benefits must have those benefits safeguarded, not only for the well-being of those persons and their communities, but also as a cost-saving measure for the health care and correctional systems. Recent research has been clear in demonstrating that people who leave jail or prison without health insurance are more likely to return (Morissey, 2006; van Olphen, Freudenberg, Fortin, and Galea, 2006). Moreover, "a recent study by Hunter College found that in the year after being released from a New York City jail, women with Medicaid coverage were more likely to participate in a residential drug-treatment program and less likely to be rearrested" (Matthews, 2007, p. 3).

According to a 2008 Pew Center on States study, in 2007 states collectively spent $44 billion of their general funds on corrections. "Adjusted to 2007 dollars, the increase was 127%" (Warren, 2008, p. 4). As the report suggests, the significant rise in prison spending is attributable to the increased payment of overtime for prison staff as well as skyrocketing prison health care costs. In fact, medical care is one of the principal cost drivers (Warren, 2008). However, as the Pew report concludes, despite high rates of incarceration and the expenditures associated with the same, there is no clear impact on crime in general nor recidivism in particular (Warren, 2008).

There are public health and economic consequences to governments and private health care payors as institutions grapple with the burgeoning prison population and the need to provide care in those institutions. As people leave prison, with no benefits and nowhere to access care, many will return, a cycle that clearly impacts both the correctional system and the communities left behind.

Medicaid Policies for Incarcerated Populations

In a letter to Herah Crawford, director of the Oregon Department of Human Resources Office of Medical Assistance, Robert Reed, acting chief of the Medicaid Branch, Division of State and Medicaid Operations, Department of Health and Human Services, noted, "Section 1905(a) (A) of the Social Security Act specifically excludes Federal Financial Participation (FFP) for medical care provided to inmates of a public institution, except when the inmate is a patient in a medical institution." Responding to Director Crawford's query regarding states' possibilities for using Medicaid funds for incarcerated persons, Reed clarified two areas. First, FPP does not "specify, nor imply" that inmates of a public institution may not be eligible for Medicaid "if the appropriate eligibility criteria are met." Second, Medicaid coverage policy does not distinguish between juveniles or adults: " . . . a juvenile awaiting trial in a detention center is no different than an adult in a maximum security prison." For FFP to be prohibited, the individual must be an inmate, and the facility in which the individual is residing must be a public institution. "An individual is an inmate when serving time for a criminal offense or confined involuntarily in State or Federal prisons, jails, detention facilities, or other penal facilities."

Suspension Versus Termination

Although federal law, as noted above, does not permit financing to federal institutions providing health care, it also does not require states to terminate a prisoner or an involuntarily confined person's eligibility to Medicaid. "In fact, the states have no authority under Medicaid law to drop inmates from the Medicaid eligibility rolls upon incarceration" (Bazelon Center for Mental Health Law, 2003). This is an important distinction that creates the conditions to suspend Medicaid benefits, as encouraged by CMS, rather than terminate them.[3,4] Suspension, as opposed to termination, recognizes an individual's eligibility and thus merely holds the benefits until the person has returned to the community.

A number of published works point to the benefit of suspension versus termination, particularly for ensuring immediate reinstatement of services and health care (Bazelon Center for Mental Health Law, 2003; Koyanagi, 2003; Koyanagi and Blasingame, 2006; Miller, 2007; Morissey et al., 2006). Although this is important for all inmates and former prisoners or detainees, this becomes particularly critical for populations living with mental illness. The repercussions of losing Supplemental Security Income (SSI) and/or Social Security Disability Income (SSDI) extend to not only the incarcerated individual but also the family with whom he or she lived before incarceration, as benefits to the family would also be revoked. Such action would directly harm and perhaps even render homeless many innocent children and families. Having some income to pay for health care and other needs is thus critical for a former prisoner or detainee and would certainly assist in family reunification.

Mental health advocates as well as the criminal justice and social justice communities argue that the investment in services must be made directly in communities so that people with mental illness do not return to prison. One way to do this is to ensure that Medicaid, SSI, and SSDI populations maintain their benefits once they return to their communities.

Indeed, access to and receipt of these services are the most powerful deterrents to recidivism for former prisoners and detainees, especially among those who are mentally ill. A federal tracking and monitoring system would not only follow these vulnerable populations, helping to ensure that they are receiving the benefits to which they are entitled, but also chart best practices for care and cost savings on a regular basis. Some promising practices exist, and these could be highlighted and practiced at the federal and state levels if they were monitored consistently (Exhibit 17.1).

Policies on this vary from state to state. Although each state has the sovereignty to decide what is best for its fiscal and administrative policies, the federal government must be able to track what is happening on a regular basis. Such tracking would inform federal policy and research as well as help to monitor quality assurance in the future.

Jails, for example, are encouraged with federal payments to inform the Social Security Administration (SSA) that a person is confined. Payments are received for supplying information that results in suspension or termination of SSI or SSDI benefits. By contrast, there is no incentive to advise SSA about those leaving prison so that benefits might be reinstated (Bazelon Center for Mental Health Law, 2001).

Jails and prisons can enter into agreements with SSA to provide monthly reports of inmates' names, Social Security numbers, dates of birth, confinement dates, and other information. The institution receives $400 when this information is sent within thirty days of the inmate's arrival and $200 if it is sent within ninety days. This information should—but does not always—include an estimated release date (Bazelon Center for Mental Health Law, 2001).[5]

Despite the options available, a 1999 survey found that all states had a policy of terminating Medicaid eligibility upon incarceration (Bazelon Center for Mental Health Law, 2001). However, these policies would seem to contradict federal government requirements that say that states must not terminate anyone from Medicaid without first determining that the person cannot qualify under another Medicaid-eligible rule. Federal law requires that those who had Medicaid eligibility when they were arrested must be "reassessed and reinstated," if still eligible upon their release. Furthermore, any person must be assisted in applying for benefits, and federal Medicaid matching funds may be used for costs incurred by state or local officials to determine an individual's eligibility (Bazelon Center for Mental Health Law, 2001;

EXHIBIT 17.1. A VIEW FROM SOME STATES.

Colorado

A draft bill for the State of Colorado's 66th General Assembly, dated September 6, 2007, recognizes a person's eligibility for medical assistance while an inmate. "To the extent permitted by federal law, the time during which a person is an inmate shall not be included in any calculation of when the person must recertify his or her eligibility for medical assistance pursuant to this article or article 5 or 6 of this title" (Colorado, 2007, pp. 2–3).

Indiana

In the October 18, 2004, minutes of a Select Joint Commission on Medicaid Oversight for the Legislative Services Agency of the State of Indiana, the discussion regarding suspension versus termination of Medicaid benefits centered on a letter received from the Centers for Medicare and Medicaid Services (CMS) that encouraged states to only suspend eligibility. At this meeting, it was suggested that suspending, versus terminating, eligibility would add little benefit, while adding significant administrative burden to the state. Instead, the alternative offered was to share in the cost with the Department of Corrections to fund case managers for inmates scheduled for release to coordinate their medical records. At the time of this meeting, the state policy was to terminate an individual's eligibility sixty days after incarceration in a correctional facility (Indiana, 2004).

Maryland

Maryland Senate Bill 960 sought to ensure that an accurate accounting was made of those individuals with mental illness—in both jails and prisons—who were receiving services in order to determine the adequacy of the mental health and related support services. This bill also sought to streamline, and thus hasten, access to services upon an inmate's release. Maryland did have provisions in place, even before this legislation, that sought to improve access to services for individuals inside the correctional system and for those exiting. An important detail to this legislation is that benefit suspension was contingent on funding for a new computerized eligibility system for Medicaid. This system was expected to be functional by 2008 (Maryland, 2006).

New York

New York State is among the few that recently passed legislation that ensures health benefits for inmates upon release. "Governor Eliot Spitzer has signed legislation that will suspend rather than terminate Medicaid benefits for prisoners while they are incarcerated so they can reenter society without having to wait 2 to 3 months for benefits to restart" (Matthews, 2007).

Ohio

In an opinion written by Jim Petro, attorney general of the State of Ohio, and provided to the Honorable Sherri Bevan Walsh on May 5, 2006, Petro makes it clear that the decision to suspend or terminate Medicaid benefits is ultimately made within a state. This opinion recognizes that federal law does not require states to terminate the Medicaid eligibility for inmates. As of May 2006, it appears that Ohio was indeed one of the majority of states that terminated Medicaid eligibility automatically when a person is jailed (Petro, 2006).

Williams, 2007). Comparatively more complicated is when a person qualifies for Medicaid as a result of eligibility for SSI. "In such cases, SSI must be restored first. If SSI has only been suspended, this should take no more than 14 days, but if it has been terminated the delay could stretch into months or years" (Koyanagi, 2003, pp. 9–10).

Ensuring that these federal regulations are upheld, and that states remain flexible in determining eligibility for their prison populations while providing case management assistance as prisoners transition and prepare for reentry makes sense for not only the prisoner but also the community to which they are returning and the prison system itself. Beyond this, it would appear to be federal Medicaid law.

Medicaid While in Prison

Another area that may assist in both the care of prisoners and their reentry is the proposition that Medicaid coverage be made available for incarcerated populations (Johnson, 2007). This proposal points out the uneven quality of care currently existing for prisoners and detainees. However, this same group suffers from illness and disease at a far greater rate than others. The contention is that they should be receiving quality health care while in prison as a protective factor in aiding these populations and their communities when they come home. Without an amendment to Medicaid that would permit states to receive federal matching funds, it becomes difficult for states to move public health programs forward and ensure quality health care to inmates. To provide adequate medical care in prison, states must have adequate resources (Johnson, 2007).

What Is Needed Right Now

Recommendations and promising practices can be effective only if, in addition to being implemented on a consistent basis nationwide, there is a real tracking and monitoring system that is accountable and identifies the gaps that must be addressed. Despite the best efforts of CMS, it remains that there is not a single agency that systematically monitors states' policies and practices regarding Medicaid suspension. As a result, data are sketchy and agencies, like CMS, meant to provide the benefits do not have an accurate accounting of who is—or is not—on the rolls. What is more, scant current data are available for those individuals and family members, which is a detriment to organizations that engage in research and advocacy. In the absence of this information, it is virtually impossible for practitioners, advocates, and researchers to accurately detect gaps and trends and to recommend or implement sound, novel practices.

Monitoring, Reporting, and Integrity and Reliability in the Process

As the federal agency that monitors Medicaid-eligible populations, CMS should report on information regarding individual state policies on Medicaid suspension or termination in cases of incarceration, or, at a minimum, make the data easily available through an accessible source like the Internet. Likewise, CMS or another federal agency must monitor the termination of benefits for those who have been Medicaid eligible as well as the restoration of coverage for those whose benefits have been suspended. In other words, we must strive for an accurate and reliable accounting of those terminated or suspended, and compare this with those who have had benefits restored. Quality control measures must be in place to assure timely restoration of benefits for eligible populations leaving the criminal justice system. Finally, a federal mechanism and/or funding must be created to support some agency, if not CMS, to routinely perform this function and to collect and report on state eligibility policies in an effort to oversee the integrity and reliability of the process.

A Federal Report Card

A federal report card must be developed to track suspension versus termination of benefits as well as what communities are doing regarding reentry and the associated best practices. A federal mandate that ensures that this information is consistently available to the public is vital. The current absence of a monitoring system that can inform on what states are doing in this respect must be remedied. Indeed, as important as it is to advocate one standard that supports the suspension versus termination of benefits, it is equally critical to have an accurate balance of what is transpiring so that subsequent recommendations and policies are produced on the sound foundation of current data.

Conclusion

Men and women, mothers and fathers, sisters and brothers, sons and daughters, friends and family, and, too often, children are populating our correctional systems. They are all of us in some category or other, but they usually share one common denominator different from many of us on the "outside:" a history of poverty, neglect, and, in too many cases, abuse. Far too many others have the additional history of mental illness and/or substance dependency.

They are vulnerable going in, and even more vulnerable coming out. Despite whatever offense they committed to put them in the system, these individuals remain members of our society who under the law do have basic rights—precisely because of their low income and/or disability status—to public assistance and, specifically, to health care in prison and benefits on the outside if they are eligible. These rights, in too many instances, are being decimated as a result of state policies that make it extremely difficult, if not impossible, for those coming back from prison to recoup their former benefits, exacting heavy prices on these individuals, their families, and communities, and ultimately on the system.

We have discussed a number of options for ensuring care for these individuals while in prison as well as when they return home. A critical corollary is the implementation of a tracking system that will enable both the federal and state funding agencies to track and monitor how these federal mandates are being implemented, allowing for corrections and constant improvements. Clearly, this would provide the dual benefit of protecting both systems and the rights of people.

Notes

1. For example, the Centers for Medicare and Medicaid Services (CMS) monitors and analyzes the accuracy of billing charges that may be viewed as erroneous or fraudulent.
2. Although prisoners and detainees may receive reasonably good care in some institutions, this is not uniform across the country's prisons. Some systems simply have not been able to provide adequate care (Warren, 2008). One example is California's prison medical system, currently under federal receivership "after a federal judge found that an average of one inmate a week was dying of neglect or malpractice" (Thompson, 2007).

3. Despite a letter issued by CMS calling for all states to suspend rather than terminate benefits for incarcerated populations (Indiana, 2004), there is still no uniform practice on this issue. A federal policy regarding suspension versus termination of Medicaid and/or Supplemental Security Income (SSI) and Social Security Disability Income (SSDI) benefits for these populations simply does not exist. There is also no federal quality assurance monitoring system for Medicaid, SSI, and/or SSDI for prisoners and former prisoners.

4. See National Commission on Correctional Health Care, http://www.ncchc.org/pubs/pubs_stbr.html, accessed August 20, 2008.

5. States do have the flexibility to implement policies that will assist ex-offenders in accessing benefits. Moreover, states can play a much needed and critical role in helping inmates before their release. The Bazelon Center for Mental Health Law regularly issues reports and issue briefs that provide recommendations and promising practices (see Koyanagi, 2003, http://www.bazelon.org).

References

Bazelon Center for Mental Health Law. *For People with Serious Mental Illnesses: Finding the Key to Successful Transition from Jail to the Community—An Explanation of Federal Medicaid and Disability Program Rules*, March 2001. Retrieved January 4, 2008, from http://www.bazelon.org/issues/criminalization/findingthekey.htm.

Bazelon Center for Mental Health Law. *Building Bridges: An Act to Reduce Recidivism by Improving Access to Benefits for Individuals with Psychiatric Disabilities Upon Release from Incarceration (Model Law and Commentary)*, April 2003. Retrieved January 4, 2008, from http://www.bazelon.org/issues/criminalization/publications/buildingbridges/index.htm.

Colorado Interim Committee Bill, LLS No. 08-0146.01, 2007. *Suspend Medicaid Benefits of Inmates*. Retrieved January 4, 2008, from http://www.state.co.us/gov_dir/leg_dir/lc-sstaff/2007/comsched/07MICJBill%204.pdf.

Estelle v. *Gamble*, 429 U.S. 97 (1976).

Gupta, R. A., Kelleher, K. J., Pajer, K., Stevens, J., and Cuellar, A. "Delinquent Youth in Corrections: Medicaid and Reentry into the Community." *Pediatrics*, 2005, 115, 1077–1083.

Indiana Select Joint Commission on Medicaid Oversight. Meeting Minutes, October 18, 2004, Indianapolis.

Johnson, R. M. A. *Report to the House of Delegates* (San Francisco: American Bar Association, Criminal Justice Section, August 2007). Retrieved January 4, 2008, from http://www.abanet.org/crimjust/policy/corrections.doc.

Koyanagi, C. *A Better Life—A Safer Community: Helping Inmates Access Federal Benefits*, Bazelon Center Issue Brief (Washington, DC: Bazelon Center for Mental Health Law, January 2003). Retrieved November 30, 2007, from http://www.bazelon.org/issues/criminalization/publications/gains/gains.pdf.

Koyanagi, C., and Blasingame, K. *Best Practices: Access to Benefits for Prisoners with Mental Illnesses*, Bazelon Center Issue Brief (Washington, DC: Bazelon Center for Mental Health Law, 2006). Retrieved January 4, 2007, from http://www.bazelon.org/issues/criminalization/publications/BestPractices.pdf.

Maryland House Bill 1594. *Benefits and Services for Individuals Who Are Incarcerated or Institutionalized*, Work Group Report, 2006. Retrieved February 2, 2008, from http://mlis.state.md.us/2006rs/billfile/HB1594.htm.

Matthews, C. "Inmates Can Get Health Benefits When Released." *Star Gazette*, Elmira, NY, July 26, 2007. Retrieved January 4, 2008, from http://realcostofprisons.org/blog/archives/2007/07/ny_inmatescan.html.

Miller, E. J. *Failing Health: The Crisis of Health Care for Indigent Offenders and for the Community* (Atlanta, GA: Community Voices, National Center for Primary Care, Morehouse School of Medicine, 2007).

Morissey, J. P. *Medicaid Benefits and Recidivism of Mentally Ill Persons Released from Jail* (unpublished research report submitted to U.S. Department of Justice), May 2006. Retrieved January 4, 2008, from http://www.ncjrs.gov/pdffiles1/nij/grants/214169.pdf.

Morissey, J. P., Dalton, K. M., Steadman, H. J., Cuddeback, G. S., Haynes, D., and Cuellar, A. "Assessing Gaps Between Policy and Practice in Medicaid Disenrollment with Severe Mental Illness." *Psychiatric Services*, 2006, 57, 803–808.

Petro, J. *State of Ohio, Office of the Attorney General, Opinion No. 2006-019*, May 5, 2006. Retrieved January 4, 2007, from http://www.ag.state.oh.us/legal/opinions/2006/2006-019.pdf.

Rosen, J. *Expediting Eligibility Determinations*. National Law Center on Homelessness and Poverty, presented at Homeless Policy Academy 3, Atlanta, GA, January 2003. Retrieved January 4, 2008, from http://www.hrsa.gov/homeless/pa_materials/pa3/pa3_rosen.htm.

Sabol, J. S., Couture, H., and Harrison, P. M. *Prisoners in 2006*. Bureau of Justice Statistics Bulletin NCJ 219416, 2007. Retrieved December 10, 2007, from http://ojp.usdoj.gov/bjs/pub/pdf/p06.pdf.

Thompson, D. "Prison Care Still Poor, Report Says." The Associated Press. *Ventura County Star*, Camarillo, CA, September 20, 2007. Retrieved August 11, 2008, from http://www.venturacountystar.com/news/2007/sep/20/prison-medical-care-still-poor-report-says.

Van Olphen, J., Freudenberg, N., Fortin, P., and Galea, S. "Community Reentry: Perceptions of People with Substance Use Problems Returning Home from New York City Jails." *Journal of Urban Health: Bulletin of the New York Academy of Medicine*, 2006, 83(3), 372–381.

Warren, J. *One in 100: Behind Bars in America 2008*. Pew Center on the States and the Public Safety Performance Project Report, 2008. Retrieved August 11, 2008, from http://www.pewcenteronthestates.org/uploadedFiles/8015PCTS_Prison08_FINAL_2-1-1_FOR-WEB.pdf.

Williams, N. *Where Are the Men? The Impact of Incarceration and Reentry on African American Men and Their Children and Families* (Atlanta, GA: Community Voices, National Center for Primary Care, Morehouse School of Medicine, 2006). Retrieved August 12, 2008, from http://www.communityvoices.org/Uploads/wherearethemen2_00108_00144.pdf.

Williams, N. *Healthcare and Incarceration: Medicaid Termination and Suspension* (Fact Sheet) (Atlanta, GA: Community Voices, National Center for Primary Care, Morehouse School of Medicine, 2007).

Young, A.M.W. *The Overtown Men's Health Study* (Miami, FL: Collins Center for Public Policy, 2006).

CHAPTER EIGHTEEN

WEB-BASED PRIMARY CARE REFERRAL PROGRAM ASSOCIATED WITH REDUCED EMERGENCY DEPARTMENT UTILIZATION

Michael Murnik, Fornessa Randal, Mary Guevara, Betty Skipper, and Arthur Kaufman

Background and Objectives

Uninsured patients without a primary care home tend to use the emergency department (ED) for primary care. We examined whether an enhanced scheduling system for follow-up care from the University of New Mexico Hospital Emergency Department (UNMH-ED) that assigns patients to a family medicine home can decrease ED utilization.

Methods

The Community AccessProgram for Central New Mexico (CAP-NM) is a consortium of primary care safety net provider organizations. CAP-NM developed a HIPAA-compliant (Health Insurance Portability and Accountability Act), web-based

This study was supported by a grant from the U.S. Department of Health and Human Services, Health Resources and Services Administration's Healthy Community Access Program and a grant from the W.K. Kellogg Foundation's Community Voices Initiative (P0060131). The content of this manuscript was presented at the Society of Teachers of Family Medicine 25th Anniversary Conference on Families and Health, February 24, 2005, in Amelia Island, Florida.

information system used by the UNMH-ED to refer uninsured, unassigned patients to family medicine practices ("homes") within the consortium. The website referral system operated twenty-four hours a day, seven days a week; printed maps to clinic sites; and listed services offered. Analysis of quality assurance data compared (1) ED utilization outcomes of eligible patients referred by the CAP-NM website to a family medicine home to (2) outcomes of controls discharged from the ED in the usual manner.

Results

The 756 patients referred to family medicine homes through the CAP-NM website demonstrated a significant 31 percent reduction in subsequent ED visits compared to controls. This reduction was most evident among those who had infrequent ED use before institution of the program.

Conclusions

Implementing an enhanced referral system to family medicine homes from the ED is associated with decreased subsequent ED utilization by uninsured patients (*Family Medicine,* 2006, 38[3], 185–189).

Emergency department (ED) overcrowding is a national problem exacerbated by ED closures, insufficient hospital bed capacity, and insufficient primary care capacity.[1-3] One factor in the problem of ED overcrowding is the rapid growth in the number of medically uninsured patients in the United States, now numbering more than forty-six million.

The uninsured are high users of ED services and relatively low users of primary care. Compared to the medically insured, the uninsured tend to delay seeking care until their medical conditions are more advanced, complicated, and costly to treat. These trends lead to higher rates of ED use and more preventable hospitalizations.[4,5] This is costly to hospitals, providers, and society, since the uninsured can pay little of what they are charged.

Previous interventions that have attempted to reduce ED visits by a high-user subset of medically uninsured by providing access to primary care have not always been successful.[6,9] The lack of reduced ED use from these interventions may reflect several barriers to care. In particular, uninsured patients have difficulty accessing primary care in a timely manner. This is a major problem at academic health centers, where the ratio of primary care to specialist providers is far lower than that in the private community and where most clinics are closed in the evenings and weekends. Kaufman et al. demonstrated that managing care through assignment of uninsured patients to primary care practices reduced the cost of care, attributable primarily to reduced hospitalizations without a demonstrable reduction in ED visits.[6] ED physicians at the University of New Mexico report that only 25 percent of ED patients referred for follow-up care after discharge ever arrive at those appointments, perhaps because the customary appointment procedure is haphazard, with many patients discharged during evening or night-time hours when appointments cannot be scheduled. Many patients have no phones or voice mail, hindering post-ED contact follow-up.

Starfield reported on the favorable effect of access to a primary care system on population health status, especially among populations with substantial income inequality.[7] However, these health benefits escape many of the uninsured, who lack a primary care home and face a fragmented health system that can be difficult to navigate.

Can assignment to a family medicine home of uninsured, unassigned patients from the ED be enhanced such that subsequent ED utilization is decreased? An opportunity arose to answer this question through a collaborative effort between the University of New Mexico Department of Family and Community Medicine and the University of New Mexico Hospital Emergency Department (UNMH-ED) working in cooperation with a safety net community health consortium known as the Community Access Program of Central New Mexico (CAP-NM). CAP-NM received federal funding from the Health Resources and Services Administration and includes six safety net provider organizations—the University of New Mexico Health Sciences Center, First Choice Community Healthcare, First Nations Healthsource, Albuquerque Healthcare for the Homeless, the Albuquerque Indian Health Service, and the New Mexico Department of Health. The primary focus of this consortium is to increase access to care for the estimated 140,000 medically uninsured in the four-county region of Central New Mexico. CAP-NM developed a system for medical information sharing to decrease duplication of services and to improve the efficiency of care. Four provider systems within the consortium redesigned their clinical operations, streamlined their services, and thereby increased capacity at each clinic site. Additionally, the consortium engaged in cooperative hiring and support of health professional staff at all facilities. Nonetheless, the majority of uninsured residents of Central New Mexico had no identified primary care home and tended to use UNMH-ED for primary care services.

The CAP-NM consortium, in collaboration with the UNMH-ED, developed a system for assigning uninsured, unassigned patients discharged from the UNMH-ED to a primary care home. We studied whether this system could reduce ED utilization.

Methods

UNM's Human Research Review Committee reviewed and approved our study methods and use of the CAP-NM database and the University of New Mexico Hospital's physician billing service and patient-tracking databases.

Referral System

CAP-NM created a HIPAA-compliant (Health Insurance Portability and Accountability Act), web-based referral program. This program, "The Primary Care Dispatch," is an appointment scheduling and referral service designed by the UNM Department of Family and Community Medicine that links the UNMH-ED to family medicine clinics within the CAP-NM safety net provider organizations via the Internet. Using this secured, password-protected site, trained discharge clerks can schedule follow-up appointments for patients twenty-four hours a day, seven days a week. Any UNMH-ED patient being discharged who has no assigned primary care provider or primary care home can be referred to any one of fifteen CAP-NM-affiliated clinics. The Internet site offers access to reserved appointments, usually within one to two days of the ED visit and scheduled at the clinic most accessible from the patient's home or workplace.

At the time of referral, the patient receives a computer-generated appointment sheet that contains the appointment date and time, a list of services provided at that clinic, and a map to the clinic site. As soon as the patient referral is made from the ED, the receiving clinic is notified electronically that an appointment has been scheduled. The receiving clinic is prompted through the CAP-NM system the day after the scheduled appointment to record appointments kept or rescheduled and primary care provider assignment. The program predominantly is used for indigent self-pay patients who are uninsured and have not qualified for Medicaid or County Indigent Assistance programs.

In the first seventeen months of the program, 834 self-pay patients were referred to clinics within the CAP-NM consortium. These referrals were made in the course of normal business in the ED by ED physicians availing themselves of the new service. Of these patients, 756 (91 percent) were eighteen years of age or older and had complete data available in all three of the data systems used for comparison: the CAP-NM program logs, the UNMH billing records, and the UNMH patient tracking database. These referred patients with complete tracking data constituted our study group of "CAP participants." The date on which each CAP participant was referred via the system was considered their "CAP index date." Preliminary data analysis revealed that the CAP participants were older on average than the general ED patient population. Therefore, control patients were randomly chosen from the group of all self-pay non-CAP patients in the same age strata as the CAP participants seen in the ED on that same day. CAP participants and controls were followed in the UNMH Patient Tracking Database from the index date to the conclusion of the study. Follow-up times ranged from two to twenty months.

Data Analysis

Analyses comparing CAP and control patients showed disparity in the number of ED visits logged during the year before the index visit. Since a major predictor of future utilization is past utilization, we decided to divide the sample into four strata based on the number of ED visits by the patients in the year preceding their index date. Groups were compared for each utilization stratum using the Z test for comparing incidence densities.[8] Annualized rates for return visits to the ED following the index visit were calculated within each stratum. Rate ratios were calculated comparing CAP participants' rates of return to their controls' rates. An estimate of the reduction in ED utilization for one thousand patient-years was then calculated using the overall return rates for CAP participants and controls.

Results

We found that patients referred via the CAP program to a family medicine home for follow-up were less likely to return to the ED than similar, unreferred controls. This decrease was most significant among those who did not use the ED frequently prior to their CAP program referral index date. While improvement trends are noted in each prior-utilization stratum, statistical significance was only achieved in the zero visits and single-visit-in-the-previous-year groups. The results of this analysis are shown in Table 18.1. Table 18.2 shows estimated reductions in visits based on the rates in Table 18.1. It is estimated that making CAP referrals should reduce the number of return ED visits by 31 percent. These were overall return rate estimates, including return rates from all prior-utilization strata.

Discussion

While some have shown a reduction in ED utilization when primary care follow-up was appointed for a specific disease entity,[10] we have shown a reduction in ED utilization without regard to disease presentations. Baren et al. demonstrated that the provision of medications, transportation vouchers, and telephone reminders from the ED increased the likelihood that asthmatic patients would keep their primary care

TABLE 18.1. COMPARISON OF ANNUALIZED RETURN VISIT RATES FOR CAP AND CONTROL PATIENTS ACCORDING TO NUMBERS OF VISITS IN THE YEAR BEFORE THE INDEX DATE.

	CAP		Control			
Prior Year Visits	#	Visit Rate*	#	Visit Rate	CAP/ Control Rate Ratio	P-Value
0	487	.71	258	1.28	.55	<.0001
1	148	7.09	228	1.55	.70	.001
2	63	1.77	101	2.14	.82	.16
3 or more	58	4.10	169	4.48	.91	.28

Notes: CAP = Community Access Program.

* The visit rate is the number of emergency room visits per patient-year following the index date.

TABLE 18.2. ESTIMATED REDUCTION IN NUMBER OF VISITS PER ONE THOUSAND PATIENT-YEARS.

Estimated Visits Using CAP Rate	Estimated Visit Using Control Rate	Differences in CAP versus Control	Percent Reduction
1,130	1,648	-518	31%

follow-up appointments.[11] However, subsequent ED use was not studied. Kaufman et al. failed to show a reduction in ED utilization despite a significant reduction in hospitalization and cost when an uninsured population was assigned to primary care providers and charged low copayments for visits, labs, and medications.[6] A recent study at the University of New Mexico comparing long-term outcomes of UNM Care patients with commercially insured and self-pay patients again failed to show a change in utilization patterns.[9] However, this study evaluated a relatively small, presumably sicker, group of patients who used services continuously over five years.

Offering uninsured, unassigned ED patients at the time of discharge a follow-up family medicine appointment within several days at a clinic near their home appeared to be associated with a decrease in subsequent ED utilization. Reduction in hospital cost is implied via reduction in uncompensated care. This success depended on a new approach to ED discharge planning and follow-up care that was timely, more comprehensive, informative, and personalized. An appointment could be made at any time, day or night, seven days a week, thus avoiding the inevitable lack of success in attempting to reach patients the next day. The ability to schedule such a follow-up appointment within days decreased the no-show rate since the appointment was at a time of immediate need. The fact that the patient was given a map to the appointed clinic located in geographic proximity to their home reduced barriers to keeping the appointment in a city with poor public transportation. Finally, the fact that patients left the ED with specific information about their new family medicine home, such as the presence of dental services, a WIC program, or a drop-in immunization clinic, may have enhanced the attractiveness of the referral.

The favorable results of the web-based appointment system on subsequent ED utilization likely are an underestimation of its potential in different systems and over a longer period of time. One reason is financial. New Mexico has one of the highest rates of medically uninsured (more than 25 percent of the under-sixty-five-years-of-age population), for whom health services received in EDs are without charge if the patient cannot afford a copay at the time of service, a rule dictated by federal Emergency Medical Treatment and Labor Act regulations. In contrast, required copays at safety net sites to which CAP referrals were made average $20—a financial disincentive for patients returning to those sites. Another reason is legal. A sizable portion of the medically uninsured in New Mexico is undocumented workers who are often attracted by the relative anonymity of services provided at the public hospital ED. And finally, in other studies,[6,12,13] the favorable benefits of a primary care assignment on utilization of resources by the uninsured are realized over several years. During the first year, the focus of this study, there is usually an increase in resource utilization throughout the health system due to pent-up demand.

Reduced ED visits of self-pay patients offer a considerable financial benefit to the hospital. The average loss to the hospital for each self-pay patient's ED visit is more than $200. An even greater savings from use of the CAP web-based referral system will be realized if the family medicine assignment is shown to lead to a reduction in hospitalizations of self-pay patients. Increased assignment of uninsured patients to a family medicine home might also reduce the disease burden in the community, a major benefit to society. Shi demonstrated that adequate access to primary care reduces disease disparities, especially in populations with significant economic disparities.[14]

This innovation depended on the collaboration of safety net health care systems in the community that offered the university a broader primary care capacity. The university had to be cautious that it was not perceived as simply "dumping" its financial burden onto others. The collaborative program has continued because the university has supported each of the community safety net partners in other ways—sharing grants, assisting in the recruitment of health professionals, providing technical support, and referring to their systems' Medicaid and Medicare patients for whom they are able to receive cost-based reimbursement. Although in most locales the primary care capacity may not exist to completely address this problem, variations on this program should be achievable wherever an overutilized ED coexists with primary care resources able to provide care for uninsured and underinsured patients, such as federally qualified community health centers.

Limitations

The results should be interpreted with caution. This was an observational, quality-assurance, data-based study of a newly launched program, not a randomized, controlled study. The majority of eligible UNMH-ED patients were not assigned CAP appointments at the conclusion of their UNMH-ED visit since not all UNMH-ED personnel were familiar with it. Access to the web-based CAP appointment system required training, and with high turnover in staff, working three shifts, training all providers and staff in this new web-based innovation was logistically difficult. While we matched each uninsured, unassigned UNMH-ED patient receiving a CAP referral in a stratified manner with a randomly selected patient who was not referred, we again emphasize that this was not a randomized, controlled study. Before stratification, characteristics of those referred differed from those not referred. The older age of referred, self-pay patients compared to controls may indicate that UNMH-ED physicians had been biased in selecting those they felt were more in need of a referral, though this was controlled for in the analysis. Other potential differences in characteristics between referred and control patients such as number of comorbidities or patient motivation toward follow-up care might exist but could not be evaluated by the current study design. And finally, not all discharging ED physicians placed the same value on a patient's need for a primary care home.

Conclusions

Future studies will assess the degree to which referred CAP-NM patients remain in their assigned family medicine home and will assess the impact of CAP-NM referrals to family medicine on subsequent hospital discharges, specialty services, laboratory tests, and medication utilization after the initial phase of "pent-up demand." It will be important to determine what factors motivate and deter UNMH-ED physicians from referring eligible patients to primary care follow-up.

A recent survey suggests that ED physicians' attitudes toward primary care are generally positive and that primary care capacity, and thus the capacity of the referral program, is the limiting factor in the follow-up process. Finally, further analyses of the influence of establishing continuity of care with a primary care physician on utilization of the ED needs to be a focus of future research.

Notes

1. L. D. Richardson, B. R. Asplin, and R. A. Lowe RA, "Emergency Department Over-crowding as a Health Policy Issue: Past Development, Future Directions," *Annals of Emergency Medicine*, 2002, 40, 338–393.

2. A. B. Bindman, K. Grumbach, D. Osmond, et al., "Preventable Hospitalizations and Access to Health Care," *Journal of the American Medical Association*, 1995, 274(4), 305–11.

3. W. W. Fields, "Calculus, Chaos, and Other Models of Emergency Department Crowding," *Annals of Emergency Medicine*, 2003, 42, 181–184.

4. R. G. Roetzheim, N. Pal, C. Tennant, et al., "Effects of Health Insurance and Race on Early Cancer Detection," *Journal of the National Cancer Institute*, 1999, 91, 1409–1415.

5. P. Franks, C. M. Clancy, and M. R. Gold, "Health Insurance and Mortality: Evidence from a National Cohort," *Journal of the American Medical Association*, 1993, 270, 737–741.

6. A. Kaufman, P. Galbraith, D. Derksen, et al., "Managed Care for Uninsured Patients at an Academic Health Center," *Academic Medicine*, 2000, 75(4), 323–330.

7. B. Starfield, "Deconstructing Primary Care," in J. Showstack, A. A. Rothman, and S. B. Hassmiller, *The Future of Primary Care*. (San Francisco: Jossey-Bass, 2004).

8. D. G. Kleinbaum, L. L. Kupper, and H. Morgenstern, *Epidemiologic Research* (Belmont, CA: Lifelong Learning Publications, l982).

9. H. Kwack, D. Sklar, B. Skipper, A. Kaufman, E. Fingado, and M. Hauswald, "Effect of Managed Care on Emergency Department Use in an Uninsured Population," *Annals of Emergency Medicine*, 2004, 43(2), 166–173.

10. D. D. Sin, N. R. Bell, L. W. Svenson, and S. F. Man, "The Impact of Follow-Up Physician Visits on Emergency Readmissions for Patients with Asthma and Chronic Obstructive Pulmonary Disease: A Population-Based Study," *American Journal of Medicine*, 2002, 112(2), 120–125.

11. J. M. Baren, F. S. Shofer, B. Ivey, et al., "A Randomized, Controlled Trial of a Simple Emergency Department Intervention to Improve the Rate of Primary Care Follow-Up for Patients with Acute Asthma," *Annals of Emergency Medicine*, 2001, 38(2), 115–122.

12. H. Bograd, D. P. Ritzweller, N. Calonge, K. Shields, and M. Hanrahan, "Extending Health Maintenance Organizations Insurance to the Uninsured: A Controlled Measure of Health Care Utilization," *Journal of the American Medical Association*, 1997, 277, 1067–1072.

13. D. P. Martin, P. Diehr, A. Cheadle, C. W. Madden, D. L. Patrick, and S. M. Skillman, "Health Care Utilization for the 'Newly Insured': Results from the Washington Basic Health Plan," *Inquiry*, 1997, 34, 129–142.

14. L. Shi, B. Starfield, B. Kennedy, and I. Kawachi, "Income Inequality, Primary Care, and Health Indicators," *Journal of Family Practice*, 1999, 48(4), 275–284.

CHAPTER NINETEEN

2007 DENVER MEN'S HEALTH REPORT CARD

Denver Health Community Voices—Level 1 Care for All

The purpose of this first edition of the Denver Men's Health Report Card is to increase awareness among policymakers, public health officials, providers, media, and the general public regarding health disparities that exist for men living in the City and County of Denver.

This report card is produced by Denver Health Community Voices, and is similar to the North Carolina's Men's Health Report Card produced by FirstHealth of the Carolinas. Denver Health Community Voices is one of eight Community Voices learning laboratories in the United States, funded by the W.K. Kellogg Foundation and administered by the Morehouse School of Medicine, National Center for Primary Care. The Community Voices initiative concentrates on policy changes to increase access to health care at local, state, and federal levels.

Why Focus on Men?

Women outlive men by an average of six years. For each of the top ten causes of death, men have higher death rates than women in the City and County of Denver, the State of Colorado, and nationwide.

The following is a short summary of areas where men in Denver are doing well and also areas of concern.

Areas Where Denver Men Are Doing Well

- *Obesity:* Slightly less than one-fifth of men in Denver County and statewide are obese (Body Mass Index ≥ 30), compared to over one-quarter of men nationwide who are obese. Although the prevalence of obesity is lower, the trend over time is getting worse.
- *Leisure-time physical activity:* Colorado is considered to be a relatively healthy state, as evidenced by only 12 percent of Denver men and 15 percent of men statewide not engaged in leisure-time physical activity. Nearly 21 percent of men nationwide do not engage in leisure-time physical activity.
- *High blood pressure:* Although one-quarter of the men in the United States report that they have high blood pressure, it is present in slightly over one-fifth of Denver and Colorado men.
- *Death rates:* Heart disease, diabetes, colorectal and lung cancer death rates are improving.

Areas of Particular Concern for Denver's Men

- *Infectious disease:* When compared to other men in Colorado and the United States, Denver men had a significantly higher incidence of infectious diseases including HIV, chlamydia, gonorrhea, and syphilis.
- *Binge drinking:* Binge drinking (five or more drinks on an occasion) is a major issue for more than one-quarter of the men in Denver, compared with one-fifth of all men in the United States.
- *Suicide:* The rate of suicide of Denver and Colorado men is significantly greater than for U.S. men.
- *Incarceration:* Almost one-fifth of Denver's men were incarcerated at some point in 2006. Of those, almost three-quarters were repeat offenders. Hispanic and African American men are disproportionately represented in the incarcerated populations in Denver, the State of Colorado, and nationally when compared to their proportion in the general population.
- *Health insurance:* One-fifth of men in the City and County of Denver do not have health insurance, a rate slightly higher than the state and the United States.
- *Poverty:* More Denver men are below the federal poverty level compared to Colorado men and men in the United States.

The existing health care safety net for men in Denver is insufficient, despite the fact that men comprise 50 percent of the adult population in Denver. Men are sons, brothers, fathers, husbands, and heads of households. It is time to make a difference in men's health in Denver. The first step is to be aware of the existing significant health disparities. The next step is for key stakeholders, including public health officials, policymakers, community leaders, and individual men to begin the conversation, review the data, and develop sustainable solutions to improve health care access for all men in Denver.

Methodology

For each of the following health indicators, rates are displayed for men in Denver and in Colorado, and for the United States. To provide information about trends over time in Denver, rates were compared over the past several years, when possible. A summary of the trends for Denver men are noted for each health indicator, including the period of time and direction of the trend as indicated below:

- *Improved* means that the trend is moving in the desired direction.
- *Unchanged* means that rates over time are basically the same.
- *Worse* means that the trend is moving in an undesirable direction.

ADULT MALES IN DENVER BY RACE/ETHNICITY (AGE 18+)[1]

African American	8.9%
Asian	3.1%
White/Non-Hispanic	54.3%
Hispanic	32.2%
Other	1.5%
Total number	**206,480**

Infectious Diseases[2–4]

HIV INCIDENCE RATES (CASES PER 100,000)

Race/Ethnicity	Denver Men 2006	Colorado Men 2006	U.S. Men 2005
African American	111.1	56.6	124.8
American Indian	113.9	28.2	19.1
Asian/Pacific Islanders	58.4	18.7	14.5
Hispanic	40.5	20.6	56.2
White/Non-Hispanic	85.0	12.2	18.2
Total	**69.5**	**17.2**	**36.2**

Denver Trend 2003–2006: Improved

CHLAMYDIA INCIDENCE RATES (CASES PER 100,000)

Race/Ethnicity	Denver Men 2006	Colorado Men 2006	U.S. Men 2005
African American	1,181.9	946.1	717.8
American Indian	227.8	158.1	305.9
Asian/Pacific Islanders	222.0	54.2	79.3
Hispanic	497.1	186.0	201.4
White/Non-Hispanic	196.7	36.7	63.6
Total	**402.0**	**189.6**	**161.1**

Denver Trend 2003–2006: Improved (Race and/or Ethnicity Missing for >50% Reported Cases)

GONORRHEA INCIDENCE RATES (CASES PER 100,000)

African American	1,122.6	731.6	666.0
American Indian	398.6	45.2	92.2
Asian/Pacific Islanders	81.8	16.8	26.6
Hispanic	212.9	73.8	67.5
White/Non-Hispanic	173.6	16.1	27.7
Total	**274.3**	**73.1**	**111.5**

Denver Trend 2003–2006: Worse (Race and/or Ethnicity Missing for >50% Reported Cases)

SYPHILIS INCIDENCE RATES (CASES PER 100,000)

African American	11.1	3.6	15.7
American Indian	57.0	5.6	3.3
Asian/Pacific Islanders	0	1.9	2.3
Hispanic	4.8	2.4	5.5
White/Non-Hispanic	18.7	2.2	3.3
Total	**12.3**	**2.8**	**5.1**

Denver Trend 2003–2006: Unchanged

Substance Abuse/Mental Health[5-8]

PERCENTAGE OF MEN AGE 18+ WHO SMOKE CIGARETTES

	Denver Men 2006	Colorado Men 2006	U.S. Men 2006
Total	22	19	22

Denver Trend 2003–2006: Unchanged

PERCENTAGE OF MEN AGE 18+ WHO BINGE DRANK IN THE PAST MONTH (FIVE OR MORE DRINKS ON AN OCCASION)

Total	28	22	20

Denver Trend 2003–2005: Improved

SUICIDE (DEATHS PER 100,000)

	Denver Men 2005	Colorado Men 2005	U.S. Men 2005
Total	26.3	27.7	17.6

Denver Trend 2003–2005: Worse

Violence/Injuries[7-11]

INCARCERATION OF MEN AGE 10+

Denver Men 2006	
Total males arrested and booked	39,501
Recidivism rate for arrest (percentage)	72
Average daily population in city/county jails	2,120

Denver Trend 2005–2007: Worse

INCARCERATION OF MEN AGE 10+

	Denver Men 2006	Colorado Men Fiscal 2006	U.S. Men 6/30/06
Total males incarcerated	39,501	20,178	2,042,100

RACE/ETHNICITY PERCENTAGE

African American	26.7	19.8	41
White	35.3	45.4	35
Hispanic	36.1	31.7	21
American Indian	<1.0	2.0	
Asian/Pacific Islanders	<1.0	1.1	
Other	<1.0	3.0	

HOMICIDE AND LEGAL INTERVENTION DEATHS (PER 100,000)

	Denver Men 2005	Colorado Men 2005	U.S. Men 2003
Total (age adjusted)	11.4	57	10.0

Denver Trend 2003–2005: Improved

MOTOR VEHICLE DEATHS (PER 100,000)

Total (age adjusted)	19.2	19.3	21.4

Denver Trend 2003–2005: Unchanged

Barriers to Health[5,6,12–18]

PERCENTAGE OF MEN 18+ WITH NO HEALTH INSURANCE

	Denver Men 2006	Colorado Men 2006	U.S. Men 2006
Total	20	18	16

Denver Trend 2003–2006: Unchanged

PERCENTAGE OF MALES (ALL AGES) BELOW POVERTY LEVEL

	Denver Men 2005	Colorado Men 2005	U.S. Men 2005
TOTAL	14	10.1	11.8

PERCENTAGE OF MALE LABOR FORCE UNEMPLOYED

	Denver Men 2006	Colorado Men 2007	U.S. Men 2006
Total	not available	2.9	4.0

Colorado Trend 2006–2007: Improved

Preventive Health Practices[5,6]

PERCENTAGE OF MEN 18+ WHO ENAGAGE IN NO LEISURE ACTIVITY

	Denver Men 2006	Colorado Men 2006	U.S. Men 2006
Total	12	15	21

Denver Trend 2003–2006: Improved

PERCENTAGE OF MEN 20+ WHO ARE OBESE (BMI ≥ 30)

Total	20	19	26

Denver Trend 2003–2006: Worse

PERCENTAGE OF MEN 50+ WHO HAVE NOT
HAD A SIGMOIDOSCOPY OR COLONOSCOPY

Total	39	42	43.2

Denver Trend 2003–2006: Improved

PERCENTAGE OF MEN 40+ WHO HAVE
NOT HAD A PSA IN TWO YEARS

Total	49	46	47

Denver Trend 2003–2006: Improved

PERCENTAGE OF MEN 40+ WHO HAVE NOT
HAD A DIGITAL RECTAL EXAM IN TWO YEARS

Total	37	40	na

Denver Trend 2003–2006: Improved

PERCENTAGE OF MEN WHO HAVE NOT
HAD A DENTAL EXAM IN PAST YEAR

Total	37	31	32

Denver Trend 2003–2006: Unchanged

Data note: Although the BRFSS did not yield enough data in any one year to get stable rates by race and ethnicity for Denver County, existing data show significant racial/ethnic disparities in all of the areas in Preventive Health Practices.

Chronic Diseases[5–8]

PERCENTAGE OF MEN 20+ WHO HAVE BEEN
TOLD THEY HAVE HIGH BLOOD PRESSURE

	Denver Men 2005	Colorado Men 2005	U.S. Men 2005
Total	21	21	25

Denver Trend 2003–2005: Unchanged

PERCENTAGE OF MEN 18+ WITH HIGH CHOLESTEROL

Total	33	35	37

Denver Trend 2003–2005: Worse

HEART DEATHS (PER 100,000)

	Denver Men 2005	Colorado Men 2005	U.S. Men 2003
Total (age adjusted)	234.4	218.3	296.3

Denver Trend 2003–2005: Improved

CEREBROVASCULAR DISEASE DEATHS (PER 100,000)

	Denver Men	Colorado Men	U.S. Men
Total (age adjusted)	37.1	46.8	42.9

Denver Trend 2003–2005: Improved

PERCENTAGE OF MEN 18+ WITH DIABETES

	Denver Men 2006	Colorado Men 2006	U.S. Men 2006
Total	4	6	8

Denver Trend 2003–2006: Unchanged

DIABETES DEATHS (PER 100,000)

	Denver Men 2005	Colorado Men 2005	U.S. Men 2003
Total (age adjusted)	22.7	21.1	24.8

Denver Trend 2003–2005: Improved

PERCENTAGE OF MEN 18+ DIAGNOSED WITH ASTHMA

	Denver Men 2006	Colorado Men 2006	U.S. Men 2006
Total	9	11	11

Denver Trend 2003–2006: Unchanged

CHRONIC LOWER RESPIRATORY DEATHS (PER 100,000)

	Denver Men 2005	Colorado Men 2005	U.S. Men 2003
TOTAL (age adjusted)	74.0	66.4	42.4

Denver Trend 2003–2005: Worse

COLORECTAL CANCER DEATHS (PER 100,000)

	Denver Men 2005	Colorado Men 2005	U.S. Men 2003
Total (age adjusted)	15.0	18.6	19.6

Denver Trend 2003–2005: Improved

PROSTATE CANCER DEATHS (PER 100,000)

	Denver Men	Colorado Men	U.S. Men
Total	29.5	27.6	20.7

Denver Trend 2003–2005: Improved

LUNG CANCER DEATHS (PER 100,000)

	Denver Men	Colorado Men	U.S. Men
Total (age adjusted)	46.9	47.7	62.9

Denver Trend 2003–2005: Improved

Data Sources

1. U.S. Census Bureau, *2005 American Community Survey*, http://factfinder.census.gov.
2. Denver County Infectious Disease data from Denver Public Health.
3. Colorado State Infectious Disease data from Disease Control and Environmental Epidemiology Section, Colorado Department of Public Health and Environment.
4. National Infectious Disease data from National Center for Chronic Disease Prevention & Health Promotion, Centers for Disease Control, 2005 surveillance report: http://www.cdc.gov/std/stats/, and http://www.cdc.gov/hiv/topics/surveillance/resources/reports/2005report/pdf/2005SurveillanceReport.pdf.
5. Behavioral Risk Factor Surveillance System (BRFSS Data): The Colorado BRFSS is an ongoing statewide random-digit dial telephone survey of Colorado adults ages eighteen

years and older. Denver County and Colorado State 2006 BRFSS data from the Health Statistics Section, Colorado Department of Public Health and Environment.

6. National 2006 Behavioral Risk Factor Surveillance System (BRFSS) data from the Centers for Disease Control: http://www.cdc.gov/brfss/index.htm.

7. 2003–2005 Denver County and Colorado Death rates from Health Statistics Section, Colorado Department of Public Health and Environment.

8. National Center for Health Statistics, Centers for Disease Control, *Deaths: Final Data for 2003, National Vital Statistics Report,* April 2006, 54(13), Table 14. Death rates for 113 selected causes by race and sex: https://www.cdc.gov/nchs/data/nvsr/nvsr54/nvsr54_13. pdf.

9. 2005–2007 Incarceration data from Denver City Jail (Pre-Arraignment Detention Facility), Denver County Jail, and Denver Sheriff's Department Technology & Support/Special Projects.

10. U.S. Department of Justice, *Prisoners in 2006,* Bureau of Justice Statistics Bulletin NCJ217675,Office of Justice Programs, June 2007.

11. Colorado Department of Corrections, *General Statistics 2007:* http://www.doc.state.co.us/ Statistics/7GeneralStatistics.htm.

12. U.S. Census Bureau, *2005 American Community Survey, Poverty Status in the Past 12 Months,* Table S1701: http://factfinder.census.gov.

13. Denver County poverty data from the Piton Foundation: http://www.piton.org.

14. U.S. Census Bureau, *Small Area Income and Poverty Estimates (SAIPE) Program:* http:www. census.gov/hhs/www/saipe/tables.html.

15. Colorado state poverty data from the State of Colorado: http://quickfacts.census.gov/qfd/ states/08000.html.

16. National poverty data from the U.S. Census: http://www.census.gov/prod/2005pubs/ p60-229.pdf.

17. National unemployment rates from the U.S. Department of Labor Bureau of Labor Statistics: http://data.bls.gov/PDQ/servlet/SurveyOutputServlet?data_tool=latest_ numbers&series_id=LNU04000000&years_option=all_years&periodsoption=specific_ periods&periods=Annual+Data.http://www.bls.gov/cps/cpsatabs.htm.

18. Colorado State labor statistics from the Colorado Department of Labor, Labor Market Information: http://www.coworkforce.com/lmi/ali/2003correct.xls,http://www.cowork-force.com/lmi/ali/2004Final.xls, and http://www.coworkforce.com/lmi/ali/2005Final. xls,http://www.coworkforce.com/lmi/ali/2006Final.xls.

CHAPTER TWENTY

2007 NORTH CAROLINA MEN'S HEALTH REPORT CARD

The purpose of the first edition of the North Carolina Men's Health Report Card is to increase awareness among policymakers, public health officials, practitioners, media, and the general public regarding the health disparities that exist for all North Carolina men. FirstHealth of the Carolinas' Community Voices project sponsored this report card production. FirstHealth Community Voices is one of eight learning laboratories in the United States for the Community Voices initiative funded by the W.K. Kellogg Foundation. The Community Voices initiative concentrates on policy changes to increase access to health care at the local, state, and federal levels. Policy work focus areas include men's health, health disparities, mental health, and oral health.

The facts are that women outlive men by an average of six years. In the 1920s, males and females lived to be about the same age. Today, the ratio of male mortality has exceeded female mortality at every age, and the gap continues to get larger. For each of the top ten causes of death, men have higher death rates than women nationwide.

In North Carolina, data show that N.C. men are improving in regards to asthma when compared to the data for N.C. men of the past. However, data are trending in the wrong direction with major health issues of diabetes and infectious disease. To complicate matters, incarceration rates and uninsured numbers are dramatically on the increase. When compared to U.S. men, N.C. men have higher rates of mortality related to stroke, prostate cancer, lung cancer, and chronic respiratory disease. N.C. men also have higher rates of smoking, motor vehicle deaths, poverty rates, and the lack of health insurance when compared to U.S. men. The health disparities are even greater than this report card reflects if N.C. men are compared to N.C. women. In general, white women comprise the healthiest population and are the benchmark for health indicators.

There is a deficit of health care safety nets for men despite the fact that men comprise 48 percent of the adult population in North Carolina. Men are brothers, fathers, husbands, heads of households, and sons. It is time to make a difference in men's health in North Carolina. The first step is to be aware of the outstanding health care disparities. The next step is for key thought leaders, public health officials, policymakers, and grassroots individuals to begin the conversation, analyze and collect the data, and explore intervention programs and safety nets that will address the health care issues.

Grading Methodology

Grades were assigned to increase awareness with regard to men's health in North Carolina. Two letter grades were assigned to each indicator. The first letter grade for trend is based on North Carolina men's progression in each health indicator over a period of time. The second letter grade represents the comparison of North Carolina men to United States (U.S.) men based on the most current data available.

The grading mechanism implemented was adopted from the North Carolina Women's Health Report card. This will allow for direct comparisons between the two report cards. The following guidelines were used for grading:

Trend Comparison

A = ≥ 20 percent improvement for the trend

B = ≥ 10–20 percent improvement for the trend

C = between a 10 percent improvement and a 10 percent worsening for the trend

D = ≥ 10–20 percent worse for the trend

F = ≥ 20 percent worse for the trend

Comparison with U.S. Men

A = ≥ 20 percent better than the U.S. for the U.S. men comparison

B = 10–20 percent better than the U.S. for the U.S. men comparison

C = between 10 percent better and 10 percent worse than the U.S. for the U.S. men comparison

D = ≥ 10–20 percent worse than the U.S. for the U.S. men comparison
F = ≥ 20 percent worse than the U.S. for the U.S. men comparison

North Carolina Men's Health: Chronic Disease

	N.C. Men	N.C. Men	Trend	U.S. Men	Grade
	1999–2000	2000–2004		2003	
Heart Disease Deaths per 100,000[1]					
All	314.4	294.5	C	286.6	C
White	307.3	285.2	C	282.9	C
Minority	343.4	334.5	C	301.4	D
Cerebrovascular Disease Deaths per 100,000[1]					
All	74.6	68.6	C	54.1	F
White	69.2	63.0	C	51.7	F
Minority	99.2	94.9	C	69.1	F
Lung Cancer Deaths per 100,000[1]					
All	88.9	86.6	C	71.7	F
White	86.8	84.3	C	71.1	D
Minority	97.9	96.6	C	75.1	F
Chronic Lower Respiratory Disease Deaths per 100,000[1]					
All	63.1	60.9	C	52.3	D
White	64.7	62.6	C	53.8	D
Minority	54.7	51.6	C	39.1	F
Diabetes Deaths per 100,000[1]					
All	27.8	30.0	C	28.9	C
White	22.9	24.9	C	27.0	C
Minority	50.2	54.6	C	42.0	F
Colorectal Cancer Deaths per 100,000[1]					
All	23.2	22.8	C	22.9	C
White	21.9	21.4	C	22.4	C
Minority	29.2	29.0	C	26.2	D

Prostate Cancer Deaths per 100,000[1]

All	33.5	31.6	C	26.5	D
White	26.5	24.8	C	24.4	C
Minority	68.4	67.2	C	43.2	F

		2002	2005	2005

Percentage Aged 18+ with Diabetes[2]

All	6.4%	8.5%	F	8.0%	C
White	6.0%	8.2%	F	7.7%	C
African American	9.9%	12.8%	F	11.0%	D

Percentage Aged 18+ Who Are Obese (BMI 30.0+)[2]

All	23.5%	25.3%	C	24.8%	C
White	21.7%	24.7%	D	24.5%	C
African American	28.4%	31.0%	C	29.9%	C

Percentage Told by a Doctor That They Have Asthma[2]

All	9.3%	8.3%	B	10.5%	A
White	9.8%	8.5%	B	10.7%	A
African American	10.3%	10.3%	C	10.9%	C

		2003	2005	2005

Percentage Aged 18+ with High Blood Pressure[2]

All	27.2%	28.0%	C	26.2%	C
White	28.1%	28.1%	C	26.8%	C
African American	35.4%	36.7%	C	31.2%	D

Percentage Aged 18+ with High Cholesterol[2]

All	33.2%	36.0%	C	37.2%	C
White	34.6%	36.8%	C	38.2%	C
African American	32.6%	36.7%[1]	D	31.5%	D

North Carolina Men's Health: Infectious Disease

	N.C. Men 2002	N.C. Men 2005	Trend	U.S. Men	Grade
HIV Cases per 100,000[3]					
All	28.5	31.2	C	37.6	B
White	11.7	14.4	F	18.7	A
African American	87.8	88.6	C*	131.6	A*
Hispanic	23.4	32.2	F	60.2	A
Primary and Secondary Syphilis Cases per 100,000[3]					
All	3.9	5.1	F	4.7	C
White	1.1	3.1	F	3.1	C
African American	13.8	12.9	C*	14.1	C*
Hispanic	3.0	4.3	F	5.5	A
Chlamydia Cases per 100,000[3]					
All	106.6	130.5	F	147.1	B
White	36.4	41.0	D	57.3	A
African American	337.3	416.2	F	645.2	A*
Hispanic	132.1	137.1	C*	183.4	A*
Gonorrhea Cases per 100,000[3]					
All	192.0	179.3	C	110.0	F
White	29.9	31.6	C	26.2	F
African American	785.6	694.7	B*	670.3	C*
Hispanic	72.1	81.0	D	64.9	F

Substance Abuse/Mental Health

	N.C. Men 2002	N.C. Men 2005	Trend	U.S. Men 2005	Grade 2005
Percentage Aged 18+ Who Are Current Smokers[2]					
All	30.5%	25.6%	B	22.6%	D
White	29.9%	25.3%	B	22.1%	D
African American	36.8%	29.2%	A	25.8%	D

Percentage Aged 18+ Drinking 5+ Drinks on One Occasion in the Past Month[2]

All	17.7%	16.4%	C	21.9%	A
White	17.6%	17.6%	C	22.6%	A
African American	13.6%	11.4%	B	16.6%	A

	1999–2000	2000–2004	2003

Suicide Deaths per 100,000[1]

All	18.9	19.5	C	18.0	C
White	21.9	21.9	C	19.6	D
Minority	9.5	10.0	C	9.5	C

North Carolina Men's Health: Violence/Injuries

	N.C. Men	N.C. Men	Trend	U.S. Men	Grade
	1999–2000	2000–2004	2003		

Homicide Deaths per 100,000[1]

All	12.5	11.2	B	9.4	D
White	7.0	6.4	C	5.3	F
Minority	28.9	26.0	B*	26.7	C*

Motor Vehicle Deaths per 100,000[1]

All	28.9	28.1	C	21.6	F
White	28.2	27.3	C	21.9	F
Minority	32.2	31.5	C	20.2	F

	1999	2005	2005

Incarceration Rates per 10,000[4]

All	102.6	113.0	D	137	B
White	42.8	50.3	D	71	A
African American	340.2	372.5	C*	468	A*

Barriers to Health

	N.C. Men	N.C. Men	Trend	U.S. Men	Grade
	2003	2005	2005		
Percentage Aged 18 to 65 with No Health Insurance Coverage[2]					
All	22.1%	25.0%	D	20.6%	F
White	15.6%	18.0%	D	17.2%	C
African American	25.0%	30.6%	F	27.0%	D
Percentage Below the Poverty Level[5]					
All	9.8%	10.7%	C	9.5%	D
White	7.7%	8.7%	D	8.1%	C
African American	5.8%	16.1%	C	17.9%	B
Percentage of Labor Force Unemployed and Looking for Work[5]					
All	6.1%	4.7%	A	4.9%	C
White	4.2%	4.1%	C	4.2%	C
African American	13.1%	8.2%	A*	10.2%	B*

North Carolina Men's Health: Preventive Health Practices

	N.C. Men	N.C. Men	Trend	U.S. Men	Grade
	2002	2004	2004		
Percentage Aged 50+ Who Have Never Had a Sigmoidoscopy or Colonoscopic Exam[2]					
All	53.2%	43.8%	B	45.7%	C
White	51.2%	40.4%	A	43.5%	C
African American	59.9%	55.6%	C	54.6%	C
Percentage of Men Aged 40+ Who Have Not Had a PSA Test in the Past Two Years[2]					
All	45.9%	44.6%	C	48.2%	C
White	45.2%	42.3%	C	47.0%	C
African American	44.9%	45.9%	C	47.2%	C

Percentage of Men Aged 40+ Who Have Not Had a Digital Rectal Exam in the Past Two Years[2]

All	42.0%	41.2%	C	45.8%	B
White	40.8%	38.2%	C	44.0%	B
African American	44.6%	46.4%	C	49.7%	C

	2002	**2005**

Percentage Aged 65+ Who Did Not Have a Flu Shot in the Past Twelve Months[2]

All	30.7%	34.2%	D	35.2%	C
White	NA	31.2%	NA	33.5%	C
African American	NA	50.9%	NA	48.9%	C

Percentage Aged 65+ Who Have Never Had a Pneumonia Shot[2]

All	37.5%	35.6%	C	38.4%	C
White	NA	31.5%	NA	36.4%	B
African American	NA	56.0%	NA	53.4%	C

Percentage Aged 18+ Who Engage in No Leisure Time Physical Activity[2]

All	25.3%	22.8%	C	23.0%	C
White	21.8%	18.9%	B	21.3%	B
African American	29.6%	28.9%	C	28.6%	C

Dental Health

	N.C. Men	N.C. Men	Trend	U.S. Men	Grade
		2002	**2004**	**2004**	

Percentage of Who Have Been to the Dentist in the Past Year[2]

All	65.5%	67.4%	C	68.3%	C
White	71.1%	72.9%	C	70.4%	C
African American	56.3%	59.0%	C	60.4%	C
Other minority	39.0%	45.4%	B	61.3%	F

*While these conditions show improvement over time, or are comparable to those at the national level, the absolute level of the condition is still higher than it should be in a healthy population and is still a burden on the population.

2005 Population Estimates for Men in North Carolina

	Total 18 and over	18–19	20–24	25–44	45–64	65+
All	3,017,004	100,436	261,970	1,240,474	998,870	415,254
White	2,253,073	64,004	179,099	884,995	776,330	348,645
African American	545,004	25,584	54,005	233,016	174,944	57,455
Other minority	218,927	10,848	28,866	122,463	47,596	9,154

Data Notes

- U.S. men were used as a comparison with North Carolina (N.C.) men with the understanding that U.S. men do not have the ideal health status. In general, white women comprise the healthiest population.
- The race breakdown of mortality in this report card is categorized as all, white, or minority, which is representative of publicly available mortality data from the North Carolina State Data Center for Health Statistics.
- Typically, mortality rates among minorities are higher in African Americans than in most other minority groups. In North Carolina, the minority group has a higher percentage of African Americans than in the U.S. minority population. This may contribute to the greater mortality rate of minorities in N.C. men compared to U.S. men.
- The U.S. incarceration data includes both state and federal correctional facility inmates while the N.C. rate includes only state correctional facility inmates.
- There can be wide variances in disease rates among the different nonwhite races, and the minority rates presented may not apply to all nonwhite racial groups. The N.C. non-white population is composed primarily of African Americans but there is a growing number of Hispanics in North Carolina. As the population shift continues, it will be important to collect health information in a manner that allows for comparisons among all the nonwhite racial groups.

Data Sources

1. North Carolina mortality data from the North Carolina State Center for Health Statistics 2000–2004 Race-Sex-Specific Age Adjusted Death Rates by County and the 1999–2000 Race-Sex-Specific Age Adjusted Death Rates by County available online at: http://www. schs.state.nc.us/SCHS/data/databook/ and http://www.schs.state.nc.us/SCHS/data/databook/2002/; All national mortality stats from National Center for Health Statistics, *Deaths: Final Data for 2003, National Vital Statistics Report*, April 2006, 54(13). Available on-line at http://www.cdc.gov/nchs/products/pubs/pubd/nvsr/54/54-20.htm.

2. North Carolina data from the state BRFSS data, with the year depending on the indicator as noted in the table. Available online at http://www.schs.state.nc.us/SCHS/brfss/; National data from the national BRFSS data with the year depending on the indicator as noted in the table, more information and data available for download here: http://www.cdc.gov/brfss.

3. North Carolina infectious disease data from the *North Carolina HIV/STD Surveillance Report*, 2005, available online at http://www.epi.state.nc.us/epi/hiv/surveillance.html; National infectious disease data from the CDC's 2004 surveillance report, available online at http://www.cdc.gov/std/stats/toc2004.htm.

4. North Carolina incarceration rates calculated from population data from the U.S. Census along with the number of incarcerated people in North Carolina from the Statistical Report generator from the Department of Corrections, available online at http://www.doc.state.nc.us/rap/index.htm; National incarceration rates from the Bureau of Justice Statistics, available online at http://www.ojp.usdoj.gov/bjs/pub/pdf/pjim05.pdf.

5. North Carolina and U.S. data from the Current Population Survey from the Bureau of Labor Statistics and the U.S. Census Bureau, abstracted using Data Ferrett, available online at http://dataferrett.census.gov; http://www.ojp.usdoj.gov/bjs/pub/pdf/pjim05.pdf (doesn't include federal prisons).

WHEN THE COMMUNITY VOICES INITIATIVE BEGAN, WE DID NOT KNOW WHAT WE DID NOT KNOW. . . .

Henrie M. Treadwell, Barbara J. Sabol, Kisha Braithwaite Holden, and Ronald L. Braithwaite

The plight of the poor continues and has, in some ways, worsened in the nation as the unserved and underserved seek health care and justice in the health care delivery and policy arenas. At present, low-income people are battered by an economic downturn—the usual reason given for failing to serve the working poor or chronically unemployed—but their alienation from health services now, as always, has been further cemented by ideologies that embrace terms that "exclude" the poor rather than embrace them as Americans, too.

When Community Voices began the initiative, the primary goal was to increase access to health care and to strengthen the fragile safety net system. The lack of insurance—or of adequate insurance—was the driving factor and represented just one of many exclusionary public policies that make some in this nation less equal than others. In addition, the fragmented system that "might have" provided primary health care and prevention did not often include access to mental health care, substance abuse treatment, oral health care for adults and for children, and the use of outreach workers to assist individuals to navigate a foreign and sometimes unfriendly bureaucracy. This was the context that we faced.

Naively, perhaps, those of us involved in leading change efforts thought initially that all we had to do was to "connect the dots." That is to say, all we had to do was to ensure patients were linked to care. However, as we looked more carefully through the lens of the community, we saw that some public policy "dots" were missing altogether (for example, no insurance coverage for poor men; no coverage of oral health for adults or those living in remote areas). We learned also that "Do no harm" does not seem to be a part of the health sector lexicon, or a practice of public policy formulation, or part of the analysis of the disparate impact of policy. As a result, Community Voices' learning laboratory leaders began an important process of discerning and then dissecting health access issues into discrete categories so that they could effectively focus on each separate piece of the health care system and work to bring it into alignment with the needs of distinct populations.

This separation of services into discrete items was a primary and important lesson. By looking carefully at the different issues that confront populations marginalized from systems of health care and social services, we were able to understand more precisely some of the public policy bottlenecks. As we analyzed the issue of mental health, for example, we uncovered a highly fragmented system offering little-to-no continuum of care, particularly for those with fewer resources. We saw how much of this disenfranchised population experienced homelessness and jails or prisons instead of receiving the community-based mental health or substance abuse treatment they so needed.[1] We learned that by focusing not only on the problems but also the solutions, like our work in effective case management and with community health workers (CHWs), we could demonstrate for policymakers and others how to make significant contributions to community health. Finally, we were also able to uncover other issues—beyond immediate health needs—expressed by the communities with whom we spoke. We learned about their need for living wages, their need for housing and safe communities with healthy food, and their desire for quality schools for their children. We learned, in short, that the social and economic determinants of health cannot be overlooked. Rather they are the foundation from which all health, or the absence of the same, will be derived.

Significant partnerships with other funders were developed along the way. These included many foundations and federal agencies. For example, our partnerships with both the American Legacy Foundation, around tobacco prevention and cessation, and the Robert Wood Johnson (RWJ) foundation, regarding oral health, helped us to strengthen the agenda for these issues and ensure that they will remain on the minds of providers and policymakers alike for some time to come. Working with others such as Health Careers Opportunity Program, The Primary Care Development Corporation, The Empire State Development Corporation, The Paula Vial Lampert Foundation, and the Colorado Trust helped us to leverage key resources in states such as New York and Colorado. On a national scale, the federal government's Health Resources Administration Community Access Program, Duke Endowment, Kaiser Permanente, Rose Foundation, Annie E. Casey, and other local and state foundations partnered with us to ensure that the initial investment made by Kellogg would be sustained beyond the life of the initiative. We worked intentionally with the U.S.

Department of Health and Human Services (USDHH) to find ways to embed mental health and oral health in the primary health care clinics funded by USDHH and the Bureau of Primary Health Care. We worked with the U.S. Surgeon General in the release of the *Surgeon General's Report on Oral Health* (2000). We would be remiss not to acknowledge these partners as well as the numerous local supports received, as none of the achievements were exclusively those of the Community Voices staff at the local or national level. Partners, friends, supporters, and collaborators were needed, and the goal was to find the common place, the "meeting ground" for a variety of issues, and to move ahead.

Community change process is something like putting together a puzzle, and the real work is to assemble the "pieces" and later organize them into the portrait of community change and community health. The ultimate goal for Community Voices was to establish a "way of working" that would always reside in the community and would continue the process of problem solving and community building. Some cross-cutting lessons have emerged from this process, including a better understanding of what is required of leadership; a heightened knowledge of who the populations are that are most affected by health disparities and inequities; the realization that useful models for the evaluation of community-led change efforts must be further developed and promoted; and clarity about the gaps in public policy that must be filled in order to ensure a more equitable health and social system in the nation.

The Power of Leadership

Wilbur and Orville Wright not only believed that they could fly—they believed that they *should* fly! In many ways, a similar attitude guided the Community Voices leadership. An overriding belief of the "possible" instead of the "impossible" drove the work and was reflected in the leadership and accomplishments over the life of the initiative. The learning laboratories viewed themselves not as the leaders who had to do everything but instead as the facilitators laying down the connective tissue across which community health services could be built. Leadership required the ability to switch between service needs; to yield to others with more skills and insight, when necessary, yet to remain firmly and tactically focused on the goal: greater access and care. Leaders in Community Voices learned to use their ability to convene; to utilize the power of their pen to write for the public in a variety of formats; to network, network, network; and to frame the issues in ways that marketplace and public policy decision makers could use as platforms for program development or expansion. Along these lines, a few thoughts on leadership have emerged from some of the project sites.

Successful community leadership is resilient and multidirectional (New Mexico Community Voices). Leadership is a process. Often a community must heighten its already existing skills, observations of multiple factors in the community environment, recognition and celebration of differences in a strength-based model, going with the "gut" on trust, and being clear about the degree of commitment and what constitutes success.

Leadership is never singular or linear. Leaders emerge during every phase of a community effort, often without the community formalizing the event. Multitiered, occasionally nonlinear leadership that can identify multiple routes and challenges is a key ingredient in addressing the diverse and often competing needs of communities.

Leadership in the nonlinear, multidirectional environment of the community must have at least a rudimentary ecological view of the world in general and the community specifically. Awareness of, and positive responses to, the shifts in the community increase both the acceptance of the leadership and the sense of positive change within the community itself. Leadership that recognizes ecological factors of community life personalizes relationships broadly across the community to honor the individual.

While current or past policy decisions (for, against, or neutral) are at the root of many problems communities face, leadership must focus on approaches derived from the community of interest to change policies that can be changed, embrace those policies that are more aligned with needs, and replace those that are not modifiable or are valueless. Simultaneous recognition of responsibility and acceptance of risk on the part of the community is also a component of leadership. Assisting each partner to evaluate his or her commitment in light of competencies and past performance and reconciling the risks to rewards from current efforts increases the sense of buy-in.

Leadership is manifested in the "white water" experience of changing policy, or stagnant or receding revenues coupled with unmet needs. Leadership is the quality of viewing the water's boiling, scanning the shore, guiding but not commandeering the raft, maintaining in the turbulence a reasoned and intuitive connection to not only the occupants in the raft, but the river, the raft, and, more important, the destination. Many of the most effective policies are the result of a process of accommodation of the various community ecosystems' needs, egos, and attributions.

While not having something for everyone, the development of more responsive policies epitomizes hope and enhances the potential for continuity and success in addressing other issues. Building upon policy change is synonymous with increasing resiliency and capacity within communities. Connecting communities through common interests, shared values, and an understanding of both policy deficits and shared gains through shared solutions builds political will while increasing capacities of all communities. We must therefore always believe that it is impossible to fail.

Making things happen (Ingham Community Voices). Sometimes the role as a "facilitator" of dialogue may be an important alternative way to exercise a different kind of power—the power to cohere diverse voices and thereby, perhaps, subvert the coercive power structures that may be responsible for the failure to commit to equity.

Community Voices played an important role in providing the space for local leaders to demonstrate the importance of dialogue in accessing a different kind of power—the power of connection, of relationship. It is the alchemy that occurs when three or more people with very disparate life experiences achieve a common understanding of the forces that have impinged upon them all, and the disparity in life opportunities that result.

Facilitated dialogue became the vehicle through which many Community Voices colleagues around the country worked to transform local health departments, health systems, provider organizations, and community thought about health in general. Is talk action? It is not. But when "talk" is facilitated and informed by certain core values that we have identified and named—compassion, enfranchisement, transparency, inquiry, stillness, and synergy—it can provide the foundation of collective will that is a prerequisite for broad social change.

Leadership at all levels! (Northern Manhattan Community Voices Collaborative). In a number of the sites it became evident that it would be critical to help create the opportunities for leadership at all levels. This meant selecting individuals who had proven track records in communities and in institutions as being trustworthy and knowledgeable in the various tasks presented. Those individuals were placed into positions with responsibilities to tackle difficult problems, and they in turn were able to rally the necessary resources to make things happen. At the same time, each of the leaders was able to develop new leadership, which kept initiatives fresh and moved them in new directions.

Oral Health: Putting the Mouth Back in the Body

Community Voices' insistence on looking at the whole person meant developing significant work around a number of other areas beyond those traditionally recognized in primary health care. In North Carolina, for example, significant children's oral health services for the three rural counties surrounding FirstHealth were initiated through Community Voices (see Chapter Six). As a result, services are fully subscribed at present and have been so almost since the clinic was opened. Because of high demand, FirstHealth is expanding the clinic and offering evening and weekend hours due to the development of an unacceptable waiting list. In the face of this demand, however, it is important to recall that *no* services were available in this community before Community Voices.

For over forty years, Ingham County Health Department (ICHD) has provided dental services at its Adult Dental Clinic at Cedar Street Community Health Center to adults who may not be able to access care through the private sector (see Chapter Three). These services have been replicated in other communities. Where children are concerned, the Oral Health Task Force (OHTF), convened by Ingham Community Voices (ICV), promoted the development of the Healthy Smiles Dental Clinic, a new dental care facility for children, most of them on Medicaid. The OHTF worked closely with ICV to increase access to oral health services in the community. It successfully sought grants from Volunteers in Health/American Dental Association to stage specific events geared to providing services to the uninsured and to raising community awareness about the need for oral health services.

The Collins Center for Public Policy in Miami worked closely with the Health Foundation of South Florida to develop a multimillion dollar oral health initiative for Miami and surrounding areas (see Chapter Four). This line of programming was only possible as a result of Community Voices Miami's earlier work on pediatric oral health in the state of Florida with previous support from the Health Foundation. Given the needs and challenges that were uncovered, the Foundation determined to make oral health a funding priority.

Northern Manhattan expanded its services in eight public schools in Washington Heights, deployed a mobile van to provide oral health services at Head Start and elderly centers in northern Manhattan and Central Harlem, worked with community-based clinics to help staff their dental clinics, and served as the hub for specialty care (see Chapter Seven). The DentCare program provides approximately forty-five thousand patient visits in the northern Manhattan community each year. This was possible because Northern Manhattan Community Voices' leadership mobilized around a prior study that showed that Harlem and Washington Heights children experienced much higher dental disease with comparatively less treatment than national groups.

Baltimore provided oral health services to adult men in their Men's Health Center and has ensured that services have continued, as men's health core services are now implemented through Total Health Care, the federally qualified health center at which the Center now resides (see Chapter One). Through their work, they have ensured that ongoing and future work will include men's health in the core of services offered through Baltimore City government networks.

Oakland Community Voices initiated oral health services for children and adults at Asian Health Services and dramatically expanded services (from one dentist to several with new operatories) and serves as a site for the training of health professions students from the University of California system (see Chapter Eight). Asian Health Services successfully raised enough government and private funds to open the first dental clinic in Oakland's Chinatown; the dental clinic was also notable because it was the first "paperless" dental clinic in the area, using dental practice management software that eliminated the need for paper files. In the same year, La Clínica de La Raza partnered with Children's Hospital-Oakland to become the provider of pediatric dental care on-site at the hospital campus.

As a result of OCV's participation in the Pipeline initiative, local dental students from University of the Pacific and the University of California at San Francisco began completing dental externships at Asian Health Services, La Clínica de La Raza, and other nearby community health centers, thereby gaining experience in providing care in a community clinic environment. Through the Pipeline program, students were exposed to the needs of low-income patients in a community-based setting, and the importance of dental services as part of the overall provision of primary medical care and chronic disease management.

Community Voices New Mexico (CVNM) developed services to refer individuals reporting to the emergency room for oral health services to an oral health home and developed a statewide oral health program with several public health dentists and ancillary personnel (only one part-time dentist functioned to meet the needs of the public without insurance before Community Voices). CVNM educated policymakers, with the result that adult Medicaid Oral Health benefits were restored, and increased the number of health professions slots in oral health for New Mexico in the Western Interstate Commission on Higher Education. It also initiated a pre-dental health professions club to increase the number of future providers in New Mexico (see Chapter Five). Multimillion dollar state and federal appropriations have resulted in a new Oral Health Center of Excellence and increased the number of residents working to provide oral health services to the poor and underserved. New Mexico has made the greatest gains in developing a state-wide oral health program.

Finally, Denver Health and Hospital Authority operates three dental clinics to meet the primary-level needs of adults and students in schools, including the use of sealants (see Chapter Two). However, its work was devoted not only to practice "on the ground" but also to the practice of communicating the lessons of implementation and policy. Policy briefs and publications highlighted the issue in the community, an important practice, as the public policy and dental community have not, generally, recognized the importance of the teeth and of oral health overall.

The loss of teeth looms large as an issue as we consider the current efforts to reduce obesity among the U.S. population. Edentulism is also worse among the poor.[2,3] Eating fresh and raw fruits is virtually impossible without teeth! We know better than what we are doing! The policy links are clear but are yet to be addressed by the profession or by policymakers.

At the Heart of Our Nation's Disparities: Valuing Men and Keeping Men in Our Homes

While Community Voices uncovered health inequities across a number of racial and ethnic minority groups as well as in rural populations across the country, as we progressed in our work it was evident that there are critical morbidity and mortality issues currently facing African American men. As we looked across the country with concern for the diverse groups of those marginalized, part of the reality that we cannot ignore is that African American men have the highest rates of HIV/AIDS and die more often of cardiovascular disease and cancer than any other racial or ethnic group in the country.[4] They are also disproportionately represented in the jail and prison systems. If we are to truly address inequity as a nation, then we must look carefully at this issue in order to address the root causes.

Much remains to be done to eliminate the damage of historically uneven social policies and to rehabilitate the image and role of the African American male and other poor men in their families and neighborhoods.[5] Emphasis by the Kellogg Foundation on the health and social disparities that contribute to early morbidity and mortality among poor men of color was initiated with the publication of a policy brief, "A Poor Man's Plight: Uncovering the Disparity in Men's Health."[6] The development of this publication was stimulated after a review of the foundation's community health service projects revealed that few men were found in clinics seeking services and no direct outreach was targeted to them, a clear difference from strategies to reach women, children, and the elderly.

One of the reasons for why men are not in clinics or health centers in the United States is directly related to policies on public health insurance (that is, Medicaid) that discriminate against men by providing coverage to only few men in the case of a proven disability or mental health issue. This is in sharp contrast to coverage for women and children. Thus the area of men's health has been even more challenging, as this nation has not yet provided guaranteed health care to working poor men who do not receive insurance through their jobs, or to the chronically unemployed whose poor health still contributes to driving up health care costs. As a whole, there have been significant efforts to address maternal and child health, compared to addressing paternal health or the health of men who also serve as the bedrock of our families. This lack of comprehensive, family-focused policies and systems continues to perpetuate the exclusion of men as valued members of our families and communities. Of concern is that this model of neglect is being exported throughout the world even though our work in the United States suggests that an overreliance on existing policies and systems may weaken the health of mother and child by contributing to the diminution of the health of the man of the household.

We believe, and the work of Community Voices and subsequent work suggests, that equity cannot be achieved if health and social policies are not equitable to men. Maternal and child health indicators, commonly used as indicators of population well-being, alone are insufficient to provide a full reading of how a community is faring and what the appropriate interventions for the health of all should be.[7] The work that has evolved around men's health, we think, is an important addition to gauging the health of a community. With the recent passage of the Patient Protection and Affordable Care Act of 2010, federal legislation calls for the expansion of Medicaid coverage in 2014 to cover—for the first time—*both* single adult women and men. This is an important step toward improving access to health care for all, and we have every hope that this public policy will work to improve poor health outcomes among low-income male populations.

However, because of the context in which Community Voices worked, in which the care for men was so glaringly absent, enactment of any programs required a comprehensive approach that included the use of national champions and advocates. As a result, the issue of men's health was further highlighted by the release of a special video performed by the actor Danny Glover that was introduced in New York at ABC News, airing for at least two years on CNN and in other venues. The actor Morgan Freeman also provided *pro bono* recordings that aired on, or around, Father's Day for two years. Throughout the initiative, the Community Voices learning laboratories acted on the premise that it was important to demonstrate that they "cared" even as they served. The recognition of the importance and value of the human spirit had, the laboratories believed, healing power in and of itself.

Baltimore Community Voices and the Baltimore City Health Department paved the way for new thinking on this issue with the opening of the nation's first full-time men's health clinic, which has now become an integral part of the Federally Qualified Health Center (Total Health Care) that serves this city. The major challenge in the early years for the survival of this clinic was the fact that most of the men had no form of health coverage and no hope of receiving support. As a result, already fragile safety nets had to ask how they could afford to serve even more uninsured clients.

Community Voices Miami worked to bring to the fore the issues of men returning from a period of incarceration, along with FirstHealth of the Carolinas and Denver Health. Many of those men who had become eligible, due to their poor health, for Social Security and Medicaid had those benefits terminated. Most are not reinstated, though reliable data from the Center for Medicare and Medicaid Services (CMS) are not available to quantify the loss of these essential social and health supports that some refer to as entitlements so as to diminish their importance. CMS does not yet have a policy to determine the degree to which benefits are reinstated, when appropriate, even though the agency did call for a national policy on suspension versus the termination of these benefits in 2004. No urgency has been put behind the call for suspension versus termination, and the result is that policymakers have had no response for the individuals or for the safety net providers and, to this date, unless health care reform is fully implemented, policies continue to make this an invisible population.[8]

Failure to count them means that they do not exist from policy, fiscal, and service perspectives. Denver, FirstHealth of the Carolinas, and the University of New Mexico all developed men's health report cards (see Chapters Two, Six, and Five, respectively). The important lesson learned through the report card development was that there are too few discrete data points that are collected about the health of poor men to accurately characterize the depth of sickness and ill health. Most reported data do not reflect the cross-section of gender, race or ethnicity, and income making invisible the realities of what is happening to poor men, especially men of color. The realities may be reflected once these men are at the morgue, and often the primary causative factor for death is unknown. So, despite the loss of health and life, it remains virtually impossible to generate a report that captures by race and gender the health status of poor men of color in this nation. Fortunately, communities have decided that they cannot wait for ethics, morality, or public policy to step into the gap to serve the men of their neighborhoods. But, at the end of the day, investment in the form of direct dollars is needed to sustain services.

Incarceration has reached emergency proportions! And again, young African American men continue to top the list, with Latino men following close behind. Despite the best efforts on the ground, what was also learned is that the collateral damage inflicted on those who have served their time and seek to return to normalcy looms larger with each passing day. While the Kellogg Foundation has contributed to some prison reentry efforts, philanthropy in general has not yet taken up this issue and education is needed to alert national and international donors alike to the fact that the "house is on fire" in African American communities and that children will perish without the rebuilding of a strong family and community as foundation for childhood development.

The nation spends $68 billion per year to house more than seven million inmates.[9] Current projections are that one in three African American men will have a prison record, given current rates of incarceration. More than two million African American children have parents in prison on any given day.[10] In addition to the cost on families there are the actual costs that have risen from $10.6 billion in 1987 to more than $44 billion in 2007, a 127 percent increase in inflation-adjusted dollars! Many in philanthropy focus narrowly on education and apparently fail to account for the impact of prison expenditures that have resulted in a lower rate of adjusted spending on higher education—an increase of only 21 percent in the period between 1987 and 2007. As a result, public education has not fared much better. This becomes a health issue, as prison expenditures and even expenditures on health care in prison far outstrip expenditures for health care for these same populations as they live in communities. Community Voices' learning laboratories all turned their attention in one way or another to the issues of criminal justice, the collateral damage of prison, the cost to society of these upside policies, and the destructive effect on the families of the poor.

Notably, the program to improve access to health care and improved health for poor men and men of color expanded rapidly among the Community Voices learning laboratories after the Community Voices program moved to the Morehouse School of Medicine (MSM). This environment, with its strong African American male and female leadership, identified immediately with the urgency of the issues and the need to act. Special funding from the Kellogg Foundation made the expansion possible. Placement of the program at MSM also imbued the program with the ability to speak more flexibly and succinctly on issues of great health and social significance. The urgency was undergirded by the fact that the largest amount of uncompensated care in clinics and the emergency rooms came from the episodic care delivered to poor men and men of color. And the mission of the institution, similar to that of other historically black colleges and universities (HBCUs), is that of caring for and uplifting the African American community overall. Further, the work at the MSM allowed the linking of health disparities to social and educational disparities, a linkage missing in most activities even though fiscal losses due to health disparities consume a huge and disproportionate amount of public funds and limit the ability of government at every level to contribute to development in other areas (for example, K–12 education). This linkage of an issue to HBCUs perhaps represents one method of moving issues in community by engaging HBCUs, Hispanic-serving institutions, tribal colleges, and Asian American/Pacific Islander (AAPI)–serving institutions in more meaningful ways to authenticate issues and provide leadership in correcting what has become a disastrous course in low-income African American, Hispanic/Latino, Native American, and AAPI communities.

Community Outreach: Leading by the Hand and from the Heart

Community outreach has been an underpinning in every Community Voices learning laboratory. Simultaneously, stimulus in this area was offered in the form of international seminars to Kellogg Foundation projects funded through its UNI programs in Peru, Nicaragua, Brazil, the Dominican Republic, and elsewhere. These provided on-the-ground examples of how community health workers (CHWs) can not only promote health but prevent disease. Publications enhanced the importance of this work and included a call for the recognition of CHWs as advocates for social justice and as natural researchers who could inform public policy[11] as well as for a policy brief calling for the sustainable financing of CHWs, arguing for their critical role as part of the integrated system of health care delivery[12] The goal in many cases was twofold: reach the community and provide a platform for career advancement among people in the population who had much to contribute to health improvement while advancing their potential to serve in other tiers in the health services industry.

While one is able to read across their work in the learning laboratories, it is important to realize that the final recognition of the importance of this group of health workers by the U.S. Department of Labor was the result of collaborative cooperation from across the nation. Work in Denver with community colleges; in New Mexico with the *promotora* network, in Ingham County with their patient navigators, in Miami with their training program, and in New York through the powerful work of Alianza Dominicana, among others, led to this success. Some learning laboratories "imported" the method of family health records as a way of monitoring and addressing family health (for example, in Miami, the UNI-Trujillo model was adapted for implementation in the immigrant-rich East Little Havana neighborhood; see Chapter Four for more details) while improving community well-being, a far departure from the fragmented approach to the health of the family in the United States. The lesson learned here is that the "global village" does have important lessons to teach to an increasingly diverse country. And, while community outreach worker programs and the training for the same remain non-uniform in the Community Voices learning laboratories and across the nation, it has become evident to all that this important group may be the vehicle through which to achieve engagement in the health system to prevent disease and promote health.

The importance of working with outreach workers who were racially, ethnically, and gender sensitive included developing men to be outreach workers, particularly among those populations most likely to be estranged from the health care system. Denver Health and Hospital Authority and its work with the county jail, and Oakland Community Voices with its extremely diverse population, were leaders in the training of this cadre (see Chapters Two and Eight). No other national effort to increase the numbers of male outreach workers exists, though the criminal justice system experiments with this group as a way of improving resettlement in community and reducing recidivism.[13] Attention to gender and to ethnic and racial diversity will be continually important as the nation moves toward including all in the health care system, improving health systems and reducing the exponentially growing early morbidity and mortality among vulnerable groups.

At the same time, the opportunity exists for the nation to address chronic un- or underemployment while also providing upward mobility training for community individuals. Linkages that go beyond simple certification to the attainment of college credit courses through alliances with community colleges may be a novel way of reducing unemployment while fostering employment in the formal sector that provides role models for the children of the outreach workers on a daily basis as they see parents at work and in the formal educational system. This variable alone may go far in breaking the chronic cycle of unemployment or underemployment that is generational in some neighborhoods.

Mental Health and Substance Abuse: The Importance of "Mind" Over Matter

The area of mental health and substance abuse treatment was most refractive to intervention in Community Voices. The reasons for the difficulty in addressing the issue were three-fold. First, the public payment streams (such as Medicaid) for mental health and substance abuse treatment were separated and continue to be so, while providers still fail to link the relationship between mental health issues (such as depression, post-traumatic stress disorder, anger as a result of alienation) and substance abuse. Mental health parity discussions are also relatively new. Second, the several organizations devoted to addressing psychological, mental health, and substance abuse issues have been slow to embrace the causes of the poor and near poor because there apparently is no income stream to support treatment for this group. Perhaps, also, there may be a tinge of "political incorrectness" when one dares to speak of poverty, racism, gender discrimination (against poor men of color), cultural competence, and so forth. As a result, it is difficult to find any movement among the groups of the profession that have united to speak out to address the mental health issues of the poor and the incarcerated, even though we know that a treatable mental health diagnosis is associated with at least 20 percent of those incarcerated.[14] Third, racially diverse and culturally competent providers, cultural harmony in the practice environment, and the incorporation of spirituality—an important component in care for many seeking help—are virtually ignored as best practices.

The Community Voices learning laboratories published documents including New York's *Mental Health: The Neglected Epidemic*. New Mexico worked with collaborators to make mental health parity a reality only to lose the gains when a Medicaid carve-out made serving the population on a timely basis with culturally competent providers virtually unimportant, an issue seen time and again across the nation. Oakland Community Voices focused on mental health issues among the general population and among the homeless (predominantly men of color), as it is well known that mental health problems are more prevalent in this population (see Chapter Eight). Oakland also, as a result of a commitment to serving its diverse constituency, worked to expand the number of bilingual and bicultural mental health providers in Alameda County, a different approach from many communities that render these populations invisible and therefore do not design public policy to reach and treat them (see Chapter Eight). FirstHealth Community Voices worked with its policymakers to inform the formation of a mental health reform effort that would affect the entire state (see Chapter Six). In the interim, it installed a skilled nurse clinician in a free clinic, a joint venture between FirstHealth of the Carolinas and the Moore County Free Clinic, to conduct mental health screenings and make referrals, as appropriate, while greater reform is formulated statewide. Baltimore did more to attempt to address substance abuse issues, as its population was visibly affected by this and related issues and was predominantly male (see Chapter One). Services included addressing substance abuse, depression, violence prevention, and services in the community.

What all of these efforts lacked, however, was a strong payment and policy framework at the level of the state government or on the national level in which the programs could have become embedded. So the problem persists. While there is more attention now to substance abuse treatment through the use of some Substance Abuse and Mental Health Services Administration (SAMHSA) funds for pilot programs to identify promising practices, states and other municipalities still find this a convenient program area in which to balance budgets and do not recognize the gains in helping individuals recover and become productive members of the community. In addition, the stigma of mental health continues to exacerbate access to care and requires that the profession and the community come together to design a social marketing program that reduces stigma while at the same time ensuring that services are available that are accessible, affordable, and gender and culturally sensitive, while embracing the spiritual aspects of healing that are important to so many, on the basis of their race, cultural, and customs.

Taking the Measure of Community-Based Intervention to Inform Practice and Policy

We must be clear that communities are different; that one-sized evaluation does not fit all. Context matters! Over the life of the Community Voices initiative, we did not spend time on logic models as we believed that designing the intervention was more important than theoretical approaches to filling in feedback loops that might have succeeded in getting people "on the same page" but which may have ultimately only served as a distant and, ultimately inaccurate, model to capture the work we were doing on the ground in very diverse communities.

In our case, we used "readiness" as the indicator of those prepared to do visionary work in novel ways, without predispositions about the ability of the community to come together or the difficulty of charting a new path. We devoted significant time to our networking meetings, to designing the innovation, and to developing themes, slogans, posters, and lists of potential partners along with strategic approaches for engaging important people, organizations, and institutions. We gave greater premium to the telling of the story, evaluating the efficacy of communicating with the media, collecting the stories of those in need or those delivering services, communicating services, and taking risks to embrace difficult issues that were not always popular.

Given this approach, our methods for evaluating our work in this journey were strongly qualitative. Along these lines, our concerns were focused on determining for ourselves and others whether what we did was actually successful—in other words, were our interventions replicable and worthy of note as "promising or best practices" for others to follow? With this in mind, Community Voices developed an evaluative approach that was both thoughtful and community-sensitive, striving to turn attention to how people worked to accomplish both community and policy-level changes.

Community Voices' approach to "evaluation" revealed important information as the initiative evolved, allowing for possible adjustments to be made along the way. We believe that one of the reasons why this was so was because of the early commitment to a community-based participatory research (CBPR) model of evaluation. In this model, community leaders and residents are as much a part of the research and evaluation design as are the evaluators themselves, allowing constant mutual learning and the possibility of making adjustments. We learned quickly that community-based work is dynamic, difficult, and ever-changing. And so the evaluation of the same must be flexible. The Community Voices experience revealed that CBPR may be a valuable method for evaluating such work. We also learned that an evaluation that looks carefully at collaboration as an indicator of cohesion among relevant stakeholders may tell us something about the possibilities for creating policy change.

However, more must be done to effectively evaluate this kind of work. As we finalize this current phase of Community Voices, a key reflection for us is that in order to best appreciate the impact of such initiatives, they must be sustained for significant periods so that the process can be best evaluated. As you have read here, much of this work has been about developing leadership and relationships; building processes that would lead to positive changes in practice and in policy. The changes that were made are real, but we must be able to develop the evidence base over time to explain why some of these more abstract components or activities actually do lead to improvements in systems and in care. This is not to downplay that much of the work is quite tangible and quantitative, as the work of health systems such as Denver Health, FirstHealth and the Ingham County Health Department reveals. However, much of what drove the success of Community Voices did rest on intangibles that are not easily measured with quantitative methods.

But the only way to continue to learn from similar work is to find the ways in which to evaluate it over time, understanding that the right evaluation needs to begin and end with the community and give as much weight to the process as to the actual outcomes. When we look carefully at the work of Community Voices, we can point across the board to common achievements in all of the sites' ability to leverage additional funds; to move the public agenda—in some cases, in very unexpected, though positive, ways (see Chapter One, Baltimore's men's health efforts; Chapter Six, North Carolina's tobacco and men's health efforts; and most of the sites' success with oral health and the promotion of CHWs); to disseminate key information through consistent publications, as demonstrated in Part Two; and to collaborate with partners and associates in efforts to improve health care access for all, beyond Community Voices funding. Finally, the leadership efforts of those most visible and those less visible must be accounted for, somehow, as a most valuable and necessary component to success.

Evaluation of this kind of work can be quite difficult, as there are many moving parts. We learned that stories play an important role in sharing the history, process, and successes. One interesting example was developed through the Northern Manhattan Community Voices Collaborative in their publication of a community health worker storybook, which provided the direct perspective of the work from communities and the CHWs on the frontlines. We combined data of this kind, whenever possible, together with more quantitative analyses such as those that were produced through Denver Health's evaluation of CHW productivity. The key for us was—and will be for others in the future, we believe—to know which kind of evaluative tool would be possible and successful in accurately capturing the work we were doing in so many different places. In the final analysis, evaluation for us was very much about the issues that we faced and the variety of creative approaches that communities were using to address the issues that would lead to the common goal: greater service venues for the unserved and underserved.

Puzzling Public Policy

The social determinants of health have their genesis in the social fabric of poor communities when wealth and health disparities continue to be ignored in a fugue of blame and disparagement. While it may feel good to discuss in moral or ethical terms health disparities that are still in need of being addressed, these hold little sway in public policy design, debate, and passage. Though it is clear that the Community Voices learning laboratories worked in the communities that were underserved and unserved, and that these were largely communities of color, it is not possible to discuss the issues from a moralistic point of view. What is far more compelling is the fiscal argument.

A recent study by the Urban Institute clearly illustrated the cost of disparities. Specifically, in 2009, disparities among African Americans, Hispanics, and non-Hispanic whites cost the health care system $23.9 billion dollars. Medicare alone will spend an extra $15.6 billion while private insurers will incur $5.1 billion in additional costs due to elevated rates of chronic illness among African Americans and Hispanics. The Urban Institute estimates that over the ten-year period from 2009 through 2018, the total cost of these disparities will be approximately $337 billion, including $220 billion for Medicare. The Institute also estimates that the dramatic changes in the demographic profile of African Americans and Hispanics that have been projected over the coming decades will have an impact on these costs. Even without taking into account projected growth in per capita spending, costs will increase further by 2050 as the representation of Latinos and African Americans among the elderly increases. The demographic imperative is a reality and nothing can change the direction of future growth in the U.S. population. Excess disease burden, particularly among the fastest-growing segments, due to failure of the system to include and serve them, imposes economic cost, which is an important element in making the "business case" for reducing disparities.[15]

With no improvement in health disparities, even with no growth in the per capita cost of health care, there will still be a dramatic growth in the cost of disparities between Hispanics and non-Hispanic whites. As the Hispanic population ages, the effect of health differences among the elderly on Medicare costs will be magnified the most, growing from $5.5 billion in 2009 to nearly $16 billion (in 2009 dollars) by 2050. Medicaid and private insurers will also bear an increased burden of disparities.[16]

It is clear that the driving factor undergirding the work of Community Voices' learning laboratories was—and is—to devise and secure a sustainable health care system that serves all, not because they cannot pay but because all of us pay exponentially for their cost when society fails to provide coverage and care. The other continuing challenge is to shine a light on other systems that are driving costs even higher, such as those being generated by the thriving criminal justice and prison-industrial complex. Much is said about the "American people" and their concern about implementing new programs. However, virtually no policymaker makes the case to those opposed to social systems reform that the taxpayer will pay anyway—and is paying already. The cost of inaction exceeds the cost-benefit of action now for health justice.

Entrenched ideology, expediency, sound bites, and divisive public discourse continue to push to the margin the need for a conversation in this nation about the legacy of racial separation, indenture, slavery, and discrimination based on race, ethnic origin, or immigrant status. These same factors obscure and make invisible the names and faces of the millions of Americans that remain isolated from primary health care and prevention that includes unfettered access to comprehensive oral health, mental health, and substance abuse care and treatment. Yet there is virtually no other way to examine the degree of disparities in some communities and not make the connection that race and ethnicity matter. Place matters if you are in a rural community, and place is confounded by race and gives those from communities of color an even greater disadvantage in gaining access to societal resources.

The Community Voices learning laboratories sought to work around the divisive discourse and to establish a protected space for dialogue and community problem solving. The learning laboratories were all successful in leaving their communities with greater services, with enhanced understanding, and with vibrant coalitions that continue to come together, though perhaps under different umbrellas, to work for many things, including national health care reform. The recommendations that are discussed in this book can assist in addressing the issues faced by all in this nation, as even those with outstanding health insurance continue to pay for the waste and devastation that is incurred when we fail to reach everyone. As Community Voices has argued and shown, extended morbidity has a fiscal and social cost.

Our recommendations embrace the World Health Organization's definition of primary health care, which states, "Primary health care is essential health care made accessible at a cost a country and community can afford, with methods that are practical, scientifically sound and socially acceptable."[17] This definition is appropriate, as most who are on the front lines and who are morally, ethically, and literate about all things fiscal in relationship to health care know that the social determinants of health are as important as access. Integrated, interpolated systems of care are needed and can be realized in our time. We have the resources to meet the health care needs of all in the nation, but we are running out of time if we wish to reverse the burden of chronic disease, family destruction, and increasing cost to the American taxpayer. Our country cannot afford to do nothing.

Notes

1. A.M.W. Young, "The Overtown Men's Health Study," Collins Center for Public Policy, 2006.
2. "Guide to Children's Dental Care in Medicaid, CMS, 2004. Available at http://www.cms. hhs.gov/medicaiddentalcoverage/downloads/dentalguide.pdf. Accessed January 21, 2010.
3. T. A. Dolan, G. H. Gilbert, R. Duncan, and U. Foerster, "Risk Indicators of Edentulism, Partial Tooth Loss and Prosthetic Status Among Black and White Middle-Aged and Older Adults," *Community Dentistry and Oral Epidemiology*, July 2008, 29(5).Available at http:// www3.interscience.wiley.com/journal/120712829/abstract?CRETRY=1&SRETRY=0. Accessed January 21, 2010.
4. *Key Facts: Race, Ethnicity and Medical Care*, The Henry J. Kaiser Family Foundation, January 2007.
5. *Where Are the Men? The Impact of Incarceration and Reentry on African American Men and Their Children and Families.* Available at http://www.communityvoices.org/Uploads/*wherearethemen2*_00108_00144.pdf. Accessed January 21, 2010.
6. J. A. Rich and M. J. Ro, *A Poor Man's Plight: Uncovering the Disparity in Men's Health*, Community Voices, February, 2002.
7. See http://collinscenter.site-ym.com/?page=HCIntlMens.
8. L. M. Pérez, M. J. Ro, and H. M Treadwell, "Vulnerable Populations, Prison, and Federal and State Medicaid Policies: Avoiding the Loss of a Right to Care," *Journal of Correctional Health Care*, 2009, 15(2), 142–149.
9. See Washingtonpost.com for January 7, 2010.
10. J. Nickel, C. Garland, and L. Kane, "Children of Incarcerated Parents: An Action Plan for Federal Policymakers," Council of State Governments Justice Center, 2009. Available at http://reentrypolicy.org/jc_publications/federa_action_plan_/Children_Incarcerated_ Parents_v8.pdf. Accessed January 21, 2010.
11. L. M. Pérez and J. Martinez, "Community Health Workers: Social Justice and Policy Advocates for Community Health and Well-Being," *American Journal of Public Health*, January 2008, 98(1). Available at http://www.ncbi.nlm.nih.gov/pubmed/18048789. Accessed January 21, 2010.
12. "Financing Community Health Workers: Why and How," National Community Voices Initiative at the Center for Primary Care at the Morehouse School of Medicine and The Northern Manhattan Community Voices at the Columbia University Center for Community Health Partnerships.
13. F. S. Taxman, D. Young, and J. M. Byrne, "Transforming Offender Reentry into Public Safety: Lessons from OJP's Reentry Partnership Initiative," *Justice Research and Statistics*

Association, Fall 2003, 5(2), 101–128. Available at http://jrsa.metapress.com/content/ g5k725n3rqm74125/. Accessed January 21, 2009.

14. A. J. Lurigio and J. A. Swartz, "Mental Illness in Correctional Populations: The Use of Standardized Screening Tools for Further Evaluation or Treatment," *Federal Probation*, 2006, 70(2). Available at http://www.uscourts.gov/fedprob/September_2006/screening. html. Accessed January 21, 2010.

15. T. Waidman, "Estimating the Cost of Racial and Ethnic Health Disparities," The Urban Institute, September 2009.

16. Ibid.

17. "Health Promotion Glossary," World Health Organization, 1998, p. 13.

NOW THAT WE "KNOW WHAT WE KNOW," WHAT IS TO BE DONE?

Gail C. Christopher

In the immediate aftermath of health care reform efforts in the United States in the early 1990s, it was no wonder that the targeted focus of Community Voices was placed on prominent access to health care for the uninsured and underserved. While this was the initial direction that set the course, the initiative's leaders knew from the outset that the goals would need to be further-reaching, more profound, and more urgent than the original idea implied. An undeniable component in this work would certainly be a commitment to ensure equity along racial and socioeconomic lines. This became abundantly clear, as time after time it was obvious that the poorest and sickest were people of color with little or no access to health and social services. Despite the best efforts of Community Voices, this fact still persists. Much must be done in order to place the social and economic determinants of the public's health, such as structural racism and segregation, squarely in the middle of the discussion and, in this way, ensure equitable access to quality health care for all. Going forward, then, the unrelenting questions must be, why do the problems persist, and what is to be done?

The work of Community Voices and its subsequent move to the Morehouse School of Medicine (MSM) ensured that the focus would remain on this question of structural oppression and violence by race and socioeconomic status. The Kellogg Foundation has remained committed to the underserved, to clearly defining more carefully who they are and what their needs are. Precisely, why is appropriate access to quality care still a race and equity issue when one looks at who is poor?

Kellogg remains focused on a number of areas of work that continue to raise the specter of inequity in health and well-being. One of these areas, for example, is oral health. The lessons derived from the Community Voices experience have created a significant portfolio of work that has made possible the continued efforts in this arena. As noted here, although much was accomplished, much remains to be done, as the demand is high and the need for qualified, minority professionals and those with the competence to provide the care are still required. Policies and practices will need to be reexamined so that the benefits can accrue to those who engage in this profession, particularly those who would serve those most underserved.

Other foundations must be credited for doing work to connect oral health to primary health. As discussed in a number of the chapters you have read here, the Robert Wood Johnson Foundation's Pipeline grant was a visionary approach to ensuring a shift in the way that dentists are trained so that the focus of care is placed back in the community, directly available through well-trained professionals situated on the front lines of care. As imagined, this work has had—and will continue to have—ripple effects on both the training and the kinds of care that might be available in some of the most underserved communities in the country. Kellogg's own continuation of this work can be seen through its commitment to the health of children and families. To address the lack of dental providers, particularly for underserved populations, Kellogg is examining how dental health therapists may serve to fill the workforce gap. The dental health therapist has the potential for addressing oral health disparities, particularly among minority communities, which are disproportionately suffering from oral disease. Still, we know that much more needs to happen; waiting lists are overflowing, and coverage for oral health services, particularly for low-income adults, is nearly non-existent. But the very good news is that through the efforts of Community Voices and others the work has begun and has set a course for more to be accomplished.

Kellogg currently is interested in looking carefully at children and families, racial equity, and civic engagement, with the notion that these three legs of the stool, as it were, are the necessary components to ensure well-being in communities. The content focus areas are education; food, health, and well-being; and family, economics, and security. Current W.K. Kellogg Foundation programming provides a tremendous opportunity to analyze the kinds of policies that might work well to ensure a strong pathway to opportunity for children, youth, and their families. We think that our support of efforts devoted to improving the health of children using a social-determinants-of-health-and-racial-equity approach will help to ensure other social and economic opportunities for children (see www.wkkf.org). This will be key, as we know that the environment in which a child is raised, educational opportunities, and the economic status of the family are key indicators for healthy and prosperous lives in the future.

The social and economic determinants of the health of children and families therefore cannot be skirted. Rather, as Community Voices shows us, many of the conversations about health *must* begin with the social and economic context. All health derives from these structures, and in determining the solutions we must be clear as to where the source of the problem begins. We know, for example, that children with parents in prison are five times more likely to follow a similar path than those without parents in prison (see Gabel and Johnston, 1997; see http://www.e-ccip.org/about_us.html and http://www.nytimes.com/2009/07/05/us/05prison.html). In a country in which the bridge between education and prison is so clear for some of our youth, what more must be done to ensure that those young people have every equal chance of promise?

Indeed, as health care reform efforts will continue for some time to come, those who persist in this work will need to think about the issues across systems; to understand that a comprehensive approach to health reform (in its most holistic sense) is linked to such things as education, safe neighborhoods, community cohesion, livable wages, and support for parents and caregivers. At the same time, understanding that so many children in the country currently live with a parent in prison, thoughtful attention must be given to the fact that the chances of these children finishing their lives in the prison system also rises as a result. What resources must we put into families and communities so that another generation of children does not follow the same path? Will we ensure that the appropriate resources are distributed equitably across all of our schools? Will our nation invest in community-based mental health and substance abuse treatment for those who need it? Will this country provide support for whole families as its members make the transition back into the community from substance abuse or from prison or both? Will communities ensure that the mothers and fathers of these children are able to find housing and jobs? In the final analysis, it will be important to remember that children will only be as well as their parents and their communities can be. If all sectors—public, private, philanthropic, and non-profit—do not invest in the kinds of issues mentioned here on the front end, we will have condemned these children to a similar, if not worse, future.

We have seen policies developed with the best of intentions; however, we must also see the shortcomings and correct them wherever possible. One example of this can be seen with child support enforcement. While on its face, this policy sought to ensure support for women and children in the absence of a partner or father, what this policy has effectively done is to increase the stranglehold on men who are in prison or just being released. While conversations with this particular population of underserved men have revealed that a priority is for them to help support their families, the challenge they face once outside of prison is that there are still too many barriers that exist for them in terms of finding jobs and housing (Pérez and Treadwell,

2009). These are not hypothetical or imagined barriers but are most real, as we know that too many organizations will not hire previously convicted people; we know that housing is limited for those who have been in prison for a substance abuse offense (quite problematic considering that a high percentage of those serving time are doing so for drug-related offenses); and there are still states that deny formerly incarcerated people the right to vote, effectively denying their individual and collective voices. What backlashes, then, is such a policy causing for men who effectively cannot provide support because of the aforementioned challenges? What of the children who will suffer in the end because fathers recidivate into prison for failure to comply? Is this the best course to travel, or would families and communities be better served by placing the focus of attention on the resources necessary in communities for all members of the family to succeed?

Despite these challenges, we must acknowledge the success gained in a number of areas that have brought awareness to the issues affecting vulnerable populations, though perhaps the area that has made the least comparative traction is mental health. While some states have enacted mental health parity laws, so much more must happen to provide appropriate care for those who suffer from mental-health-related illnesses. Although the parity laws—which must be applauded—do much for recognizing mental health as an integral part of primary care, they are positioned to serve only those with health insurance. As we continue the struggle for universal coverage and access, effective mental health treatment remains an elusive luxury for millions. Again, we can see a direct connection to the dearth of care in community-based settings and the subsequent incarceration of people (70 percent of those incarcerated have some form of mental illness or co-occurring disorder such as substance abuse). How many more people must we incarcerate before we heed the overwhelming evidence that shows that better social and health outcomes are achieved by providing community-based treatment on the outside, on demand (Freudenberg, 2005; and see http://www.bazelon.org/).

Although many challenges have been faced and addressed, so many still remain to be acknowledged and changed! Community Voices set an unprecedented path toward asking very hard questions and insisting on the answers. Even more compelling is that many of the people directly affected by state and national policies have spoken in this endeavor about what must be done to shift the pendulum toward equity. We are in this together, community-based organizations, academia, philanthropy, government, and private sector alike. Community Voices has taught us that it takes many kinds of voices from different places and experiences to move this agenda forward. We have learned the value, then, of working not only with community organizations but also with community institutions such as the Morehouse School of Medicine and other historically black colleges and universities across the country that are linked directly to the communities they serve while developing the necessary thinking in policy arenas. A lasting legacy of Community Voices undoubtedly will be its institutionalization at the Morehouse School of Medicine, ensuring a continuity of this work in the nation and a voice for the poor, the historically marginalized.

For all of us, the work is not over. In many ways, despite the covering and dissection of so many perverse policies that continue to hold people captive in poverty, in ill health, or in prison, the work of insisting on some of the specific policy changes that must occur has just begun. Through our individual and collective work, we must continue to insist that parents have the resources to care for their children; that children are kept healthy, ensuring for them quality education, good food, and safe environments; and that communities can thrive. This is our call to action. This is what we must do lest another generation be lost.

References

Freudenberg, N., Daniels, J., Crum, M., Perkins, T., and Richie, B. E., "Coming Home from Jail: The Social and Health Consequences of Community Reentry for Women, Male Adolescents, and Their Families and Communities" *American Journal of Public Health*, October 2005, 95(10), 1725–1736.

Gabel, K., and Johnston, D. "Public Policy and the Children of Incarcerated Parents," in K. Gabel and D. Johnston (eds.), *Children of Incarcerated Parents* (New York: Lexington, 1997).

Pérez, L., and Treadwell, H. M., "Homeward Bound and Homeless: The Challenge of Those Returning Home After Incarceration," in E. P. Hammond and A. D. Noyes (eds.), *Housing: Socioeconomic, Availability and Development Issues* (Hauppauge, NY: Nova Science Publishers, 2009).

INDEX